DESIGN IN

The Cranbrook Vision   1925~1950

AMERICA

HARRY N. ABRAMS, INC., PUBLISHERS, NEW YORK IN ASSOCIATION WITH

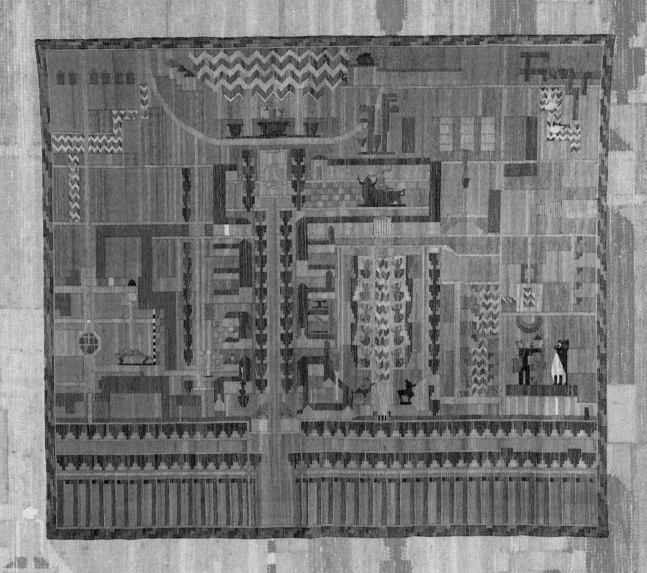

TEXT BY ROBERT JUDSON CLARK, DAVID G. DE LONG, MARTIN EIDELBERG, J. DAVID FARMER, JOHN GERARD, NEIL HARRIS,

THE DETROIT INSTITUTE OF ARTS AND THE METROPOLITAN MUSEUM OF ART

DESIGN IN

The Cranbrook Vision 1925~1950

AMERICA

JOAN MARTER, R. CRAIG MILLER, MARY RIORDAN, ROY SLADE, DAVIRA S. TARAGIN, CHRISTA C. MAYER THURMAN

Front cover

CARL MILLES. *Orpheus Fountain*. 1934–37, installed 1938. Bronze. Each figure approx. h. 96″. Cranbrook Academy of Art/Museum

Back cover

ELIEL SAARINEN. *Drawings for Living Room Furniture Suites: Armchairs*. c. 1929. Colored pencil on brown paper on black board. Each 3 ½ × 5 ¼″. Suomen Rakennustaiteen Museo

Frontispiece

ELIEL AND LOJA SAARINEN (DESIGNERS) AND STUDIO LOJA SAARINEN (WEAVERS). *Hanging Showing Cranbrook Map*. 1935. Linen warp, linen, silk, and wool weft; plain weave with discontinuous wefts. 104 × 124″. Cranbrook Academy of Art/Museum

Ill. p. 8

See caption, fig. 83

Library of Congress Cataloging in Publication Data

Design in America.

   Bibliography: p.
   Includes index.
   1. Cranbrook Academy of Art—Exhibitions.
2. Art, Modern—20th century—Michigan—
Bloomfield—Exhibitions.   3. Design—Michigan
—Bloomfield—History—20th century—Exhibitions.
I. Clark, Robert Judson.   II. Belloli, Andrea P. A.
III. Detroit Institute of Arts.   IV. Metropolitan
Museum of Art (New York, N.Y.)
N330.B55C74   1983   709′ .774′ 38   83-6343

ISBN 0-8109-0801-8
ISBN 0-89558-097-7 (Detroit Institute of Arts : pbk.)
ISBN 0-87099-341-0 (Metropolitan Museum of Art : pbk.)

The exhibition has the following itinerary:

THE DETROIT INSTITUTE OF ARTS
December 14, 1983 through February 19, 1984

THE METROPOLITAN MUSEUM OF ART,
NEW YORK CITY
April 18, 1984 through June 17, 1984

SUOMEN RAKENNUSTAITEEN MUSEO/
SUOMEN TAIDETEOLLISUUSYHDISTYS, HELSINKI
August 1, 1984 through September 19, 1984

MUSÉE DES ARTS DÉCORATIFS, PARIS
October 24, 1984 through January 21, 1985

VICTORIA AND ALBERT MUSEUM, LONDON
April 1, 1985 through June 30, 1985

Catalogue Coordinator:
Andrea P. A. Belloli
Photographer:
Dirk Bakker
Editors:
Adele Westbrook and Anne Yarowsky
Designer:
Kenneth R. Windsor

This book is published in conjunction with a major exhibition of objects generously loaned by the following institutions and private collections:

The Art Institute of Chicago
Ascension of Christ Lutheran Church, Birmingham, Michigan
Benjamin Baldwin, New York City
Florence Knoll Bassett, Coconut Grove
Mrs. Brigitta Bertoia, Barto
Carolyn Farr Booth, Bloomfield Hills
CBS, Inc., New York City
Christ Church Cranbrook, Bloomfield Hills
Cranbrook Academy of Art/Museum, Bloomfield Hills
Cranbrook Educational Community, Bloomfield Hills
Cranbrook School, Bloomfield Hills
The Detroit Institute of Arts
Dianne Dwyer, New York City
Mrs. Ray Eames, Venice, California
The Episcopal Archdiocese of Northern Michigan, Marquette
Everson Museum of Art, Syracuse
Flint Institute of Arts
Marshall Fredericks, Royal Oak, Michigan
Theodore R. Gamble, Jr., New York City
Mrs. Leigh Gerdine, St. Louis, Missouri
Marianne Strengell Hammarstrom, Wellfleet, Massachusetts
Herman Miller Museum Collection, Zeeland, Michigan
Mr. and Mrs. Austin E. Jones, Scottsdale
Ronald S. Kane, New York City
Margueritte Kimball, Cambridge, Massachusetts
Kingswood School Cranbrook, Bloomfield Hills
Mrs. Arthur Nevill Kirk, Phoenix
Kleinhans Music Hall Management, Inc., Buffalo
Knoll International, New York City
Don Knorr, San Francisco
Mr. and Mrs. Joseph N. Lacy, Bloomfield Hills
Jack Lenor Larsen, New York City
The Metropolitan Museum of Art, New York City
Millesgården, Lidingö
The M.I.T. Museum, Cambridge, Massachusetts

I. Wistar Morris, III, Philadelphia
National Museum of American Art, Smithsonian Institution, Washington, D.C.
National Park Service, Jefferson National Expansion Memorial, St. Louis
Pennsylvania Academy of the Fine Arts, Philadelphia
Don Petitt, New York City
Ralph Rapson, Minneapolis
Joseph J. and Carolyn Roberto, New York City
Tony Rosenthal, New York City
Charles E. Rossbach, Berkeley
David Rowland, New York City
Royal Institute of British Architects, London
Lilian Swann Saarinen, Cambridge, Massachusetts
Robert D. Sailors, Cortez, Florida
Smålands Museum, Växjö
The Solomon R. Guggenheim Museum, New York City
Suomen Rakennustaiteen Museo, Helsinki
Robert Saarinen Swanson, Bloomfield Hills
Ronald Saarinen Swanson, Bloomfield Hills
Richard Thomas, Bloomfield Hills
Harry Weese, Chicago
Yale University, Sterling Memorial Library, New Haven
Yolande and Waylande Gregory Foundation
Private Collections

The exhibition was organized by The Detroit Institute of Arts and The Metropolitan Museum of Art and made possible through grants from the IBM Corporation, The National Endowment for the Arts, The National Endowment for the Humanities, and Founders Society Detroit Institute of Arts.

CONTENTS

PREFACE

As the Cranbrook Academy of Art embarks upon its second fifty years of activity, The Detroit Institute of Arts and The Metropolitan Museum of Art are pleased to present "Design in America: The Cranbrook Vision 1925–1950." This exhibition is the first major presentation to document the emergence of modern American design in the second quarter of the twentieth century and could not have been realized without the continuous cooperation of the Academy. Cranbrook has long been one of the most important institutions in arts education in the world, and the larger Cranbrook community—which includes Brookside School Cranbrook, Cranbrook School, Kingswood School Cranbrook, the Cranbrook Institute of Science, and the Cranbrook Academy of Art—is one of the most significant architectural complexes of its type.

The beginnings of the Academy marked a unique moment in the development of American architecture and decorative arts. Cranbrook was one of the few institutions in this country that offered instruction in design during the 1920s and thirties, and its influence on architecture, interior design, art, and crafts after World War II was crucial and extensive. Although many of the important artists who taught or studied at the Academy have received international recognition, the significance of their shared experience at Cranbrook has not, nor has the influence that Cranbrook exerted on their sensibilities ever been extensively explored. In addition to its significance in the area of arts education, Cranbrook's physical facility is one of the modern masterpieces of institutional architecture; the largest work of Eliel Saarinen, one of the finest architects of his age; and a building complex too little known, given its importance in its creator's oeuvre.

The exhibition includes over 200 objects and photo-panels and surveys the history of the Cranbrook facility itself as well as the achievements of the teachers and students who were present at the Academy by the time of Eliel Saarinen's death in 1950. The work of these artists and designers is traced through the early 1960s to give a sense of their mature accomplishments and of the aspects of their Cranbrook training that they continued to carry with them. This survey makes it clear that the Cranbrook Academy of Art has had a unique position in the history of modern architecture, design, and art. The reaffirmation of hand fabrication, of clarity of design, and of revival styles that characterized the Arts and Crafts approach was continued there into the early modern period. The ancestors of George G. Booth, the patron who initiated and sponsored the creation of Cranbrook, were English craftsmen, and Booth's own interests in this area eventually led to his conception of a community that would make it possible for students to explore a wide range of the visual arts (as well as the sciences) and their interrelationship in one educational complex.

By happy chance, Eliel Saarinen was in Michigan when Booth made his decision to initiate this ambitious project. Saarinen's extensive experience in his native Finland in the Arts and Crafts tradition made him an ideal choice as the designer to realize Booth's vision, and in cooperation they developed Cranbrook's unique architectural facilities and educational program. The history of

Cranbrook illustrates the transition from Arts and Crafts concerns to industrial design, exemplifying an approach that respected tradition while exploring avantgarde concepts of form, technique, and mass production.

The story of the Cranbrook exhibition itself clearly illustrates an increasing interest in the architecture and design of the second quarter of this century. The idea of a show that would present the history of Cranbrook in its early years was first suggested by Frederick J. Cummings in early 1978. This idea was immediately and enthusiastically taken up by Roy Slade, President of the Academy, who, since his arrival there in 1977, had been aware of the extraordinary level of achievement that had marked the institution's beginnings. At the same time The Metropolitan Museum of Art was exploring the idea of an international exhibition devoted to Eliel and Eero Saarinen; a meeting between Slade and R. Craig Miller, Assistant Curator in The American Wing of the Metropolitan Museum of Art who was completing his doctoral research on the Saarinens, led to a joint venture by the three institutions. The Metropolitan's participation in the organization of the show was secured with the support of James Pilgrim, Deputy Director, and Lewis Sharp, Curator and Administrator of the Department of American Art. A group of scholars was then invited to serve on a Scientific Committee to organize the exhibition; their contributions to the realization of the show and enthusiastic involvement in the assembling of this catalogue cannot be overestimated.

We would like to take this opportunity to convey our deep appreciation to the staffs of The Detroit Institute of Arts, The Metropolitan Museum of Art, and Cranbrook Academy of Art for their exceptional work on behalf of this exhibition. In particular, we wish to recognize several individuals whose contributions were crucial to the success of the project. Jay Belloli, former Curator of Modern Art at The Detroit Institute of Arts, ably co-administered the show's organization through the fall of 1982; Davira S. Taragin, in addition to her role as author, assisted Mr. Belloli with the coordination of the show until his departure, at which time she assumed the duties of co-administrator. MaryAnn Wilkinson worked most effectively and with great effort as Research Assistant, organizing many aspects of the exhibition. Edwinna Gardner provided support in the areas of typing and logistics. Chiyo Ishikawa provided excellent freelance assistance on archival research. We are also grateful to Abraham Joel, Head Conservator, and Carol Forsythe, Mary Ballard, Valerie Baas, Jerri Nelson, and Uziel Sasson of The Detroit Institute of Arts' Conservation Services Laboratory; Boris G. Sellers, former Director of Development, and Patricia Miller, Marianne DePalma, and Janet McDougal, Development Department; and to Robert T. Weston, Administrator, Susan Weinberg, Assistant Administrator, and Karen Serota, Registrar's Office, for their contribution to the organization of the exhibition tour. We are also grateful to Margaret DeGrace, Acting Director, Public Relations.

At The Metropolitan Museum of Art, R. Craig Miller, as well as participating in the project as an author, served throughout as the exhibition co-administrator. John K. Howat and William S. Lieberman, Chairmen respectively of the Departments of American Art and Twentieth Century Art, have been unfailing in their belief in the importance of this exhibition. Numerous people in various departments at the Metropolitan have also lent their assistance: Ellin Rosenzweig and Terese Bienfait Blake, Department of American Decorative Arts; John Canonico, Rudolph Colban, Susan Klim, and Hermes Knauer, Objects Conservation; Dianne Dwyer, Paintings Conservation; Marjorie N. Shelley and Margaret Holben Ellis, Paper Conservation; Nobuko Kaijitani and Elena Phipps, Textile Conservation; Herbert M. Moskowitz and Laura Rutledge Grimes, Registrar's Office; and Richard Dougherty and Emily Rafferty, Office of the Vice-President for Public Affairs. In particular, Amelia Peck, Research Assistant to Mr. Miller, has contributed greatly to the organization of the exhibition.

The assistance of Cranbrook Academy of Art, particularly of its President, Roy Slade, who has been continuously involved in the development of the exhibition, has been crucial; the show could not have been conceived without his participation. John Gerard, Curator of Collections, deserves special appreciation for his constant effort and care, as do Lucy Harper, Roberta Stewart, Susan

Waller, Beverly Hoffman, and Diane Vogt-O'Connor. George Sexton and Russell Culp of George Sexton Associates, Washington, D.C., are responsible for the splendid installation of the show.

Elsewhere, we wish particularly to thank Juhani Pallasmaa, former Director, Suomen Rakennustaiteen Museo, for his continuing support. Also to be acknowledged are the President of Knoll International, Stephen C. Swid, as well as Donald M. Rorke and Georgina Walker, for their assistance and generosity.

Finally, for the catalogue, special thanks are due Andrea P. A. Belloli, former Coordinator of Publications and Editor of the *Bulletin* at The Detroit Institute of Arts, who on short notice was willing to assume the position of Catalogue Coordinator and who is responsible in large part for the book's success. We also wish to acknowledge the dedicated assistance of Cynthia Jo Fogliatti, Publications Department, and June Kompass Nelson, who provided freelance editorial assistance. The outstanding photography of Dirk Bakker, Chief Photographer, The Detroit Institute of Arts, assisted by Robert Hensleigh, Timothy Thayer, and Marianne Letasi, Photography Department, has added significantly to our appreciation of the objects. We are grateful to Harry N. Abrams, Inc., New York, for their commitment to the exhibition and its catalogue and wish especially to mention Margaret Kaplan, Executive Editor, who first expressed interest in the book and oversaw its development, and Adele Westbrook and Anne Yarowsky, for their tireless efforts in editing the catalogue and seeing it through production. Ken Windsor, a graduate of Cranbrook now on the Abrams staff, brought a special sensitivity to the design of this publication.

"Design in America: The Cranbrook Vision 1925–1950" would not have been possible without the extraordinary generosity of the IBM Corporation. We also wish to convey our thanks to the National Endowment for the Arts and the National Endowment for the Humanities for grants received. Finally, we would like to express our gratitude to all the lenders who have so generously allowed objects to be shown throughout the American and European tours.

FREDERICK J. CUMMINGS, *Director*
The Detroit Institute of Arts

PHILIPPE DE MONTEBELLO, *Director*
The Metropolitan Museum of Art

ACKNOWLEDGMENTS

The Scientific Committee wishes to express its gratitude to the following persons and institutions whose assistance and support have been invaluable in the preparation of this book:

Ulf Abel; Mrs. Frederick Ahlson; Don Albinson; Rita Alexandrides; Geraldine Funk Alvarez; Harold E. Armstrong; Edmund N. Bacon; James Russell Bailey; Benjamin Baldwin; Marianne Bamberger; J. Henderson Barr; Dennis Barrie; Quinta Scott Barry; Edward Charles Bassett; Florence Schust Knoll Bassett; Sonya Bay; The Rev. John Bean; Robert Beauchamp; Mrs. James Beresford; Ingrid Bergman; John Berry; Brigitta Bertoia; William Bigglestone; Richard J. Bilaitis; Mrs. Rachel D. Black; Joseph and Yvonne Palmer Bobrowicz; Henry S. Booth; John L. Booth; John M. Booth; Tom Bower; Helen Brown; C. William Brubaker; William H. Calfee; Cynthia J. Cannon; Betty Carbol; Nancy Richards Clark; Mrs. R. E. Clark; Frederick Colby; Joy Hakanson Colby; William W. Comstock; Robert P. Conway; Roger L. Crispel; W. L. Cunning; Sharon Darling; Marshall H. Daugherty; D. J. De Pree; Max De Pree; Peggy DeSalle; Harry Devlin; Daniel Dickerson; William R. Dickson; Niels Diffrient; Lucy Dippold; Margaret Dismore; Lou Dorfsman; Larry Dowler; Shirley Driks; Jeanne Duperreault; Charles Y. Dusenbury; Dianne Dwyer; Ray Eames; Andrew Euston; Sha Fagin; David Fan; Ulla Fant; Carl L. Feiss; Joan DeWolf Fiore; Mr. and Mrs. William S. Ford; Lavina Franck; Miriam Kellogg Fredenthal; Marshall Fredericks; Mrs. Theodore Robert Gamble; Theodore R. Gamble, Jr.; Mrs. Leigh Gerdine; Marilyn Ghausi; Mrs. T. Harrison Gibbs; Elsa Gilbertson; Vito Anthony Girone; John Parker Glick; Allan Greenberg; Eloise A. Greene; Carl Gronberg; Hermann Gurfinkel; Genevieve Karr Hamlin; David A. Hanks; Joseph K. Hanson; Noma Hardin; John Harris; Steve Harrison; Marika Hausen; Virginia Heckert; Anne Hedmark; George F. Hellmuth; Marion Henley; William Hewitt; Mrs. Walter P. Hickey; Rosemary Lamond Higby; Martha Hilligos; Olle Holmquist; Margie Hughto; Judith Hull; Owen Hungerford; Timothy Husband; Jane Hutchins; Robert J. Iorillo; Mary Ison; Frederick James; Inga Johansson; J. Stewart Johnson; Marion Kirk Jones; William Vogt Kaeser; Louise Lambert Kale; Donald Kalec; Pat Kane; Ronald S. Kane; Signe Karlstrom; Mrs. Thomas C. Kavanagh; Robert Kidd; Margueritte Kimball; Vera Kirk; Svea Klein; Robert Kline; Gerhardt Knodel; Don Knorr; Betty Kondayan; Balthazar Korab; Frank Kowsky; Mr. and Mrs. Joseph N. Lacy; Catherine Lambert; Philip Langdon; Jack Lenor Larsen; Martha Middleton Lauritzen; William Lebovich; Nancy Leitch; Catherine Woerman Lewis; Kelvyn Lilley; Edward J. Lindsay; Marta Lindstrom; Harvey Littleton; Nils Luderowsky; Betty Lundquist; Winifred Lunning; Kendall P. Lutkins; R. B. Lytle, Jr.; Lydia Winston Malbin; Mrs. Lloyd Marentette; Helene Margolies; Mervin Martin; George Matsumoto and staff; Frederick W. Mayer; Thomas J. McCormick; George McCue; Donal McLaughlin; Leza and William McVey; Valerie Mendes; Ralph Metcalf; Francis Merritt; C. Michaelides; J. Irwin Miller; Rolf Milles; Jack Mitchell; Jill Mitchell; George Moon; I. Wistar Morris, III; Anders Mortner; William C. Muchow; Arlee Murphey; Albert L. Neibacher, Jr.; June Kompass Nelson; Mrs. Matthew Nowicki; Gerda Nyberg; Gyo F. Obata; Harry Ormston; Fred Overcash; Peter C. Papademetriou; C. Ford Peatross; Jarno Peltonen; Jeanne K. Perabo; Tapio Periainen; Thomas Perry; Don Petitt; Dipl. Ing. Von Pfaler; Mary Walker Phillips; Buford Pickens; Adolf K. Placzek; Warren Platner; Jan Pokorny; Joe Ann Polster; John Pratt; Howard Preston; Jessica Price; Walter Prokosch; Gary Quesada; Catha Rambusch; Mr. and Mrs. Ralph Rapson; Charles P. Reay; Laura Macomber Rice; Charlotte Robbins; Mr. and Mrs. Joseph Roberto; Jay Robinson; Kevin Roche; Laurance S. Rockefeller; Don Rorke; Tony Rosenthal; Charles E. Rossbach; Mr. and Mrs. David Rowland and staff; Dorothy Rudzki; Mr. and Mrs. Robert Rynbrandt; Eric Saarinen; Lilian Swann Saarinen; Robert D. Sailors; Asko Salokorpi; Ernst Scheyer; Arthur O. Schmidt; Herb Schmidt; Jerry L. Schobert; Fitzhugh Scott; Pamela Scott; Warren Seamans; Mrs. Dorothy Sepeshy; Janet Sielaff; Stuart Silver; Robert Simha; Frank Stanton; Patricia B. Stark; Jack Steele; John and Susan Stephenson; R. Jay Stewart; Erica Stoller; Ezra Stoller; Carol Strahl; Marianne Strengell; Robert S. Swanson; Ronald S. Swanson; Sigrid Synnergren; Mrs. Robert S. Tangeman; Rebecca St. L. Tennen; Angelo Testa; Richard Thomas; Thomas B. Thompson; Bradford Tilney; Marc Treib; James E. Tucker; Erkki Vanhakoski; Rebecca Venable; Louise Virgin; Linda Wagenfeld; Georgina Walker; Axel Wallenberg; Antoinette Lackner Prestini Webster; Mr. and Mrs. Harry Weese; Shirley Weese; Louis B. Wetmore; L. M. Wetzel; Bill White; William and Charlotte Whitney; John M. Whittlesey; Billy Wilder; Ellin Wineberg; Mrs. Milo Winter; William E. Woolfenden; Marie Louise Wulfcrona-Dagel; Thomas Wyman; Karol Yasko; Christopher R. Young; Shirley Dinowitzer Zimmerman; Alice Zrebiec; John Zukowsky.

Archives of American Art; The Art Institute of Chicago; Burton Historical Collection of the Detroit Public Library; Chicago Historical Society; The Cloisters; Columbia University, Avery Architectural Library; Crow Island School; Deere and Company; The Detroit Institute of Arts Museum Archives and Record Center; First Christian Church, Columbus; Flint Institute of Arts; Furniture Conservation Associates; General Motors; Harry Weese and Associates; Hellmuth, Obata and Kassabaum; Jefferson National Expansion Memorial; Kleinhans Music Hall; Library of Congress, Prints and Photographs Division; Massachusetts Institute of Technology; The Metropolitan Museum of Art, Watson Library; Millesgården; The M.I.T. Museum; Nationalmuseum, Stockholm; Office of Charles and Ray Eames; Orrefors Glass; Perkins and Will; Ralph Rapson and Associates; Rice University, School of Architecture; Roche, Dinkeloo and Associates; Royal Institute of British Architects; Skidmore, Owings and Merrill; Smålands Museum, Växjö; Smithsonian Institution; Suomen Rakennustaiteen Museo, Helsinki; Taideteollisunsmuseo, Helsinki; University of Michigan, Ann Arbor, Bentley History Library, Michigan Historical Collections; Washington University, School of Architecture; W. C. Muchow and Partners; Yale University, School of Architecture and Sterling Memorial Library, Manuscripts and Archives.

1 | NORTH BY MIDWEST

The founding of Cranbrook was a twentieth-century variation on an old American theme: creation of a dedicated community, a special world constructed in the service of some higher ideal. It had particular meaning to the Middle West. By the 1920s the middle part of the country, from western New York all the way out to Utah, had been hosting experiments in group living for almost one hundred years. The energies supporting these enterprises drew from secular and religious visions of a higher life. Fourierists, Christian Socialists, Mormons, Rappites, Dunkers, Mennonites, often beginning on the eastern seaboard, spread their doctrines of collective salvation across Ohio, Indiana, Illinois, Missouri, and beyond to the Rockies. The American West possessed so rich a sense of possibility that it was natural for enthusiasts to see this Garden of the World as a setting for reformation by example.[1]

On the surface George Booth, aesthete, wealthy newspaper baron, and founder of the Cranbrook community, might seem distant from this tradition of radical experiment. But it was Booth's commitment to Michigan and the larger region, together with his passion for reform, that permitted Cranbrook's birth. Booth was not alone. Arts and Crafts enthusiasm swept the Middle West in the 1890s and thereafter. Its analogues in Boston and New York were inspired by the same master, William Morris. But private presses and local societies multiplied with special intensity in the Middle West, evidence of the region's hunger for artistic improvement and confidence in the power of aesthetic reform.[2]

Arts and Crafts supporters such as Booth had large goals. They wanted tasteful designs to replace the garish objects filling the American home, such poor competition for foreign products. But they also wanted something else: an integration of daily life, social values, and the act of production. They sought unities which had been separated by industrialization, technology, and urbanization. Honest craftsmanship was more than simply an instrument to produce more handsome objects; it could lay the basis for an ethically responsible collective life. The monotonous ugliness of contemporary design stunted moral sensibilities as powerfully as it deformed taste.

The English and Americans were not the only ones awakening to the links between taste and social responsibility. In Northern Europe, Germans, Austrians and Scandinavians actively worked on the problems that Morris and his disciples isolated. The Finland where Eliel Saarinen studied and established his practice dramatized the designer's social role. Elsewhere in Europe the new forms termed Art Nouveau, Jugendstil, Stile Liberty—in architecture, ceramics, graphics, and furniture—had become ways of transcending the historicist tyrannies of artistic orthodoxy. Creative independence and autonomy could apparently flourish in this new stylistic vocabulary. Art would no longer be hedged in by didactic moralizing; its highest justification lay in its own being.

In Finland, however, the arts, the applied arts especially, were viewed as instruments to protect an authentic cultural inheritance. The arresting combinations of folk motifs and sinuous applications which form the Finnish ver-

Colorplate 1

MAJA ANDERSSON WIRDE (DESIGNER) AND STUDIO LOJA SAARINEN (WEAVERS). *Study Hall Lobby Carpet for Kingswood School Cranbrook* (detail). 1931. Linen warp, wool weft, wool pile; plain weave with eight picks of weft between each row of knots. 22′ 10″ × 11′ 3″. Kingswood School Cranbrook

sion of Art Nouveau suggested how nationalist aims could exploit the audacious new shapes. For Finns the visual arts made up an arena of recovery, a means of resisting the Pan-Slavism being trumpeted by their Russian rulers. Handicrafts, architecture, design itself suggested a new basis for cultural identity.[3]

There is, then, an interesting convergence of aims and experiences which ties Eliel Saarinen and Scandinavia with George Booth and the aspirations of the Middle West. This convergence makes Cranbrook a special cultural achievement. Although Booth and Saarinen discovered one another under specific, even arbitrary and coincidental circumstances, the match between them built upon a certain historical logic. Like turn-of-the-century Finland, the Middle West labored under the constraints of a cultural province. While its talented young artists sought reputations in distant centers, it had begun to provide within itself the means for their training and support. Museums, art schools, academies of design, and societies of connoisseurship began to appear. The Polytechnical Institute in Helsinki, the Architectural Club, the Friends of Finnish Handicrafts, the School of Arts and Crafts, had Midwestern counterparts in the *Inland Architect*, the school of The Art Institute of Chicago, The Detroit Museum of Art (later The Detroit Institute of Arts), the Minneapolis Chalk and Chisel Club, *House Beautiful*, and a series of publications and institutions concerned with training, certifying, and educating.[4]

There were other parallels between Finland and the Middle West. Both were dominated by the presence of Nature. The harsh winter climate combined with an abundance of summer sunlight, innumerable lakes, and large forests to pull Finns back to outdoor living, even after they had moved to cities like Helsinki or Turku. Nature as weather was omnipresent in Scandinavia. In the Middle West it was the scale of the landscape, the endless prairies and huge inland seas, that tended to impress residents, along with the severity of summer heat and winter cold. Nature in the Middle West was less easy to admire than it was in Finland. Its power was immense but its beauty more subtle, with uniformities cloying to eyes seeking the contrasts of mountain and plain, or ocean and sea coast. Architects rather than painters proved best able to translate the qualities of the prairies into symbolic and representational forms. Sullivan, Wright, George Maher, Purcell and Elmslie, as well as others of the Prairie School created their version of a distinctively organic domestic architecture at just the time that Saarinen was building the flats, villas, and civic structures that would ensure his reputation in Europe. In both situations respect for Nature and provincial traditions combined to aid the architects. Local needs were challenging, not constricting.[5]

Cosmopolitan as they were, Booth and Saarinen demonstrated their preferences by moving outside the city, Saarinen constructing his famous studio-home, Hvitträsk, more than twenty miles from Helsinki, George Booth founding a new community in Bloomfield Hills, just about the same distance north of Detroit. For there was also, in Finland and the Middle West, a tension between a rural past and an urban future. Despite the persistent power of the natural landscape, growing cities would have much to say about the social and intellectual development of the two regions. Small as it was, Helsinki had become surprisingly sophisticated by 1910, while Chicago and her less populous urban neighbors were developing into significant economic powers in their own right. Much of this Midwestern area's character would be hammered out in cities and towns. Visiting the Middle West just after World War I (and defending its high ambitions) Meredith Nicolson described the "alert young cities" watching each other "enviously—they are enormously proud and anxious not to be out-bettered in the struggle for perfection."[6] Julian Street, who made his tour just before the War, likened Buffalo, Cleveland, and Detroit to three sisters living amicably on the same block. As the youngest, Detroit was the "belle of the family" with a "sweet, domestic kind of beauty, like that of a young wife. . . ."[7] Midwestern cities were big with plans for cultural palaces and civic centers, even while the region itself continued to be suspicious of urban life as an ideal.[8]

Saarinen's career showed evidence of the same split. While some of his most important commissions involved country houses, urban needs made his large-scale projects possible, among them the Helsinki Railway Station (figs. 1 and 21) and the National Museum. Even decentralization, which Saarinen supported fervently, required extensive planning, and he favored a dispersed monumentality in the 1915 scheme for Munksnas-Haga, a section of Helsinki.

Urbanization was creating new links between Northern Europe and the Middle West. However ancient their origins, the North German and Scandinavian cities were new to large populations. Helsinki itself had been a small town before political events thrust prominence upon it. Its lengthy past had left few relics, because periodic fires had ravaged its wooden buildings. But by century's end Helsinki had a particularly concentrated mixture of architectural forms and was a fortunate place for a young architect to grow up in. One early twentieth-century visitor, A. M. Scott, found in it a "strange, freakish personality that is alien to the rest of Europe," suggesting Japan or Egypt. Its mixture of soberly German, elegantly neoclassical, and bizarre modern buildings made it seem like "an enchanted palace" rising from the sea, right out of the Arabian Nights. But there was a variety and wanton energy to Finnish urban design that pleased Scott, "a freshness, a verve, an intense delight in artistic representation that we miss in the prosaic banalities and arid scholasticism with which we are so familiar at home. There is movement, life, effort, experiment here."[9]

With a few changes Scott's last comments might have been the response to Chicago architecture of an Easterner impressed by the novelty and energy of the region's approach to building, different from the academicism that clung to the seaboard. Finland, on the periphery of a world culture, and the Middle West, deep within the interior of another, were linked by their special provincial versions of cosmopolitanism. Far enough from the capitals to be permitted their own voices, they were close enough to benefit from established masters and accepted practices, to absorb the lessons of technical competence and stylistic literacy. The result was plain-style exoticism in the Prairie School's Middle West and exuberant Jugendstil in Finland, each uniting a massive simplicity of form to dazzlingly original ornamentation. Both architectural schools were similar in their insistent individuality, awaiting discovery by visitors weary of derivative academic design and seeking new models for the future.

Cultural exchanges between the two regions formed a counterpoint to the immigration of people. As scholars have shown, Germans, Austrians, and Scandinavians were quickest to appreciate the Prairie School, while this group was alert to developments in Berlin, Vienna, Darmstadt, and Amsterdam.[10] City-building tasks stimulated exchanges of ideas. Although Daniel Burnham's 1909 Chicago Plan was inspired heavily by Paris, it made its journey abroad to be exhibited at Berlin, and American engineers and city planners were eager to learn about German zoning and municipal land banks. Pooling information on the electrical, sewerage, public works, and rapid transit systems being constructed in both areas also furthered this cross-pollination.[11] And just before the War, Scandinavian art shows appeared, the first, sponsored by the American-Scandinavian Society (founded in 1908), opening in New York, and then being shown in Buffalo, Toledo, and Chicago, before returning to Boston, and then home. American reviewers commended the closeness to nature represented by the landscape paintings, the Swedes displaying the "youthful spirit of a widely scattered Northern nation awakening to a new sense of national life."[12] In 1913 an exhibition of the Danish Handicraft Society came to Detroit, sponsored by the Boston Arts and Crafts society. Scandinavian art was emerging as an attractive complement to the Mediterranean and Gallic sources which had been dominant for so long.

The new influence of Northern Europe was demonstrated after the War in the famous Chicago Tribune Competition (fig. 20) which first brought Saarinen to American attention. Half of the more than one hundred foreign entries came from Germany, Scandinavia, and the Netherlands.[13] The remainder were divided among sixteen countries, from Cuba and Luxembourg to Mexico and New Zealand. Wartime struggle and economic dislocations combined with American prosperity to suggest emigration to some European artists and architects. Saarinen's journey, first to Chicago and then to Michigan, was to a region feeling the surge of steel, rubber, glass, and automobile production, and planning immense quantities of industrial, commercial, and residential construction.[14]

But the Middle West in the twenties was also experiencing— or suffering from—an unprecedented literary and journalistic coverage. Since the days of Mark Twain, Hamlin Garland, Edward Eggleston, and Theodore Dreiser, Midwestern writers had been a major force in national literature.[15] They were associated with realistic, carefully documented, and often heavily ironic descriptions of the area's social geography. The Middle West endured an arresting combination of boosterism and self-denigration. By the 1920s it was not only the harsh realities of farm life that were receiving attention; towns and cities, as Sherwood Anderson, Sinclair Lewis, and Edgar Lee Masters presented them in their classic texts, were filled with a series of philistine voices.[16] When Ernest Gruening published his symposium volume *These United States* in 1923, Leonard Lanson Cline entitled his essay on Michigan "The Fordizing of a Pleasant Peninsula." Detroit he presented as "the consummation of the salesman's ideal." Its orchestra, library, and museum were simply the "outward and visible sign of an inward and spiritual salesmanship," a gesture like the Mother's Day carnation "in the buttonhole of the man who has not written home for twelve years." Michiganians, he insisted, were "a people without identity, without community of purpose or past, without tradition," and their commitment to culture seemed complacent and hypocritical.[17]

The rest of the Midwest also fared badly. "Have you a city that smells worse than Akron," Sherwood Anderson asked in his essay on Ohio, or "is a worse junk-heap of ugliness than Youngstown, that is more smugly self-satisfied than Cleveland. . .?"[18] What Kansas lacked, William Alan White confessed, was "a sense of beauty. . . . Nothing is more gorgeous in color and form than a Kansas sunset; yet it is hidden from us. . . . Why is the golden bowl broken. . . ?"[19]

But affection lingered. After lining up his targets, targets lampooned unmercifully in *Babbitt, Main Street,* and *Dodsworth,* Sinclair Lewis wrote that Minnesota, like the rest of the Middle West, had one supreme merit. Admittedly, its rulers were reverent toward automobiles, golf, bridge, and banking. But whereas Easterners desired nothing else, the "golfocentric" Midwesterner was not altogether satisfied; "wistfully he desires a beauty that he does not understand."[20] Surrounded by the symbols of twentieth-century prosperity, Midwesterners continued to search for cultural leavening, and to complete a civilization that seemed, perennially, still unfinished.

George Booth's attempt to bring an extraordinary tripartite institution—school, atelier, and art colony—to a Detroit suburb was, in one sense, an answer to this inchoate demand. Cranbrook would educate artists, supply art and artifacts of quality, and, most of all, exemplify the possibilities of a community committed to art. It was the integration of art with daily living which made Cranbrook special. And for this the total setting, provided by Saarinen's buildings, Milles' sculpture, and the landscape, was crucial. Saarinen had created his own such world at Hvitträsk thirty years before; there were few American models for Booth to replicate. American art colonies were recent, created usually to provide inexpensive vacation retreats for artists and writers.[21] Rarely were they comprehensively planned. They were usually perched on some strip of attractive seashore or along a pretty lake, battening off landscape beauty in a modest way. Cranbrook, however, was a designed entity, intended to integrate dozens of separate lives on a year-round basis. Like many European cities it would suggest a finished, a completed world. This sense of spatial integration was one of Saarinen's legacies from Helsinki; and his continuing interest in monuments, evidenced in both his urban plans and his competition entries, revealed a concern with centering lives around common goals and visions.

It was vision and an enlarged sense of possibility that brought Booth and Saarinen together. The problem was learning how to extend the vision to others. Cranbrook could be perfect in itself yet limited in its impact if it remained isolated from the city that lay twenty miles away. While some visitors in the thirties and forties marveled at Cranbrook's special combination of creative art and community, others found an air of unreality, a distancing from the problems of the larger society.[22]

This was a dilemma facing utopian communities more generally, struggling to perfect a way of life and make it simultaneously relevant and appealing to a large audience. The solution was to exemplify, to supply a model for others to admire and imitate. In the twentieth century this has become a Scandinavian role, and occasionally a Scandinavian conceit: to demonstrate to other industrialized societies the possibilities of designing an environment at once humane, beautiful, and efficient. Several generations ago, this was a Midwestern ideal as well. George Booth's goals were broad. America, he told Detroit's second annual Arts and Crafts Society exhibition audience, "is peculiarly the land of hope. . . . We are, as it were, in the laboratory of life experimenting, seeking the truth." The purpose of the Society was to "spread the gospel of good work" along with higher standards of art, "to the end that American life may progress in simplicity and purity. . . ."[23] There was size to Booth's ambitions. At a time when the Middle West is afflicted by diminished expectations and economic disappointments it is useful to recall this period of optimism and amplitude. And to see in institutions like Cranbrook not simply a source for great design, but testimony to an exemplifying ideal and even hope for its renewal.

2 | CRANBROOK AND THE SEARCH FOR TWENTIETH-CENTURY FORM

Late in his life, George G. Booth, founder of Cranbrook and chief American patron of Eliel Saarinen, admitted privately that he did not like the "city fathers," as he called them, that guard the main entrance of Saarinen's railway station in Helsinki (figs. 1 and 21).[1] The gigantic figures of pink granite that stare into the Finnish capital perhaps embodied, for him, too much Nordic strength and stubbornness. Booth respected good Scandinavian work. But in Saarinen, his architect and collaborator of twenty-five years, he appreciated gentleness, flexibility, and a rare visual sensitivity. By the 1940s, the heraldic iconography in Helsinki may therefore have seemed ostentatious and crude.

In their time, however, these four robust bearers of light were surely seen as emblems of the search for architectural, as well as political, independence in Finland. They can also be regarded, in retrospect, as symptomatic of the creative life of Saarinen and the intentions of his eventual American benefactor. For the lanterns are like glowing crystals, held forth as Holy Grails. Several scholars have recently pointed out that such imagery, rooted in the Middle Ages and revived in German Romantic literature, refers to the cathartic power of art in a dreary world.[2] The crystalline lamps, connoting metamorphosis and perfection, are therefore symbols of the transformation of everyday life through the arts.

Such potent ideas of aesthetic rejuvenation underlay many aspects of the Arts and Crafts movement at the turn of this century. Although it originated in England during the 1860s, the movement soon became international and served diverse regional functions—as well as more personal, therapeutic ones. Eventually, it addressed the problem of the designer's role in the industrial context, especially in Germany. Protagonists in the most fruitful years of the movement, that is, about 1895–1910, were usually of the generation born in the late 1860s or early 1870s. They included, for example, Peter Behrens and Joseph Maria Olbrich, Josef Hoffmann and Adolf Loos, Charles Rennie Mackintosh and Edwin Lutyens, Frank Lloyd Wright and Bertram Goodhue. Some of the architects had been academically trained, while others were without much formal education at all. Still others were converts to architecture from other media. Yet they had in common a concern for the single-family house, and even those who were not British were touched by a certain Anglophilia. Eventually a desire to go beyond quaint solutions brought them through a cleansing period of elegant stylization; in their search for an appropriate twentieth-century style, some went on to a more tectonic classicism.[3]

Eliel Saarinen and George G. Booth were members of this generation and they shared Arts and Crafts ideals. This conflation of beliefs was to engender the Cranbrook Academy of Art, officially founded in 1932 after years of gestation.

ELIEL SAARINEN IN FINLAND AND AMERICA

The architectural firm of Gesellius, Lindgren and Saarinen, founded in Helsinki in 1896, had a prominent role in the surge of National Romanticism in Finland before

1

GESELLIUS AND SAARINEN. *Railway Station, Helsinki* (main entrance). 1904–16. Photo courtesy Wayne Andrews

the turn of the century. The partners explored the possibilities of granite construction in the manner of H. H. Richardson, injecting Nordic elements to make it their own. Then came several towered country houses that owed something to the Shingle Style.[4] Their interiors, after 1900, were more English. Large living halls, fireplace nooks, prominent stairways, details of hammered copper, stenciling and appliqués, were clues to an admiration of things British (fig. 2). By the middle of the decade, however, the firm (now Gesellius and Saarinen) had found aesthetic kinship with Vienna, where modernism, although lately arrived, was more elegant than anything else on the Continent (fig. 3). Thus one remote capital of European culture supplied encouragement and examples to another, even more detached, artistic center.

Germanic influence, which hovered over almost every aspect of Finnish life, can be observed even more clearly in Saarinen's vocabulary between 1908 and 1910. This is best seen in a little-known project that he designed in 1910

2
GESELLIUS, LINDGREN AND SAARINEN. *M. Neuscheller House ("Suur-Merijoki") near Viipuri, Finland* (library). 1902–03. Reproduced from *Dekorative Kunst* 6 (1903)

for an exhibition of 1913 (fig. 4). The forms were taken from J. M. Olbrich's last monumental work in Darmstadt, the Exhibition Building of 1905–08; yet Saarinen made much more of the individual motifs. In his project there were several courtyards along one main and three minor axes, all accented by entrance pavilions, galleries, and a variety of towers and roofs. Envisioned on the edge of a pond, this proposal also recalled the buildings of Olbrich and Behrens in the Flora Park, Cologne, which were built for an exhibition of Rhenish art in 1906.[5]

Saarinen, almost more than anyone else of his generation, was concerned with the whole gamut of the applied arts and architecture. His interests ranged, quite literally, from sofa pillows to the cityscape. By the second decade of the new century he was busy with plans for suburbs and the renewal of cities, seeking an architectural order for his native land. But unlike Otto Wagner in Vienna, Saarinen was not independently wealthy and could not keep his draftsmen busy without real clients. He therefore depended increasingly on his patron, Julius Tallberg. When Tallberg died in 1921, Saarinen was left to the vicissitudes of postwar civil strife and economic doldrums.

In 1922 Eliel's wife, Loja, had a dream in which she found a lost jewel and returned it to its grateful owner in Chicago.[6] Within a few months her husband had entered the Chicago Tribune competition and won second prize

23

(see De Long). A trip to America followed in 1923. By 1924 he had met George Booth, who wanted to develop his Michigan farmland to serve the public good (see Taragin). It was later reported that Saarinen had long carried the "idea of establishing an institution for architectural schooling, where all related arts, sculpture and handicraft included, should be gathered together."[7] However nebulous the concept may have been, it meshed with the ideas of Booth, who now became Saarinen's "patron-for-life."

GEORGE G. BOOTH AND THE ARTS

Nine years older than Saarinen, George Booth represented the earlier end of the same generation. Born in Canada, by 1924 he had become a naturalized American and a millionaire. Although he was not without artistic accomplishments of his own (see Farmer), his fortune had come through marriage and newspaper publishing. Booth was, therefore, a natural propagandist, and a dedicated chauvinist of things American—especially Midwestern. He was also a confirmed Anglophile. A religious man, he was the donor of a church to serve his suburban neighbors. Further, he was a patron of museums and a founder in 1906 of the Detroit Society of Arts and Crafts. And, although he was not himself an educator, in his ultimate role as founder of Cranbrook he almost functioned as one. As a gentleman of Bloomfield Hills, aged sixty, he began to combine his strengths and obsessions to create on his pastoral estate three private schools and an academy of art. It was an American millionaire's sense of noblesse oblige, together with a persuasive ability to realize his private wishes, that brought Cranbrook into being.

4
ELIEL SAARINEN. *Arts Building Project, 1913 Industrial Exhibition, Helsinki.* 1910. Reproduced from *Arkitekten* 6 (1910)

In the story of Cranbrook the year 1922 looms large. In February George Booth and his wife, while on a tour of Europe, visited the American Academy in Rome, which had been founded in 1894. They admired the building and visited with the Fellows—the American artists and scholars who had come to study for appointed periods. A history of the Academy published in 1915 emphasized the philosophy of the place:

24

The Academy is not a school; it is not for technical training or the teaching of any rudiments; it does not have classes nor does it even impose a very rigid, prescribed course. . . . The primary object[ive] . . . is to afford to persons of advanced training an opportunity for residence and study in Rome and Europe, generally under conditions such, that while they are given every freedom for individual development, each member is brought into contact with other members working in the various allied arts. This fellowship of the students among themselves, and their informal contact with the members of the Faculty, are the means by which influence is brought to bear on them rather than by any formal instruction.[8]

In 1922 Booth's newspaper, the *Detroit News,* carried photographs of, and an article—as well as an editorial—about the American Academy, which was described as "nourishing the flower of this nation's artistic genius in an atmosphere and under circumstances which, of all the world, are best designed to cause that flower to bloom."[9] In that same issue of the *News,* an article announced an exhibition of handcrafts by the Wiener Werkstätte that was planned at Detroit's Society of Arts and Crafts for the end of the year. Continuing a policy of enriching the Detroit Institute of Arts with decorative arts, George Booth purchased six pieces from the Viennese workshop for the collection.[10]

Also in 1922, there appeared an exhaustive study compiled by Charles R. Richards, *Art in Industry,* which surveyed the state of American education in the applied arts. "This country finds itself unexpectedly today the richest

5

ELIEL SAARINEN (DESIGNER) AND LOJA SAARINEN (FABRICATOR). *Model of Cranbrook School and Academy of Art.* 1925. Photo: Nyholm. Courtesy Cranbrook Academy of Art/Museum

6

JOSEF HOFFMANN. *Preliminary Sketch for the Austrian Pavilion, "Exposition Internationale des Arts Décoratifs et Industriels Modernes," Paris, 1925.* 1924. Reproduced from Eduard F. Sekler, *Josef Hoffmann: Das architektonische Werk,* Salzburg and Vienna, 1982

country in the world. Economic leadership is forced upon it. . . . In many fields we are sadly unprepared for such world ascendancy and in none is this more true than in the field of art."[11] Richards and his assistants had examined the curricula of fifty-five schools that gave instruction in the "industrial arts." From the Maryland Institute (founded 1847), Cooper Union (1859), the Rhode Island School of Design (1877), Pratt Institute (1887), and even the California School of Arts and Crafts (1907), data were gathered, conclusions and recommendations made. A large chapter of the book was devoted to "Industrial Art Education in Germany," comparing it with the situation here at home:

> The Arts and Crafts Movement [in America] . . . has had little influence in raising the general level of design. . . . Its main result has been to stimulate a comparatively small group of men and women to produce "applied art" such as stained-glass windows, work in silver, needlework, bookbinding and the like, but at this point the movement has apparently stopped. This . . . is in contrast with the history of such work in Germany, where . . . instruction in the arts and crafts is not only carried on very effectively in the schools but, what is more important, exerts a very large influence in the production of the factory and of the workshop.[12]

Richards' book surely did not go unnoticed in Detroit or in Bloomfield Hills. Within two years Saarinen and Booth had met. The architect later recalled their conference of May 1925:

> Mr. Booth revealed his plans for Cranbrook and for the first time told the story of what he intended to do about it. . . . He was full of vigor and energy. . . . He spoke as one who has something close to his heart and embraces it with warmth and enthusiasm.
>
> [Booth] explained how he, because of ancestral inclination, keen interest, and good advice, learned already in his earliest years to understand and appreciate the realm of beauty in nature, in art, and wherever he turned his attention. This fact, he accentuated, had become his great opportunity in his enjoyment of life. . . . [Now] he was eager to share with others the same happy opportunity. . . .
>
> In the search for various methods . . . to advance his ideas, he fell upon the happy thought that his ideas could be advanced best when started from the youth. That is, when sensitiveness to beauty is grafted into minds that are still young and receptive, the result is bound to be most effective.
>
> Indeed, in all its simplicity, this was the central core of the Cranbrook idea.[13]

From these vague, but admirably altruistic beginnings developed the three schools for young people, out of which, it was hoped, talented artists would be chosen and joined together with promising students from elsewhere in the crowning institution of the whole complex: an academy of art. Although the Academy was not officially opened until 1932, it was always regarded as both the goal and physical center of Cranbrook. In fact, when Saarinen made his drawings for the school for boys, which was the first major building of the complex (1925 ff.), the Academy was conceived adjacent to it at a slightly higher ground level. The model of 1925 by Loja Saarinen gave three-dimensional form to these suggestions and reveals the most fascinating aspects of Eliel Saarinen's concept of the grand plan (figs. 5 and 29). There were to be several major axes and many minor ones. Courtyards were slightly irregular, and they opened to ponds or great vistas. The whole was ambitious; yet the effect was to be intimate and cloistered.

Although various details of the drawings and model bespeak the Scandinavian background of the designer, the overall result recalled English Gothic Revival quadrangles.[14] Inevitable, therefore, is the analogy with work being done on American campuses in the first three decades of the century, especially at Princeton and Yale.[15] It was in 1903 that Andrew Fleming West, Dean of the Graduate School at Princeton, had written that the campus should consist of "quadrangles enclosing sunny lawns, towers and gateways opening into quiet retreats, ivy-grown walls looking on sheltered gardens, vistas through avenues of arching elms, walks that wind amid the groves of Academe."[16] Saarinen described his own vision more architecturally:

> The general scheme is arranged to obtain a good mass-effect and rhythm of line in the landscape and harmonious and varied place-formations in conformity with the character of the buildings. . . . In suitable places a richer form treatment has been suggested to further support a varied picturesqueness as a deviation from the symmetry and seriousness of the basic motif. . . . The ornamental treatment . . . will grow out of the production of the Academy in these arts. . . .
>
> Thus the institution grows successively into a historic document of the work executed and of the currents that moved within the youth studying at the Academy.[17]

So there was an organic principle in Saarinen's plan. Despite the exacting details of the model, there were to be modifications and additions as the complex evolved, as well as sculptural embellishments by faculty and students (see Taragin and Marter). In actuality, changes were sometimes made because of George Booth's fear of ostentation;[18] more often they were made because of other demands on his funds. Some changes, however, reflected Saarinen's developing sense of an American architecture. Thus the Kingswood School (1929–31) has an air of Frank Lloyd Wright's prairie architecture (see De Long)—and, even more interestingly, a similarity to Behrens' Wrightian buildings for the Gutehoffnungshütte in Oberhausen, Germany (1921–25).[19]

When the Cranbrook Library and Museum (1937–42) were finally built at the end of the fountain axis leading from Lone Pine Road, the open portico had the unmistakable air of European abstracted classicism of the 1930s (pl. 61). Close examination suggests, however, that this was not simply a gesture paralleling the spare compositions of totalitarianism. Rather, it is Arts and Crafts classicism that goes back to Viennese work of the 1920s—for example, the preliminary scheme by Josef Hoffmann for the Austrian Pavilion at the Paris Exposition of 1925 (fig. 6). The debt to Vienna was only slowly abandoned by Saarinen, as is obvious when his ironwork at Cranbrook is compared with the artifacts of another of the Wiener Werkstätte's most inventive designers, Dagobert Peche (figs. 7, 125, 126, 127; pls. 30 and 31).

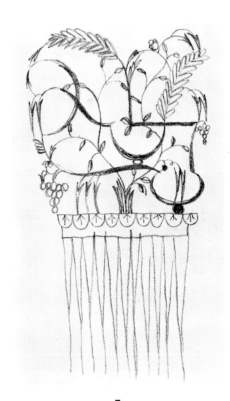

7

DAGOBERT PECHE. *Sketch for an Ivory Comb.* Before 1923. Reproduced from M. Flögl, *Die Wiener Werkstätte, 1903–1928: Modernes Kunstgewerbe und sein Weg,* Vienna, 1929

Parallels in imagery between the Cranbrook buildings and European examples point to the consideration of European precedents for such an academy of the arts. Like so much else in the Cranbrook story, threads lead back to England. For it was the land of the Industrial Revolution that brought forth the most imaginative responses to and reactions against it. London was the site of the first international exposition, held in 1851. That event, in turn, led to the founding of the South Kensington Museum (now the Victoria and Albert Museum) in 1852. When the Museum's new building was opened in 1857, the School of Design (later the Royal College of Art) was transferred to the same premises. This influential precedent of having a school of design in connection with a museum of ornamental art came to be known as the "South Kensington principle."[20]

Gottfried Semper, the German architect and theorist, had been involved with the London exposition of 1851. The following year he published *Wissenschaft, Industrie und Kunst,* in which he argued for the judicious use of machinery, workshops with a spirit of community between master and apprentice, and the improvement of public taste through museums of the decorative arts.[21] It was in Vienna that the first such institution on the Continent, the Österreichisches Museum für Kunst und Industrie, was established, opening in May 1864. Within four years a school of applied arts had been added. When the latter institution celebrated its fiftieth anniversary in 1918, Alfred Roller, its director, could boast of three major departments (architecture, painting, and sculpture) as well as studio courses in metal sculpture, ceramics, enamelwork, and textile and fashion design. Many of the faculty members were, or had been, associated with the Wiener Werkstätte (founded in 1903), which Roller rightly regarded as the perfect model of combining art and small industry.[22]

Developments in Vienna from the 1860s onward were soon emulated in other major cities of the German-speaking world. These schools of applied arts were carefully organized according to a methodical approach that continued to thrive into the twentieth century thus warranting the praise of Charles Richards and his colleagues in 1922, as mentioned earlier.[23] But in Germany another innovation developed around the period of the First World War when, for example, the Academy of Fine Arts in Berlin was combined with the School of Applied Arts under the general directorship of the architect Bruno Paul.

The most famous example of such amalgamation in Germany was, of course, the chain of events in Weimar that led to the founding of the Bauhaus in 1919. Henry van de Velde, the Belgian neoimpressionist-turned-architect, had been called to Weimar in 1901 by the Grand Duke of Saxony to be a consultant in matters of the arts and commerce. Eventually he designed a new art academy there, as well as a building for the school of applied arts which he eventually headed. Van de Velde chose not to publish a fixed *Lehrplan* for his school. Rather he sought to establish good relationships between teachers and apprentices as had "existed in the great times of handcraft in the past."[24]

The First World War forced Van de Velde out of Germany. His replacement after the conflict was Walter Gropius, who was a full generation younger. Gropius unified the academy and the school in an attempt to eradicate the differences between the fine and the applied arts. The result constitutes a major chapter of twentieth-century history. The first *Programm* of the Bauhaus, published in 1919, urged architects, sculptors, and painters to return to the crafts. "There is no essential difference between the artist and the craftsman. The artist is an exalted craftsman. . . . Proficiency in a craft is essential to every artist." To train architects was the ultimate goal, but the way was through the craftsman's workshop. Gropius and his co-workers embarked with almost religious zeal.

> Together let us desire, conceive, and create the new structure of the future, which will embrace architecture and sculpture and painting in one unity and which will one day rise toward heaven from the hands of a million workers like the crystal symbol of a new faith.[25]

By the late 1920s when the Bauhaus had been moved to Dessau and the first Americans began to attend,[26] the students were being adventurously trained in the use of machinery and new materials for household objects. In the more traditional media, such as weaving, complete abstraction was soon the rule.

In addition to the many European schools founded in the nineteenth and early twentieth centuries, one other phenomenon must be considered. It is the artists colony, an invention of the mid-nineteenth century.[27] The most telling example in this context was that in Darmstadt. It was the only such group that was called an "artists colony" from its beginning. In fact, it was not a group that had come together of its own accord because of mutual interests. Rather, it was the invention of Ernst Ludwig, the Grand Duke of Hesse, who in 1899 called to Darmstadt seven artists, not one of whom was known principally as a painter, to live and work in the colony.[28] A grandson of Queen Victoria, and an artist and composer of some achievement, Ernst Ludwig was a political figure of little significance.[29] He thus chose to preside over a world of the arts.[29] J. M. Olbrich was one of the seven artists; having designed their communal studio building, he spoke optimistically at the laying of the cornerstone in May 1899:

> In this peaceful stillness . . . [we dedicate ourselves] to providing, in firm and unmistakable forms, a reflection of modern culture, thereby placing a sign post on the way to the renewal of life.[30]

To emphasize the general good, the artists were encouraged to help raise the level of public and commercial taste in the grand duchy through the work in their studios. The idea was adventurous, but its achievements seldom matched the initial promise. At one point (1907–11) there was an attempt to bolster the colony by introducing a plan of studio teaching for tuition-paying students.[31]

Despite all of these historical precedents of raising public taste and joining the fine and applied arts under one roof, it was the American Academy in Rome that furnished the most direct inspiration for what George G. Booth brought about on his acreage in the cause of the arts. For the policy in Rome of adopting no curriculum and inviting artists and scholars to come together for informal creative activity remained the idealized mode for Cranbrook.

DEVELOPMENT OF THE CRANBROOK ACADEMY

The Cranbrook Academy evolved slowly as an idea and as a working institution. Booth, in his Trust Indenture of 1927, had foreseen an arts and crafts school in conjunction with the Academy, the latter eventually to include departments of architecture, design, (interior) decoration, drawing, painting, sculpture, drama, landscape design, music, and artistic craftsmanship (see Taragin).[32] By August 1930 he had formulated a concept of four master artists-in-residence: an architect, a painter, a sculptor, and a designer. These master artists would reside and work at Cranbrook, and "give general talks to students on art matters." They would also help in planning the architectural development of the immediate properties by "submitting schemes or sketches without charge for any work contemplated, but for actual work performed . . . [they] would be fairly compensated."[33]

In April 1931, a full year before the Academy actually opened, Eliel Saarinen addressed the national convention of the American Institute of Architects at San Antonio on the subject of "the Cranbrook Development."

> [The purpose of the] Cranbrook Academy of Art . . . is to afford talented and highly trained students the opportunity of pursuing their studies in a favorable environment and under the leadership of artists of the highest standing. . . .
>
> [It] is not an art school in the ordinary meaning. *It is a working place for creative art.* The leading idea is to have artists . . . live at Cranbrook and execute their work there. Those artists form a more or less permanent staff of the Art Council. Besides these artists we will have . . . visiting artists from various parts of the country or from foreign countries

[who] will bring freshness and new impulses to the Cranbrook art life and will help us to a richer and closer understanding of the contemporary movement in various minds and in various countries. . . .

Creative art cannot be taught by others. Each one has to be his own teacher. But [contact] with other artists and discussions with them provide sources for inspiration. . . .

Many think the Academy with its Craft Studios tries to revive the medieval spirit of craftsmanship against our machine age. That is not so. The main idea . . . is not to develop craftsmanship, *but the design*. . . .

There is no use for skillful craftsmen if we do not know the form of our time. The first thing and the most important one is to develop an adequate design to express our contemporary life. And if the form is there, it is of minor importance if we use the hand of man or the machine. . . . Both are necessary.[34]

The philosophy of education at Cranbrook was seldom committed to paper, and never reduced to a manifesto; so one hunts in vain for a truly definitive document (see Taragin). But the essence of Booth's and Saarinen's thought was that "self-education under good leadership" was the only way "that leads toward the wisdom of life."[35] Instruction at first was principally in architecture, which—because of Saarinen's presence—included a spectrum of subjects from furniture design to city planning.

One of the first of seven full-time students in architecture was Carl Feiss (1932–33) who later recalled the atmosphere in the studio. Saarinen "was a small man, solid but not stout, and of a very self-effacing color. He merged into any crowd, disappearing like the Cheshire cat leaving nothing but twinkling gray eyes. Those eyes missed nothing—ever. He had inexhaustible energy." Feiss continued:

Eliel was constantly wandering in and out. He never gave what, in common architectural school parlance, would be called a "crit." Our relationships were different. His genius as a teacher was to make it appear that he believed that we knew as much about architecture as he did. The only differences were in kinds of experience and points of view. Since we knew that that was nonsense, we did everything we could to prove that it wasn't nonsense. The result was that we all worked harder and learned more in our few years at Cranbrook than ever before (or probably after). . . .

There was such a genuine intensity of purpose and so eager a search for order and beauty that none seemed ever to get bored or mad with anybody. . . . Both the winters of 1932 and 1933 were bitter cold and since we were all broke—in a sense exiled both physically and economically to the cultured wilds of Bloomfield Hills, Michigan—there was a real kinship amongst us. . . . It was an educational experience. It was an immersion into a little Shangri-La which gave some prevision of what a center of culture of the future could be.[36]

So from the beginning the emphasis was on place, people, and experience—rather than on curriculum and methods.

The Academy soon encountered the problem of attracting students worthy of its intentions. In many cases when candidates arrived for their postgraduate work, they were not well enough prepared. Thus, by 1936 an Intermediate School was developed to provide a quasi-remedial function (see Taragin). Although Eliel Saarinen constantly resisted any tendency to formalize the approach, classes were organized and eventually a system of credits was adopted. Degrees were finally awarded in 1943. Thus the free spirit of Cranbrook became more institutionalized in inevitable steps that were taken as students demanded certification of their prowess and experience.

Out of economic depression, trial and error, and by sheer will, the school had entered a golden age by the end of the 1930s. In fact, the two academic seasons before the American entry into the Second World War crystallized the magic of the place. The foundation laid by the older masters inspired and supported the new energies and ideas of the younger faculty and students. The staff for 1940–41 bears scrutiny. Eliel Saarinen was President, as well as Director of the Department of Architecture and Design. Carl Milles, who had come in 1931, was Director of the Department of Sculpture. The Department of Painting was headed by Zoltan Sepeshy, a Hungarian who also arrived in 1931. Other teachers and their titles were: Harry Bertoia, Metal Craftsman; Charles Eames, Instructor of Design; Marshall Fredericks, Instructor of Modelling; Maija Grotell, Instructor of Ceramics and Pottery; Wallace Mitchell, Instructor of Painting and Drawing; Eero Saarinen, Assistant in the Department of Architecture; Loja Saarinen, "In Charge of the Department of Weaving" (a special title, because she was not officially a teacher); and Marianne Strengell, Instructor of Weaving.

Only three of the above were native-born Americans, and this did not go unnoticed by outsiders,[37] some of whom also worried about the possibility of a "monastic mentality" at Cranbrook.[38] Nevertheless, there was an impressive sequence of guest lecturers,[39] and there were immensely productive days and nights in the Cranbrook studios. Although these glorious years were brief, they were stellar. The spirit and inventiveness of Eames and of Saarinen's son, Eero, who was his father's assistant, seem to have accounted for much of this period's verve (see De Long and Miller).

For several months in 1940–41, there was contact with Gordon M. Buehrig, designer of the 1936 Cord, regarding the possibility of founding a department of automobile design.[40] It was an appropriate place, in the shadow of Detroit, for such a plan. But this came to nothing. Nevertheless a concern about industrial design increased at Cranbrook. In the spring of 1941 correspondence began with Walter Baermann, an industrial designer who was then Director of the California Graduate School of Design in Pasadena. A native of Germany, Baermann had come to the United States in 1929 at the invitation of Joseph Urban, the Viennese architect in New York. Later he had worked for the designers Norman Bel Geddes and Henry Dreyfuss. In 1931–32, while working in the Philadelphia architectural offices of Howe and Lescaze, he had designed the interiors of the Philadelphia Savings Fund Society office building. By September 1941 he had been hired to replace Charles Eames and had become head of the new Department of Industrial Design at Cranbrook.

Eliel Saarinen asked Baermann to prepare a thorough "Report on the Present and Future of the Cranbrook Academy of Art." It was submitted by mid-October. The author found that the school did not measure up to Germanic expectations, nor to some American ones. "Its success and great esteem is based solely on the outstanding reputation of its leader and his associates and their success with single individual apprentices, as well as on the widely known excellence of its plant and its largely romanticized atmosphere."[41] Baermann recommended that the Academy, which was largely a postgraduate institution with little academic structure, be augmented with a complete undergraduate curriculum, a college curriculum, and even a junior college. By the following month there was considerable resistance to the proposals. In the summer of 1942, Baermann went to Washington as a consultant in the Office of Civilian Defense. His contract with Cranbrook was not renewed. The loss of Baermann represents the end of Cranbrook's short-lived first golden age.

World War II, of course, changed many things. Some classes were suspended and others served a new clientele. As students were diverted to war, there was more room for fee-paying local residents to come for occasional classes and to paint. Then the G.I. Bill was introduced in 1944. This all helped Cranbrook to survive (see Taragin). There were efforts to make the curriculum more viable for the mid-century—and for wartime. The 1942–43 *Announcement* contained a slightly altered statement of the Academy's "Educational Philosophy":

Conscious that arts and crafts are increasingly the servants of both war and peace, art, in its historic character, remains for the Academy the most natural and highest expression of man's effort to create and recreate his spiritual surroundings. The conception of art is all inclusive, and embraces architecture, sculpture, painting, the crafts, design, and all things which develop taste and reach toward achievement.[42]

By the end of the war, Eliel Saarinen was old and ready to retire. His resignation was accepted in 1946, and his place was taken by Zoltan Sepeshy, who was given the title of Director in 1946 and of President in 1959. This administration was not an entirely positive interlude for the Academy, at least not in retrospect. As a painter, Sepeshy's strength was in technique and materials; his style, and that of many of his students, was a variety of post-Cubist realism that became popular among W.P.A. muralists and magazine illustrators (see Marter). As an administrator he was gracious on the one hand, and a determined master of order and requirements on the other. Although his Department of Painting often had the most students, it did not become Cranbrook's strongest discipline under his aegis. As Eliel Saarinen and his sculptor-colleague Carl Milles faded from the scene, emphasis passed to other areas, especially to the ceramics workshop of Maija Grotell (see Eidelberg).

8

BENJAMIN BALDWIN AND HARRY WEESE. *Tea Wagon.* 1940. Reproduced from Eliot Noyes, *Organic Design in Home Furnishings,* New York: The Museum of Modern Art, 1941

SIGNIFICANCE OF THE CRANBROOK VISION

By 1950 Eliel Saarinen was dead, as was George G. Booth. Together they had founded an academy in the wilderness, based on the principles of flexibility and diversity. As J. S. Sirén emphasized in a memorial oration, the elder Saarinen had always felt that "life is too richly faceted to be encompassed in a single theme. The voice of the twentieth century must sound orchestral, and personality must have its alotted place in art."[43]

The influence of Eliel Saarinen had been noticeable in America early. For instance, the forms and decoration of the 1928 Bullocks Wilshire Department Store in Los Angeles, designed by John and David Parkinson, were surely derived from Saarinen's work.[44] His solution for the American skyscraper with a gentle profile of setbacks became an immediate paradigm. Saarinen's exhibition interiors for the Metropolitan Museum in 1929 and 1934–35 effectively summed up the decorative tendencies of the 1920s and anticipated interest in the *moderne* of the 1930s and 1940s (see Miller). He continued as a gentle and persuasive teacher until the next generation assumed his mantle after the Second World War.

The Academy's students and faculty had helped contribute to the tentative modernism of both the New York and San Francisco expositions in 1939.[45] It was at that pivotal point, 1939 to 1941, that the greatest Cranbrook-related innovations occurred. For example, it was in 1940 that The Museum of Modern Art announced its competition for home furnishings of "organic design." The award-winning drawings and prototypes were exhibited at the Museum the following year.[46] Eero Saarinen and Charles Eames, in perfect demonstration of the ideal of collaboration that had been encouraged at Cranbrook, produced the most important work in the competition. Their chair designs and subsequent work have become American classics. Yet Saarinen and Eames were not the only representatives of Cranbrook in the 1940 competition. Less familiar are the entries by Harry Weese and Ben Baldwin, particularly the tea wagon of tubular and perforated steel with a wicker basket (fig. 8). It was Alvar Aalto's cart of laminated wood updated and transformed by an American vision (see Miller).

With the furniture that Eero Saarinen and Charles Eames produced in the 1950s, the world saw thoroughly convincing applications of industrial methods and materials to physical and aesthetic needs. Eero and Eames produced the major American "look" of the 1950s for homes and, more usually, for offices. In this they were aided by Florence Knoll, who had participated in the "Cranbrook experience" exactly as the founders had originally intended. As a young woman, Florence Schust had come to Kingswood School Cranbrook, and through her studio work there had become acquainted with the Saarinens. They guided her further studies at the Academy, treated her as one of the family, and encouraged her travels abroad. After the development, with her husband, of the firm of Knoll Associates, the production of furniture designs by her Cranbrook colleagues, as well as by herself, put the name Knoll into every collection of good design in post-World War II America and abroad (see Miller). Her interiors of 1965 for the CBS Building in New York were the archetypes for corporate modernism of their time (pl. 26).

The CBS Building, one of the last works of Eero Saarinen, stands in New York as a brooding but eloquent statement of skyscraper design in opposition to the tall glass box (fig. 75). It has aged well, and gives little hint of the tumultuous searching for forms that typified the mature career of its designer. For, after his inventive variations on Miesian themes at the General Motors Technical Center (figs. 48, 98, 99), he produced a decade of remarkable buildings, responding almost expressionistically to their varied functions. Some of them, such as the TWA Terminal (figs. 71 and 101), were so personally interpretative that they fell short as architecture.[47] But there was more to Eero Saarinen than his extravagances. When he died in 1961, he was just getting over being "interesting" and was becoming one of the greatest American architects of his generation (see De Long and Miller).

The influences of Cranbrook are still with us, and still being renewed. The history of the Academy is complicated, and not without its uneven moments and missed opportunities. But who would expect otherwise of a continuing experiment? What is amazing and laudatory is the quality of the work of its founding faculty in creating the place and the precedent, and in successfully passing on its obsessions. We can look at the over 200 works in this exhibition with a certain critical distance and sense the romantic urge of their makers to push life to a higher register through the useful arts with which we surround ourselves.

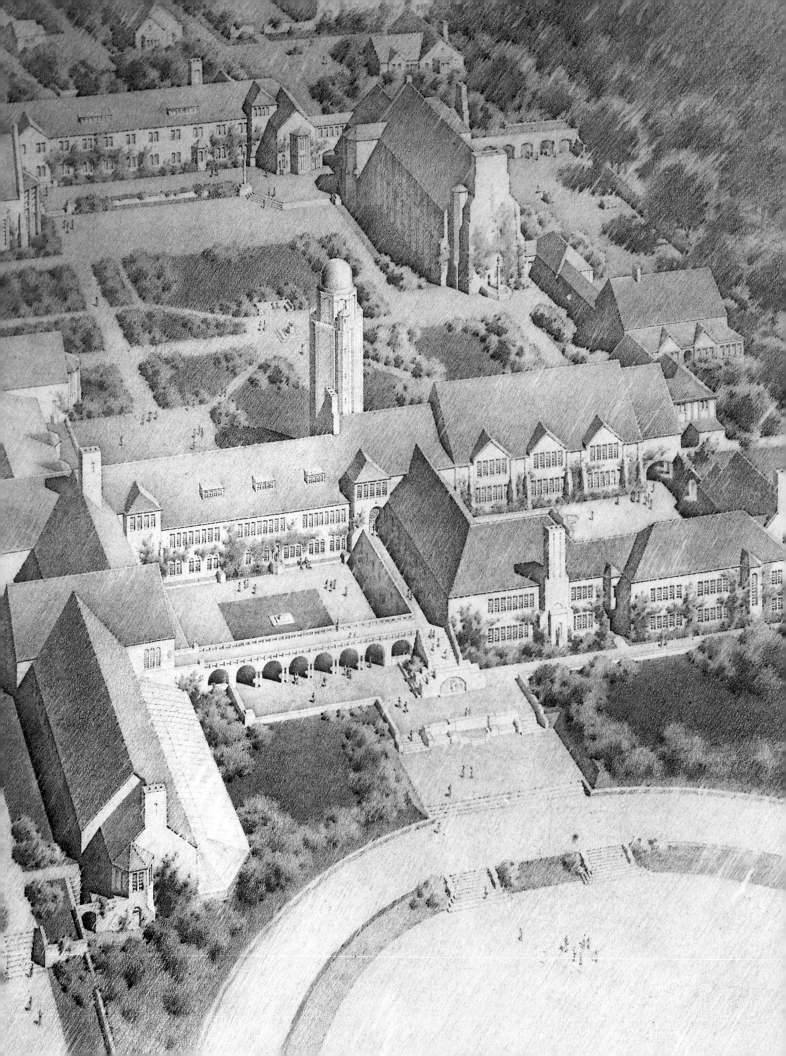

3 | THE HISTORY OF THE CRANBROOK COMMUNITY

In 1927, as part of the Trust Indenture for the Cranbrook Foundation, the Detroit newspaper publisher and patron of the arts George G. Booth (fig. 10) authorized the establishment of an educational community in Bloomfield Hills, Michigan, that would stress the knowledge and appreciation of the arts. The nucleus of this complex was to be an academy unlike any in America since it would be a working place for the creation of art, not an institution devoted entirely to theoretical teachings. At the time, Booth did not closely define the nature of this academy because he had not as yet developed a comprehensive plan for it.[1] The community, which would ultimately consist of the Episcopal Christ Church Cranbrook; Brookside School Cranbrook, an elementary school; two preparatory schools, Cranbrook School (for boys) and Kingswood School Cranbrook (for girls); Cranbrook Academy of Art; and Cranbrook Institute of Science, was founded in response to the existing policies of cultural institutions in metropolitan Detroit toward the decorative and applied arts. He appears to have felt that the isolation of his farm estate in a suburb twenty miles from the city would provide an excellent opportunity to put his ideas into effect. Since Booth and the architect Eliel Saarinen, the first President of Cranbrook Academy, conceived the community's development along fairly broad lines, the Academy grew in an *ad hoc* manner for the first twenty-five years of its existence,[2] changing frequently in response to the political and economic climate of the United States.

From the turn of the century on, Booth had been one of the leading proponents in America of the Arts and Crafts movement. Born in 1864 in Toronto, Booth's interest in architecture and the decorative and applied arts can be traced to his family background. He himself felt that his ancestors' involvement in the arts and crafts in the village of Cranbrook, Kent, in England was the primary cause of this fascination.

> . . . In [Cranbrook, Kent] . . . my father was born, and my grandfather and great-grandfather lived and worked as craftsmen. My grandfather, whom I as a child remember seeing only once or twice was a coppersmith, and a master of the craft. He made those wonderfully-formed ewers, kettles, and flagons of which the antiquarian is so proud—made them by hand as his father before him did. He was proud of his handiwork, and this characteristic has clung tenaciously to each branch of the family since, and I am certain it accounts for my own love for the artistic work of the handicraftsman . . .[3]

There were, however, many other artistic influences on Booth throughout his youth. After receiving the equivalent of an eighth-grade education, Booth worked for a short time in Toronto for his uncle, the architect Henry Langley. This experience was important but Langley's home filled with objets d'art made an even greater impact upon the young man.[4] In 1883, two years after his family's move to Detroit, George was hired as salesman and designer in the ornamental ironworks company his father was managing in Windsor, Ontario; by the mid-1880s George had purchased the firm himself and was running a lucrative

9
ELIEL SAARINEN. *Cranbrook School.* 1925 ff., aerial perspective (detail) 1926. Pencil on paper (signed *Cranbrook 1926/Eliel Saarinen*). 21 ½ × 25 ⅜″. Cranbrook Academy of Art/Museum

10
George G. Booth (1864–1949). c. 1916.
Photo courtesy Cranbrook Archives

11
Ellen Warren Scripps Booth (1863–1948).
1918. Photo: Francis Scott Clark. Courtesy
Cranbrook Archives

business. His marriage in 1887 to Ellen Warren Scripps (fig. 11), daughter of James E. Scripps, founder of the *Evening News,* brought Booth into close proximity with the Detroit art scene. James Scripps was an early patron of The Detroit Museum of Art. Upon his father-in-law's insistence, Booth became business manager of the newspaper in 1888, then general manager in 1897, and finally President of The Evening News Association in 1906 upon Scripps' death. Booth was to remain in this position until 1929 when he retired in order to devote all his time to Cranbrook; he was to serve as a member of the Board of Directors of the *Detroit News* until his death on April 11, 1949.

Being a financially cautious man, Booth's active involvement in arts patronage did not begin until after 1900 when his monetary success was guaranteed. He was then in a position to fulfill any obligation he might have felt to the vast number of Michiganians who, by supporting the *News,* were responsible for his wealth.[5] For the next twenty years of his life Booth worked actively at the state and national levels to promote the arts and crafts. His activities included the founding in 1900 of the Cranbrook Press, based upon William Morris' Kelmscott Press (see Farmer), and active participation in the Art Alliance of America, as well as in the American Federation of Arts. His work in the latter association, for example, culminated in a large-scale exhibition of American handicrafts which opened in 1922 under the auspices of the Smithsonian Institution at Washington's National Museum. Perhaps Booth's most extensive effort to show his personal support for the Arts and Crafts movement occurred in 1907 when the Detroit architect Albert Kahn designed a home for him on his farm estate (fig. 12). This residence eventually would contain Booth's sizable art collection and library.[6]

Metropolitan Detroit was, however, Booth's primary target, for he felt a need existed for good design in a city with a growing automobile industry.[7] Prompted by the outcome of the 1904 and 1905 applied arts exhibitions at The Detroit Museum of Art, in which he had participated,[8] Booth helped found the Detroit Society of Arts and Crafts in 1906. Since the city lacked a first-rate art school, the Society, under Booth's leadership as President, founded the independent Detroit School of Design in 1911.[9] Two years later, as a result of Booth's efforts, the School became affiliated with the Museum.[10] Booth had been a member of the Board of Trustees of The Detroit Museum of Art intermittently between 1908 and 1914. From 1915 onward, prompted by his brother Ralph Harmon Booth, who was then active in the Museum, Booth donated to the same institution more than one hundred works, primarily by contemporary craftsmen and sculptors, in the hope of familiarizing both the public and Museum officials with contemporary trends in the handicrafts and securing a foothold for the Society within the Museum's structure (see Thurman).[11]

By the early 1920s Booth appears to have been frustrated by the lack of results his efforts had produced. In 1918 the Detroit School of Design was closed for economic reasons. In 1926 Booth was instrumental in the formation of the Art School of the Detroit Society of Arts and Crafts, but his involvement with the Society decreased in the late 1920s since he felt that the Society was not realizing its original goal of exhibiting and selling the highest quality decorative and applied art objects in the salesroom.[12] Similarly, by 1923 Booth had become disenchanted because Museum officials could not decide whether the works of contemporary crafts and sculpture that Booth had donated should be installed in the contemporary painting and sculpture galleries or used as architectural ornamentation for the building. In 1944 Booth asked that a number of works he had donated to the Museum be returned in exchange for Carl Milles' *Sunglitter.*[13]

Booth became involved with the University of Michigan's architectural program in the early 1920s; this activity heightened his awareness of the status of art education in Michigan. His son, Henry Scripps Booth, who was a student of architecture at the school from 1918 through 1924, wrote to him frequently about the rigidity of the program and the instructors.[14] The reinstitution of architectural studies at the University in 1906 under the direction of Professor Emil Lorch had led to a long-term consideration within the academic community of this program's position in the University's structure as well as its need for a new building. Because of his willingness to help state institutions, Booth was asked to lobby in favor of the dissolution of the architectural division's affiliation with engineering. At the time, in fact, he may even have been approached to partially finance the new structure for the proposed College of Architecture "in which the 'applied arts' of design would be taught parallel with architecture and decorative design and drawing and painting."[15] Yet the bureaucratic delays involved in both the separation of architecture from engineering and the institution of a George G. Booth Traveling Fellowship in Architecture in 1923 disillusioned Booth considerably.[16]

The idea of forming a community where artists could live and work in Bloomfield Hills may have been proposed initially to Booth in 1919 by William Tyler Miller, a Detroit landscape architect.[17] During the next few years, Booth researched the structure of art academies and museums abroad—always in relation to the state of the arts in Detroit. He was aware of the endeavors of George Grey Barnard who, at the time, was assembling a collection of medieval art that would eventually be incorporated into The Cloisters in New York. Like Booth, Barnard recognized the importance of having works of art from various periods available to students.[18] Finally, approximately two years after a 1922 visit to the American Academy in Rome, Booth decided to develop his own experimental art educational community.[19] He had already begun to develop his farm estate (fig. 13) in response to the immediate needs of his family and neighbors. He had the Greek Theater designed in 1915 because of his personal interest in the Little Theater movement; the Meeting House which preceded Christ Church Cranbrook provided George's father with a place to preach; and Bloomfield Hills School, later

12
ALBERT KAHN. *Cranbrook House.* 1908, Library wing 1918, photo c. 1919. Photo courtesy Cranbrook Academy of Art/Museum

13

Cranbrook Farm Estate. 1906. In background is the future site of Cranbrook House. Photo courtesy Cranbrook Archives

Brookside School Cranbrook, was intended for the elementary education of the neighborhood children.[20]

In 1924 Booth told Eliel Saarinen, then Visiting Professor in Architectural Design at the University of Michigan, of his plan for the Cranbrook community and asked the architect not only to prepare master plans for an art academy, but also to provide counsel concerning the nature of education at the proposed art academy. Saarinen's work bore the strong recommendation of architect Albert Kahn and of Emil Lorch, who had initially brought Saarinen to the University of Michigan in November 1923. Above all, Saarinen was recommended by Booth's son, Henry, who, as a student in Saarinen's first undergraduate seminar, had prepared a series of drawings for a proposed art academy as part of his thesis. In early 1924 Booth had helped to provide the financial support to enable Saarinen to submit a scheme for the proposed Memorial Hall project in Detroit; Saarinen's proposal for the Detroit Riverfront project was the result (see De Long). Booth's initial discussions of the Cranbrook concept with Saarinen led the architect to cancel his plans to return permanently to Finland in the summer of 1924.[21]

The physical development of Cranbrook, which Booth believed to be the first priority, proceeded slowly since construction of each building was determined by the availability of funding. Saarinen did several master plans for the Academy and the school for boys but none of them was followed exactly because Booth felt that they were too pretentious (fig. 29). Booth initially had asked Saarinen to remodel Cranbook's original farm buildings for the school for boys. He acquiesced to the erection of a new structure only when informed that renovation would be more costly. Construction of the Art School buildings proceeded slowly in the latter part of the 1920s since Booth wanted to be sure that adequate funds would be available for the successful completion of Christ Church Cranbrook, Brookside, and the school for boys. Similarly, Booth delayed the establishment of Kingswood School, a preparatory school for girls, until 1931 since he did not feel that such a school was vitally important to his plans for the Cranbrook community.[22]

From 1933 to 1935 the severity of the Depression caused a curtailment in the physical growth of the complex. During this period construction was limited to the renovation of one of the original buildings on Booth's farm estate, the Cranbrook Pavilion, into a much-needed lecture hall and temporary exhibition space. Improved economic conditions in 1936 enabled ground to be broken for the Institute of Science designed by Saarinen. In the same year, increased student enrollment at the Academy led to another building campaign which lasted for more than three years. When the Institute of Science was completed, plans were developed for a museum and library to replace earlier facilities; construction began on this segment in 1940. World War II and Booth's advancing age brought to a halt any further expansion of the campus.[23]

The development of the Academy's educational philosophy proceeded slowly for several reasons. First, Booth wanted to complete necessary construction for the entire community before dealing specifically with the needs of the Academy. More to the point, when he had started to build Cranbrook in the mid-1920s, Booth's concept of the Academy had been somewhat nebulous and it had taken several years to clarify it. Initially, he had conceived of an academy of art that would have closely paralleled the American Academy in Rome (see Clark). According to this idea, master artists in painting, sculpture, architecture, and design would have been invited to work at Cranbrook, provided with private residences, studios, and honoraria—all on the condition that they would create works to enhance Cranbrook's physical plant and execute their own commissions. In addition, each was to have supervised a few highly qualified "fellows" who would have received just remuneration for work executed in cooperation with the masters. The architectural development of the complex was envisioned as being part of the educational experience as a paradigm of good design.[24]

Booth's original scheme was to have been introduced gradually. In actual practice, Saarinen's presence at Cranbrook, Booth's great interest in

14
Original Cranbrook Academy of Art/Museum. c. 1930. This space is part of the present-day Administration Building. Photo: George Hance. Courtesy Cranbrook Academy of Art/Museum

architecture, and the construction of the first of the art buildings (in 1925) to house the Cranbrook Architectural Office (in which Saarinen worked), the original museum (fig. 14), and the library provided the foundation for the first stage of art education at Cranbrook. By mid-1926 the Architectural Office was employing several former University of Michigan students to prepare the drawings and specifications for the school for boys. Booth saw the relationship between Saarinen and these draftsmen as a rudimentary educational system. "The young men and women engaged in the draughting rooms are students under Prof[.] Saarinen as well as employees performing a business service—They are getting their advanced education and earning full compensation at the same time."[25] The museum and library, which evolved from Booth's own propensity for collecting, were established to pro-

15

Cranbrook Cabinet Shop. c. 1930. Tor Berglund, Cabinetmaker, is in the foreground. Photo courtesy Cranbrook Academy of Art/Museum

vide these young people with both printed images and actual examples of good design. The time spent in these facilities was considered an important part of their work at Cranbrook.

With the establishment of a functional architectural office, Booth began to consider the formation of craft studios to embellish Saarinen's architectural scheme. In 1927, the Hungarian sculptor Geza Maroti was brought to Cranbrook to create the sculptural decoration for Cranbrook School (fig. 185); within the next two years, master craftsmen such as Tor Berglund and Arthur Nevill Kirk set up studios for cabinetry (fig. 15), silver, iron, bookbinding, and weaving (see Miller, Farmer, and Thurman). Some of these artists chose to work with assistants or apprentices, thus following Booth's original idea. Since Booth intended the artists to both live and work at Cranbrook, residences were also needed. Therefore, in 1928 Booth authorized Saarinen to begin designs for artists' living and working spaces (fig. 16). At first, Booth felt obliged to provide some work for the craftsmen and so he not only gave them commissions for the educational community and for his own home but also, beginning in 1927, attempted to have them hired both at Cranbrook School and at the Art School of the Detroit Society of Arts and Crafts. Their employment as art instructors at the school for boys and later at Kingswood was to become an important aspect of the cooperative art effort among the Cranbrook institutions. However, in 1930, finding it increasingly difficult to support these artists by himself, Booth instituted a plan by which the craft studios were gradually to become self-sufficient by creating their own markets and, more importantly, by conducting classes for the public.[26]

With construction on the various buildings well under way by 1930, Booth realized he had to turn his attention to the development of the educational program. At the time he found himself increasingly responsible for the administration of the craft shops, although Henry P. Macomber, former President of the Boston Society of Arts and Crafts, had been hired to manage them. A year earlier Booth had engaged Charles Harris Whitaker, a former editor of the *Journal of the American Institute of Architects* who was recommended by Emil Lorch, to prepare a survey of art schools abroad. Whitaker's survey, however, did not provide Booth with a definite direction to follow. In addition, for almost two years beginning in 1928, Booth had searched unsuccessfully for an art director who could unify the existing art activities at Cranbrook into a working academy and organize an overall plan of instruction for the Cranbrook institutions. Finally, in November 1930 the painter and educator Frank Leonard Allen, who had previously been affiliated with Pratt Institute and the Yonkers School of Design, was hired as the Academy's first Supervisor of Art Education. This appointment lasted less than two years; in 1932 Allen was relieved of the position.[27]

Booth formally established Cranbrook Academy of Art in 1932, with Eliel Saarinen as its first President. Booth's choice of Saarinen was probably influenced by the fact that by 1931 the first advanced architectural student was already working at Cranbrook under Saarinen while residing on campus at the recently completed student residence, the Art Club (fig. 16).[28] The Detroit architect Richard Raseman, who had little experience in art education or administration, was chosen as the Academy's Executive Secretary.[29]

Eliel Saarinen's remarks concerning his own interest in educational theory are revealing. "Never before till I had to tackle the educational

16
Construction of Art Club, 1929. Photo courtesy Archives of Laura Macomber Rice

problems in connection with the Cranbrook development, had I been particularly interested with education—art-education, or otherwise. My limitations in this respect were concentrated to one and sole pupil, stubborn and unconcerned, that is, to myself."[30] By the time he accepted Lorch's invitation to teach at the University of Michigan, Saarinen had become a strong advocate of "self-education under good leadership" and he tried to institute this policy in his seminars at the University. He was to write, "During the passing years I had become accustomed to the conviction that any art education must grow *from personal experience with the life problems of today, and under the good guidance of a creatively alert mind.* Mere theoretical study could not bear proper fruit."[31] Saarinen never fully agreed with Booth's concept of a master-apprentice situation at Cranbrook because of its similarities to the medieval guild system. Saarinen believed strongly in the close relationship between art and life; as early as 1925, he conceived of Cranbrook as a place where students would learn the fundamental principles of art so that they could develop a mode of artistic expression that would reflect modern existence.[32] His major statement of 1935 on education combined his long-held belief in the primacy of architecture over the other arts with his desire to eradicate any differences between the philosophies of art education and education in general:

> . . . every child—from the earliest childhood—is eager to plan and to organize—to "build"—in sand, with stones, cubes, cardboard and the like. In this play there is always a subconscious dreaming about future deeds. Certainly the germ of planning and building is in the nature of the child and properly nursed it may begin to take roots and grow to a lasting hobby or, perhaps, to an inclination of a positive value in the future. Therefore, if the pupil—from the very first and during the whole school time—were given the opportunity to dream about his future environment, his future home, its suitable neighborhood, and so on, he then would gradually be educated to see things in terms of organic order, regardless of whether this means art—as the word is generally understood—or general organic order in society, business, or the various phases of life.[33]

These ideas constituted the basis for Saarinen's theories on education that were published in the 1940s.[34]

    Due to the Depression and, above all, the National Bank Holiday of 1933, Booth's scheme to make the craft studios financially independent failed. The public simply could not afford the high cost of objects produced at Cranbrook. In that year all of the craft studios except Studio Loja Saarinen were closed.[35] To save the Academy as the Depression deepened, in the early 1930s Saarinen and Rasemen redefined the school and its role within the art community of metropolitan Detroit. The Academy was not to be an informal "free scholarship school" based upon master-apprentice relationships but a post-graduate institution with departments in architecture, sculpture, and painting, and with established tuition fees. Particular emphasis was to be placed on architectural design rather than on craftsmanship; there were to be no formal classes, specific hours, established school terms, formal critiques, or requirements; students were to pursue their own interests. Full scholarships for advanced students were no longer available. Those in painting and sculpture would have to pay tuition (room and board if appropriate); only architecture students would receive tuition waivers. To guarantee the Academy's continuing existence, Saarinen and Raseman worked to reaffirm the Academy's involvement with the other Cranbrook schools and with art institutions in metropolitan Detroit. It was hoped that the former would develop curricula based upon Saarinen's theory of education and also employ teachers sympathetic with the architect's ideas. Then graduates from the preparatory schools would be able to do advanced work at the Academy; eventually these students would comprise the basis of the Academy's student body.[36] Further efforts were made to collaborate with the University of Michigan's architectural program and to share teaching staff with the Art School of the Detroit Society of Arts and Crafts.[37]

17
Throne Designed for Second Crandemonium Ball, Drafting Rooms, Cranbrook Academy of Art, March 20, 1936. Photo courtesy Cranbrook Archives

In fact, the severity of the Depression initially made Saarinen's and Raseman's scheme highly impractical. It was difficult to attract qualified, mature students without full scholarships. The unusual nature of the program also may have intimidated prospective students. The total freedom to pursue one's own projects was a concept alien to American ideas of education (see Clark). Saarinen's reputation did help to bring some architectural students to the Academy in 1933 and again in 1934.[38] Efforts to establish a cooperative program with the University of Michigan never materialized, perhaps due to the two schools' varying educational philosophies. The idea of having Cranbrook and the Art School of the Detroit Society of Arts and Crafts jointly employ the same artists never progressed beyond Arthur Nevill Kirk's working at both institutions.[39]

Although Saarinen tried to develop an overall policy on art education for the various Cranbrook institutions, his inexperience in educational matters made it difficult for him to formulate his ideas completely and convince others of the need for such a unified approach. When he did discuss his thoughts with the heads of the various schools, their reaction was immediate—Saarinen was "dictating" the educational policies of their respective institutions, which they felt fell within their own jurisdiction.[40] Although Academy artists would increasingly be employed to conduct Kingswood's art classes, only a few graduates of the two preparatory schools ever did postgraduate work at the Academy.

Increased attendance during 1935–36 can be attributed to a further decision of Saarinen's to institute several full scholarships in architecture, painting, and sculpture, and to his personal efforts to recruit students by contacting various architectural offices and universities throughout the country. By 1936, the Intermediate School had been established within the Academy to provide art instruction on an elementary level for students who were not able to compete with the more advanced graduate students but who could afford to pay tuition. Although Saarinen designed additional facilities for the Intermediate School,[41] he was not especially interested in its educational development.[42] In 1936 a new women's dorm was constructed, thus making the formerly coed Art Club for men only. Two years later, due to the growing popularity of the Intermediate School and the subsequent rise in student enrollment, work was begun on four additional faculty residences, another dormitory, a garage, and a painting studio.[43]

In spite of the Academy's economic problems and geographic isolation, the spirit that developed there in the 1930s and 1940s was primarily responsible for the uniqueness of the educational experience. Adequate facilities now existed within which the student was expected to learn by doing his own art work and by interacting with those around him. The absence of formal critiques, classes, or numerous requirements enabled students to devise their own projects and pursue their own interests. They were encouraged to experiment in various media, and this led to numerous artistic collaborations involving several areas of study (see De Long and Miller). In fact, it was quite common for students, upon completion of their stay at the Academy, to be working in different areas than when they had started. Since there was no established curriculum of study, national and international art competitions often provided the stimuli for exploring new concepts in the arts (see De Long and Marter). Saarinen himself encouraged students to enter these competitions since he felt that his own participation in them had led to his personal success. The wide diversity of the students' backgrounds and their professional experiences added an important dimension to the educational process and "made Cranbrook a rich melting pot for the exchange of ideas and design principles."[44]

The complex's physical isolation from Detroit and other institutions of higher learning played a major role in determining life at the Academy. Students were together both in informal class situations in their studios and at mealtime. It was common for students to work long hours in the studios and to live on campus. The community devised its own entertainment; elaborate costume parties such as the Crandemonium Balls of 1934 and 1936 (fig. 17) provided both recreation and important learning experiences because of the emphasis on the collaborative production of costumes and sets.[45]

Student and faculty exhibitions were frequent and open to the public. Booth's continual efforts to expand exhibition space at Cranbrook provided increased opportunities for a broad exhibition program. Formal lectures were also held at the Academy. Major figures, such as Le Corbusier, Frank Lloyd Wright, Leon Volkmar, Lewis Mumford, Alvar Aalto, and Ely Jacques Kahn, whose work was particularly relevant to the interests of the students were invited to address the community. Many well-known figures in the arts came to see Saarinen (fig. 18), although this phenomenon was not as prevalent in the other departments.

One of the most important elements of the Cranbrook experience was the opportunity to work with the European-born faculty. Students came to Cranbrook to work with major figures such as Saarinen himself, Carl Milles, Marianne Strengell, and Maija Grotell. The Academy owed the high quality of its faculty almost exclusively to Saarinen; many members had been his acquaintances in Europe. Cranbrook's growing reputation was directly attributable to the fact that its faculty was readily accessible to the students. Very few other art institutions in America could boast of the existence of similarly open channels of communication between instructors and students.[46]

The start of World War II in Europe brought a decrease in the number of advanced students at the Academy since degrees were needed to obtain jobs, for example, in teaching and the increasingly industrial job market. In addition, the Academy did not offer comprehensive work in industrial design. Thus it was out of pace with educational developments elsewhere. In the 1930s Zoltan Sepeshy, then Instructor of Painting, had recognized the necessity of instituting a formal degree program at the Academy; however, Saarinen had delayed in doing this because of his own disinterest in structured education. As a result of the decrease in enrollment, however, an extensive two-year review of the entire Cranbrook community took place, with particular emphasis on the Academy, to determine what could be done to make Booth's educational community perform as a self-perpetuating unit. Walter Baermann, head of the newly-formed Department of Industrial Design, was asked by Saarinen to examine the situation and suggest an alternate scheme. Baermann's report, which advocated—among other things—the development of a strong undergraduate program in the preparatory schools and the Academy, did not appeal to Saarinen (see Clark).[47]

During the early 1940s Saarinen, Sepeshy, and Raseman actively worked on a plan—to involve only the Academy—which would allow that institution to grant graduate and undergraduate degrees. By 1942, when the State of Michigan conferred upon the Academy the power to do this, elements of a more formalized educational situation had been instituted; for example, procedures to take attendance were initiated to determine the number of hours spent in the studios. The introduction of a formal degree program meant that, for the first time in the Academy's history, specific programs of study had to be outlined, course credits had to be assigned, and students had to satisfactorily complete their coursework in order to receive degrees. A few required courses were instituted which were held at assigned hours, a unique situation at the Academy.[48]

Initially, this program had only a limited effect upon the Academy's student body because of the War. After 1944, however, combined with the educational benefits offered to war veterans under the G.I. Bill, it helped attract an increasing number of qualified students to Cranbrook. In spite of the optimistic turn of events, there was concern during the last two years of the decade that once the G.I. Bill's financial assistance decreased, the Academy might be forced to admit less qualified students in order to insure its financial security and continuity.[49]

During this period the vanguard at Cranbrook was changing. From the late 1930s on, the level of Booth's activity decreased due to illness and old age. In 1946 he resigned as Chairman of the Cranbrook Foundation, a position he had held since its inception in 1927; his responsibilities were to fall to his son, Henry. Until his death in 1949, however, George Booth was to remain interested in the administration of the Cranbrook Museum. Further, in 1943, shortly after Raseman resigned his position as Executive Secretary of the Academy, Saarinen asked to be relieved of the presidency, claiming that he was an architect, not an administrator. He felt that he had accomplished at the Academy what he had been hired to do: form a strong faculty. Saarinen wanted his successor to possess national renown.[50] In 1943 Zoltan Sepeshy, who had been a strong advocate of the degree program, was appointed Registrar *ad interim* and, later, Educational Director to assist in the administration of the Academy until a new head was found. In fact, Saarinen did not leave the presidency until 1946, when Sepeshy was chosen as Director of the Academy (see Clark).

In 1950 Saarinen began work on his version of "The Story of Cranbrook."

> It was . . . my first endeavor to have a statement from Mr. Booth about his ideas about the whole Cranbrook situation. We discussed this matter again and again and although Mr. Booth was in full agreement with those ideas I had developed in our mutual discussion, he seemed reluctant to put his ideas down on paper. His inclination seemed to be at first freedom to every institution, I grant that, but a common idea should have been accepted by them all, otherwise, the whole [of] Mr. Booth's idea could go into pieces.[51]

Saarinen's concern at the end of his life was understandable. However, despite numerous difficulties he clearly had succeeded in realizing Booth's original dream. Cranbrook Academy of Art was recognized as a center where mature, advanced students would receive training that would enable them to make major contributions to the arts.

18

Eliel Saarinen (left) and Frank Lloyd Wright at Kingswood, April 1935. Photo courtesy Cranbrook Archives

4

Eliel Saarinen and The Cranbrook Tradition in Architecture and Urban Design

As modern architecture gained acceptance in the decades following the first World War, the fact that it was a style with complicated and overlapping currents was not widely discussed. To arrive at a clear and easily transmittable doctrine, these currents were often seen as subordinate to modernism—that is, the single current represented by the International Style and its descendant modes.[1] Beginning in the early 1960s and more persuasively during the last decade, a broader view has been taken, and it now seems probable that not modernism alone, but some more inclusive image will form the standard by which our century is judged. In this light, the work of Eliel Saarinen and his students gains special prominence.

Taken together, this work would not constitute a mode or school in the sense of work by architects who studied at the Bauhaus or Taliesin. For the design philosophy that was developed at Cranbrook encouraged diverse expressions linked not by appearance or even clearly specified principles of design, but rather by a consistent attitude toward place and materials. It was a philosophy that safeguarded both values of personal expression and public good, that was derived from a pragmatic rather than an intellectual approach, and that led to a tradition of modern architecture perhaps best defined by Eero Saarinen. The development of this tradition can be seen in selected works by Eliel and Eero Saarinen, supplemented by certain works of those who studied with them.

The design that brought Eliel Saarinen to the attention of the American public, that resulted in his coming to America, and that expressed the basic principles underlying his work was his entry in the 1922 Chicago Tribune competition. More than 260 entries were submitted, and they reflect a broad range of historical and modern motifs, their diversity having been encouraged by a program that stressed the need for an appropriate architectural symbol.[2] The winning entry by Raymond Hood (1881–1934) and John Mead Howells (1868–1959) was praised for its integration of overtly Gothic references.[3] By contrast, Saarinen's was heralded as being modern. Louis Sullivan (1856–1924), whose own achievements in skyscraper design lent substance to his opinion, wrote enthusiastically of Saarinen's entry that, "in its single solidarity of concentrated intention, there is revealed a logic of a new order."[4] Thomas E. Tallmadge described the design as "bursting the bonds" of precedent, and shortly afterwards Sheldon Cheney characterized Saarinen as ". . . one of the most brilliant of the radicals working in America today."[5] In retrospect, such praise seems exaggerated, for while Saarinen's design is less archaeologically derived than Hood's and its massing simpler, it still evokes a strongly medieval spirit. It also stands in marked contrast to entries that seemed truly modern to a later generation, such as that by Walter Gropius (1883–1969).

A preliminary study of the south elevation (fig. 20) illustrates an early stage of Saarinen's design, before he further emphasized the verticality of the building by treating a portion of the lower floors as a link to existing facilities on the east.[6] In his final scheme, more carefully proportioned setbacks appear to buttress the central portion of a slimmer tower, its verticality emphasized by the continuous mullions that sweep up on all sides. Its appeal to Sullivan suggests that

19

ELIEL SAARINEN. *Cranbrook Academy of Art.* 1924 ff., plan and elevations of proposed Art Club entrance (detail) 1927. Pencil on paper (signed *Cranbrook 1927/Eliel Saarinen*). 24 ¼ × 36″. Cranbrook Academy of Art/Museum

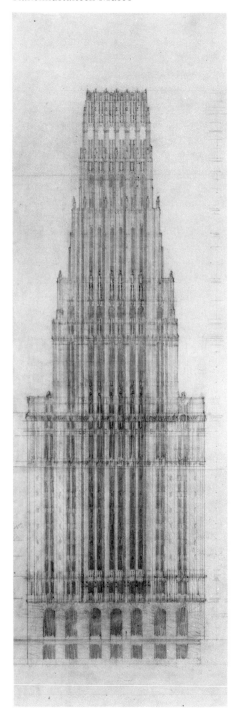

20

ELIEL SAARINEN. *Chicago Tribune Project* (south elevation). 1922. Pencil on tracing paper. 31 ⅛ × 10 ⅛″. Suomen Rakennustaiteen Museo

he saw it as a sympathetic extension of his own principles, and that its stepped profile seemed to develop the potential of his own much earlier project incorporating boldly scaled setbacks, the Odd Fellows Temple, Chicago (1891).[7]

Saarinen's Tribune entry influenced an entire generation of skyscrapers, recognizable by symmetrical and plastically interwoven setbacks and by a subdued, vaguely medieval detailing.[8] There are several immediate precedents for such towers in his own work, including his project for the Finnish House of Parliament, Helsinki (1908), or the final version of the tower (fig. 21) for the Helsinki Railway Station (1904–14).[9] Both are less medieval in feeling than the Tribune, and incline away from his earlier embodiment of National Romanticism toward the Austrian Secession, an influence that began to be apparent in his work following a series of trips through Europe in the early 1900s.[10] The tower of the Railway Station as completed can thus be compared to the Palais Stoclet (1905–11) by Josef Hoffmann (1870–1956), as can the station's entrance to the Ernst-Ludwig House, Darmstadt (1899–1901) by J. M. Olbrich (1867–1908). More immediately before the Tribune project, Saarinen had sometimes incorporated overtly classical elements in his work, once more following the lead of Hoffmann, Olbrich, and other European architects in the second decade of the century. Such examples (fig. 22) as his Villa Keirkner, Helsinki (1915/16–18), have been omitted from many surveys of his work, yet they display a sympathetic knowledge of classical detail that is otherwise only suggested in his writings. Such knowledge underlies a more general classicism that is often apparent in the clear massing of certain designs, and is even present in the Tribune project. At that time, Saarinen believed a balanced attitude toward classical and medieval traditions was essential to achieve an expression fully responsive to human memory, and wrote:

> Our traditions are founded on two great spheres of ideas: classical antiquity (clarity, humanity) and gothicism (depth and intensity of feeling) . . . . classical antiquity created . . . universal human values . . . . gothicism is . . . consummate in organic and constructive unity. . . .[11]

Saarinen believed that only through an intuitive approach could such a union be properly effected, and warned against reliance on strictly academic principles.[12] Through such an intuitive search for an appropriate symbol, he had produced a prototypical skyscraper without exact precedent. His Tribune project successfully abstracted past tradition so as to seem new, yet retained sufficient imprint of the past to appeal as an accessible image. It is this approach that underlies much of Saarinen's subsequent work in America.

In his letter awarding Saarinen second prize, the manager of the Tribune suggested that he might visit Chicago.[13] Accepting, the architect left for Chicago in February, 1923.[14] During his stay there he developed a visionary scheme that explored the urbanistic potential of the Tribune prototype.[15] His earlier experience in urban design understandably led him in such a direction, and his interest was probably reinforced by a suggestion that there was need for such vision in Chicago.[16] The lack of commissions then available to Saarinen in Finland—the result of that country's civil war and subsequent economic as well as political crises—no doubt enhanced the appeal of possible work in the United States.

The resulting Chicago Lakefront project was developed in considerable detail.[17] As seen in the site plan (fig. 23), Saarinen envisioned a major boulevard paralleling the lake, integrated with adjoining parks and terminated at each end by a plaza. The boulevard was planned to continue either under or around these plazas, connecting with major arteries in such a way that traffic would be routed through the area, relieving existing congestion. Much of the boulevard was to be built below grade, and linked on each side by an elaborate series of ramps to a mammoth, three-level parking garage designed to hold 47,000 cars (fig. 24).[18]

Towers resembling the Tribune project provided visual terminals at each end of the central portion of the boulevard, their effect suggested by the perspective looking south (fig. 26). Rows of trees shown on each side emphasized the tall silhouette of the Chicago Tower, as Saarinen called the major structure planned at the south plaza. Placed to one side of the plaza and linked by arcades to lower structures on each side (fig. 25), it was meant to define urban space rather than merely occupy it. The north plaza was developed in greater detail. There, a fifty-seven-story hotel was to contain 4,000 rooms and be connected to a major railway station below, its location determined by Saarinen's proposed relocation of existing rail lines in the area. Restaurants and waiting lounges located below grade were to be lit by vast light courts located in the plaza north of the hotel. Saarinen wrote that such underground terminals seemed the way of the future, as indeed New York's rebuilt Pennsylvania Station sadly confirms. The plaza south of the hotel was to be partly enclosed by the Art Institute, which Saarinen suggested be balanced by a major concert facility across the sunken boulevard to the east.[19]

21
ELIEL SAARINEN. *Railway Station, Helsinki.* 1904–16. Photo courtesy Cranbrook Archives

22
ELIEL SAARINEN. *Villa Keirkner, Helsinki.* 1915/16–18. Photo courtesy Cranbrook Archives

   The Chicago Lakefront project proved Saarinen's skill as an urban designer and reflected his interpretation of concepts developed by Camillo Sitte.[20] Like Sitte, he envisioned buildings not as freestanding structures that dominated their settings, but as related elements that defined exterior spaces.[21] Because Saarinen thought in terms of physical design rather than statistics, he avoided the term "planner" in describing his own work. As Chairman of the American Institute of Architects Committee on City and Regional Planning, he wrote, "city planning . . . is primarily an architectural problem. . . ,"[22] a view illustrated by the Chicago project.

The design of Cranbrook provided the opportunity for Saari-
nen to realize certain ideals related to architecture and urban design. The series of
events that led directly to this commission apparently began early in 1923, when
Saarinen was completing his Chicago Lakefront project. In April of that year, he
was recommended to Cranbrook's future founder, George G. Booth, as one of the

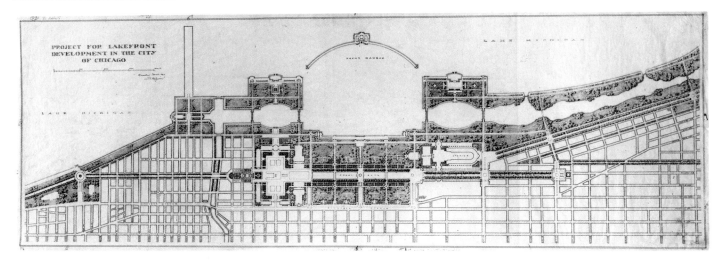

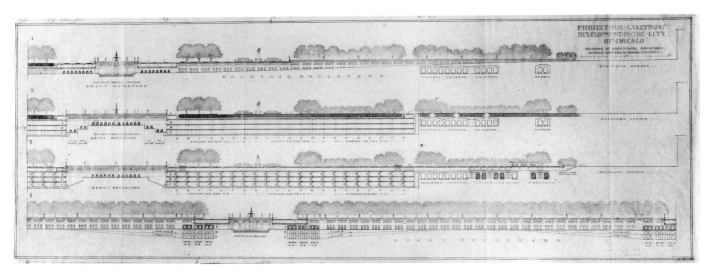

world's leading architects.[23] In the fall of 1923, when Saarinen returned from a
summer visit to Finland to teach at the University of Michigan, Booth's son became
his student, and prepared studies for an academic complex to be located on the
family estate.[24] The problem was not hypothetical and the elder Booth was sufficiently impressed by Saarinen's guiding interest to offer him the actual commission
in the spring of 1924.[25]

Booth's confidence must have been reinforced by Saarinen's de-
sign for the Detroit Riverfront, a project executed for the local chapter of the American Institute of Architects with Booth's financial support.[26] Designed in the early
months of 1924, this project is of architectural interest as a link between the Chicago Lakefront project and Cranbrook, for its informality and varied vocabulary
suggest a quality of design not immediately apparent in the earlier and larger Chicago proposal (fig. 27). The buildings are grouped about a plaza reminiscent of St.
Mark's, a favorite example of urban design for both Saarinen and Sitte, and they
incorporate a mixture of classicizing and medievalizing details.[27] The interior of
the domed Memorial Hall reflects an Early Christian character premonitory of
later work by Saarinen, and the towered city hall recalls that in Stockholm (1902–
23) by Ragnar Östberg (1866–1945).[28] Saarinen's knowledge of contemporary

Evanston Illinois 1923
Eliel Saarinen

26

ELIEL SAARINEN. *Chicago Lakefront Project*
(perspective view to South Plaza). 1923.
Pencil on tracing paper (signed *Evanston Illinois 1923/Eliel Saarinen*). 15 × 24 ¼″.
Suomen Rakennustaiteen Museo

27

ELIEL SAARINEN. *Detroit Riverfront Project*
(perspective). 1924. Pencil on paper (signed
Eliel Saarinen/Ann Arbor 1924). 16 ⅞ ×
23 ½″. Photo courtesy Suomen Rakennustaiteen Museo

Scandinavian work was reinforced by direct contact with such figures as Östberg
and Martin Nyrop (1849–1925), architect of the influential City Hall in Copenhagen (1892–1902), and in these years many parallels can be drawn.[29]

The first buildings at Cranbrook reinforce the continuity with
contemporary Scandinavian work by Östberg and Nyrop. In the fall of 1924 Saarinen had again returned to Ann Arbor from a summer in Finland, and by early
October he had submitted drawings of his proposed scheme for Cranbrook to
Booth.[30] Saarinen produced several studies during the next few months, returning
yet again to Finland in the summer of 1925. On his return to America in fall of
that year he moved to Bloomfield Hills and concentrated his efforts on the school
for boys, the first component of the plan to be realized.[31] Originally conceived to
incorporate the farm buildings that had been designed for Booth by Marcus R.
Burrowes in 1912, the plan was soon enlarged by Saarinen so that ultimately only
a few fragments of the farm buildings were retained. Construction on the School
began in 1926; the first sections were finished late in 1927, though work on related
components continued for many years (fig. 28).[32]

The 1925 site plan (fig. 29) resembles several others in the
1924–25 series and indicates locations of major elements that did not vary greatly:
the school for boys, residences and Academy buildings along Academy Way, and

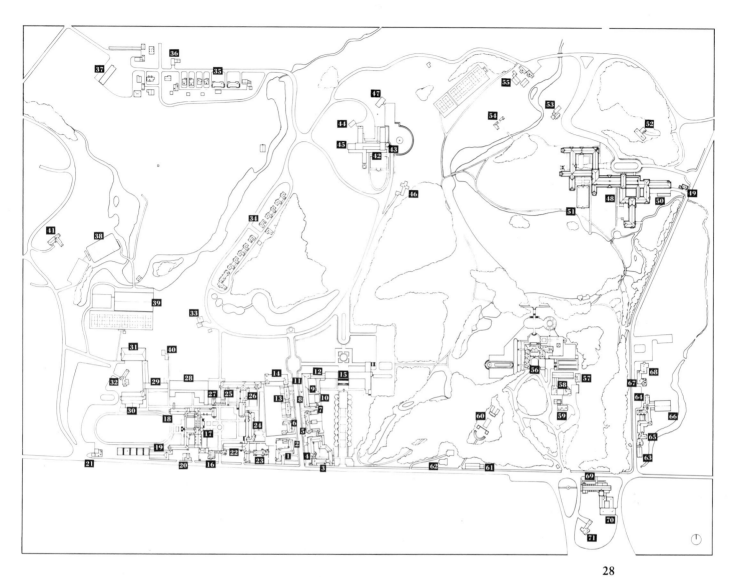

28

Site Plan of Cranbrook Educational Community. 1982. For legend, see p. 351

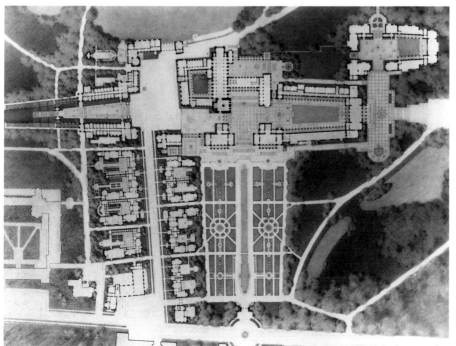

29

ELIEL SAARINEN. *Cranbrook Academy of Art.* 1924 ff., proposed site plan 1925. Ink and pencil on paper (signed *Ann Arbor 1925/Eliel Saarinen*). 29 × 39″. Cranbrook Academy of Art/Museum

the formal garden axis leading from Lone Pine Road to a linked pair of monumental buildings that were later to be realized as the Museum and Library.[33] These related to proposed elements of an expanded academy that were never built: additional dormitories and studios, dining and assembly halls, and facilities for such specialized components as a music and drama school. Other plans are still larger, showing a continuation of buildings to the north, perhaps meant to house a school of landscape architecture. For by 1925 Booth envisioned no less than a major academy of fine and applied arts similar to the American Academy in Rome, and encouraged Saarinen in the development of increasingly grandiose schemes.[34] In these there is a consistent sense of architectural order that is always humanly scaled. Saarinen showed an underlying concern for the exterior spaces themselves, creating a series of courts and gardens defined by building elements and linked by walks and roads (fig. 186). Organizing axes provided a sense of unity and led to such focal elements as fountains or sculpture (fig. 188 and pl. 61). These axes were manipulated by subtle angles and turns that departed from strict Beaux-Arts models and yielded a looser, more informal connection of elements. Even the shapes of the smaller spaces were varied from conventional regularity, so that everywhere vistas were created in a manner suggesting endless variety.[35] The buildings themselves were never isolated monuments, but connected in a manner that defined carefully devised spaces of differing hierarchies, emphasizing the planned experience of spatial continuity.

30

ELIEL SAARINEN. *Cranbrook School.* 1925 ff., perspective showing Dining Hall 1928. Pencil on paper (signed *Cranbrook 1928/ Eliel Saarinen*). 11 ¾ × 15 ⅜″. Photo courtesy Cranbrook Academy of Art/Museum. Cranbrook School

The Cranbrook School for boys not only illustrates Saarinen's deep concern with planning and with the building as it related to a larger whole, but also affirms his equal concern for the component parts of the building itself. His vision encompassed a full range of scales: the chair or light fixture as it related to its room or space, the room as it related to its composition within a building and the building as it related to its broader setting. As the design is examined at each of these levels, Saarinen's ability to maintain consistent control becomes apparent. Thus the compositional variety portrayed in the site plan is sustained in the aerial perspective (fig. 9), and in turn is transferred to the architectural details of the buildings themselves. As rendered in the perspective study of the dining hall (fig. 30), building masses are plastically enriched by such elements as porches, bay windows, and stepped chimneys; these, in turn, are further embellished by a variety of openings and indentations that vary the surfaces. At a smaller scale still—the means by which these openings and indentations are defined—the sense of varied richness continues. This is shown in the proposed Art Club entrance (fig. 19) realized with simpler trabeated forms as part of the first dormitory unit for the adjacent Academy. Nor is this quality lost inside, where, in the intricate flow of connected spaces, in the definition and embellishment of those spaces, and in the design of furniture or sculptural elements, the sense of exacting concern continues, each part controlled by Saarinen's clear vision.[36]

31
ELIEL SAARINEN. *Cranbrook School.* 1925 ff., Dining Hall from east. Photo courtesy Cranbrook Archives

In terms of composition and detail, the school for boys evokes a loosely medieval feeling that can be tied to no single moment of the past. As with the Tribune project, Saarinen abstracted freely from a variety of sources, avoiding specific references. His design contrasts with such examples of literal interpretation as the nearby Christ Church Cranbrook, commissioned by Booth in 1923 and designed in a Gothic mode by the office of Bertram Grosvenor Goodhue (1869–1924).[37] Saarinen's design is more plastically massed, more inventively varied in its parts, and more complicated in derivation. There are echoes of Östberg and Nyrop, and the varied niches within the pediment above the main gate (fig. 126) recall by their placement, though not by their specific shape, gables of medieval Finnish churches.[38] Elsewhere, as on the east facade of the Dining Hall (fig. 31),

32

ELIEL SAARINEN. *Christian Science Church Project, Minneapolis.* 1925–26, exterior perspective 1926. Pencil on cream paper (signed *Cranbrook 1926/Eliel Saarinen*). 18 ⅛ × 32 ¹³⁄₁₆″. Suomen Rakennustaiteen Museo

squared stone panels and fluted columns suggest classicizing inspiration. On the east facade of the academic building, the brickwork has an Early Christian appearance.[39] Nowhere is there a lack of associative references, yet in their skillful combination Saarinen transcended conventional eclecticism. His achievement was more a matter of sustained quality and of creatively adapted details than of bold innovation.

Eliel Saarinen's renderings of the early Cranbrook buildings illustrate remarkable technical ability. He usually began these in the upper left-hand corner, moving diagonally across the sheet to achieve a finished image in one pass. In more complex perspectives, preliminary guidelines might first be scribed on the sheet.[40] His concern for clearly delineated details extended to actual construction, which he carefully supervised whenever possible, refining variations in brick and stone in a way that reflected a master builder's sympathy for materials. Critics at the time noted his care and suggested that a new architecture could develop from such understanding dedication to a crafts tradition.[41]

Saarinen extended the architectural manner of the school for boys in the first buildings of the Academy and in his own house, designed in 1928 and completed by 1930.[42] Inside Saarinen House, the easy movement along connecting interior axes, the dramatic studio space, and specially designed features recall his earlier home at Hvitträsk (1902 ff.).[43] Also between 1924 and 1928, while he was designing the first buildings at Cranbrook, Saarinen entered two architectural competitions: one for a Christian Science Church in Minneapolis (1925–26), and the second for the League of Nations in Geneva (1926–27). A stepped octagonal drum with low dome dominates each, relating to a major assembly space within. The simple arcuated treatment of the church exterior (fig. 32) and skylit foyer (fig. 34), the direct translation of uncomplicated interior volume to exterior form, and the visual dominance of the domed rotunda recall late Antique or Early Christian examples more readily than conventional classical sources, a recurring theme in Saarinen's work during this period.[44] Inside (fig. 33), such details as the ribbed skylight, trabeated expression of the wall planes, and fluted columns complicate any single comparison and are a reminder of Saarinen's inclusive attitude toward the past.

33

ELIEL SAARINEN. *Christian Science Church Project, Minneapolis.* 1925–26, interior perspective 1925. Pencil on paper (signed *Cranbrook 1925/Eliel Saarinen*). 17 × 19 ¾″. Collection Richard Thomas

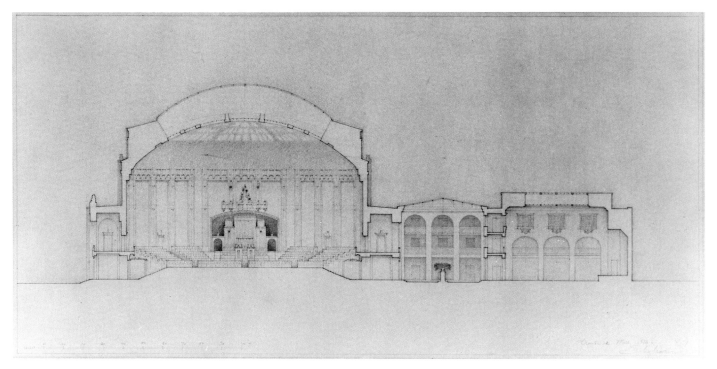

34

ELIEL SAARINEN. *Christian Science Church Project, Minneapolis.* 1925–26, section 1926. Pencil on paper (signed *Cranbrook Mich 1926/Eliel Saarinen*). 11 ¾ × 22 ⅛″. Cranbrook Academy of Art/Museum, Gift of Dorothy M. and Edgar R. Kimball

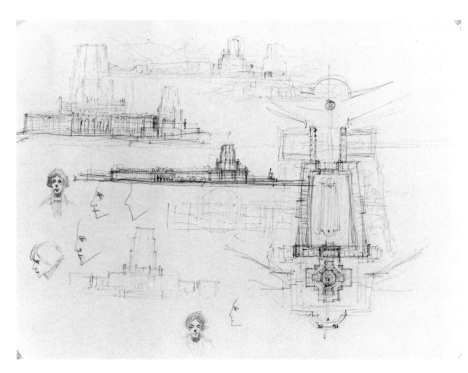

35

ELIEL SAARINEN. *Architectural Studies.* Pencil on paper (both sides). 9 ¹/₁₆ × 12 ¹⁵/₁₆″. Suomen Rakennustaiteen Museo

The conditions of the competition for the League of Nations provided for a larger and more dramatically sited design.[45] Like the church, the elements of the central mass are fully integrated so that no single part seems detachable. The fenestration is more severe and the taller drum more impressive, as befits the proposed assembly hall for 2,700 people (pl. 2). The central element is treated as a tower, a compositional element expressive of place that was much explored by Saarinen. Several projects during this period combine tower-like forms with lower building elements that relate to monumental plazas and pools. In one group of sketches, Saarinen explored possible configurations for a project, or projects, that resemble both the major Finnish folklore museum (the Kalevalatalo of 1919–20), and the League of Nations. Some (fig. 35) appear to be conceptual studies for the latter, and others in the series suggest its evolution as a design. Such drawings indicate Saarinen's preoccupation with certain thematic elements and his reworking of those elements to suit different situations.[46]

The designs so far considered constitute Saarinen's first phase of American practice. Each manifested a connectedness of parts, a kind of sculptural wholeness that Saarinen used the word "organic" to describe. Various historical sources are suggested by details, as well as by massing, and are handled in ways that avoid specific reference to any single period. As indicated earlier, his was an intuitive rather than academic eclecticism, and the abstracted results appealed to critics of the time as being modern. Saarinen was by no means alone in producing designs of this sort, as even a cursory review of contemporary periodicals indicates. Yet he was among the leaders in terms of sensitivity to scale and finish, and in terms of the sophisticated inventiveness with which he reinterpreted the past.

Beginning in 1929 Saarinen entered a transitional phase in which the majority of his references were to a more recent past. The Kingswood School for girls at Cranbrook offers the first clear evidence of this transition. A school for girls had been contemplated for some time at Cranbrook, and discussions were held in 1927 and 1928 relating to its size and location.[47] Saarinen's early design drawings for Kingswood are dated 1929; construction began in 1930, and work was substantially completed by late the following year.[48] The warm tan brick and copper roofs contrast with the dark red brick and slate roofs of the earlier Cranbrook buildings (fig. 36). The massing of the building is simpler, and the ornamental details show variations on fewer themes. The telescoping motive, a minor detail in the boys' school chimneys and in such earlier designs as the Helsinki Railway Station (fig. 21), is here carried throughout the building, giving shape to columns as well as chimneys, and imposing pattern on brick panels, leaded windows, rugs, and other elements (fig. 153 and pl. 35). Flared columns had been used sparingly and in conjunction with fluted columns of other persuasions in the school for boys. Here they predominate, and as abstractions of floral motives they strongly recall the sort of decoration popularized in the 1925 "Exposition Internationale des Arts Décoratifs et Industriels Modernes" in Paris, which Saarinen had attended. Both have Austrian roots.

Saarinen also altered his method of presentation in these years. Instead of deeply shaded pencil, he used a lighter watercolor technique for the perspectives. In preparation for the working drawings, he executed simple plans

36
ELIEL SAARINEN. *Kingswood School Cranbrook.* 1929–31, view from main entrance. Photo courtesy Balthazar Korab

and elevations in different colored inks (fig. 38), again indicative of a lightened technique.[49] There is no less care with details, rather an attitude of simplification through reduction of decorative themes. The sheet detailing the columns of the entrance loggia (fig. 37) illustrates the degree of intensity with which he still addressed even the smallest part.

The basic inspiration for Kingswood is clearly in the low, hipped-roof houses that Frank Lloyd Wright (1867–1959) designed in and around Chicago in the first decade of the century.[50] Saarinen was seeking an appropriately American mode of expression, and he turned naturally to Wright, who, he believed, had made the most effective beginning in that direction.[51] The low, extended wings of Kingswood reinforce a Wrightian image with their hipped roofs, broadly overhanging eaves, and horizontal bands of windows. The informally linked axes of the interior volumes—already explored in earlier Cranbrook buildings—further extend the Wrightian feeling, as do the changing levels of both floors and ceilings, and the broad openings connecting major interior spaces. Yet Saarinen defined these volumes in ways that depart from Wrightian prototypes, for walls are treated as massive elements with solid corners, not as visually lightened screens. Windows and doors are cut into these walls rather than being treated as openings left between screening elements. This is clearly apparent where windows relate to roof soffits: in Wright's examples, such windows are rabbeted into the soffit so that the window as a formally defined part disappears. At Kingswood, the windows are detailed with a rowlock course of brick placed between window and soffit, emphasizing the wall as a continuous masonry enclosure into which windows are inserted. Saarinen's attitude toward ornament also differed from Wright's. Both believed that ornament was essential to meaningful architecture, and that it should relate to some theme of the building's purpose, materials, or construction. Yet

Colorplate 2

ELIEL SAARINEN. *League of Nations Project.* 1926–27, perspective 1927. Colored pencil on paper (signed *Eliel Saarinen 1927*). 21 ½ × 43 ¹³/₁₆″. Suomen Rakennustaiteen Museo

Wright's ornament, even in such extreme examples as the Imperial Hotel in Tokyo (1917–22), is integrated in a way that Saarinen's often is not, and at Kingswood the flared columns are differentiated from adjacent shapes in a way that Wright's ornamental parts never were. Clearly Saarinen drew from Wright, but subjected that work to the same transforming process that he had applied in adapting earlier precedents.

Saarinen combined four enlarged versions of the fluted, telescoping columns at Kingswood to form the baldachino of the Alexander Hamilton Memorial project. A preliminary design of 1932 (pl. 3) shows simpler columns, but with a terraced base and upper crown similar to the later scheme of 1933. Both were conceived as an open pavilion that bridged a long channel of water, illustrating Saarinen's assured handling of monumental forms and his urge to unify architectural forms with the plazas, pools, and landscaping of urban parks.[52] The crown was to have been of gilded bronze, with lights concealed in the fluted concentric circles of the oculus.[53] Again, the design recalls motifs popularized in the Paris Exposition of 1925. A similar feeling permeates the Hudnut Building, New York (1929–30), on which he collaborated with Ely Jacques Kahn (see Miller).[54] Other designs of the period develop related themes.

During these same years graduate students in architecture began to be accepted at Cranbrook, the first coming in 1931, a year before the Academy was officially opened.[55] Eliel Saarinen, who continued to be in charge of the Cranbrook architectural office and to accept independent commissions, was elected President of the Academy in June 1932.[56] Graduate students in architecture were admitted only if they had prior professional training, and while at Cranbrook were expected to work on large-scale design problems of their own choosing, generally related to their home communities. Saarinen acted as critic and usually visited the

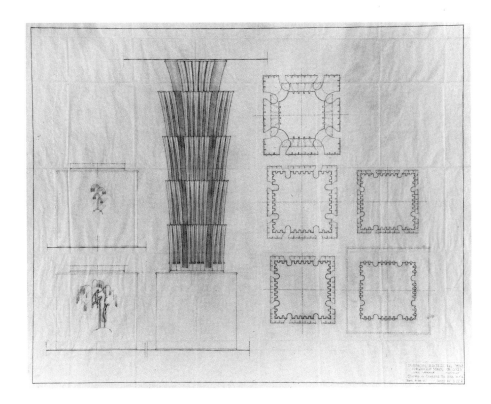

37 and 38

ELIEL SAARINEN. *Kingswood School Cranbrook.* 1929–31, column details c. 1931. Ink, pencil, and colored pencil on tracing paper. 31 ⅛ × 38 ½″. Partial plan and north elevation c. 1930. Colored ink and pencil on tracing paper. 33 ¼ × 69″. Cranbrook Academy of Art/Museum

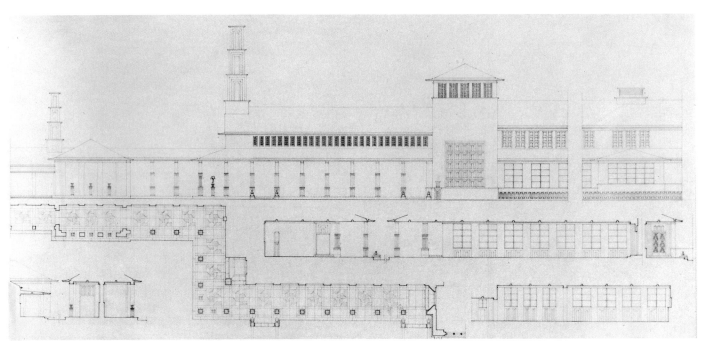

architecture studio each day. No formal classes were required.[57] Among the first students were Carl Feiss and Edmund N. Bacon, both of whom have had major careers as teachers and planners.[58] As Saarinen influenced his students, they may have influenced him, reinforcing an awareness of new developments useful to his redefined approach. It seems certain that his son Eero, who studied with him longer and more intensely than anyone else, had this effect.

Eero Saarinen had collaborated informally with his father on several projects, including Kingswood as well as the school for boys, and was an accomplished draftsman before entering Yale in the fall of 1931.[59] Eliel Saarinen supported his son's decision to study at Yale and was no doubt pleased by Eero's success there, for his designs were often commended and he completed the five-year course in three, receiving his degree in June 1934.[60] A traveling fellowship provided the opportunity for extended travel in Europe, and during this time Eero began to work in the Helsinki office of Karl Eklund, where he eventually settled until summer 1936.

Although Yale's architecture program was then organized in the accepted tradition of the École des Beaux-Arts, students were not restricted to traditional architectural modes, as Eero's own designs sometimes indicate.[61] For while certain examples of his student work are historical and none of those known could be described as an example of the International Style, several reflect an American trend toward a simple, pictorial modern. Because such work is shorn of the sort of applied ornament that characterizes Art Deco examples, yet stops short of the International Style in the handling of mass and volumetric expression, it is sometimes termed *moderne* to distinguish it from the decorative on one hand and the modernist on the other. One example by Eero is the design for a monumental clock, awarded a mention in the Emerson Prize competition of December 1932 (fig. 39).[62] Curvilinear window details, and the very curve of the facade, suggest the "streamlined" forms popularized by Norman Bel Geddes (1893–1953), in whose office Eero worked for a brief period.[63]

Surviving drawings done by Eero Saarinen during the period he worked with Eklund in Helsinki reveal a deeper understanding of modern architecture, more specifically of the International Style as interpreted and reworked by Scandinavian architects. Work with Eklund included drawings for alterations to the Swedish Theater in Helsinki, and a competition entry for the Finnish Pavilion at the 1937 Paris Exposition, but it is perhaps his "Forum" drawing that shows this most clearly (fig. 40).[64] Done in competition for a commercial complex in downtown Helsinki, its taut transparency and curvilinear form recall Asplund's Paradise Restaurant at the 1930 Stockholm Exhibition.[65] Both look back to work by Eric Mendelsohn (1887–1953) and suggest a kind of "Northern modernism," in which the underlying philosophy of European modernism was accepted, but its

39
EERO SAARINEN. *Design for a Monumental Clock* (perspective). 1932. Pencil on paper. 58 × 39″. Photo courtesy Joseph Szaszfai. Private Collection

40
EERO SAARINEN. *Forum Project, Helsinki* (perspective). c. 1934. Pencil and charcoal on tracing paper. 13 ½ × 14 ⅛″. Suomen Rakennustaiteen Museo

Colorplate 4

ELIEL AND EERO SAARINEN. *First Christian Church (formerly Tabernacle Church of Christ), Columbus, Indiana* (exterior). 1939–42

architectural expression modified by the incorporation of more diverse materials, textures, and shapes than were the norm for the major monuments of the International Style. It is a more personal, more flexible approach. This attitude is nowhere more apparent than in the work of Alvar Aalto (1894–1976), who had led Finland toward modernism in the late 1920s and who had begun to modify it by 1935.[66]

Eero Saarinen returned to Cranbrook during the summer of 1936 and entered into practice with his father.[67] During the next three years they produced a series of designs that marked the end of the elder Saarinen's transitional phase, established the manner of expression that characterized his last decade of practice, and served as a point of departure for Eero's independent work. Those in the office at the time recall Eero's increasingly important role in the years prior to World War II,[68] a role suggested by new elements in the designs produced.

The Institute of Science at Cranbrook, constructed from 1936 to 1937, indicates the direction of these designs. Its awkwardness as well as early date suggest that it was one of the very first such designs by the firm. The blocky, sharply articulated parts with flat roofs and simply cut openings resemble Eero's design for a police station that had won a mention at Yale in June 1932, a few months after Eliel had become involved in preliminary planning for the Institute.[69] Also similar to the Institute and leading toward the mature work of the later 1930s are the Community House in Fenton, Michigan (1937–38); the Civic Center project, Flint, Michigan (1937 ff.); and early designs for the music shed and related buildings of the Berkshire Music Center, Tanglewood, Massachusetts, begun in 1937.[70] With its curved auditorium openly expressed as a major design element, the latter leads directly to the Kleinhans Music Hall.

In October 1938, Eliel and Eero Saarinen were commissioned to design the Kleinhans Music Hall in association with the Buffalo firm of F. J. and W. A. Kidd. Construction was underway by fall 1939, and the building was officially opened on October 12, 1940.[71] The major elements of the building are clearly expressed on the exterior, with the curved shapes of the large auditorium and small chamber music hall joined to a two-story lobby between them (fig. 41).[72] The massive exterior of the steel-framed structure is clad in a warm tan brick, lightened visually by thin concrete canopies that cantilever over the entrances and varied by the panels of buff Mankato stone that enclose the chamber hall. A reflecting pool, now filled in, originally surrounded this hall and enriched the composition by completing the curve of the auditorium at ground level. Inside, the strong, ship-like curves of the lobby and grand, simple sweep of the auditorium impart a sense of great calm.

Eliel Saarinen likened the design of Kleinhans to that of a musical instrument, such as a violin, that was shaped entirely according to need.[73]

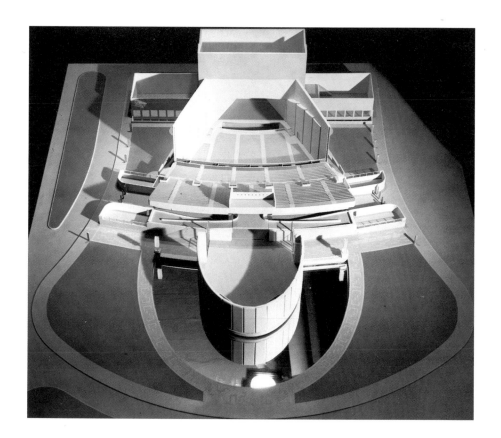

41

ELIEL AND EERO SAARINEN WITH F. J. AND W. A. KIDD. *Kleinhans Music Hall, Buffalo.* 1938–40, model. Photograph: Askew. Courtesy Cranbrook Archives

42

ELIEL AND EERO SAARINEN WITH PERKINS,
WHEELER AND WILL. *Crow Island School,
Winnetka.* 1938–40, view toward entrance.
Photo courtesy Hedrich-Blessing

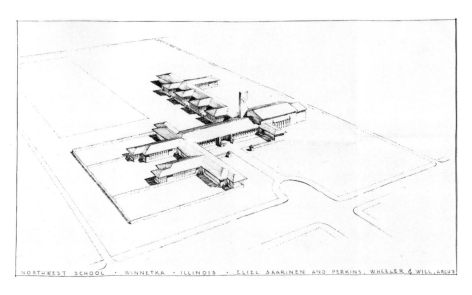

43

ELIEL AND EERO SAARINEN WITH PERKINS,
WHEELER AND WILL. *Crow Island School,
Winnetka.* 1938–40, aerial perspective,
preliminary study [Eero Saarinen, c. 1938].
Photo courtesy Cranbrook Academy of Art/
Museum

While there was ample European precedent for such a design, similar projects by Bel Geddes may have had special appeal for Eero, as had been reflected in his 1933 student project for a monument to J. S. Bach.[74] The general character of the building contrasts with Eliel Saarinen's previous phase, though such details as the stone cladding of the chamber music hall retain a conservative image as do similar details of Aalto's theater entrance in the Workers' Club, Jyväskylä (1924).[75] Such detailing, the general massiveness of the building, and its very shape led Swiss historian Sigfried Giedion, then visiting at Harvard, to criticize its design in 1939. His remarks were later echoed by Joseph Hudnut, Dean of Harvard's school of architecture.[76] Regarded in America as leading spokesmen for the International Style, they indicated by such criticism the tightening of standards by adherents of modernism. That Saarinen's work did not conform proved ultimately to constitute much of its strength.

Concurrently with Kleinhans the Saarinens were working on the Crow Island School, Winnetka, Illinois (figs. 42 and 43). Again it was a collaborative effort, for they were associated with the Chicago firm of Perkins, Wheeler and Will, an office then recently established that received the commission on the condition that they entrust its design to a more experienced architect. Eliel Saarinen, a friend of Perkins' father, was the young firm's choice. Work began on the design early in 1938, construction in 1939, and the building was completed in 1940.[77]

Even more than Kleinhans, the Crow Island design is conceived as a series of distinctly articulated parts, similar to such obvious parallels as the Bauhaus, Dessau (1925–26). It seems again to reflect Eero's presence, for it is quite unlike Eliel Saarinen's earlier, more visually cohesive designs and seems instead a direct reflection of attitudes expressed by Eero in Finland.[78] The visual separateness of classroom units emphasizes their independent function, reinforcing educational philosophies advocated by Winnetka's Superintendant of Schools at the time, Carleton Washburne. Richard J. Neutra (1892–1970) had earlier pioneered in the design of such schools in America. Yet the low, spreading wings and grouped windows of Crow Island (fig. 42) evoke a Wrightian feeling not unlike Kingswood. An early study in Eero's hand, with hipped roofs and overtly Wrightian details, confirms this link (fig. 43). Again, the tie was tenuous: discontinuous windows, blocky proportions, and an abbreviated overhang (reportedly cut to reduce costs) obscure the similarity. The tall pylon marking the entrance—in function a chimney—partly reestablishes the parallel. Its picturesque quality was criticized by Hudnut.[79]

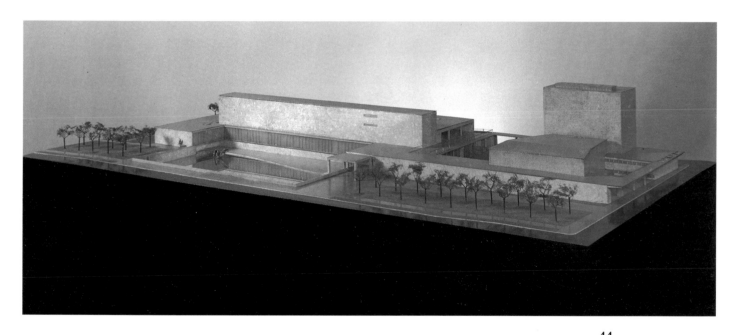

44
ELIEL AND EERO SAARINEN WITH J. ROBERT F. SWANSON. *Smithsonian Gallery of Art Project, Washington, D.C.* 1939–41, model. 48 × 96 × 16″. Photo courtesy Smithsonian Institution. National Museum of American Art, Smithsonian Institution

The Tabernacle Church of Christ (now the First Christian Church) in Columbus, Indiana, commissioned while designs for Kleinhans and Crow Island were reaching completion, shows greater assurance. Eliel Saarinen was first contacted by members of the building committee in February 1939 after more conventional proposals by other architects had been rejected. He and Eero were given the commission in April of that year; construction began in the summer of 1940, and the church was dedicated on May 31, 1942.[80] Its major components—sanctuary, offices, and educational wing—are placed in three clearly defined rectangular wings, the two along each side being connected by a third that is raised on columns and bridges across a sunken garden (pl. 4). The larger of the two side wings contains the sanctuary, its entrance emphasized by a tall, freestanding bell tower rising from the sunken court that originally contained a large reflecting pool. Earlier designs for a stepped tower, flared like the Kingswood columns, were revised to express a simpler statement of form. The treatment of the building masses with flat roofs and sharply cut openings, as well as the combination of warm tan brick with buff stone panels and trim, reinforce themes of Crow Island and Kleinhans. Cryptic geometric ornament on column and wall surfaces imparts an immediacy to the planar surfaces. While Eliel Saarinen avoided obvious iconography in much of his ornament, the angular shapes leading to the cross above the entrance seem meant to suggest its worldly setting, contrasting with the image within which the cross appears suspended in light, symbolic of resurrection.[81] The asymmetrical composition of the sanctuary reflects the elder Saarinen's urge toward the particularization of space.

While the Columbus church seemed to lack immediate precedents in America, it did follow an approach clearly established by slightly earlier designs by Finnish architects including Aalto and Erik Bryggmann (1891–1955), among others.[82] It seems certain that Eero was familiar with at least some of these, for they had been published in Finnish periodicals, and in a letter written from Finland he includes sketches for a church that links Columbus with its Finnish prototypes.[83] Further, interior details including railings, light fixtures, and wood screens closely resemble similar designs by Aalto. Yet it is not simply a matter of direct translation. Other details, including built-in seating and fireplaces, recall work by Wright, and thus partly nationalize the design. Moreover, masonry textures and detailing reflect the elder Saarinen's stablizing hand and establish continuity with his earlier practice in America.

With the Columbus church, the manner characterizing Eliel Saarinen's last phase of American practice was firmly established. Though obviously more modern than his independent work of the previous decade, it should not be judged as an attempt at modernism, which it was not, but as an attempt to achieve a fully modern expression while retaining selected traditional references. The functionally organized plan generates an architectural expression of articulated parts that contrasts with the cohesive unity of his earlier work, as did Crow Island School. Yet these parts are defined by familiar means: by brick walls with strong textures, by corners detailed to emphasize mass, by stone-framed openings, by ornamented columns and railings. These insured a level of acceptance by their very familiarity, and thus eased the passage through a gradually evolving modern style. Wright's work represented another extreme—more intensely personal, it included traditional references so fully transformed by his genius that perception of them could be obscured. Eliel Saarinen incorporated elements that Wright had identified as essential in certain situations, including the sense of sheltering eaves and relaxed perimeters, yet he did so guardedly, and with ties to familiar devices. As in his work of the previous decade, Saarinen, now working with his son, proved himself a master of adaptation, achieving brilliant results through craft and synthesis rather than through innovation. His son would move further, and in working within the established boundaries of his own, slightly later time would develop a potential for invention inherent in his father's approach.

Two designs produced at the same time as the Columbus church—each for an art gallery—suggest emerging differences in the approaches of Eliel and Eero Saarinen. The first, for the Smithsonian Gallery of Art, seems to have been largely Eero's, while the second, for the Cranbrook Academy of Art Museum and Library, seems more attributable to the elder Saarinen. In July 1939, the Saarinens' Smithsonian design was declared winner of the first prize in a national competition that had been initiated in January. Two earlier designs in which Eero's dominant role is clearer are strikingly similar: the 1938 project for the Wheaton College Art Center competition, submitted by Eero alone, and the project for a theater at the College of William and Mary, on which he collaborated with Ralph Rapson and Frederic James. The latter, also submitted in competition, won first prize in April 1939, and according to Rapson its final form was due largely to Eero. Rapson's first sketches, done independently, confirm the change Eero brought to the design. Rapson also concurs that Eero, not Eliel, was largely responsible for the Smithsonian design.[84]

The major components of the Smithsonian project were almost diagrammatically separated (fig. 44), as they had been in the Columbus church, but with a changed attitude toward the expression of mass. The main entrance led from the mall through an open pavilion and foyer to the grand gallery beyond, a one-story, loft-like space.[85] A long passage also led from one side of the vestibule to a theater at the south end. Above the main block, an L-shaped element contained offices and a library, with a long segment left open to create a double-height space in the gallery below. A large pool set within the wings was planned to contain a sculpture by Carl Milles. The building, designed with cladding of marble and glass slabs set in thin metal frames, drew closer in appearance to the International Style than had any earlier design by the Saarinen firm, for textural effects were minimized and forms expressed as simply as possible. The Saarinens now earned the approval of Hudnut, who served as professional advisor to the jury. Their design was also praised by jury member Walter Gropius, then teaching at Harvard and considered an even more persuasive advocate of the International Style than

45

ELIEL AND EERO SAARINEN. *Cranbrook Museum and Library.* 1938–42, perspective 1940. Pencil on paper (signed *Cranbrook 1940/Eliel Saarinen*). 11 ½ × 24 ¾". Cranbrook Academy of Art/Museum

Hudnut. This support signaled a recognition of modernism that ultimately proved its undoing. The Saarinens' design was criticized for its lack of cohesive unity, and for being "too stylish."[86] The controversy surrounding what would have been the first clearly modern building on the mall led to delays, and eventually the project was cancelled.[87]

This level of criticism had not plagued the Saarinen office in other commissions, nor had their work invited it. The easier acceptance of their more traditional work again prevailed in the Cranbrook Museum and Library (fig. 45). In its classical balance and solid monumentality, with reliance on textured materials and surface ornament, it seems clearly, at this date, to have been more Eliel's than Eero's. The Cranbrook trustees had, in fact, asked Eliel Saarinen to begin drafting the program for its design in 1937, though actual planning does not seem to have begun before 1938, and work continued through most of 1939.[88] Construction started in May 1940, and the building was essentially completed by late 1942.[89] While it followed the general dictates of his earlier master plan and continued to reflect his sensitive integration of such related elements as pools and sculpture, its manner contrasts with earlier Cranbrook buildings and confirms Eliel Saarinen's acceptance of a modern vocabulary. Yet it was still a compromise with modernism that relied on the vocabulary much popularized by the 1937 international exposition in Paris. Saarinen had visited that exposition and his design seems

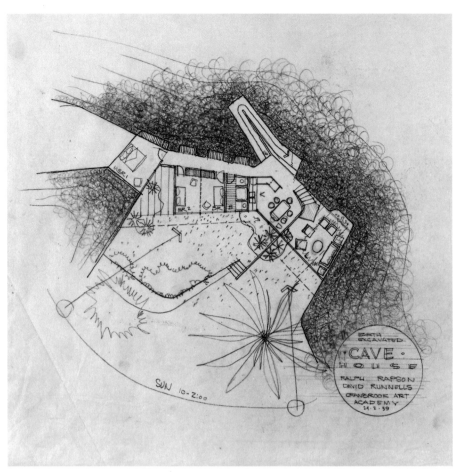

46
RALPH RAPSON AND DAVID RUNNELLS. *Cave House Project*. 1939–40, plan study 1939. Pencil on yellow tracing paper. 15 ¼ × 21″. Ralph Rapson and Associates

partly inspired by the Musées d'Art Moderne, erected there as a permanent monument.[90] The grandly ceremonial propylaeum connecting the Museum and Library in Saarinen's design (pl. 61) also recalls Asplund's Woodland Crematorium, Stockholm (1935–40), as well as still earlier work by Hoffmann (fig. 6).

During these years, from the fall of 1939 through December 1941, Eero taught at Cranbrook, appointed officially as assistant to his father.[91] Even before that time he had taught informally, acting as design critic in the Cranbrook studio. Eliel Saarinen's hope that his son would eventually succeed him at Cranbrook was ended when Booth terminated Eero's appointment and asked the Saarinens to move their office from Cranbrook premises.[92] To Cranbrook students that included Ralph Rapson and Harry Weese, Eero's presence was important, partly because he seemed closer to recent developments in the field.

Understandably, student work at Cranbrook reflected an increasing awareness of advanced practice in the United States as well as Europe. Collaborative work was encouraged in keeping with the Cranbrook ideal of integrated arts, and Cranbrook students were frequent winners of such competitions as the Collaborative sponsored by the Alumni Association of the American Academy in Rome. In 1940, they won both first and second prizes in the Rome competition, announced in October 1939, for a "people's forum" in Washington. The second-place entry (figs. 201 and 202) shows a level of competence typical of several, and in recalling an amphitheater designed in 1931 by Bel Geddes, suggests an eagerness to stay abreast of the times.[93]

Ralph Rapson's work in the late 1930s and early 1940s gives further indication of the directions Cranbrook students were taking. In 1939, he collaborated with David Runnells on a design for a Cave House to be built partly underground (fig. 46). Its angled and curved forms reflect an awareness of Aalto's 1938 design for the Finnish Pavilion at the New York World's Fair, and it contrasts strongly with Eero's buildings of the same date, though not with the organically shaped furniture that he and Cranbrook students Rapson, Charles Eames, and others were beginning to design. The Cave House project was reworked by Rapson and Runnells in 1942 as a fabric house, and seemed to reflect a free approach that Eero would only take up in later years.[94]

Other work by Cranbrook students in these and slightly later years drew from more predictable precedents. Runnells, together with another former Cranbrook student, George Matsumoto, designed the Kansas City Art Institute (1948 ff.) in a manner that recalls the Crow Island School.[95] Rapson's Gidwitz house, Chicago (1941–46), shows ties to Gropius' own house at Lincoln, Massachusetts (1937).[96] In 1944, Rapson won the competition for the Legislative Palace of Ecuador (fig. 47), its components clearly defined like earlier work by the Saarinens, but its details closer in appearance to contemporary work by Le Corbusier.[97]

Charles Eames had more professional experience than most when he began his studies at Cranbrook in September 1938.[98] After studying architecture at Washington University in St. Louis from 1925 to 1928, he worked until 1931 as a draftsman for the St. Louis firm of Trueblood and Graf, then entered private practice with Charles M. Gray, and later Walter E. Pauley. Following an extended trip to Mexico between 1933 and 1934, he associated with Robert P. Walsh.[99] Early work by Eames and Walsh included a medievally detailed church, St. Mary's in Helena, Arkansas; and at least one Williamsburg-inspired house in Webster Groves, Missouri.[100] With the John Philip Meyer house in St. Louis, designed in 1936 and constructed from 1937 to 1938 (pl. 5), Eames shifted focus from his earlier, more obvious sources to work closer in spirit to Eliel Saarinen's of the late 1920s. It was a major commission for Eames, and included such special items as rugs by Loja Saarinen (see Thurman) and ceramic plaques designed by a St. Louis sculptor.[101] As work progressed through 1937, Georgian pediments and other details shown on the drawings of 1936 sometimes gave way to simpler, more abstract forms. Inside, fireplace arrangements, silver-leafed light coffers, and other details correspond to similar motifs in Saarinen House.

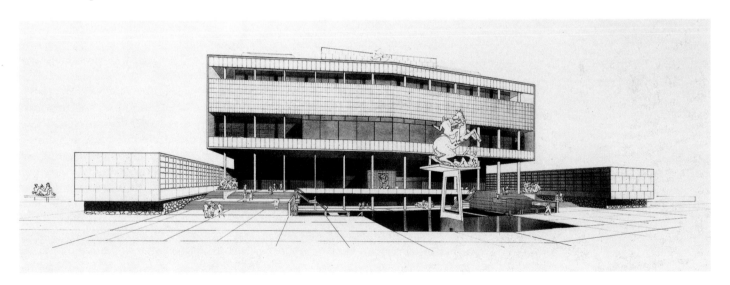

47

RALPH RAPSON WITH ROBERT TAGUE. *Legislative Palace Project, Quito.* 1944, perspective. 23 ¹⁄₁₆″ × 29 ½″. Photo courtesy Ralph Rapson. Ralph Rapson and Associates

Eames' approach changed dramatically while he was at Cranbrook. After studying for one year, he served as Instructor of Design in the Intermediate School from September 1939 to June 1941. During this time he became a close friend of Eero Saarinen, with whom he began his experimental chair designs. Eames moved to California in June 1941, and following the War resumed his collaboration with Eero.

Eero Saarinen spent the war years working for the Office of Strategic Services in Washington. He returned to Bloomfield Hills in 1945 to rejoin his father, drawn by the promise of a commission for the design of the General Motors Technical Center. Different attitudes toward design within the firm continued to be apparent. In later work that Eliel Saarinen directed in the office, he refined the manner of designs dating from the late 1930s. Thus the Des Moines Art Center (formerly the Edmundson Museum) (1944–48) relates to the Cran-

48

SAARINEN, SWANSON, AND SAARINEN. *General Motors Technical Center, Warren.* 1945–56, exterior. Photo courtesy Ezra Stoller

brook Museum and Library; and Christ Church, Minneapolis (1949–50), is a small, beautifully detailed version of the Columbus church. During this same period, planning work by the firm related largely to college campuses, such as the 1938 competition for Goucher; the Drake University plan (1946–47 ff.); and the Brandeis University campus plan (1948–51). These also suggest a continued collaborative effort.

Eero's approach, as demonstrated by the Smithsonian project, and even earlier by his 1938 entry for the Wheaton Center, developed gradually into something quite different. In his design for the General Motors Technical Center, elements that had been connected in the Smithsonian project disengage and spread across the landscape, creating a campus of independent parts unified by the vast pool at the center (fig. 48). This project was underway by 1946 after a more ambitious scheme that he and his father worked on in the previous year had been set aside. Postwar material shortages delayed construction on the later scheme until 1949; the first buildings were completed by 1951, and the complex was essentially completed by 1956.[102] It is Eero's most complete essay in modernism and obviously derives from the Illinois Institute of Technology, Chicago (1939–41 ff.) by Mies van der Rohe (1888–1969). Yet that vocabulary is modified by brightly glazed panels of brick and by an exaggerated emphasis on industrial materials. Pioneering developments in enameled panel and glass construction, structurally dramatic stairs designed in partnership with his office associates, and the very prominence of the domed auditorium and water tower suggest a fascination with traditional forms transformed by new building techniques. Eero's pursuit of new technologies as a means of architectural expression eventually led away from the more conservative forms advocated by his father, yet in his respect for structure and materials a sense of continuity is retained. There is also a sense of continuity in his belief that the integration of commissioned works of art was essential to modern design, signaled at General Motors by examples including Alexander Calder's fountain, Harry Bertoia's screen (see Marter), and Antoine Pevsner's sculpture, *Bird in Flight.*

As work on General Motors was beginning, Eero collaborated with Charles Eames on two designs that were commissioned as part of the influential Case Study House series sponsored by *Arts and Architecture* magazine.[103]

This series was intended to elicit prototypical solutions for postwar houses, and those by Eames and Saarinen were among the first group announced in 1945: Number 8 for Charles and Ray Eames, and Number 9 for John Entenza, editor of *Arts and Architecture* and the guiding force behind the ambitious program (figs. 49, 50, 51, 52).[104] Both were conceived as open pavilions with geometrically clear boundaries. They relate not only to earlier designs by Mies van der Rohe, but also to California work by Rudolph M. Schindler (1887–1953) and Neutra. More immediately, both recall designs of the early 1940s by Eero Saarinen: the raised wing of his 1941 Bell house project anticipates the Eames house (No. 8), as the open plan of his 1943 design for a prototypical house does the Entenza house (No. 9).[105] Curvilinear elements in Saarinen's 1943 design as well as radiating segments in the Entenza house also recall Rapson's and Runnells' 1939 Cave House project, and suggest a degree of interaction among the many talented designers who were together at Cranbrook in the late 1930s and early 1940s. Thus Eames' 1940–41 project for a studio for Frances Rich closely resembles the Saarinens' Wermuth house of the same date,[106] and a city hall design of 1943 combines elements used by Rapson in his preliminary designs of 1938 for the William and Mary theater competition.[107]

The Entenza house was completed by 1950, elegantly detailed with an open interior made palpable by slim steel columns and a freestanding fireplace.[108] The Eames house was never built as originally designed, but instead the

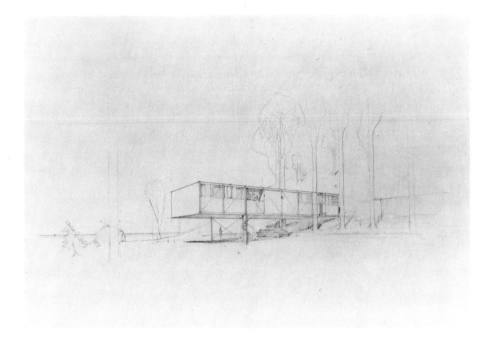

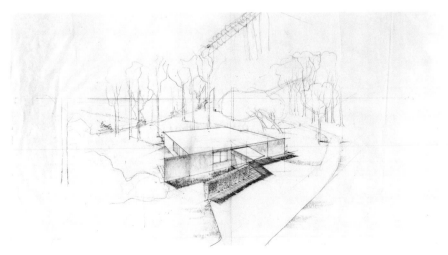

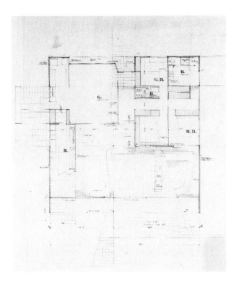

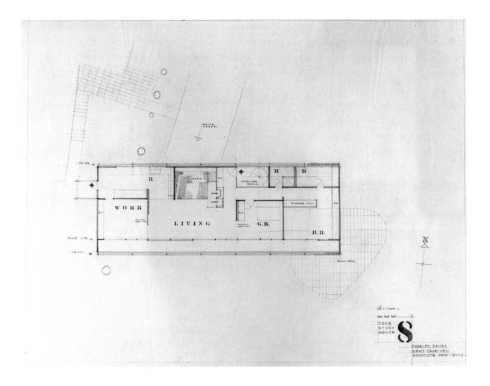

51 and 52

CHARLES EAMES WITH EERO SAARINEN. *Case Study Houses No. 9 (Entenza House), 1945–50, and No. 8 (Eames House), 1945–48, Pacific Palisades,* plans. Pencil on tracing paper. 26 × 36 ⅜″; 28 ¼ × 36 ½″. Office of Charles and Ray Eames

steel that had been ordered for its dramatic frame was adapted to a simpler, and ultimately more significant, design (fig. 53). In the fall of 1948, with materials already delivered, Charles (together with Ray Eames, since 1941 his wife and office partner) redesigned the house so that a greater volume was enclosed with essentially the same structural members. Perhaps sensitive to the way the elder Saarinen sited buildings, they shifted the house's location from a central to an edge position, enhancing the sense of place.[109] More importantly, they transformed their image of the building as a specific and observable object to one that was a more neutral container of space, achieving what Eames had sometimes sought as "unselfconscious architecture." The steel was used to define a regular frame, or grid, of changeable parts, its pure form dependent on work by Mies van der Rohe, but with an added potential for variety. The colors, textures, and different translucencies of the enclosing panels indicate this, as do the collections of objects contained

53

CHARLES AND RAY EAMES. *Eames House (Revised Case Study House No. 8), Pacific Palisades.* 1948–49, exterior. Photo courtesy Julius Shulman

comfortably within. For its time, there had been no clearer realization of an adaptable architecture achieved by regularly assembled industrial materials. The sensitivity to scale, materials, and building techniques surely depends on an understanding of Eliel Saarinen's work, as the determination to exploit new technologies does on Eero's. Yet in this design, Charles and Ray Eames established a position independent from both that was almost immediately noticed by perceptive critics.[110]

Ideas implicit in the Eames house were carried further in the Billy Wilder project. Designed in 1949, it, too, was conceived as a generalized enclosure (fig. 54). Here the organizational sense of the structural grid was reinforced by the paving pattern of an expansive entrance court. Brunelleschi would have envied the sleekly thin wall planes that followed modular lines to enclose a regular, clearly organized volume (fig. 55). Yet Charles and Ray Eames kept it purposely without a dominant focus—one looked through it rather than at it. Conceptually similar but differently rendered sketches show the two-story living area as a composition of clearly perceivable but informally joined planes, to be given individual character by attitudes of use (figs. 56, 57, 58).[111]

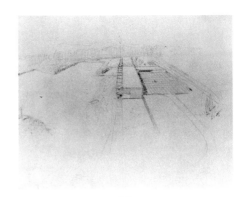

54

CHARLES AND RAY EAMES. *Billy Wilder House Project, Beverly Hills.* 1949, aerial perspective. Pencil on yellow tracing paper [Charles Eames]. 8 ⅝ × 11″. Office of Charles and Ray Eames

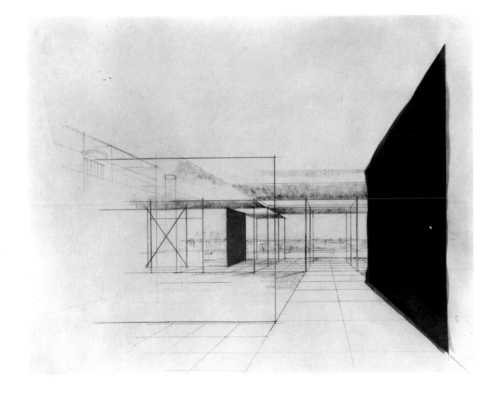

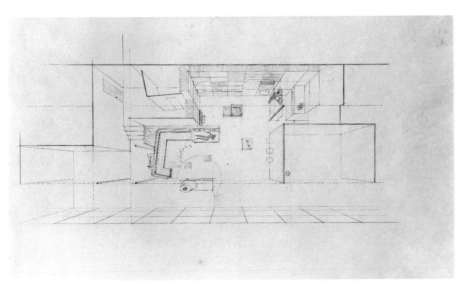

55

CHARLES AND RAY EAMES. *Billy Wilder House Project, Beverly Hills.* 1949, perspective of entrance. Pencil, colored pencil, and colored paper on tracing paper. 16 ½ × 21 1/16″. Office of Charles and Ray Eames

56

CHARLES AND RAY EAMES. *Billy Wilder House Project, Beverly Hills.* 1949, plan perspective. Pencil on tracing paper. 21 1/16 × 36 ⅜″. Office of Charles and Ray Eames

57

CHARLES AND RAY EAMES. *Billy Wilder House Project, Beverly Hills* (interior perspective of living and dining areas). 1949. Blue ink on yellow tracing paper [Charles Eames]. 8 ½ × 10 ⅞″. Office of Charles and Ray Eames

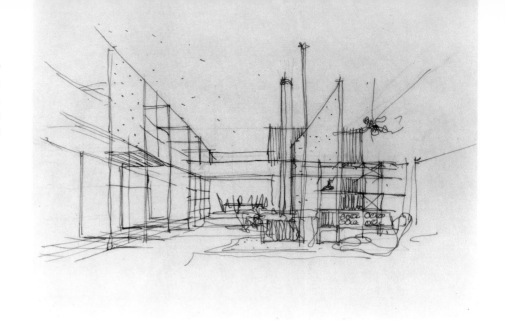

58

CHARLES AND RAY EAMES. *Billy Wilder House Project, Beverly Hills.* 1949, interior perspective of living area. Pencil on yellow tracing paper [Ray Eames]. 10 ½ × 11 ¹³⁄₁₆″. Office of Charles and Ray Eames

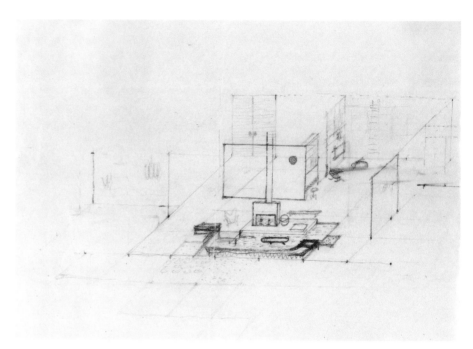

59

EERO SAARINEN AND ASSOCIATES. *Irwin Miller House, Columbus, Indiana.* 1953–57, exterior. Photo courtesy Balthazar Korab

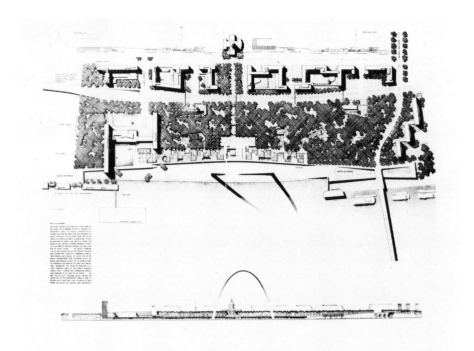

60

EERO SAARINEN. *Jefferson National Expansion Memorial, St. Louis.* 1947–66, plan and elevation (first submission) 1947. Ink and pencil on board. 38 × 49 ¾". Photo courtesy Balthazar Korab. National Park Service, St. Louis

61

EERO SAARINEN. *Jefferson National Expansion Memorial, St. Louis.* 1947–66, model. 84 ⅝ × 91 ½ × 15 ¾". Photo courtesy National Park Service, St. Louis

Eero Saarinen and his associates realized aspects of the Wilder project in the Miller house, Columbus, Indiana (1953–57) (fig. 59). It further extended the image of the Case Study houses and was intended, like houses by Eames, to provide a universal enclosure that would allow change within.[112] The ease with which Alexander Girard's interior arrangements fit testifies to its success, and in its luxury of finish and quality of detail it is surely unsurpassed for its time (pl. 15). Eero had first proposed a raised pavilion located on a lower portion of the site, and next a house built partly underground. His final scheme—a simple pavilion supported on a regular grid of steel columns—is placed within a landscaped setting that expands its architectural boundaries.[113] Linear skylights delineate the column grid and relieve the ceiling plane of visible weight. They also transform the walls of thin marble or slate panels into translucent planes that seem themselves a source of light. Enclosed suites, located at each of the four corners in a pinwheel arrangement, reinforce the logic of the enclosure. In one important aspect it departs from comparable work by Eames, for the attention given to details is part of a passionate search for form that distinguishes Eero's later career. He sought associative meanings appropriate to a modern architecture, yet avoided specific historic references. For him such meanings must have seemed possible in the handling of such recognizable and essential elements as columns, which could be given rich yet timely meaning if transformed by new uses of materials and advanced building techniques. The welded steel column capitals of the Miller house, carefully detailed in a manner he approved, illustrate one instance of this.

Eero Saarinen's winning entry in the Jefferson National Expansion Memorial competition had earlier demonstrated his determination to find new meaning in the redefinition of traditional forms (figs. 60 and 61). The competition was announced in May 1947; five finalists were chosen in September, and Eero's monumental catenary arch was awarded first prize in February 1948.[114] Several of the more than 160 architects who entered had studied at Cranbrook, including Charles and Ray Eames, George Matsumoto, Ralph Rapson, and Harry

62 and 63

ELIEL SAARINEN. *Jefferson National Expansion Memorial Project, St. Louis.* 1947, perspective and plan. Pencil on tracing paper (J. Henderson Barr). Each 26 × 46 ³⁄₈″. Cranbrook Academy of Art/Museum, Gift of E. Charles Bassett

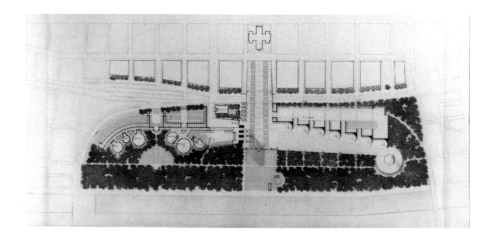

64

EERO SAARINEN AND ASSOCIATES. *M.I.T. Chapel and Auditorium, Cambridge, Massachusetts.* 1950–55, model. 54 × 72 × 10 ¼". Photo courtesy M.I.T. Museum

65

EERO SAARINEN AND ASSOCIATES. *M.I.T. Chapel, Cambridge, Massachusetts.* 1950–55, perspective showing exterior detail. Pencil on paper (probably Edward Charles Bassett). 15 ⅛ × 21 ¼". M.I.T. Museum

66

EERO SAARINEN AND ASSOCIATES. *M.I.T. Chapel, Cambridge, Massachusetts.* 1950–55, interior. Photo courtesy M.I.T. Museum

Weese. Many of the schemes included monumental arches. But the bold scale of Eero's stood apart, as did the ease with which it relegated to a minor position the museums and amphitheaters encouraged by the program.[115] When construction was delayed by complications related to the preparation of the site, Saarinen refined his design. Changes were made to the section of the hollow concrete core that is reinforced by its stainless steel enclosure. The height of the arch was increased from 590 to 630 feet, its location was moved back from the river's edge, and its landscaped setting simplified. Begun in 1961, it was at last completed in 1966, its evanescent image a moving symbol of its time.

Eliel Saarinen's entry reaffirms a difference in approach that had become apparent by the late 1930s (figs. 62 and 63).[116] It is comprised of more carefully integrated parts, though (like his son's) the major monumental form is a spatial frame rather than an impermeable object. Yet this conventionally shaped frame carried the weight of a more traditional age, evoking an image of massiveness that was less appealing in 1947 than it had seemed a decade earlier in the propylaeum connecting the Library and Museum at Cranbrook.

Although in certain ways problematic, the M.I.T. Chapel and Auditorium are even more prophetic of Eero's later career than his Jefferson Arch

67

EERO SAARINEN AND ASSOCIATES. *Thomas J. Watson Research Center for IBM, Yorktown.* 1957–61, exterior. Photo courtesy Ezra Stoller

(figs. 64, 65, 66). They were commissioned in October 1950; construction on the Auditorium began in May 1953, and on the Chapel in May 1954; both were dedicated in May 1955.[117] Saarinen conceived the Auditorium as a segment of a sphere, its concrete shell roof supported at three points and its walls largely glazed.[118] By contrast the chapel is a windowless brick cylinder set within a moat, lit within by a single skylight and by light reflecting up through a glazed band at the perimeter of the undulating interior wall. The immediate precursor of the Chapel is Eliel Saarinen's 1947 project for a similar chapel at Stephens College, still being designed by the elder Saarinen at the time of his death in 1950. Both of these centralized chapels relate ultimately to Early Christian prototypes, and the connection may have been a conscious one.[119] The varied shapes of the supporting arches in the M.I.T. Chapel (fig. 65) also correspond in feeling to those in the entrance gate and elsewhere in the first buildings at Cranbrook, affirming continuity between father and son, as did the inclusion of sculpture. The screen by Harry Bertoia, animated by light, provides extraordinary interior focus. Theodore Roszak's spire, also integral to Saarinen's concept, seems less effective, perhaps diminished by the sculptural qualities of the building itself. Eero persisted in his quest for sculpture that might extend and strengthen architectural form, yet his own, larger creations remained dominant.[120]

In the M.I.T. buildings Eero departed consciously from designs restricted primarily to rectangular shapes. Significantly he did not regard this as reacting against the work of such established modernists as Mies van der Rohe, but rather as being sympathetic to it for the choice of form honored functional need and structure was honestly expressed.[121] In seeking appropriate expression of function, he examined needs with the intent of selecting specific, observable shapes. He argued that a triangular shape offered the most appropriate plan for an auditorium, while a circle epitomized a timeless, non-denominational quality ideal for the Chapel. Its textured walls of brick related to existing M.I.T. buildings, expressing a sensitivity to setting that Eero also believed essential.[122] In accordance with precepts of modern architecture as he interpreted them, he also felt obliged to examine forms made possible by new building techniques; his M.I.T. dome was one of the first examples in the United States to exploit the possibilities inherent in thin shell construction.[123] Preliminary sketches for the Auditorium recall buildings in the first proposals made for General Motors in 1945 and anticipate such later designs as Dulles International Airport (fig. 73). In seeking variations of a fundamental sort, Saarinen was almost certainly aware of similar departures being made in that same period by such leading figures as Le Corbusier (1887–1965).[124] A more immediate example was Aalto's Baker House dormitory (1946–49), adjacent to Eero's M.I.T. buildings. By joining an international shift toward a more varied modern architecture, Eero Saarinen embarked upon a demanding course that encouraged the invention of a new architectural vocabulary for each commission.

During the brief decade of his fully independent practice, Eero Saarinen's office received an extraordinary number of major commissions. Several of the resulting designs utilized relatively conventional framing and were developed for situations without the contextual restraints of an urban setting. In these designs, form was determined primarily by use, and Saarinen continued to explore various geometries. Among the best is the Thomas J. Watson Research Center for IBM, Yorktown, New York (1957–61). Its curved plan yielded advantages in office arrangement and provided visual relief within the 1000-foot-long corridor (fig. 67).[125] The elegantly detailed, dark-tinted curtain wall is anchored to fieldstone elements at each end and along the inner face of the curve, providing a sense of fixed location. This and other complexes for major corporations—such as the Bell Telephone Laboratories at Holmdel, New Jersey (1957–62)—offered persuasive, influential models for suburban office complexes.

In situations restricted by a more constrained site, where architectural form was determined partly by the need to relate to adjoining buildings, Eero appeared less at ease. His allusions to architectural motifs of a more eclectic age seemed almost apologetic, as in the Emma Hartman Noyes House, Vassar College (1954–58), or the Law School at the University of Chicago (1956–60). Large numbers of design studies for the similarly restricted U.S. Embassy in London (1955–60) reflect an approach that Eero usually followed, with all possible alternates being reviewed as a means to a more perfect solution.[126] Yet the focus of these studies on facade variations rather than volumetric concerns implies a certain degree of frustration. In other, later instances he achieved better results, as in the Samuel F. B. Morse and Ezra Stiles Colleges, Yale University (1958–62). There through texture and irregular form generated by a revived technique of

68
EERO SAARINEN AND ASSOCIATES. *Samuel F. B. Morse and Ezra Stiles Colleges, Yale University, New Haven.* 1958–62, exterior. Photo courtesy Ezra Stoller

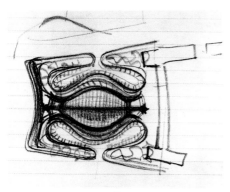

poured stone construction, Eero produced a picturesque and effective evocation of another age (fig. 68).[127] The cohesiveness of related parts, and the care with which exterior areas were shaped, recall the spirit of Cranbrook itself.

In designs where form was determined largely by structure, Eero realized his greatest successes. In these he gave careful consideration to problems of use and setting as they affected design, but one senses an underlying stimulation that came from an expanded opportunity to sculpt space. Study models that he routinely used to record ideas were much employed in the development of these designs. Following the M.I.T. Auditorium, his next two major works exploring new structural systems were the David S. Ingalls Hockey Rink at Yale University (1956–58), and the Trans World Airlines Terminal at Idlewild (now J. F. Kennedy) Airport, New York (1956–62). In both, Eero believed the particular nature of the major function to be housed was best served by the visibly dramatic form he chose.

The Ingalls Rink was the first to be designed.[128] Eero began with a concrete arch that could span the length of the rink without intermediate supports, honoring the oval shape of the rink itself. The suspended roof enriches the sense of curved form, its outer edge anchored to walls that are themselves curved in plan. Preliminary sketches (fig. 69) show one of several variations, tried before the arch itself was lifted up at each end, its actual support partially concealed by entrance doors (fig. 70).[129]

In the TWA Terminal, Eero sought an expression of flight itself (fig. 71).[130] Comparisons are often made with expressionistic sketches done by Mendelsohn in the late teens and early 1920s that Eero may have seen as a valid statement of twentieth-century architecture, and one too long ignored.[131] Any interpretation of Mendelsohn was surely encouraged by Joern Utzon's Sydney Opera House (completed 1973), a design strongly defended by Eero as a member of the jury for that competition.[132] In America, the most immediate parallel was the more conventionally shaped Lambert Airport Terminal Building, St. Louis (1953–56), by the firm of Yamasaki, Leinweber, and Associates.[133] Eero's terminal is far more personal and more complexly shaped, composed essentially of four sculpturally formed barrel vaults, each supported at two points and so balanced that the entire structure rests on only four Y-shaped columns. The sensuously formed interior generates a feeling of continuous motion that was without exact parallel, and

71

EERO SAARINEN AND ASSOCIATES. *Trans World Airlines Terminal, John F. Kennedy (formerly Idlewild) Airport, New York.* 1956–62, exterior. Photo courtesy Balthazar Korab

72

EERO SAARINEN AND ASSOCIATES. *Deere and Company Administrative Center, Moline.* 1957–64, exterior. Photo courtesy Balthazar Korab

the lack of scale-giving elements enhances the sculptural effect of the building, emphasizing a futuristic, machine-like quality that was no doubt intentional. It was a significant attempt at revised spatial definition, partly based, as were many of Eero's designs, on a subjective interpretation of structural technology.[134]

Eero Saarinen's tragic death cut short his evolution as an architect. That he was moving toward a brilliant resolution of divergent forces is demonstrated by three late works: the Deere and Company Administrative Center, Moline, Illinois (1957–64); the Dulles International Airport near Washington, D.C. (1958–63); and the Columbia Broadcasting System Headquarters, New York City (1960–65). Each reflects a creative interpretation of function, place, material, and structure that is balanced by intelligent logic.

The Deere Center celebrated steel as no other building ever had. At first, Eero proposed an inverted pyramid, but next conceived the building as a bridge connecting two gentle hills (fig. 72).[135] Interpreting an essential quality of the farm implement company the building was to serve, he developed an architecture of metal parts that was meant to honor machinery. These parts were shaped and connected with a sensitivity suggestive of Japanese wood detailing. Glazed

73

walls were protected by exposed structure and by shading devices of the same material; these enhanced a permeable appearance. Characteristically seeking underutilized technologies, he specified steel that would protect itself by a layer of corrosion: its color and texture added extraordinary finish.[136]

In Dulles (fig. 73) more convincingly than in the TWA terminal, Eero gave universally appreciable form to an airport, achieving for that new building type what Sullivan had managed for the skyscraper. Its success depended as much upon Eero's analysis of function as upon his intuitive grasp of structure, for his concept of a mobile lounge allowed the weakening complications of airport walkways to be eliminated, and thus justified a single form deserving monumental expression. It is a terminal as place, as essentially one building that is the anchor of movement rather than its imitator. Surpassing the more personal shapes of TWA, there is a visible logic to Dulles' regular structure. The smooth integration of its suspended canopy with lower terraces, and the dramatic accent of the control tower, recall aspects of Eliel Saarinen's Helsinki Railway Station: both architects grasped a potential inherent in buildings specific to their time. And with Dulles, as much as with any of his later designs, Eero Saarinen returned to an architectural concept of cohesively connected parts.[137]

The CBS Building also balances the achievements of father and son, for the vertical rise of its expressive masonry supports realizes a potential inherent in the Tribune project of 1922. Eero's first schemes called for a sculptural frame that was to rise from a terrace located on a level below the street (fig. 74).[138] He moved gradually toward his final scheme, a single, unbroken shaft that to him epitomized simplicity (fig. 75).[139] It was not the simplicity of blank planes, but rather of a surface enriched through a logical manipulation of structure and services. Such pleated treatment can be found in German skyscrapers of the early 1920s, and has its roots in Expressionist towers.[140] For Eero there were other justifications. It was New York's first major skyscraper to be built of reinforced concrete, and he celebrated its structural weight through the repeating pattern of partly hollow triangular piers. These imparted depth to the building's outer walls and the hollow upper portions provided spaces for mechanical services. The doubling of these piers at the corner sustained the logic of the alternating pattern, yet left unresolved the definition of the walls themselves. There is a certain nobility in the very lack of compromise.[141]

Essentially, Eero Saarinen's approach was intelligently pragmatic rather than consciously intellectual. The symbolism of his buildings related to their immediate function and was largely self-contained. He did not actively seek connections with broader intellectual currents in his work—such issues began to be reintroduced in America only in the late 1950s, beginning especially with the

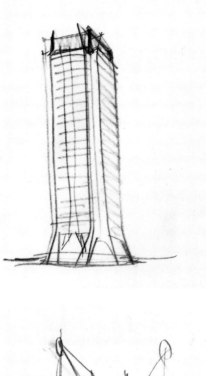

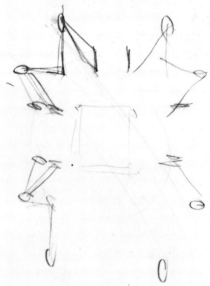

74

EERO SAARINEN AND ASSOCIATES. *Columbia Broadcasting System Headquarters, New York City.* 1960–65, perspective diagram and preliminary plan. Pencil on yellow tracing paper (Eero Saarinen). Manuscripts and Archives, Sterling Memorial Library, Yale University

75

EERO SAARINEN AND ASSOCIATES. *Columbia Broadcasting System Headquarters, New York City.* 1960–65, exterior. Photo courtesy CBS, Inc.

CHARLES EAMES. *John Philip Meyer House, St. Louis.* 1936–38

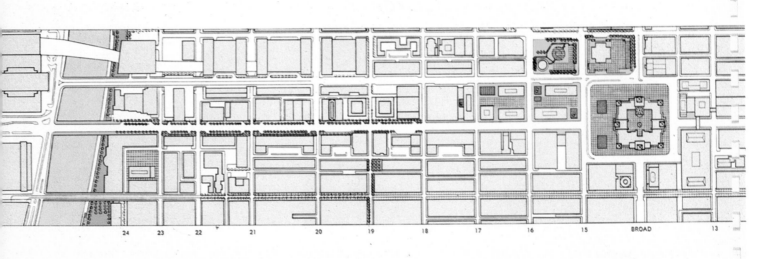

Colorplates 6 and 7

PHILADELPHIA CITY PLANNING COMMISSION, EDMUND N. BACON, EXECUTIVE DIRECTOR. *Plan for Center City, Philadelphia, Market Street Development.* 1946–63 ff. Reproduced from Philadelphia City Planning Commission, *Center City Philadelphia,* Philadelphia, 1963

work of Louis I. Kahn (1901–74) and others in his circle. A major stimulus in the intellectualization of American architecture, the first section of Kahn's Alfred Newton Richards Medical Research Building at the University of Pennsylvania (1957–61) was only completed in the year of Eero's death. Yet before that time, Eero was an acknowledged leader among American architects seeking new architectural expressions appropriate to the 1950s.[142] His office, its productive force guided by such valued associates as Kevin Roche, John Dinkeloo, and Joseph N. Lacy, attracted people of unusual talent.[143] There they assisted Eero in his passionate search for form and witnessed his determined, often brilliant invention of new vocabularies for major commissions. That he sought new answers within the established framework of modern architecture, through exploitation of various materials and structural systems, is understandable. For in accepting the immediate past by problem solving rather than seeking to explore abstract concepts, he reinforced a belief in cultural continuity that is essential to an understanding of Cranbrook students' basic tie to a crafts tradition. That his invention of vocabularies within this framework could not be sustained at the level Eero demanded, nor its results appreciated without an extended period of development, was soon recognized. Robert Venturi, who worked in Saarinen's office from 1951 to 1953, and who later taught with Kahn at the University of Pennsylvania, was perhaps most articulate in calling for an architecture that established meaning through the manipulation and refinement

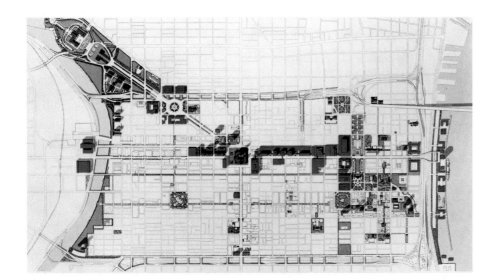

76

PHILADELPHIA CITY PLANNING COMMIS-SION, EDMUND N. BACON, EXECUTIVE DI-RECTOR. *Plan for Center City, Philadel-phia.* 1946–63 ff., site plan. Reproduced from Philadelphia City Planning Commis-sion, *Center City Philadelphia,* Philadel-phia, 1963

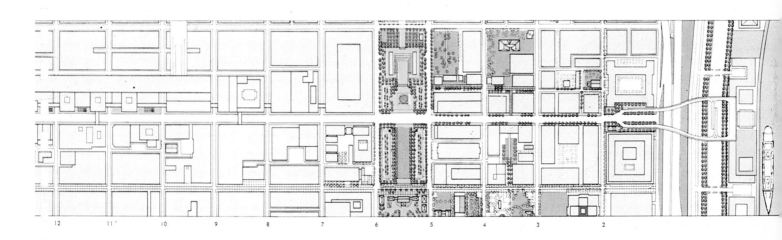

of certain architectural details rather than whole building forms.[144] Changing fash-ions led to critical evaluations of Saarinen's work that often overlooked his sincere efforts to arrive at just such details (as in the Miller house), but according to his own terms, and in an essentially modern rather than historic guise.[145]

During the 1950s, Eero's achievements partly overshadowed those of other architects trained at Cranbrook. Yet their work consistently reflects a concern for detail and an understanding of urban scale that is not always so easily observed in Eero's work. Examples by Harry Weese and Edmund N. Bacon illus-trate this.

In his design for a summer house begun the very month of Eero's death, Weese evoked a traditional sense of shelter through the manipulation of recognized architectural elements (fig. 77).[146] These elements are not overtly eclectic, but instead recall an evolving modern tradition developed by such archi-tects as Wright, Aalto, and Eliel Saarinen. The branching wings of the house, shown in the first conceptual sketches (fig. 79), recall Wright's 1937 design for

Wingspread, a house that also related to a specific place. The sheltering effect expressed by the folded wood planes of the roof and walls (fig. 78) is sympathetic to Aalto, and the very placement of the house on its island setting, as well as the play of towered elements against low wings, evoke images of Hvitträsk. Yet these elements have been assimilated without self-conscious reference to another age, and thus support a sense of cultural continuity as it had been taught at Cranbrook. Also reflected was a belief in architecture as a primary form of expression not requiring the consciously intellectual support of literary analogy.

At larger scale, Bacon's design efforts are exemplary. He grasped the need for cohesive physical design of cities as taught by Eliel Saarinen, and applied that understanding to the development of Philadelphia, where he began work in 1940 and was named Executive Director of the City Planning Commission in 1949.[147] The resulting plan for Center City provided for urban spaces as experiential realities, defined by elements that respected traditions of place and form. He sensed the essential role of axis as an appropriate urban connector, and in such applications as the Market Street development (fig. 76 and pls. 6 and 7) realized

77

HARRY WEESE AND ASSOCIATES. *Island House, Muskoka, Ontario.* 1961–63, exterior. Photo courtesy Balthazar Korab

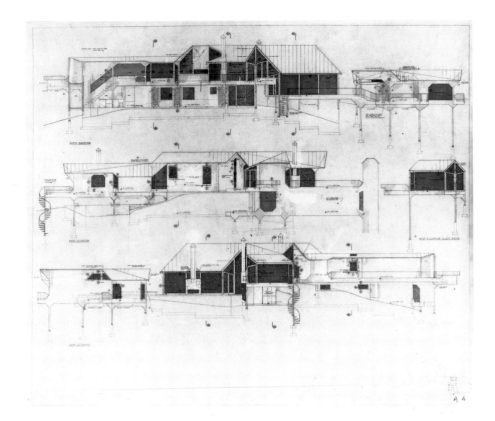

78

HARRY WEESE AND ASSOCIATES. *Island House, Muskoka, Ontario.* 1961–63, elevations/working drawing sheet A-4. Pencil and film laminates on plastic film. 35 × 41 ⅞″. Harry Weese and Associates

potentials implicit in Eliel Saarinen's plan for the Chicago Lakefront. In both, necessarily complex levels of vehicular and pedestrian movement were provided with natural light and open courts. Treated as noble and monumental spaces, they reflect a sense of designed place rare at such scale.

Later work by Cranbrook students, done in the decades following Eero Saarinen's death, extends the tradition promulgated by the school. It is a tradition bound by sensitivity to place, by a sympathetic as well as practical understanding of materials, by an ability to design at scales that extend from individual objects to entire cities, and by an understanding of how to relate such differently scaled elements. Major works by such architects as Edward Charles Bassett, William C. Muchow, George Matsumoto, Gyo Obata, and others illustrate this. If there is a reticence to depart from precedent, it is a reticence born of respect for continuity, and of a desire to reinforce an accepted attitude toward the development of modern architecture. Such ideas give meaningful shape to our time.

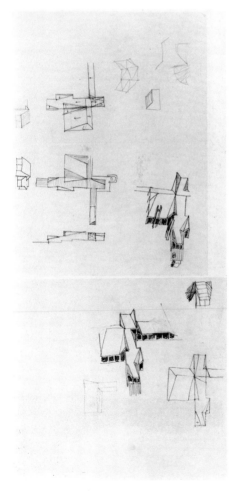

79

HARRY WEESE AND ASSOCIATES. *Island House, Muskoka, Ontario.* 1961–63, design diagrams [1961]. Pencil on tracing paper (Harry Weese). Harry Weese and Associates

5 | INTERIOR DESIGN AND FURNITURE

The story of interior and furniture design at Cranbrook is one of the most important chapters in the history of twentieth-century American design. On the one hand, it is an account of events that happened at a specific place and time: the founding of the Cranbrook Academy of Art in 1932 and the resultant developments over the next quarter century involving two generations of faculty and students. The first generation consisted mainly of Europeans—most notably Eliel Saarinen and his family, particularly his son, Eero. The second—Midwesterners such as Charles Eames and Florence Knoll—studied at Cranbrook in the 1930s but with the second World War were dispersed between California and the East Coast. On the other hand, Cranbrook's history is symptomatic of the decisive developments occurring in American design during this century.[1] First and foremost, it chronicles the struggle for a reconciliation between the ideals of the Arts and Crafts movement and the demands of industrial design. Moreover, it affirms the paramount role played by architects in the battle for modern design. The story also involves an assessment of the impact of European émigrés who came to the States around the first World War and in the thirties.[2] Most importantly, it entails the work of a brilliant generation of American designers that emerged after World War II as leaders of western design for some two decades. It is a remarkable story that concurred with the founding of one of the most influential design schools in America, the Cranbrook Academy of Art.

When Eliel Saarinen came to the United States in 1923 at the age of fifty, he had had a long and distinguished career in Finland and Europe (see Clark).[3] During the late 1890s and early 1900s, Saarinen's work was very much in the manner of the Arts and Crafts movement or what the Finns call National Romanticism. Increasingly after 1904 the influence of more abstract German and Austrian design was evident, and in the succeeding decade Saarinen produced neoclassical projects similar to German work of the teens. In short, his work was very much a part of the mainstream of modern European design—individual and memorable without being overtly avant-garde.

Prior to coming to Cranbrook, Saarinen worked on several American projects which show his work in transition. The most important interior in the 1923 Chicago Lakefront project (figs. 23, 24, 25, 26) was for a waiting room in the train station—a square room lit by four large skylights and divided into four parts by semicircular-headed colonnades.[4] The Memorial Hall in the Detroit Riverfront project (1924) was a decidedly neoclassical building (fig. 27); the auditorium was a centralized space dominated by a glazed dome which emitted light into a sunken crypt.[5] Saarinen's most important design for a centralized space, however, was the proposed sanctuary for a Christian Science Church (1925–26) in Minneapolis, Minnesota (figs. 32, 33, 34). The tripartite plan recalled Wright's Unity Temple (1906), and the foyer, in particular, was reminiscent of Edward Thomsen's and G. B. Hagen's Gentofte Komune, Øregaard School (1923–24), in Denmark. The sanctuary had a square base from which an octagonal mass rose. The interior walls were boldly articulated with pilasters and a corbelled cornice,

Colorplate 8

ELIEL SAARINEN (DESIGNER) AND THE COMPANY OF MASTER CRAFTSMEN (MANUFACTURER). *Side Chairs*. 1929–30. Fir (?) with black and ocher paint, red horsehair upholstery. 37 3/8 × 17 × 19"; seat h. 18 1/2". Cranbrook Academy of Art/Museum

80

ELIEL SAARINEN. *Dining Hall, Cranbrook School.* c. 1927–28. Photo: Nyholm. Courtesy Cranbrook Academy of Art/Museum

81

ELIEL SAARINEN. *Armchair.* 1928. Oak and bronze. 44 × 19 ½ × 17 ⅜"; seat h. 17 ¾". Cranbrook Academy of Art/Museum

but the most prominent feature was the ceiling—a saucer dome with an intricate glazing pattern. Had the project been executed, the sanctuary would have been one of the most monumental ecclesiastical spaces to have been built in America in the 1920s. These transitional projects show Saarinen's work in relation to two contemporary currents in Scandinavian architecture—the medievalism of Ragnar Östberg (1866–1945) and the neoclassicism of Gunnar Asplund (1885–1940).

Eliel Saarinen's most important American undertaking was the series of buildings he designed for George Booth at Cranbrook. The first complex was for the school for boys (begun 1925), whose somewhat eclectic exteriors and interiors recall Östberg's Stockholm City Hall (1909–23), though similarities to English collegiate architecture have also been noted (see De Long). In discussing his American career, one can never forget that the elder Saarinen was a true believer in the Arts and Crafts ideal of total design; and the interiors and furnishings for his buildings must always be viewed in this larger context. Moreover, it is important to remember that if Saarinen's interiors for the school for boys were not so traditional as James Gamble Rogers' Gothic Revival Harkness Quadrangle (1921) at Yale University, neither were they as avant-garde as Walter Gropius' Bauhaus at Dessau (1925–26)—two contemporary institutional designs. Rather, they occupied a middle ground and may be seen as a late manifestation of Arts and Crafts design.

Although Saarinen's energies seem to have been spent largely on the superb exterior detailing of the Cranbrook buildings, there are several masterly spaces within them. The academic building (constructed c. 1926–27) features two impressive halls (see De Long). One entrance hall has a two-story space with plaster walls, beamed ceiling, and an inglenook with extremely fine brick detailing around the fireplace; the beautifully detailed wood stair and balcony recall Saarinen's Villa Keirkner, Helsinki (1915/16–18) (fig. 22). The other entrance lobby has sculpted plaques by Eero Saarinen and a blue and gold stenciled design on the concrete beams by Pipsan Saarinen Swanson, perhaps the earliest American collaboration by Saarinen's son and daughter.[6] The most prominent feature in the library is a fireplace inglenook with sculptural panels by Geza Maroti (see Marter).[7]

Clearly the most impressive space at the school for boys is the Dining Hall (constructed c. 1927–28), a long rectangular room with plaster walls and barrel vault lit by semicircular-headed windows on both sides (figs. 30, 31, 80). The leaded windows—particularly the five-bay window on the west end wall—are one of the glories of this imposing room.[8] A low wood wainscoting and herringbone floor give a human scale to this large space. Lighting is provided by two rows of fixtures—each consisting of four glass bowls on a brass pendant—which were made by Orrefors, Sweden, to a modified Saarinen design.[9] Furnishings for the hall consisted of oak banquet tables and simple but subtly proportioned side chairs and armchairs (fig. 81).[10] A certain Englishness may be noted here in Saarinen's use of vernacular furniture forms; the quality of the wood and the fine detailing impart a gracefulness and elegance to the chair designs, as was characteristic of such British contemporaries as E. W. Gimson (1864–1919) or Gordon Russell (1892–1980).[11] Though the Dining Hall has a certain spartan quality in its furnishings, it has a true dignity in its ample proportions as befits a preparatory school for young men.

While working on the plans for the school for boys, Saarinen began a series of designs for dormitories and faculty housing along Academy Way. The most complete of these was a residence for his family. Saarinen House (1928–30) is, in fact, one of the most significant houses built in America during

82

ELIEL SAARINEN. *Living Room, Saarinen House.* 1928–30. Photo courtesy Cranbrook Archives

83

ELIEL SAARINEN. *Dining Room, Saarinen House.* 1928–30. Photo courtesy Cranbrook Archives

the 1920s.[12] The extraordinary interiors featured Saarinen's meticulous detailing and mostly custom-designed furnishings. The two most important spaces were the living and dining rooms. The first is a formal rectangular room with a cove ceiling (fig. 82); its most prominent feature is a fireplace on the south wall faced in dull brown tiles edged in silver, which were made by Mary Chase Stratton at the Pewabic Pottery, Detroit, from Saarinen's design (see Eidelberg).[13] The predominant colors of the room were grey and rust—the former a distinctive color now called "Saarinen grey." Door frames were maple stained grey, and the walls were covered in a Dupont fabric of rayon and jute in the same color palette.[14] The furniture (pl. 9) was arranged formally around the edges of the room; a rug by Loja Saarinen ran down the center of the dark oak floor.[15] Particular note should be made of the couch with the traditional Finnish rya rug draped from the wall to the floor (visible at the rear left in fig. 82).

In designing the furniture for this room Saarinen produced a set of beautifully delineated drawings (c. 1929) for ten suites of furniture (Back Cover; pls. 10, 11, 12, 13).[16] Each set included an armchair, tea table, tall cabinet, low cabinet, and lounge chair; all were similar in form and varied mainly in their inlay pattern and upholstery. The final ensemble was executed by Tor Berglund, the gifted Swedish cabinetmaker who came to Cranbrook in 1929, and at least four other inlaid table designs by Eliel Saarinen are attributed to him.[17]

At the north end of the room one entered the dining room through striped velvet portieres (fig. 83). This formal and elegant room is octagonal in shape with a stepped, domed ceiling.[18] The walls were covered in rectangular fir panels; the interiors of the corner niches were painted Chinese red. The dome was gilt.[19] The focal point of this room, however, was the Art Deco dining room suite made from Saarinen's design by the Company of Master Craftsmen.[20] Two versions of the table are known; both have octagonal bases and circular inlaid tops. One design featured a single pedestal (fig. 84); the executed version has a base made of four fluted panels (fig. 83).[21] The side chairs of fir with black linear decoration were originally upholstered with horsehair in a reddish coral color (pl. 8).[22]

The decidedly Art Deco quality of the living room and dining room furniture was, no doubt, a response to the work of the French *ébénistes* that Saarinen had seen at the "Exposition Internationale des Arts Décoratifs et Industriels Modernes" of 1925. The elegant armchairs for the living room (pl. 9) have tapered panels and legs veneered in exotic woods with fine geometric decoration. The fluted backs of the dining room side chairs (pl. 8) are a further extension of Saarinen's concern for subtle modelling highlighted with linear decoration. Both the living room and dining room tables have graceful, although attenuated, bases; the tops feature complex geometric inlays. Together the furnishings for these two rooms are among the finest Art Deco furniture produced in America.[23]

Saarinen's next commission at Cranbrook (figs. 36, 37, 38) was Kingswood School Cranbrook (1929–31), an immense complex on multiple levels. A hallmark of Saarinen's style is a restrained and somewhat conservative elegance, and nowhere at Cranbrook was it displayed more completely than in the richly detailed interiors at Kingswood. The major ones are simple geometric spaces: Saarinen employed domes, barrel vaults, octagonal recesses, or coves for spatial enrichment, and the beauty of these interiors is derived in large part from their fine proportions and, most especially, the natural and artificial lighting.[24]

As in the school for boys, the Kingswood dining hall (fig. 85) is a large vaulted space; but in this instance, Saarinen employed a considerably more complex lighting system. General illumination is provided on the north and

Colorplate 9

ELIEL SAARINEN (DESIGNER). *Armchairs and Table for Saarinen House.* 1929–31. Chairs (TOR BERGLUND [CABINETMAKER]): greenhart, African walnut, rosewood, and maple veneers (?) with silk and linen upholstery. 30 ¾ × 25 ½ × 22 ½″; seat h. 18″. Table (TOR BERGLUND [ATTRIB.]): greenhart, African walnut, rosewood, and maple veneers (?). 26 × 30 × 30″. Cranbrook Academy of Art/Museum

ELIEL SAARINEN. *Dining Table.* 1929. Pencil, colored pencil, and ink on tracing paper. 17 ⅛ × 11″. Suomen Rakennustaiteen Museo

south sides by rows of large windows on the lower level. The flattened portion of the vaulted ceiling is lit by a row of leaded clerestory windows in the upper walls. Artificial lights were concealed in a vertical plane from which the low vault sprang. The lighting was wired ". . . for three circuits which may be switched independently of each other to form a most interesting angular pattern of light and shade on the ceiling arch."[25] The finishes and furnishings were meticulously detailed but restrained as befitted the Saarinen style.[26] The walls and ceilings were of sand-finish plaster in tones of warm, flat grey. The wainscot and paneling were of oak with a waxed silver grey finish; the floor was also oak, though finished in a dark acid-

85

ELIEL SAARINEN. *Dining Hall, Kingswood School Cranbrook*. 1929–31. Photo courtesy Cranbrook Archives

stain and waxed to a dull gloss. Colorful accents were provided by the furniture and textiles. The tables and side chairs (pl. 14, right) were made of silver grey birch with coral painted decoration; the latter were upholstered with a linen damask of the same color. The wool and rayon curtains repeated the same colors in patterns of vermillion, silver, and gray. The focal point of the room, though, was the *Festival of the May Queen* hanging flanked by two aluminum *torchères* (figs. 128 and 139).

The other major interior at Kingswood is the auditorium (fig. 86). The rectangular room had an oak floor and wainscoting; the grey upper walls

86

ELIEL SAARINEN. *Auditorium, Kingswood
School Cranbrook*. 1929–31. Photo: George
Hance. Courtesy Cranbrook Archives

were articulated by pilasters with silver leaf decoration and triple rows of light
amber and green leaded windows.[27] The most exciting feature was the ceiling with
aluminum reflectors and silver leaf decoration by Pipsan Swanson.[28]

The furnishings for Kingswood are quite important for they
mark the debut of Eero Saarinen as a furniture designer. The sketches for Kingswood (figs. 87 and 88) and the executed designs (pl. 14) indicate the facility with
which the precocious young man—barely out of his teens—could design traditional
wood furniture or avant-garde tubular steel chairs.[29] This dichotomy in the younger
Saarinen's work is most evident in his furniture designs from the thirties but can
also be seen in his "romantic" architectural designs in the 1950s, which aroused
much controversy since they seemingly departed so sharply from the then-current
version of the International Style. The wood side chairs for the dining hall (pl. 14,
right) are a handsome Art Deco design featuring tapered legs and a curved crest
rail; they are, in fact, remarkably similar to one of Saarinen's sketches (fig. 88).[30]
Another drawing (fig. 87) shows a massive, crisply geometric lounge chair with
almost *moderne* streamlining. The auditorium armchairs (pl. 14, left), on the other
hand, have chromium plated steel frames and are upholstered in a light green fabric; this cantilevered design recalls the tubular version of the Brno chair (1929–30)
by Ludwig Mies van der Rohe (1886–1969).[31] Lastly, there was the more traditional wood furniture designed for the dormitory rooms and made in four color
schemes of yellow, rose, green, or blue to harmonize with the general color treatment of the rooms.[32]

A large project like Kingswood required the services of virtually all the artists at Cranbrook to be completed in such a brief time (1929–31). The interiors are a remarkable ensemble in their overall conception and in the richness of the detailing (fig. 152). Kingswood remains one of the Saarinen family's most impressive accomplishments.

The years from 1929–36 were a somewhat amorphous period. With the onset of the Depression, Eliel Saarinen executed few projects outside Cranbrook. He traveled frequently to Finland in the summers and maintained a career in his homeland.[33] Most importantly, Eero Saarinen departed to study sculpture in Paris and architecture at Yale University;[34] subsequently he practiced in Finland for approximately two years. His return to Michigan in 1936 to work in his father's office opened a new phase not only at the Saarinen firm but also at Cranbrook.

Eliel Saarinen's interior designs during this period (1929–36) consisted mainly of two exhibition rooms and the interiors for the Hudnut Building in New York. After the 1925 Paris Exposition, there was a concerted effort on the part of American designers, museums, department stores, and manufacturers to foster modern design in this country. One of the most popular means was installations featuring furnished rooms and exhibits.[35] Saarinen participated in two of the most important shows held at The Metropolitan Museum of Art under the direction of Richard Bach.[36]

Saarinen was, in fact, the principal designer for "The Architect and the Industrial Arts—An Exhibition of Contemporary American Design" held in 1929.[37] Two of the guidelines established for the show are of interest: first, architects—rather than industrial designers—were chosen to participate because of their ". . . strong position in relation to the manufacturing world and . . . [their] strategic position with regard to the dictation of styles to be used . . ."[38] and secondly, ". . . the objects shown [were] all of American conception and execution throughout . . . [and] they have been designed for the specific purpose of this showing."[39] Although it was a goal of the exhibition that many of the objects could be mass-produced, in reality the rooms were so luxurious and involved so much custom-finishing that few of the designs lent themselves to industrial production.

A dining room by Eliel Saarinen was one of the finest interiors in the 1929 exhibition (fig. 89). Conceived in shades of brown and tan,[40] it was a rather squarish interior with a wood floor and rug designed by Saarinen;[41] the baseboard, corner piers, and cornice provided a border for the patterned wallpaper designed by Pipsan Swanson.[42] The most striking feature was a fireplace of Pewabic tiles, which was later reinstalled in the living room at Saarinen House along with a pair of magnificent peacock andirons (fig. 82 and pl. 31). The dining room table was circular but had a much more massive octagonal base than the example in Saarinen House (fig. 83). The furniture was dark and had an elaborate inlay much like the living room suite at Saarinen House (fig. 82). The side chairs (fig. 90) of American black walnut, in particular, are remarkable for the "fluting" in the rear stiles and are reminiscent of tall-back chairs designed at the turn of the century by Saarinen and architects such as Charles Rennie Mackintosh (1868–1928) or Frank Lloyd Wright (1867–1959).[43]

By 1934, modern design had become more a part of the public consciousness.[44] The economic realities of the Depression had also caused a change; the room settings in "Contemporary Industrial Art" (1934–35) at The Metropolitan Museum of Art were less opulent and conveyed a greater sense of the everyday.[45] Many of the items—furniture, household wares, etc.—were indeed intended for mass production; and the younger generation of participating designers—William Lescaze (1896–1969), Donald Deskey (b. 1894), Raymond Loewy (b. 1893), and Russel Wright (1905–1977)—contributed very stylish *moderne* interiors and objects. Saarinen's "Room for a Lady" was a sleek salon in shades of eggshell, coral, and black.[46] Compared with the 1929 room, patterning had been greatly reduced; the furniture was largely built-in; and there was a pronounced horizontality in the drapery pattern and furniture trim. Saarinen's silver designs (pl. 32), however, were the finest feature of the interior[47] and represent one of the few in-

87 and 88

EERO SAARINEN. *Chair Designs, Kingswood School Cranbrook.* c. 1929. Pencil and colored pencil on paper. Lounge chair: 4 ⅜ × 3 ¾"; side chair: 3 ⅛ × 2 ⅝". Cranbrook Academy of Art/Museum

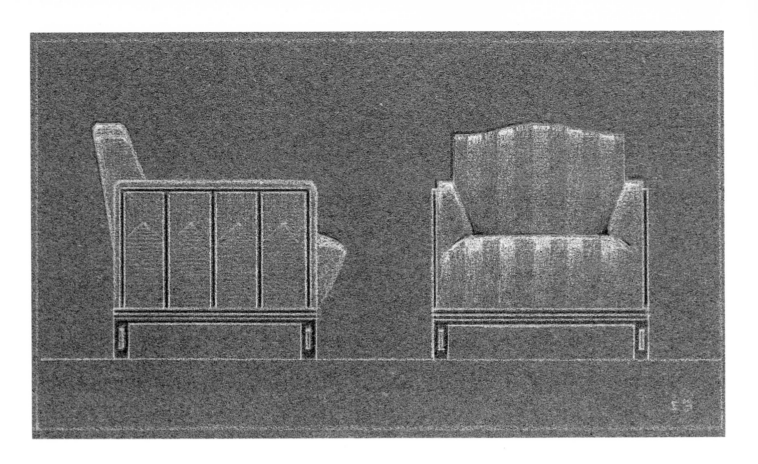

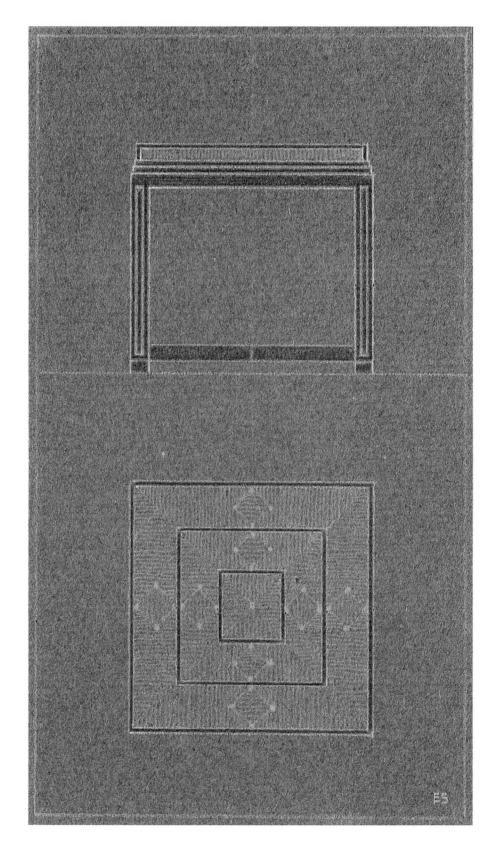

Colorplates 10, 11, 12, 13
ELIEL SAARINEN. *Drawings for Living Room
Furniture Suite*. c. 1929. Colored pencil on
brown paper mounted on black board.
Lounge chair 3 ½ × 6 ¼″; armchair 3 ½ ×
5 ⅓″; table 6 ½ × 3 ¾″; low cabinet 4 ⅛
× 5 ¼″. Suomen Rakennustaiteen Museo

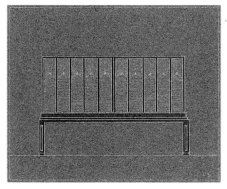

stances in which he designed an object which lent itself to commercial mass production.

The Hudnut Building (c. 1929–30) in New York was designed
in conjunction with Ely Jacques Kahn,[48] a collaborator with Saarinen at both of
the exhibitions held at The Metropolitan Museum of Art. The Villaret marble
facade was restrained, but the interiors were luxurious as befitted the deluxe clientele of this beauty salon. The most impressive room was the entrance lounge,[49]

89

ELIEL SAARINEN. *Dining Room, "The Architect and the Industrial Arts," The Metropolitan Museum of Art.* 1929. Photo courtesy The Metropolitan Museum of Art

which had a terrazzo floor covered with a yellow and grey rug made by the Cranbrook Shops under the direction of Loja Saarinen. The walls were paneled with zebra and prima vera wood. The ceiling was also of prima vera and featured a gold-leafed recessed dome with concealed lighting. Metal trim in this room was nickel-silver. The side and armchairs with their "fluted" upholstery were a variation of the dining room seating at Saarinen House (pl. 8); the slender "bamboo" metal legs added a further note of luxury. The Hudnut commission was Eliel Saarinen's only building in New York; and the demolition of the salon with its sumptuous interiors—an ensemble of grey, exotic woods, and accents of gold—is particularly unfortunate.

Eero Saarinen's career in Finland was brief,[50] and there was only one project in which he was involved with the interiors: the remodeling of the Swedish Theater, Helsinki (1934–36), on which he collaborated with his father and Jarl Eklund.[51] The principal interiors were the theater itself, lobby spaces, and the restaurant facing the Esplanade. The majority of the drawings for the interiors were for furniture,[52] and these furniture designs were an outgrowth of the earlier work done for Kingswood. They included Empire and Louis XVI revivals for the lobby and board room, Windsor chairs, and *moderne* designs for the restaurant and theater seating.[53] There was, strangely enough, no follow-up on the earlier tubular metal designs inspired by Mies van der Rohe.

The Swedish Theater designs showed no influence of the work of Alvar Aalto (1899–1976) either, but shortly after his return to America the younger Saarinen did a project for *Architectural Forum* (October 1937) for a combined "living-dining room-study," which showed that he was very familiar with the Finnish designer's work.[54] The rectangular paneling of the dining area and the horizontal built-in cabinets recall his father's work. Saarinen, however, chose three chairs by Aalto for this interior which presage his own designs in laminated and bentwood in the late 1930s and early forties.[55]

On Eero Saarinen's return to the United States in 1936, three important commissions came into the office that renewed the national position of the Saarinen and Saarinen firm after the building lull caused by the Depression: the Kleinhans Music Hall, Buffalo, New York (1938–40), the Tabernacle Church of Christ (now First Christian Church), Columbus, Indiana (1939–42), and the Crow Island School, Winnetka, Illinois (1938–40). These buildings rank among the finest work produced by the office and indicate the younger Saarinen's growing influence as a designer in the firm (see De Long).

The basic composition of the Kleinhans Music Hall consists of two horseshoe-shaped auditoriums sharing a long, slightly bowed lobby, which has a wide stair at either end leading to a large balcony (fig. 41).[56] The space has a flowing quality because of the repeated use of *moderne* streamlined curves throughout: stair details, curved walls, coved ceilings, and even the profiles of the sofas. What makes the space so distinctive, though, is the low indirect lighting, which seems dim by contemporary standards.

90

ELIEL SAARINEN (DESIGNER) AND THE COMPANY OF MASTER CRAFTSMEN (MANUFACTURER). *Side Chairs, Dining Room, "The Architect and the Industrial Arts," The Metropolitan Museum of Art.* 1929. American black walnut, silverplate buttons, leather reupholstery. 43 3/8 × 17 1/2 × 18"; seat h. 19". The Metropolitan Museum of Art, Purchase, Theodore R. Gamble, Jr., in honor of his mother, Mrs. Theodore Robert Gamble; Gift of Lenore Ann Cisney

Colorplate 14

EERO SAARINEN. *Auditorium Armchair and Dining Hall Side Chair, Kingswood School Cranbrook.* 1929–31. Armchair: tubular steel and wood with green woven upholstery. 31 ⅛ × 21 ⅝ × 27 ½″; seat h. 16 ¾″. Side chair: birch, pink paint with reproduction linen upholstery. 35 ½ × 16 ⅞ × 19 ¼″; seat h. 19″. Cranbrook Academy of Art/Museum

The major interiors at Kleinhans are the main auditorium and the smaller chamber music hall. They represent one of the earliest usages by the Saarinen office of a wedge-shaped space for a public building, a portent in particular of Eero Saarinen's fascination with large sculptural interiors in the late 1940s and fifties.[57] The elder Saarinen's hand may be seen in the detailing of the walls of the chamber music hall with their rosewood paneling with pink painted decoration.

Most of the furniture designed for Kleinhans was not exceptional,[58] but the armchairs (fig. 91) for the chamber hall appear to be the earliest experiment by the Saarinen office with two-dimensionally molded plywood.[59] The form of a molded plywood shell suspended in a continuous U-shaped leg and armrest is very much indebted to a similar armchair (1930–33) by Aalto.[60] The stretcher

detail of the Kleinhans chair, however, recalls an American design (1934–35) by Gilbert Rohde (1894–1944).[61] Aalto's influence is further apparent in a lounge chair and stool used in the bar on the lower level; both designs had thick upholstered pads on wood cantilevered bases reminiscent of an Aalto lounge chair of 1936. The most prominent visual feature in Aalto's cantilevered chair is the wide arm. In Saarinen's armless lounge chair, the seat cushion sits directly on the frame, and the junction between frame and upholstery is thus more dramatic. The form is, in fact, more reminiscent of Mies van der Rohe's Tugendhat chair (1929–30), which had a steel frame.[62]

The Tabernacle Church of Christ (pl. 4) remains one of the finest buildings by the Saarinen office. The obvious indebtedness to the ecclesias-

tical interiors of Erik Bryggmann (1891–1955) could perhaps be attributed to Eero Saarinen's stay in Finland and illustrates his growing influence in the design process of the office.[63]

The most imposing interior of the Columbus church is the sanctuary (fig. 92), one of the most magnificent ecclesiastical spaces built in America in this century. Entered from a low narthex, the nave is a lofty, serene space separated by a row of cylindrical columns from a low side aisle on the left.[64] The chancel is reached by a flight of steps: pulpit, organ, and screen on the left; choir stalls and a large tapestry (fig. 155 and pl. 41) by Loja Saarinen on the right. To the rear is a low wood screen above which hangs a large cross on the end wall; both elements are illuminated by a hidden window from the left.[65] The beauty of this space—as with other Saarinen interiors—is derived from the superb proportions, beautiful lighting, and dexterous handling of materials. Illumination comes from a mixture of indirect lighting in the chancel, direct from the floor-to-ceiling windows on the right side of the nave, and artificial from the suspended metal fixtures, which recall Aalto. The floor is of stone. The vertical walls are a mixture of natural and painted brick and a rough plaster which creates subtle geometric patterns.[66] A change in the texture of plastering also occurs on the ceiling between the chancel and nave. The wood screens in the chancel—a mixture of cylindrical and rectangular members also in the manner of Aalto—add warmth to the masonry interior. Likewise, the laminated wood pews and chancel chairs are a continuation of the experiments noted earlier at Kleinhans. The sanctuary is a restrained ensemble of natural stone, off-whites, and blond woods bathed in an everchanging pattern of light and soft shadows. Here the Saarinens achieved a quiet lyricism appropriate for a house of worship.

These same elements are repeated at a smaller scale in the chapel.[67] Other parts of the building, however, have a strangely eclectic quality as if several hands or ideas were in evidence. The pastor's study is quite Wrightian in the handling of space. The stairwells recall Aalto in the use of vertical poles in the balustrades and the sculptural wood light troughs. Even more perplexing are the traces of Le Corbusier in the nursery in the plan of the toilet and the free-standing curved walls. Such details reveal an office in transition.

The last building (figs. 42 and 43) in this series is the Crow Island School.[68] The important planning innovation was the layout of the classrooms for the primary and intermediate grades. Each unit is an L-shaped room with its own garden, workroom, and toilets. The design was praised for its homelike quality and the generous amount of light and air it provided.

The classroom furniture was custom-designed for a child's scale. The chairs have a basic geometric quality in the junction of a two-dimensional bent plywood seat panel on cylindrical wood legs, but the design may also be seen as a portent of the revolutionary chairs that were done shortly thereafter for the "Organic Design in Home Furnishings Competition" held at the Museum of Modern Art (1940–41; see below). Classroom tables were also made up of simple geometric shapes; furniture for the entrance lobby was quite similar to the more conservative designs done for Kleinhans.

A characteristic of the Saarinen office was a proclivity to continue exterior materials in interiors. Brick is used for the walls of the Crow Island lobby and corridors, as well as vertical and horizontal wood paneling for a contrasting texture. The auditorium is a particularly handsome space with its undulating ceiling and almost "brutalist" masonry walls of alternating courses of brick and block.[69]

The Cranbrook Museum and Library (fig. 45) is something of a coda to this group. It was Eliel Saarinen's last executed building for the Cranbrook complex and was certainly his most formal and monumental. The design has traditionally been attributed to him,[70] and the interiors undeniably lack the excitement of Kleinhans or the Tabernacle Church where the younger Saarinen was actively involved. The composition is a tripartite arrangement of two rectangular blocks separated by a propylaeum. The Museum is by necessity a closed volume and reflects the now-familiar subtle palette preferred by Eliel Saarinen: in this in-

92

SAARINEN AND SAARINEN. *First Christian Church (formerly Tabernacle Church of Christ), Columbus, Indiana* (sanctuary). 1939–42. Photo courtesy Suomen Rakennustaiteen Museo

stance, travertine floors and fabric-covered walls and plaster ceiling originally finished in shades of warm grey.[71] The most interesting features were the sculpted plaster coffers in the ceiling. The Library, on the other hand, is a sunny reading room, and the light blond wood bookcases and furniture lend a sense of added warmth. Of particular interest are the low wood tables with their S-shaped laminated bases and the desk chairs with their cantilevered wood bases which are reminiscent of an Aalto side chair (c. 1929).[72]

  Although Cranbrook Academy was founded in 1932, there were few students formally studying interior or furniture design in the early years.[73] Cranbrook, moreover, did not produce a single design philosophy or aesthetic in the sense of that formed at the Bauhaus (see Clark). In seeking to characterize Cranbrook's approach to design, one would naturally mention the freedom of the students to work in all media, as well as the fact that furniture and interior design were always conceived of in an architectural context. Finally, one would add the importance of the physical environment at Cranbrook—i.e., the integration of the landscape, buildings, sculpture, and interiors. Above all, there was always the example of Eliel Saarinen's own work: he believed deeply in the unity of a design concept from its broadest characteristics to the smallest detail. Together with his son, he exemplified the belief that an artist's work was the paramount force in his life, for the Saarinens were notorious "workaholics." All of these concepts helped to establish an identity for Cranbrook as an institution, but this condition is alto-

93
CHARLES EAMES (DESIGNER) AND JOHN RAUSCH (MANUFACTURER). *Table, John Philip Meyer House, St. Louis.* 1936–38. Bleached cherry, cherry veneer, European walnut veneer, harewood, and black paint (?). 30 ⅛ × 36 × 36″. Collection Mrs. Leigh Gerdine

gether the more remarkable since these were qualities that may be learned more readily by example than by formal academic study.

By the late thirties, a younger generation of students and faculty gathered at Cranbrook (see Clark) that was to exert a profound influence on American design after World War II: Charles Eames, Florence Knoll, Benjamin Baldwin, and Eero Saarinen. The important friendships that began among this circle were to affect profoundly their personal and professional lives over the succeeding decades. The last years before World War II were a germinal time for modern design in America, and it is these years that have often been called the "golden moment" at Cranbrook. Certainly it was an exceptional, although brief, time. With the departure of both Charles Eames and Walter Baermann as industrial design instructors in the early forties, a period of difficulty ensued for the Design department at Cranbrook.[74] The national reputation of the Academy, however, continued to attract good students during the forties, and postwar graduates included such remarkable designers as David Rowland, Don Knorr, and Niels Diffrient, who form an important addendum to the Cranbrook story.

Charles Eames (1907–78) was in many ways the ideal student sought by Cranbrook in the early days when its model was the American Academy in Rome (see Taragin and Clark). He had practiced as an architect in St. Louis (see De Long) but had tried his hand at painting, stage design, stained glass, and furniture during the 1930s. Here was a young artist who would benefit from a year or two of study with Eliel Saarinen and Carl Milles free of financial considerations. Eames' career in St. Louis is still somewhat obscure, but his known works vary from Georgian revival to modest *moderne* houses. The change that was to occur in his work while at Cranbrook was nothing short of miraculous.

The John Philip Meyer house in Huntleigh, outside St. Louis (1936–38), was an imposing country residence with formal gardens and was perhaps Eames' most important commission from his St. Louis period (pl. 5). The design appears to have been changed after the house was underway, and the principal interiors clearly show the influence of the elder Saarinen.[75] The elegant tone of the house was set by the entry way: the hall had a maple-inlaid parquet floor, terracotta plaster walls, and a silver-leaf coffered ceiling.[76] The space was visually enlivened by a marble stair with aluminum railing that was lit by a stained glass window made by Emil Frei to an Eames design.[77]

The two most imposing interiors were the *en suite* living and dining rooms, for which Eames was asked to design supplementary furnishings. A large rectangular space with coffered ceiling, the living room featured a marble fireplace flanked by grey niches.[78] The color scheme was rich but subdued: a terracotta rug made by V'Soske, pink plaster walls, grey draperies designed by Loja Saarinen, and furniture upholstered in grey and terracotta. Eames designed a veneered card table (fig. 93) and set of four armchairs for the room.[79] The former with its tapered legs, Art Deco carved elements at the junction to the skirt, and inlaid top in geometric patterns is obviously indebted to Eliel Saarinen's furniture from the late twenties (pls. 8, 9, 10, 11, 12, 13). Such conservative work, moreover, may be taken as an indication of Eames' lack of awareness of avant-garde design during his St. Louis years.

The dining room was even more formal with its Federal furniture and French doors leading to a terrace. Eames designed an inlaid sideboard and acanthus-leaf chandelier for this room. The color scheme rivalled the living room in its richness: silver-leafed doors, grey plaster walls, a white rug (made by V'Soske to an Eames design), lemon yellow draperies with a coral and silver pattern, and brocaded upholstery fabric in coral. The Meyers were exceptional clients who provided Eames with an opportunity not only to build a large house but to design a series of interiors that are the epitome of thirties taste.

The Meyer house was the culmination of Eames' St. Louis career, and in 1938 he enrolled as a student at Cranbrook.[80] The following year he was asked to join the faculty and, most importantly, joined the Saarinen office on a part-time basis.[81] As Eames himself said later, ". . . it really wasn't until I started to work for Eliel Saarinen, and with Eero, that I had any conception of what 'concept' was."[82] Moreover, Eames often went to Chicago on weekends to confer with László Moholy-Nagy.[83] It was at this point, too, that Eames met his second wife, Ray Kaiser, at Cranbrook.[84] Two designs done there indicate the rapid metamorphosis that occurred during this period in his work.

In 1939 Eames and Eero Saarinen designed an exhibition of the resident faculty's work, which was installed at Cranbrook Pavilion.[85] It was an architectonic installation with wood structures used to define areas and act as display surfaces. The exhibit seems to be the first collaborative design by Saarinen and Eames to have been executed and was a harbinger of the highly influential exhibition installations that Charles and Ray Eames were to do in the 1940s and fifties.

Saarinen's and Eames' most famous collaborative efforts were, of course, their entries for the "Organic Design in Home Furnishings Competition" held at The Museum of Modern Art in 1940–41, for which they won two first prizes for a series of chairs, modular storage units, sectional sofa, and tables.[86] That competition may now be seen as the presage of the important developments in American furniture design in the third quarter of the twentieth century, and it clearly established Saarinen and Eames as leaders in the modern design movement.[87]

The significance of Saarinen's and Eames' Organic Design entries can be properly understood only if one views them in relation to the developments in furniture design in the previous fifteen years.[88] The year 1925 was a critical point in time. The influence of the Paris Exposition on the furniture designs of Eliel Saarinen has already been noted. The exhibit was an impressive showcase for the work of the more conservative Art Deco designers such as Jacques-Emile

94

EERO SAARINEN AND CHARLES EAMES (DE-SIGNERS) AND HASKELITE MANUFACTURING CORPORATION, CHICAGO, AND HEYWOOD-WAKEFIELD COMPANY, GARDNER (MANU-FACTURERS). *Armchair for "Organic Design in Home Furnishings Competition," The Museum of Modern Art, 1940–41.* Molded plywood shell, maple legs, and wool upholstery. 45 ½ × 33 × 29″; seat h. 18″. Collection Ray Eames

95

BENJAMIN BALDWIN AND HARRY WEESE. *Drawings for Chairs for the "Organic Design in Home Furnishings Competition," The Museum of Modern Art, 1940–41.* Pencil on yellow tracing paper, 34 ¾ × 14 ½″. Collection Harry Weese

Ruhlmann, but it also featured examples of the International Style, most notably Le Corbusier's Pavillion de L'Esprit Nouveau. It was also in 1925 that Marcel Breuer (1902–1981) designed his first tubular steel chair at the Bauhaus.[89] This was followed in the late twenties by a series of remarkable designs by Breuer and Mies van der Rohe that formulated a new conception of the chair[90] with tubular steel cantilevered frames and minimal upholstery.[91] By the mid-thirties, Breuer and Aalto had extended this aesthetic of minimal mass and a clear articulation of frame and seating area to include two-dimensionally laminated wood forms.[92] Saarinen's and Eames' achievement in 1940 was in bending laminated wood in a third dimension and in creating a new aesthetic featuring a lightweight molded shell on an attenuated base. As Eero Saarinen himself later noted, "New materials and techniques have given us great opportunities with structural shells of plywood, plastic and metal. . . . The problem then becomes a sculptural one, not the cubist, constructivist one . . ." [of the De Stijl and Bauhaus designers in the early decades of the century].[93] Saarinen's and Eames' work over the next fifteen years may be seen as a development of these initial technological innovations and sculptural forms.

The most important entries for the Organic Design competition by Saarinen and Eames were for a side chair and several versions of an armchair and lounge chair (fig. 94). All had three-dimensional plywood shells and were available with foam rubber padding and fabric upholstery.[94] There were several modifications between the designs submitted and the prototypal pieces executed.

The drawings show chairs with aluminum legs attached by a rubber-weld joint, whereas wood legs were finally used.[95] Likewise, the chairs were designed to have their wood veneer backs exposed but because of surface imperfections had to be fully upholstered. The one exception was the side chair, which had its Honduras mahogany veneer exposed on the back, though even here the drawing showing a bare wood shell could not be achieved.[96]

Modular case units were certainly not a new idea,[97] but the Saarinen/Eames design of Honduras mahogany veneer was a handsome, straightforward solution for flexible storage. The series was based on an 18-inch module. Cabinets and raised bases came in a variety of sizes; the former were to be made with interchangeable shelves, drawers, or doors. The Saarinen/Eames design was thus not only adaptable, but the modular construction facilitated packaging and shipping. Knockdown furniture was an idea that Eames addressed directly in several later designs.

Likewise, sectional sofas were not a novelty but Saarinen and Eames envisioned a sofa that would be physically and visually light instead of typically heavy and upholstered. Their design employed a molded plywood shell for a base and flat—rather than helical—springs with foam rubber padding for the seating surface.[98] An interesting detail was a zipper along the edge to join the units together.

Two other Cranbrook designers entered multiple categories in the competition and won prizes: Benjamin Baldwin (b. 1913) and Harry Weese (b. 1915).[99] Their most important entries were for lighting fixtures and outdoor furniture—tables, chairs (fig. 95), chaise lounges, and barbecue wagons. The most interesting design in the outdoor furniture category was for a tea wagon (fig. 8) which had a grey tubular metal frame, birch plywood and metal shelves, wicker basket, and pneumatic tires. While the form is obviously indebted to Aalto's tea cart (1936) with a laminated wood frame, the Baldwin/Weese design is unmistakably American in the straightforward expression of its function and materials.[100] The patio furniture had tubular or wrought-iron frames and a variety of seats: wire mesh, cedar slats, canvas sling, or upholstery. The floor and table lamps employed materials so favored by designers in the 1940s: stems of painted or chromed tubing and shades of parchment, Japanese paper, or plastic. One of the Organic

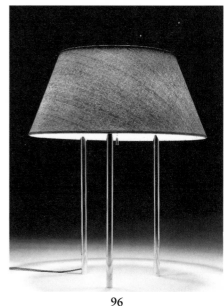

96
BENJAMIN BALDWIN. *Lamp*. c. 1940. Brass with linen shade. 20 ⅜ × diam. 17 ⅛". Collection Benjamin Baldwin

97
RALPH RAPSON. *Rocking Chair for the "Organic Design in Home Furnishings Competition," The Museum of Modern Art, 1940–41.* Black painted frame, reupholstered with linen webbing. 32 × 28 ¾ × 39"; seat h. 14 ¾". Collection Ralph Rapson

Design entries was executed as a prototype for Baldwin (fig. 96) and subsequently manufactured by George W. Hansen, New York.[101]

Another Cranbrook student, Ralph Rapson (b. 1914), submitted an entry for a rocking chair (fig. 97) which had a black wood frame and white webbing.[102] Although Rapson's prototypal chair is constructed of straight lengths of wood, the design is derived from the gracefully curved bentwood chairs produced by Bruno Mathsson (b. 1907) in the 1930s, an example of which Rapson purchased in Detroit in 1939.[103] Although the Rapson rocker did not win a prize in the competition, the chair and other variations were produced by Knoll in the early 1940s.[104] Rapson thus seems to be the first of many Cranbrook designers to have worked for Hans and Florence Knoll.

The early forties saw the departure of many of the students and faculty who had formed such an important circle at Cranbrook during the late 1930s.[105] Any discussion of design in the post-World War II period thus stretches beyond the confines of the Academy to California, Chicago, and the East Coast as this younger generation reached its maturity. Friendship and work were to bring this group together frequently over the succeeding years, and there was no more illustrious group in modern American design than the Cranbrook circle.[106]

Of the younger generation at Cranbrook, Eero Saarinen was certainly the most universal designer. As he said in a 1960 speech in Munich, "My father, Eliel Saarinen, saw architecture as everything from city planning to

Colorplate 15

EERO SAARINEN AND ASSOCIATES. *Irwin Miller House, Columbus, Indiana* (living room). 1953–57. Photo courtesy Ezra Stoller

the ash tray on a living room table. This is what I also believe. . ."[107] Eero Saarinen's approach to the design of interiors and furniture was characteristic of a significant segment of American design in the late 1940s and fifties.[108] First, Saarinen conceived of an interior and its furnishings in terms of the overall architectural conception of a building. Everything down to the smallest detail had to be a part of this "organic unity," a concept which Saarinen acknowledged he had learned from Frank Lloyd Wright. "A room is like a piece of art—it is just one idea."[109] Secondly, contemporary design should be expressive of a twentieth-century *Weltanschauung,* particularly avant-garde painting and sculpture. Moreover, the Industrial Revolution had necessitated fundamental changes in our society; to meet the demands of the modern age, furniture had to be mass-produced, and interiors must assume a certain anonymity. "The . . . mass-produced walls and spaces and the mass-produced furniture must never lose their impersonal character. These mass-produced elements are to the interior as structure is to architecture."[110] One's identity could be expressed by "ornamental or non-structural elements": flowers, paintings, books, handcrafted objects. Eero Saarinen brought an additional richness to his buildings—particularly in the case of sculpture and color treatments—through a continuation of the Cranbrook tradition of a collaboration with other artists, although he did not note this point in his Munich speech.[111]

Saarinen's design approach, moreover, is indicative of rather fundamental changes which occurred in the postwar design movement in America. First of all, the emphasis was clearly on mass-produced furniture, not custom designs. The majority of the commissions for modern interiors and furniture were for contract—i.e., commercial—not residential use. This shift toward large-scale projects and industrial production implies a staff or studio effort; for a design to go from conception to production requires many contributions. In the case of the Saarinen office, a generation of talented designers was involved.[112]

The majority of the postwar domestic designs by Eero Saarinen belong to the 1940s. The A.C. Wermuth house in Fort Wayne, Indiana (1940–41), and a project for the Sam Bell house (c. 1941) repeat many motifs used by Marcel Breuer and Walter Gropius (1883–1969) in a series of houses built on the East Coast from the thirties onward: raised sections on pilotti, the use of fieldstone and wood siding for exteriors and for the curved or askew interior walls.[113] Considerably more original was a project (1943) done by Eero Saarinen and Oliver Lundquist for a competition sponsored by *Arts and Architecture.*[114] Important features were the preassembled components which were delivered from the factory with everything built in. Of particular interest is the multiple-use and multilevel living space which was a prototype for the later Entenza residence (figs. 50 and 51). A perspective with a cut-out revealing the interiors showed prototypal sketches for the "womb" settee and chair (c. 1946–48) (figs. 102 and 104, right).

The two most important domestic commissions jointly designed by Saarinen and Eames from the forties were the Entenza and Eames residences, a pair of houses built in a meadow overlooking the Pacific Ocean in Pacific Palisades, California (figs. 49, 50, 51, 52, 53).[115] The Entenza house (1945–50), with its open plan and generous terraces, took advantage of the California climate. In contrast to the primary colors on the exterior, the interior was rather neutral; the living room had a wood ceiling, beige carpeting, a fireplace accented in orange-red, and a large built-in sofa covered in Belgian linen.[116]

In many ways, the Irwin Miller residence (1953–57) in Columbus, Indiana (fig. 59 and pl. 15), was an outgrowth from the Entenza house in plan and in the use of metal structure. The Miller house, however, was much more formal in its arrangement of family spaces in a modified Greek cross plan with private areas in each corner. The steel frame was decidedly Miesian in its fine detailing and pristine white finish, recalling Mies' elegant pavilion for Dr. Farnsworth, Plano, Illinois (1950).[117] Saarinen personally supervised the design of this sumptuous villa for the Millers with the assistance of Alexander Girard for the interiors.[118] The principal spaces have a travertine floor, white marble walls of book-matched panels, and an exposed steel structure with skylights illuminating alternating interior walls. Color is provided by the upholstery, art collection, and plants. Special features of interest are the sunken conversation pit, the pedestal dining room table, and a storage wall designed by Girard.[119] The Miller residence was Saarinen's finest domestic commission, and with the possible exception of the Farnsworth residence, it was perhaps the most beautiful modern house built in America during the 1950s.

The acclaim awarded the Tabernacle Church of Christ brought other ecclesiastical commissions to the Saarinen office. While some of these jobs came into the office in the late forties, the majority were executed after Eliel Saarinen's death in 1950. The younger Saarinen was increasingly concerned with how architecture could convey "emotionally the purpose and meaning of the building . . . Conveying significant meaning is part of the inspirational purpose of architecture and, therefore, for me, it is a fundamental principal of our art."[120] For these ecclesiastical commissions, Eero Saarinen employed three building types, which while different, nevertheless share certain characteristics. The circular chapel was perhaps the most original spatially, and its most fully realized example was the Chapel (figs. 64, 65, 66) at the Massachusetts Institute of Technology, Cambridge (1950–55).[121] For the Lutheran Concordia Senior College, Fort Wayne, Indiana (1953–58), Saarinen designed an A-frame structure whose pronounced verticality he felt recalled the tradition of Northern European churches.[122] In contrast, the last churches designed before his death in 1961—such as the North Christian Church, Columbus, Indiana (1959–63)—are partially sunken buildings which rise out of the earth, in a Wrightian sense, to a central belfry.[123] All of these sanctuaries

98

EERO SAARINEN AND ASSOCIATES. *General Motors Technical Center, Warren, Research Administration Building* (Lobby). 1945–56. Photo courtesy General Motors Technical Center

were envisioned as spaces that would have a powerful emotional effect on the worshiper. They were unadorned interiors finished in exterior materials. Most importantly, their beauty was largely derived from dramatic lighting effects, whether from oculi or indirect sources.

The majority of the commissions for office complexes that came into the Saarinen office during the forties and fifties were for suburban or rural sites. The landscape was thus of the greatest importance. The grounds in many cases were conceived on the scale of the gardens of André Le Nôtre (1613–1700) with their *allées,* lakes, and fountains; interior views were very carefully planned to coincide with these beautiful vistas. Most importantly, as Eero Saarinen reached his maturity in the late forties, he developed an individual design approach. Charles Eames noted:

> Eero intensified his pursuit of the concept and the structure peculiarly appropriate to each particular problem . . . each building is in effect a model of the particular problem it seeks to answer. . . [Saarinen's] legacy [is thus one] of concept and procedure, rather than of form.[124]

The office buildings of the fifties most readily reflect this design approach.

The General Motors Technical Center (fig. 48), Warren, Michigan (1945–56), was the first large postwar commission executed by the Saarinen office, and it further marked the transition from father to son there. A prodigious complex of twenty-five buildings, the entire center was laid out with a Miesian

99

EERO SAARINEN. *Lounge Chair for General Motors Technical Center.* c. 1950. Tubular aluminum with brushed chrome finish, and vinyl reupholstery. 26 ¼ × 36 ½ × 32 ¾"; seat h. 18 ¾". The Metropolitan Museum of Art, Gift of General Motors Corporation

100

EERO SAARINEN (DESIGNER) AND KNOLL ASSOCIATES, INC. (MANUFACTURER). *No. 71 Armchair.* c. 1950. Aluminum with black painted and chrome finish, steel, wool and leather reupholstery. 33 ¼ × 25 ¾ × 24 ¼"; seat h. 19". Collection CBS, Inc.

rigor on a five-foot module which completely determined the planning of the interiors. The interiors, though, are considerably richer in color and texture than the German master would have allowed. The public reception areas received particularly dramatic treatments. The lobby of the Research Administration building (fig. 98) has walls of glazed brick and floor to ceiling glass.[125] A dramatic contrast is achieved in the juxtaposition of embossed wood ceiling panels with the exposed steel columns. Visually striking are the somewhat theatrical stairways in the lobbies; the floating spiral stair of granite suspended on stainless steel rods in the Research Administration lobby is certainly the most virtuoso example.[126] Senior executive offices in the Styling Administration building approach sumptuousness with their wall-to-wall carpeting and silk-paneled ceilings. Of particular interest are the undulating walls of extruded metal and the extravagant continuous built-in sofa and desk of laminated wood.[127] One of the important innovations in the GM interiors was the ceiling treatment. With the development of curtain wall buildings in the fifties, lighting levels and air conditioning systems grew increasingly complex, and a major goal of interior designers was to clean up this clutter. The five-foot-square luminous ceiling panels have all of the mechanical systems integrated into the structure, which is also integral to the movable wall system.

In outfitting the interiors of a complex of this scale, Saarinen relied largely on general furnishings produced by Knoll. It was at GM that the no. 71 and no. 72 chairs—known the world over as the chair with the hole in the back—were first used (fig. 100).[128] Eero Saarinen also produced a custom design for a lounge chair and sofa used in several of the lobbies (figs. 98 and 99). Obviously inspired by Le Corbusier's Grand Confort (1929), Saarinen's design differs in that it is a solid upholstered unit suspended in its aluminum frame, rather than loose cushions inside a steel frame.[129] Further decorative treatments were provided by the custom rugs designed by Marianne Strengell for the library and other major interiors (see Thurman). A pacesetter for American corporate architecture, the GM Technical Center was one of the largest building projects to be undertaken in the United States during the postwar period and required more than a decade for completion. It established Eero Saarinen as one of the major American corporate architects.

In the headquarters for Deere and Company (fig. 72), Moline, Illinois (1957–64), the relationship between the interior and exterior is as subtle and complex as with a Japanese house and its gardens.[130] One stands in a highly articulated structure of cor-ten steel and gold-tinted glass with the landscape always present. This feeling of transparency is further enhanced in the innovative layout of the offices: secretarial areas are open spaces on the exterior, and the interior private offices have glass partitions. Since the interiors were largely completed after Eero Saarinen's death, the furnishings are mainly the work of Warren Platner, a senior designer in the office, although Alexander Girard did lend assistance.[131]

The Thomas J. Watson Research Center for IBM (fig. 67) in Yorktown, New York (1957–61), also featured a remarkably innovative plan. All the laboratories and offices were designed as interior spaces, and the peripheral window areas are used as the main corridors. The laboratories and offices are laid out back to back, so that each section shares a utility core.[132] Perhaps the most interesting space in the crescent-shaped building is the long, glazed peripheral corridor behind the front facade; there is a certain anomaly here in the use of glass exterior walls and fieldstone interior walls. The two-story entrance lobby, however, is enlivened spatially by the use of a rather baroque double stair with balcony, although it is not quite the tour de force of the GM examples. The plan of the mammoth Bell Laboratories in Holmdel, New Jersey (1957–62), is a further development from the IBM building, but the principal innovation is the introduction of an interior court which is Piranesian in scale.

Eero Saarinen explored the idea of interior courts in several public buildings during the fifties. The American Embassy in London (1955–60) has a modest pool in the lobby area, but the Oslo Chancellery (1955–59) has a multi-story, diamond-shaped courtyard of impressive proportions. Perhaps the most significant space is the multi-level court in the Women's Dormitories at the University of Pennsylvania (1957–60); the planting, fountains, and shuttered balconies add texture and life to this space. These interior courtyards were antecedent to the extremely popular atrium hotels built in America during the 1960s and seventies.[133]

Concurrent with this concern for innovative plans and interior courts, Eero Saarinen's preoccupation with strong sculptural forms enclosing large interior spaces was increasingly explored in a series of postwar buildings. The use of the wedge- or horseshoe-shaped auditorium in the late thirties, as in the Kleinhans Music Hall, has been noted earlier; this was followed by a fascination with domed structures for large interior spaces in the late 1940s.[134] At the GM Technical Center, the dome was expressed on the exterior and interior, while at the MIT Auditorium (1950–55) the concrete shell simply served as a means of spanning the space (fig. 64). By the early fifties, the younger Saarinen had begun to employ bold structural systems—reinforced concrete and suspension cables—which allowed him to design some of the most visually exciting and original spaces produced at mid-century. The important transitional work in this series was the Ingalls Rink (figs. 69 and 70) at Yale University (1956–58). As Saarinen noted shortly before his death:

> . . . I would agree the Hockey Rink marks an important moment in my work. You could say it strengthened my convictions about making everything part of the same "form-world" and gave us confidence about handling vaults and

101
EERO SAARINEN AND ASSOCIATES. *Trans World Airlines Terminal, John F. Kennedy (formerly Idlewild) Airport, New York* (interior). 1956–62. Photo courtesy Ezra Stoller

102

EERO SAARINEN (DESIGNER) AND KNOLL AS-
SOCIATES, INC. (MANUFACTURER). *No. 73
Settee ("Womb" Sofa)*. c. 1946–48. Black
painted tubular steel, wool blend reuphol-
stery. 35 ¾ × 61 ½ × 35″; seat h. 18″.
Collection Mr. and Mrs. Joseph N. Lacy

103

EERO SAARINEN (DESIGNER) AND KNOLL IN-
TERNATIONAL (MANUFACTURER). *No. 174
Table (Pedestal Table)*. 1955–57. Steel with
fused plastic finish and cremo marble. 28 ⅜
× 78 ⅛ × 48 ⅜″. Collection Knoll International

104

CHARLES AND RAY EAMES. *Living Room,
Eames House, Pacific Palisades*. 1948–49.
Photo courtesy Julius Shulman

suspended roofs which have interested me since some projects of the 'Fifties
and the Aspen tent [1949]. It influenced both TWA and the Washington airport.[135]

This search for strong sculptural forms enclosing large interior
spaces culminated in these three buildings: the Ingalls Rink, TWA Terminal, and
Dulles Airport. With its massive concrete spine and wood deck supported by longitudinal cables, the Ingalls Rink is not unlike an inverted boat's hull.[136] The vaulting space with its sense of movement and energy embodies the speed and action of
the game on the ice. This desire for expressive interiors reached its culmination in
the soaring vaults of the terminal for Trans World Airlines (figs. 71 and 101), at
Kennedy Airport, New York (1956–62). Here Saarinen wanted to create an interior that would express the "excitement of travel."[137] The bilateral terminal consists
of four enormous vaults divided by bands of skylights. A central soaring bridge
separates the two main areas for ticketing and waiting. Stairs, counters, and seating
are all integral to the sculptural whole; the red seating area provides an accent of
color to the off-white and light grey surfaces.[138] TWA and Dulles (fig. 73), outside
Washington (1958–63), personify the sensation of flying as no other twentieth-
century buildings do. Dulles is a serene pavilion which seems to be suspended above
the Virginia plains. From the exterior, it is certainly one of Saarinen's most arresting forms; the interior, however, seems less successful than TWA. The space is
too low for such a long building, and the counters, shops, and service areas inter-
rupt the unity of the dramatic space. Such temple-like structures cannot easily ac-
commodate numerous functional demands.

Eero Saarinen's furniture was an integral part of his work as
a designer. While the office certainly continued to produce custom designs for a
client's specific needs, his major interest from the 1940s onward was in mass-
produced furniture. It is a measure of his commitment to his work that he was able
to pursue in essence two careers (as an architect and furniture designer) at the
same time.

The first evidence of Saarinen's maturity as a furniture designer was his entries with Charles Eames for the Organic Home Furnishings competition (1940–41) noted earlier. The outbreak of the Second World War prevented
their manufacture. After Florence Knoll joined Knoll Associates (c. 1943), one of
the primary achievements of the company was enlisting a generation of young designers.[139] Eero Saarinen joined Knoll around 1943.[140] His first design, still working with wartime limitations, was the no. 61 lounge chair and ottoman (c. 1946).[141]
The profile of the laminated wood base with multiple bends was contrasted against

Colorplate 16

EERO SAARINEN (DESIGNER). *Sketches for Pedestal Chair*. c. 1955. Ink and colored pencil on paper. 11 × 8 ½". Collection Don Petitt

a sculptural seating panel. The chair was quite comfortable and was available upholstered or with webbing. The design was not especially innovative, though, since the frame was an amalgamation of the detailing of Aalto and Mathsson.

The material that was to have the greatest impact on furniture design at mid-century was plastic.[142] A new material for the furniture industry, its potential was realized during the 1940s by a number of designers working on innovative chairs. Eero Saarinen and Ralph Rapson published sketches in the March 1946 issue of *Interiors* showing several prototypes for molded shell chairs,[143] but perhaps the most noteworthy design of the forties was Mies' conchoidal chairs.[144] Saarinen began his designs for his no. 70 lounge chair (popularly called the womb chair) as early as 1946, but it was not manufactured until 1948 by Knoll, making it the first fiberglass chair to be mass-produced in America.[145] The chair has a molded, reinforced plastic shell with foam rubber padding and fabric cover; a seat and back cushion were added for additional comfort.[146] The base was of metal rod with a chrome or painted finish. Prototypes of the chair show Saarinen's struggle to find a base for the powerful shell that would work structurally and aesthetically;[147] the junction of the plastic or plywood shell with its base was, in fact, one of the major problems facing furniture designers at mid-century. The introduction of a successful design to the Knoll line invariably resulted in spin-offs: in this case the no. 74 ottoman (c. 1950)[148] and the no. 73 settee (fig. 102), Saarinen's only mass-produced sofa.[149]

A follow-up to the no. 70 lounge chair, the no. 71 armchair (fig. 100) was first introduced at the GM Technical Center (c. 1950) and has become one of the most widely used office chairs of the twentieth century.[150] Saarinen's experiments with plastic are continued in the fiberglass back, but the seat is a standard wood panel with foam rubber upholstery.[151] The design is derived directly from the Organic Design entries. The soft sculptural forms, though, belie their simplicity: a close examination of the detailing of the base, shell, and upholstery reveals a masterful design.[152]

Eero Saarinen's last furniture design for Knoll was the so-called "pedestal" series (1955–57).[153] Saarinen felt that he had resolved the problem of "the slum of legs" in a room,[154] and he achieved perhaps the most successful resolution—at least visually—of a plastic shell to its base, though not his goal of a sculptural shell in one piece and of one material.[155] The chairs (pl. 16) rise out of the floor on a single stem to a shell of soft folds, almost flower-like.[156] In reality, the shell is made of molded plastic but a stable base could only be achieved in cast aluminum with a matching fused plastic finish. While the chairs have been justly praised, it is perhaps the line of tables which is most pleasing.[157] The large tables (fig. 103), in particular, with their composition of a floating plane on a single thin pedestal, have an elegance—if not an ethereal quality—that makes them one of the assured classics of the twentieth century.

Like the Saarinens, Charles Eames conceived of ". . . everything as architecture and has practiced architecture in all his work."[158] His wife, Ray Kaiser, studied as a young painter (c. 1933–c. 1939) under Hans Hofmann before coming to Cranbrook in 1940. What was so phenomenal about the Eameses was their range of interest and mind: urban planning, architecture, interiors, furniture, toys, stage and movie sets, film, graphics, and exhibitions. In any discussion of the Eameses' careers, their work must be viewed in terms of the world they created around themselves and the multitude of interacting activities that were always going on. In dealing with such a husband-and-wife team, there is no clear division of responsibilities, and the number of talented people working in the Eames studio over the years makes the problem even more complicated.[159]

With their move to California in 1941, Charles and Ray Eames' energies were increasingly devoted to furniture designs rather than architecture. Nevertheless some important house designs did follow. Charles Eames' collaboration with Eero Saarinen on the Case Study Houses no. 8 and no. 9 (figs. 49, 50, 51, 52, 53) was noted earlier. The former was revised by Eames in late 1948 and completed in the fall of 1949. As executed, the Eames house consists of two steel-framed pavilions—a residence and study—separated by a courtyard, a modular composition seventeen bays in length. In contrast to the primary colors and gold leaf of the exterior, the interiors were quite neutral. The most dramatic space was the two-story living room, a soaring glass pavilion (fig. 104) with an adjacent inglenook nestled under the bedroom balcony.[160] The largely glazed steel frame of the buildings in essence created a three-dimensional grid, which was continued in the tatami floor mats of the living room. This grid provided a framework for an ever-changing display of objects: furniture, toys, plants, folk art, or floor pillows. In contrast to the almost stripped interiors of the International Style, the Eameses—who were avid collectors—increasingly filled their interiors with "found objects" to a point approaching Victorian clutter. They proved, as perhaps no other American designers did, that ornament was no longer a crime, and this was indeed one of their most important contributions to mid-century interior design.[161] The decorativeness and informality of their interiors stand in marked contrast to the polished and spare elegance of designs by Florence Knoll, their contemporary and equal as an arbiter of taste in the fifties.

In 1949, Ray and Charles Eames began work on an extraordinary project for the Billy Wilder residence (figs. 54, 55, 56, 57, 58) in Beverly Hills, California. The interiors were a continuation of the Case Study houses with their open plans, planar walls, and exposed metal structures. The Wilder house's rectangular plan was, in fact, a development from the first version of the Eames house. The exterior walls were largely without fenestration, with the exception of

CHARLES AND RAY EAMES (DESIGNERS) AND
HERMAN MILLER FURNITURE CO. (MANU-
FACTURER). *Modular Storage Units*. c.
1946. Maple. Base: 12 ¼ × 71 ⅞ × 16″;
unit: 14 ¾ × 35 ⅞ × 16″. Photo courtesy
Ray Eames. Collection Ray Eames

the longitudinal wall to the garden, which was completely glazed and sheltered by a continuous pergola. Moreover, all the interior walls were pulled back from this garden facade, in essence repeating the pergola. It was thus an extremely rich design spatially, particularly as shown in the sketches for a two-story interior. Several innovations deserve special note since they became characteristic features of modern homes in America during the postwar years: multilevel living spaces which flowed together, a built-in sofa and freestanding fireplace in the living room, as well as a storage wall in the library. Of particular interest are sketches for the dining room which show several versions of a pedestal table.[162] The Wilder drawings indicate a project that would have rivaled the Irwin Miller house in its sumptuousness had it been executed, and its lack of realization must rank with Wright's ill-fated McCormick house (1907).

Although the number of interior design commissions given to the Eameses was limited, they designed several exhibitions in the 1940s and fifties so distinctive as to constitute an "Eames style" which was recognized internationally.[163] The exhibits (figs. 116 and 117) generally consisted of a strong architectural background for mass-produced objects arranged in domestic groupings; to these Charles and Ray Eames added household accessories: flowers, books, ceramics, textiles, glass, and plants. Distinctive Eames touches came in such individual color combinations as pink with raspberry; subtle textures provided by the use of European or Chinese papers for wall coverings; and photographic panels made from enlarged details of natural forms. These installations were especially influential in dispelling the popular notion that modern design was cold and inhuman.

Particular note should be made of the Eameses' display done for the exhibition "For Modern Living" at The Detroit Institute of Arts in 1949.[164] This was not an exhibition room for a specific purpose but rather an almost surreal space for the interplay of objects. Two pieces of furniture displayed are of interest: the serpentine lounge chair, La Chaise (1949),[165] and the colorful knockdown storage system, the ESU series (pl. 20, rear right) discussed below (1949–50). Distinctive interior finishes were the "peg-board walls" and the floor of white cement and rocklite.

These temporary exhibits survive only in photographs, but Ray and Charles Eames' innovative furniture has been produced by the thousands, making them perhaps the most influential American furniture designers of this century. While some of their pieces were in the deluxe category, the majority of the Eameses' designs were for inexpensive, well-designed everyday objects. Their imagination found new solutions for sofas, occasional chairs, a variety of tables, lounge chairs, storage units, and even the chaise lounge; not surprisingly, the results were equally appropriate for a home, office, or institution. These new forms, however, were not capricious designs but were derived from technological breakthroughs in handling molded plywood, fiberglass, wire, and aluminum. All of these concerns resulted in an aesthetic characterized in general by a soft, flowing line, in contrast to the crisp geometry and right angles of Florence Knoll.

During the 1940s, the Eameses' major work was in molded plywood following the designs done for the Organic Design competition.[166] A series of children's furniture (c. 1943) was made of two-dimensionally molded plywood, but the major breakthrough came in about 1946 with an extensive furniture series that was shown at The Museum of Modern Art: chairs, modular storage units, a variety of tables, and folding screens (fig. 116).[167] The designs were initially made in California in conjunction with the Evans Products Company but were shortly thereafter transferred to the Herman Miller Furniture Co. after George Nelson, senior design consultant for the Midwestern manufacturer, enlisted the Eameses.[168] The tables were mass-produced with varying dimensions and bases;[169] likewise, the folding screens (FSW series) of molded plywood sections with canvas hinges (pl. 17, left) were issued in two heights and various lengths.[170] The modular storage units (fig. 105) were an outgrowth of the earlier Organic Design series but are a considerably more assured design; the fact that they never got beyond the prototype stage was a loss for postwar American design. The most innovative—if not revolutionary—designs were for the lounge and side chairs (pl. 17, right).[171]

Colorplate 17

CHARLES AND RAY EAMES (DESIGNERS) AND
HERMAN MILLER FURNITURE CO. (MANU-
FACTURER). *FSW Folding Screen and Side
Chair.* c. 1946. Screen: ash, plywood and
canvas. 34 × 3 × 59 ⅛″. Collection Theodore R. Gamble, Jr. Side chair: birch plywood, rubber mounts, with ponyskin upholstery. 28 ¾ × 21 ⅜ × 19 ½″; seat h.
17 ¾″. Lent by I. Wistar Morris, III, courtesy of The Metropolitan Museum of Art

The enveloping shell of the Organic Design entry (fig. 94) was here reduced to a minimal seat and back panel; the base was conceived as a sculptural cradle of metal or wood, rather than a four-legged appendage. Both the lounge (LCW) and dining (DCW) chairs with wood bases were exhibited in the New York installation designed by the Eameses (fig. 116), and a variety of three-legged chairs with metal bases were also shown. The classic side chairs (fig. 117, center) with a four-legged metal base (LCM and DCM), however, had apparently not been developed.[172] The Eames chair (popularly called the potato chip chair) is a twentieth-century classic; perhaps no American chair since Wright's wood side chair for the Larkin Building (1904), Buffalo, New York, has had a comparable impact on modern design.[173]

The winning entries submitted by Charles and Ray Eames for the "Low-cost Furniture Design" competition sponsored by The Museum of Modern Art (1947–50) were equally as prophetic.[174] Like Eero Saarinen's almost contemporary no. 71 armchair for Knoll, the Eameses' designs (pl. 18) for armchairs and side chairs were remarkably similar in form to the Organic Design chairs of molded plywood a decade earlier. The Low-cost chairs were originally envisioned as having molded shells of stamped metal with a variety of wood and metal bases. The cost for the necessary molds proved prohibitive for Herman Miller, however, and the chairs were manufactured in 1949 with fiberglass shells.[175] Although Saarinen's no. 70 lounge chair of fiberglass was earlier, the Eameses' design was "the first one-piece plastic chair to feature the natural surface of its material."[176] Moreover, the plastic shell chair was colorful, comfortable, and remarkably inexpensive.

By the 1950s, then, Charles and Ray Eames had produced molded shell designs of plywood, metal, and plastic. The following year they continued their experiments with steel wire and aluminum and produced a series of attenuated designs.[177] These tables and chairs are indicative of an increasing use of metal in the Eameses' furniture during the fifties. Surprisingly, wire was used

for only one shell design, a series of diminutive side chairs (1951) which came with a variety of fanciful bases.[178] Harry Bertoia, a Cranbrook alumnus who had worked in the Eames studio for many years, exploited a similar construction in a remarkable series of wire shell chairs (pl. 19) for Knoll (1952) which were available with a painted, chrome, or colored fused plastic finish.[179] At the same time Charles and Ray Eames used wire strut bases for two tables which had plastic tops over a wood laminated core: the miniature LTR table (c. 1951) which could be used as an occasional table or stool (fig. 104, right) and the oval ETR table (c. 1951) which is elephantine in its eighty-nine-inch length (pl. 20, foreground). Distinguishing

106

CHARLES AND RAY EAMES (DESIGNERS) AND HERMAN MILLER FURNITURE CO. (MANU-FACTURER). *Lounge Chair and Ottoman.* 1956. Rosewood plywood, cast aluminum with chrome and black painted finish, steel, and leather upholstery. Chair: 32 ¼ × 33 ½ × 32 ¾"; seat h. 15 ⅜". Ottoman: 16 × 26 × 21 ½". Collection Dianne Dwyer

features of the two tables are the ten-inch height and the frank expression of the plywood in the table edge.

Inspired by industrial shelving, the Eameses designed the ESU series (c. 1949–50) with a steel angle and diagonal rod bracing (pl. 20, rear right). What made the modular storage cabinets so appealing was the colorful inter-changeable parts: shelves, drawers, doors, and side panels were made of wood, plastic-coated plywood, or lacquered masonite.[180] The ESU series was envisioned as a knockdown system like an erector set to simplify shipping, an important change from the two wood storage units designed in the forties.[181]

Likewise, shipping was a major consideration in the design of the compact sofa (c. 1952) whose two back pads fold down for compact packaging (pl. 20, rear left). The design was not as innovative technologically as the earlier Organic Design sofa entry, but it was visually light in its arrangement of three pads on a chrome-plated and black enameled steel frame.[182] This combination of matte and shiny—i.e., black and chrome—became a common method of articulating the various parts of metal bases during the late 1940s and fifties.

Certainly the most famous Eames design of the decade was the ES 670 lounge chair and ottoman (1956; fig. 106).[183] The three-piece shell design had been achieved a decade earlier in a prototype which had a steel cantilevered base.[184] Revised in the fifties, the Eames lounge chair had rosewood plywood shells, a black and polished aluminum pedestal base, and tufted leather upholstery.[185] Like Mies' Barcelona chair (1929), the Eames lounge chair has achieved a mythological aura afforded few objects in modern design, although in this instance, it is an extremely comfortable status symbol.

Lastly, the work with cast aluminum bases led to a new design series, the aluminum group (1958). It included a variety of tables and seating pieces, the most appealing of which were the pedestal chairs (fig. 107).[186] They featured a completely polished aluminum base softer in profile than the Eames lounge chair, but it was the chair frames with their exquisitely sculptured die-cast aluminum members that earned this series its renown. An important upholstery innovation was the manner in which the thin pads were fitted into the side stretchers. The seating panels were of two kinds: a Saran sling seat with stiffening panels or naugahyde with horizontal "trapunto" stripes executed with electronic welding.[187]

During the 1960s, Ray and Charles Eames continued to design even more sophisticated aluminum frame pieces, as well as constantly updating earlier furniture designs. For every design that was produced, though, there were

107
CHARLES AND RAY EAMES (DESIGNERS) AND HERMAN MILLER FURNITURE CO. (MANUFACTURER). *Lounge Chair and Ottoman.* 1958. Cast aluminum, black painted steel, and Saran upholstery. Chair: 38 ⅝ × 25 ⅝ × 31 ¼"; seat h. 16 ⅜". Ottoman: 18 × 21 ⅛ × 21 ⅜". Lent by Ronald S. Kane, courtesy of The Metropolitan Museum of Art

Colorplate 19

HARRY BERTOIA (DESIGNER) AND KNOLL IN-
TERNATIONAL (MANUFACTURER). *Lounge
Chair, Ottoman, and Screen.* Lounge chair
1952–53. Steel rod painted black, rubber
mounts, cotton reupholstery. 38 × 38 ×
35 ⅞"; seat h. 15 ¾". Ottoman 1952–53.
Steel rod painted black, cotton reupholstery.
15 × 24 ⅝ × 17 ¾". Lent by Mr. and Mrs.
Joseph Roberto, courtesy of The Metropolitan Museum of Art. Screen c. 1950. Brass-
coated steel. 55 × 23". Collection Mrs. Brigitta Bertoia

an equal number of prototypes never realized: ideas that were too advanced technologically or too expensive but which nonetheless are an important part of American design at mid-century. Increasingly their energies were devoted to a remarkable series of films and traveling exhibitions.

Florence Knoll and the Eameses were certainly the most pro-
lific furniture designers in the Cranbrook circle. Before turning to the work of
Knoll and another designer, Benjamin Baldwin, notice should be taken of the work
of Ralph Rapson, Don Knorr (b. 1922), and David Rowland. Rapson and Knorr
worked primarily as architects, and their most interesting furniture designs were
done in their early careers. Knorr's most famous design was for a conical chair
(fig. 108) which won a first prize over the Eameses in the Low-cost Furniture competition noted earlier. The entry had a Versalite plastic shell and chrome-plated
steel rod legs; the no. 132 version manufactured by Knoll was made of sheet metal
with black legs.[188] Rapson's entry for the Organic Design competition, a wood
rocker (fig. 97), was noted earlier. While at Cranbrook, Rapson and David Runnells designed a project for a Cave House (fig. 46); an interior perspective (dated
January 1940) shows molded furniture with compound curves (probably of wood),
illustrating the degree to which such ideas were in the air at Cranbrook at the time
of the Museum of Modern Art competition. During the Second World War, Rapson worked for the Knoll company for two or three years and did a series of unex-
ecuted designs (figs. 109 and 110) in stamped metal, molded plywood, and fiberglass.[189] Rapson's furniture sketches show an extremely facile draftsman on the
cutting edge of modern design.[190]

Rapson often reworks a concept for a chair over many years,
but few designers have been more painstaking in their work than David Rowland

Colorplate 20

CHARLES AND RAY EAMES (DESIGNERS),
ALEXANDER GIRARD (FABRIC DESIGNER),
AND HERMAN MILLER FURNITURE CO.
(MANUFACTURER). *Compact Sofa, ESU
Storage Units, and ETR Oval Table.* Sofa
c. 1952. Steel chromed and painted black.
34 ¾ × 71 ¾ × 30″; seat h. 16 ¾″. Storage
units c. 1949–50. Steel, plywood, lacquered
masonite, and plastic laminate. 32 ⅝ × 47
× 16″; 58 ¾ × 46 ⅝ × 16 ¾″. Herman
Miller, Inc. Table c. 1951. Plastic laminate,
plywood, steel rod painted black. 9 ¾ ×
29 ⅛ × 89″. The Metropolitan Museum of
Art, Theodore R. Gamble, Jr., in honor of
Mrs. Theodore Robert Gamble

Colorplate 21

DAVID ROWLAND. *Prototypal Chair Designs.* c. 1960. Sof-Tech side chair: black vinyl over tubular steel frame and flat springs.
31 ¼ × 17 × 16″; seat h. 17 ½″. 40/4 side
chair: grey crackle paint over steel rod with
Saran reupholstery. 29 ¼ × 18 ½ × 21″;
seat h. 17 ¼″. Collection David Rowland

(b. 1924), who will continue on a project for ten to fifteen years.[191] He is an industrial designer who calls himself an "architect of products."[192] Rowland belongs to the postwar generation, but his interest in industrial design seems to have been formed even before he came to Cranbrook.[193] Compared to the oeuvre of Eero Saarinen or the Eameses, both the scope and quantity of Rowland's work might seem limited, for the goal he has chosen for himself is the design of a minimal stacking chair—minimal in the sense of materials, weight, volume, and cost. He has already produced two intelligent solutions that rank among the best chair designs of the third quarter of the twentieth century. In contrast to the shell forms seen earlier, Rowland's work is a further development of the Bauhaus or modern aesthetic, with its emphasis on a clearly articulated frame and minimal upholstery. A prototype for the 40/4 chair (c. 1960)—the first design—recalls a series of tubular metal side chairs designed by Breuer (1925–27).[194] It has a steel rod frame with a gray crackle paint finish and was originally upholstered in a striped Saran (pl. 21, right).[195] The 40/4 series has become one of the most widely used chairs of the last quarter century because of its stacking and ganging properties. Likewise, his second chair design was equally adaptable. Flat spring upholstery was not a new idea,[196] but Rowland worked for more than twenty years in perfecting the idea for a mass-produced chair.[197] A prototype for the Sof-Tech chair (c. 1960; pl. 21, left) approaches Marcel Breuer's ideal of sitting on "resilient air columns"[198] with its spare composition of four-legged, tubular metal frame and exposed springs coated in black vinyl.

The two Cranbrook alumni who have practiced largely as interior designers are Ben Baldwin and Florence Knoll.[199] Baldwin's entries for the Organic Design competition have already been noted. From 1945 to 1946 he worked in New York with Skidmore, Owings and Merrill; his principal project was the Terrace Plaza Hotel, Cincinnati, Ohio (1943–48), on which he served as designer in charge of the interiors and furniture.[200] While in New York, Baldwin established a partnership (c. 1948–56) with William Machado, which lasted through moves to Montgomery, Alabama, and Chicago. Since 1956 he has practiced independently.

Unfortunately, few of Baldwin's early interiors survive intact, and many of these were not photographed. In Baldwin's work there is not a readily recognizable style so much as an individual design approach (figs. 111 and 112). His interior designs characteristically reveal a strongly architectural approach with a primary interest in space and light. Baldwin has said: "I am against clutter. My work in interior design is my expression of opposition to the chaotic world man creates. It is a constant search for the tranquility one finds in nature. . . . In nature I find a sense of order, logical and lyrical, which I would like my work to express."[201] Therefore it is no surprise that in his work furniture is kept to a minimum; his preference is for built-in sofas, shelves, or storage. For seating he uses traditional or modern chairs with equal ease—bergères, wicker lounge chairs, or upholstered club chairs, chosen for comfort, texture, or their lines. This sensitivity to other art no doubt accounts for the fact that so many of his clients are collectors. This is not to say, however, that there are no distinctive Baldwin touches: repeatedly one sees large library tables for reading, eating, or working; attenuated Chiavari chairs; Venini vases; and low shelves for the display of objects. His choice of colors and materials reflects a consistent aesthetic: a subtle palette of off-whites and beiges; natural materials such as cotton, linen, silk, or leather; and restrained materials such as English oak, limestone, and granite. Baldwin's interiors do not have the machinelike elegance of Knoll or the color and clutter of the Eameses. Rather there is a serenity and simplicity that is almost Far Eastern in feeling. Baldwin has acknowledged this association himself:

Japanese artists and craftsmen have worked in the same basic vernacular for centuries, with endless variations on modular structure and natural materials. There one really sees that interior design is an architectural process, that its first concern is with space—the poetic relation of solids and voids and the play of light and color to delight the senses. Lin Yutang summed it all up: "It is the unoccupied space which makes a room inhabitable."[202]

108

DON KNORR (DESIGNER) AND KNOLL ASSOCIATES, INC. (MANUFACTURER). Side Chairs. c. 1949. Sheet metal and steel legs painted black. 28 1/4 × 22 1/8 × 20 7/8"; seat h. 17 5/8". Photo courtesy Knoll International. Collection Don Knorr

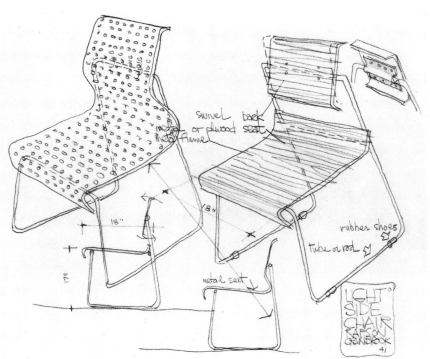

109 and 110
RALPH RAPSON. *Sketches for a Lounge Chair and a Side Chair.* 1942, 1941. Pencil on tracing paper. 8 ½ × 10 ¾″; 9 × 11 ¼″. Collection Ralph Rapson

111 and 112

BENJAMIN BALDWIN. *Living Room, Cowles House, Wayzata, Minnesota, and Dining-Living Room, Baldwin Apartment, Chicago.* 1965, c. 1960. Photos courtesy Ezra Stoller and Benjamin Baldwin

Baldwin, of course, continues to practice, and some of his more accomplished designs have been completed in the last two decades, which serves to remind us that the Cranbrook tradition lives on in the present.

Eero Saarinen and the Eameses have rightly been awarded prominent positions in twentieth-century American design; the other Cranbrook designer to achieve equal fame was Florence Schust Knoll Bassett (b. 1917). While attending Kingswood School (1932–34), Knoll established a close personal friendship with the Saarinen family.[203] She attended Cranbrook Academy intermittently (1934–39), as well as the Architectural Association in London (1938–39).[204] With the outbreak of the War, she returned to the States and worked for Breuer and Gropius in Cambridge during the winter of 1940.[205] Her architectural studies were completed under Mies van der Rohe at the Illinois Institute of Technology, Chicago, in 1941.[206] Eliel Saarinen and Mies van der Rohe were her two most important teachers, and Knoll later remarked that from Saarinen she learned the totality of design to the smallest detail and from Mies a "greater clarification of design" and the importance of the juxtaposition and detailing of materials.[207]

Following her graduation in 1941, Florence Knoll moved to New York and worked initially for Harrison and Abramovitz. Shortly thereafter, she met Hans Knoll and joined the Hans G. Knoll Furniture Co. as head of the Planning Unit (c. 1943).[208] With Hans Knoll as businessman and Florence Knoll as chief designer, the Knoll firm quickly became one of the most important modern design companies in America.

Prior to the arrival of Florence Knoll, Jens Risom, a Dane, had been the major designer for the company.[209] The nature of commissions was shifting from residential to contract work during the forties, and Florence Knoll changed the aesthetic of the company from a Scandinavian line favoring wood furniture to a look reflecting industrial design.[210]

In talking of her furniture designs, Florence Knoll has somewhat modestly said: "I never really sat down and designed furniture. I designed the fill-in pieces that no one else was doing."[211] Knoll did not, in fact, so much develop new furniture forms as perfect existing ones. Her designs for seating do not reflect major innovations in materials or technology, as is the case with Eero Saarinen or the Eameses' work. Rather it is the form that has been redesigned. Her sofas and lounge chairs maintain a clear separation between base and seating. The innovations are in the upholstery: the details of profile and contour; the junction of a cushion to its base; and welting, stitching, or buttoning techniques. It is particularly in the design of bases that her perfectionism is most evident. Wood legs from the forties tended to be tapered or splayed forms.[212] By mid-century, however, Florence Knoll had found her medium in metal frames, and she detailed

Colorplate 22
FLORENCE KNOLL (DESIGNER) AND KNOLL INTERNATIONAL (MANUFACTURER). *Custom Credenza.* 1950s/c. 1965. Aluminum with chrome finish, rosewood, and cremo marble. 25 ½ × 163 ⅞ × 18 ⅛″. CBS, Inc.

her furniture with a rigor rivaling Mies, as if she were designing a steel frame building. In the late forties, she used painted metal rod and tubular steel,[213] but it was the T-angle frame tables (fig. 114) that were the first evidence of her "constructivist" designs to come.[214] The parallel-bar base series (fig. 113, right foreground) was almost De Stijl-like in its composition of intersecting black and chrome bars (c. 1955);[215] this was followed by square tubular chrome bases (c. 1962) which could be treated as minimal frames for tables (fig. 113, center) or as highly articulated bases for sofas and chairs (fig. 113, left and rear). For custom designs such as Frank Stanton's office (1954), Knoll designed a steel base for a desk whose section was a Greek cross.[216] Knoll realized that offices and homes continued to need traditional upholstered sofas and chairs for comfort, but she refined the forms until they achieved a crisp, sleek profile.

In the design of tables, Knoll was equally practical, producing a series of dining, conference, coffee, and end tables for the home or office. The no. 301 dining table, which is similar in form to the so-called "Parson's table," best illustrates the crisp, geometric look Knoll sought for the company in the late forties; it also seems to reveal a close examination of Mies' lesser-known furniture designs.[217] During the 1940s and fifties, Knoll developed this aesthetic in innumerable tables with glass, wood, or marble tops, and the frames—whether wood or metal—were variations of the bases noted above. Two important innovations for the office that deserve special note were the boat-shaped conference table and the executive table desk.[218]

Storage units, the other major furniture form in a room, did not escape Knoll's attention. The no. 121 and no. 123 wood modular wall units from the 1940s were obviously inspired by Breuer's design for the Piscator apartment, Berlin (1927).[219] Knoll, however, soon developed them into a wall-mounted credenza for the executive office and a series of sideboards. Mies van der Rohe's influence on Knoll's work in the postwar years seems to be evidenced in the no. 116 sideboard which had a wood cabinet with pandanus sliding doors and a recessed, painted metal base; the design recalls a cabinet designed for the study of the Tugendhat house, Brno, Czechoslovakia (1930).[220] In the fifties, Florence Knoll produced a series of elegantly detailed sideboards (such as the no. 2542; pl. 22) that equalled—or surpassed—the German master with their marble tops, matched veneer sides, and chrome or bronze bases. Moreover, Knoll redesigned another storage unit, the chest of drawers, as monolithic units eliminating all visible hard-

113

FLORENCE KNOLL (DESIGNER) AND KNOLL INTERNATIONAL (MANUFACTURER). *(Clockwise from left) No. 2551 Lounge Chair, No. 2520 Table, No. 67 Sofa, and No. 51 Lounge Chair. 1950s, 1960s.* No. 2551 lounge chair: tubular steel with chrome finish and wool reupholstery. 30 ½ × 24 ⅞ × 29 ½"; seat h. 15 ½". No. 2520 table: steel with chrome finish and cremo marble. 17 × 36 × 36". No. 67 sofa: steel with chrome finish and wool reupholstery. 32 ⅛ × 84 ⅝ × 30 ⅝"; seat h. 16". No. 51 lounge chair: steel with chrome finish and black paint, and wool reupholstery. 30 ¾ × 29 ¾ × 25"; seat h. 15". Collection CBS, Inc.

114
FLORENCE KNOLL (DESIGNER) AND KNOLL INTERNATIONAL (MANUFACTURER). *No. 304 Table.* c. 1954. T-angle aluminum with chrome finish and cremo marble. 15 × 23 ¾ × 23 ⅝". Collection Florence Knoll Bassett

115
FLORENCE KNOLL. *Anonymous Office, New York City.* c. 1945.

ware by making the handles integral to the construction (pl. 23, rear).[221] This reductionist tendency is, in fact, a primary characteristic of Knoll's work, particularly in interiors.

Florence Knoll was an original and prolific furniture designer, but it was her work as an interior designer that made her reputation. During the

Colorplates 23 and 24
FLORENCE KNOLL. *Showrooms in New York and San Francisco.* 1951, 1957. Photos courtesy Knoll International

116 and 117

CHARLES AND RAY EAMES. *Exhibition Installations: Eames Exhibition, The Museum of Modern Art, 1946, and Herman Miller Showroom, Beverly Hills, c. 1949.* Photos courtesy The Museum of Modern Art and Ray Eames

second quarter of this century, modern design—with its emphasis on white interiors fitted with steel and glass furniture—was often thought to be cold or sterile. Knoll's importance as an interior designer lies in the fact that she translated the International Style into a look acceptable for American offices and homes, but like Mies, her style was one of elegance and fine detailing, not the everyday. During the two decades that Knoll was actively involved with the company, she designed interiors for hotels, banks, universities, hospitals, and embassies both here and abroad. Although much of the company line was appropriate for a home, she had relatively few domestic commissions herself.[222] It was in the Knoll showrooms and a series of offices that she developed her style.

The showrooms for the 1940s seem to have been largely in remodeled townhouses; an inherent plan of small rooms did not afford much spa-

Colorplate 25
FLORENCE KNOLL. *Office, Connecticut General Life Insurance Company, Bloomfield, Connecticut.* 1954–57. Photo courtesy Florence Knoll Bassett

tial play. The interiors mainly featured natural materials: birch, brick, grass matting, fishnet curtains, and bamboo or pandanus screens. Colors tended to beige, grey, and green with accents of lemon or black. An important display technique was the "fabric wall": a floor-to-ceiling arrangement of Knoll's textile collection.

It was the New York showroom (1951) that marked a dramatic change in Florence Knoll's work and the beginning of the "Knoll look" (pl. 23).[223] The loft space of a skyscraper allowed considerable flexibility, and here she introduced a structural system of black steel channels with suspended colored panels for walls and ceiling. Against a white background, she juxtaposed a palette of brilliant colors: orange, citron, red, black, violet blue, and fuchsia. The furniture was arranged in groupings at a domestic scale, and an assortment of accessories—flowers, books, sculpture, and paintings—provided an additional richness. While the showroom was striking, it nonetheless allowed the visitor to see the objects first and not the designer's installation. In a larger sense, this showroom signaled a shift away from wood to metal frames and fiberglass shell designs in the future. Moreover, a change in clientele allowed increasingly richer materials: marble and thick glass for

Colorplate 26
FLORENCE KNOLL. *Dr. Frank Stanton Office, Columbia Broadcasting System Headquarters Building, New York City.* 1965. Photo courtesy Florence Knoll Bassett

Colorplate 27
FLORENCE KNOLL. *Sketch for Hans Knoll Office, New York City.* 1949. Ink, crayon, fabric, leather, and rattan on tracing paper. 9 × 11 ⅞". Collection Florence Knoll Bassett

table tops, teak and rosewood rather than birch, and custom V'Soske wool carpets in place of matting. Though it was expensive the company was producing good design. The New York showroom had a clean, colorful, and stylish quality that came to signify the elegance of a Knoll interior. Along with the Eameses' installations, a new look in American interior design had been established for the 1950s.

With the phenomenal growth of the Knoll company, a rapid succession of showrooms followed. Chicago (c. 1953–54) was a reversal of New York with its black interiors.[224] San Francisco—Knoll's favorite (pl. 24)—featured two-story spaces with balconies and an open plan with brightly colored planar walls (1957).[225] Even more spatially exciting were the butterfly ceilings in Milan and Dallas (1957) and the elegant, plaster vaulting in Los Angeles (1961) done in the manner of Sir John Soane (1753–1837).[226]

By the mid-fifties, Knoll had become an international operation; Florence Knoll's showrooms had made modern American design truly an "international style." At home, the "Knoll look" became an accepted standard for American corporations through a series of executive offices designed by Knoll and the Planning Unit.

A seminal design in Florence Knoll's career was a suite of private offices in a New York skyscraper (c. 1945). The complex was U-shaped in plan with a central reception area. In opposition to the static grid of the structural columns of the building, Knoll introduced undulating walls covered with cork for this room (fig. 115).[227] Other features, which recurred often in her later work, were a built-in sofa with low circular conference table and sliding wall partitions at either end of the room. The adjoining library has what appears to be Knoll's earliest use of a boat-shaped conference table. The remarkable spatial innovation was the translucent glass walls between the exterior executive offices and the interior secretarial areas.[228] In the senior executive's office, moreover, Knoll introduced a new definition of a businessman's needs: a wall credenza for papers, a table desk for conferences, and a sofa grouping for informal business conversation. These planning concepts and details were to be refined over the next two decades in her office interiors.

One of Knoll's best designs was for Hans Knoll's office (1949) in New York (pl. 27). The fifteen-foot-square room was one of the first economically planned executive offices, and Knoll reduced the height of the furnishings to achieve a larger scale. The treatment of the room as planar surfaces may also be seen as an important antecedent to the New York showroom of 1951: the wall-to-wall carpeting; the black accent wall with horizontal credenza; the window wall with floor-to-ceiling curtains of wheat-colored Indian silk; and even the teak slab desk. Knoll recalled—as the perspective (pl. 27) reveals—that she was among the first designers to use swatches of materials on their drawings or models as an aid in the design process.[229]

Florence Knoll's greatest period as a designer of corporate offices was the 1950s. The commissions varied in scale from entire buildings to executive suites. For the Connecticut General Life Insurance Company (pl. 25), Bloomfield, Connecticut (1954–57), the Knoll Planning Unit was responsible for the layout of the interiors and furniture of the entire complex; here they further developed the idea of open-plan office areas and modular executive offices.[230] However, it was Frank Stanton, the President of CBS, who was to be Knoll's most important patron. The first offices for CBS (1954) in New York established her as a designer for presidential office suites where generous budgets allowed the finest materials and detailing. Her goal was to eliminate the clutter: ". . . the simpler the background, the easier the thought process."[231] Knoll used wall credenzas to conceal telephones and other office equipment, as well as storage walls to hide televisions, bars, and so on. This reductionist tendency was further evidenced in the painstaking detailing of the ceiling plane to conceal mechanical and lighting systems. CBS was followed by even more elegant interiors for the H.J. Heinz Co., Pittsburgh (c. 1958), and for Cowles Magazine, Inc., New York (c. 1962).[232] Ironically, Knoll's greatest and final commission came from Frank Stanton to complete the interiors for Eero Saarinen's last design, the CBS Building (1960–65), New

York (figs. 74 and 75). Having retired from the company in 1965, Knoll returned to design the presidential suites (pl. 26) and other executive floors.[233] All of her brilliant planning, superb taste, and elegant detailing were marshaled to create the most sumptuous executive offices in America of their time. There could have been no greater swan song.

Florence Knoll's importance was as an interior designer and entrepreneur—perhaps the most influential American interior designer of the post-war generation. She helped establish the position of the interior designer, as Henry Dreyfuss (1904–72) and Walter Dorwin Teague (1883–1960) had for the industrial designer in the preceding quarter-century. With Hans Knoll, she sought out many of the most talented designers of the century in both Europe and America. Through the facilities of the Knoll company, they produced a dazzling series of furniture, textiles, and graphics. As a planner, Florence Knoll had a significant impact on the layout of the modern office. In her showrooms, she indicated how modern design could be adapted to the home or office. Her work shows that she learned the lessons of industrial design from the Bauhaus, a purity and elegance from Mies, and the concept of total design from Eliel Saarinen. The resultant style—the "Knoll look"—was so pervasive that it came to symbolize American interior design in the 1950s and sixties. It was a singular union: a designer of objects and interiors of international renown and a principal of one of the most influential design firms of her time. No American designer since Louis Comfort Tiffany (1848–1933) could claim such a mantle.

This outline of the careers of the Cranbrook circle, ranging from Eliel Saarinen to Florence Knoll, indicates the preeminent position the Cranbrook Academy of Art holds in the history of American interior and furniture design. It chronicles the work of two generations over a period of some four decades. While there are individual stylistic differences among the artists, there are underlying similarities that may be attributed to Eliel Saarinen's teaching and example at Cranbrook. All of the artists surveyed approached interior and furniture design in an architectural context, and they all believed in the totality of design from the largest to the smallest detail. What is remarkable about the Cranbrook experience, though, is that furniture and interior design were not relegated to a secondary position in relation to architecture. In fact, if one considers the number of major designers—as opposed to architects—produced by Cranbrook and the influence of their work on their contemporaries, one can readily see that interior and furniture design equal—if they do not exceed—the architectural production in influence. Cranbrook thus seems to occupy a unique position for an American institution in achieving the Arts and Crafts ideal of raising the applied arts to a fine art. The Cranbrook story, however, is incomplete, for several of the designers are still active, and the impact of the Cranbrook circle on younger designers both here and abroad is yet to be assessed. Moreover, Cranbrook—unlike many other influential twentieth-century art colonies—not only survives physically as a complex but also as a vital teaching institution. Cranbrook possesses a tradition of achievement and challenge as it moves into its second half-century.

6 | METALWORK AND BOOKBINDING

George Booth's patronage and personal creativity were manifest throughout Cranbrook's early years, but nowhere more so than in the creation of the Metalwork and Bookbinding departments.[1] The initial development of these craft workshops, two of the earliest at Cranbrook, strongly reflects Booth's Arts and Crafts ideology even though, at the same time, Eliel Saarinen was making numerous designs for metalwork with an eye to commercial production. Both goals—achieving integrity for the handcrafted object and raising the quality of design for machine-made pieces—existed side by side at Cranbrook in varying degrees of importance for many years. In general, the craftsmen and faculty members in the Cranbrook programs reinforced their tradition of hand-wrought technical excellence and experimentation, while Eliel Saarinen participated actively in industrial art exhibitions and produced elegant designs for mass-produced objects, reflecting an attitude that was held in common—surprising as it seems at first—by Booth himself and the renowned Bauhaus in Germany.

Booth's own taste was formed and applied long before his conception of Cranbrook was implemented. By 1900, he had established the Cranbrook Press, located under the eaves of the *Detroit Evening News* building. His model was William Morris' Kelmscott Press, and he used Morris typefaces as well as outfitting the facility with furniture of his own—traditional—design. Following the style of the first years of letterpress printing, Booth published a series of small, handsome volumes, among them a 1902 history of the Press itself.[2] He derived its name from the town in England where his grandfather had worked as a coppersmith; this is among the earliest manifestations of the Cranbrook name and implies Booth's own anglophile, revivalist sympathies. The Press, however, functioned for only a few years, although its name was later revived for the printing operation at Cranbrook Academy.

It was certainly Booth who personally hired Jean Eschmann to set up the bookbinding workshop at Cranbrook in 1929, for Booth's connections with like-minded patrons and other arts and crafts societies in America provided him with special knowledge of many fine craftsmen. Eschmann, a native of Switzerland, was then working for the well-known Riverside Press in Cambridge, Massachusetts, as a hand-binder and probably became known to Booth through a common friend.[3] Eschmann's European background, with traditional training in a local crafts school, followed by apprenticeship to a master craftsman, must have fitted Booth's criteria perfectly.[4] Like a true medieval artisan, Eschmann traveled throughout Europe in his youth, learning his métier through experience in a variety of situations until 1919, when he followed other members of his family to the United States.

As one of the early craftsmen at Cranbrook, he was expected to fulfill practical duties for Booth and the nascent Academy, as well as to instruct students, an arrangement formalized in contracts between Eschmann and the Cranbrook Foundation.[5] The pervasive medieval spirit of his employment not only required Eschmann to provide fine leather bindings for Booth's personal library

118
Wrought Iron Shop at Cranbrook. c. 1930.
Photo courtesy Cranbrook Academy of Art/ Museum

119

JEAN ESCHMANN. *Binding for Cupid and Psyches by Apuleius.* c. 1931. Tooled leather. 7 ¾ × 6 × ½″. Cranbrook Educational Community

and books in the Cranbrook collection, but also to perform such journeyman tasks as making up pads of paper and fashioning three-ring binders.[6] Still, Eschmann's main duties were centered around instruction, and George Booth encouraged greater participation by Cranbrook students in this workshop.[7] Eschmann's brochure of this period announces his class schedule, his availability for private commissions, and his special skills, which included the restoration of old books. Photographs of the workshop in those days record considerable activity, showing Eschmann supervising students as they work with traditional hand-binding tools and equipment.[8] Mrs. Eschmann recalls that many early students were professional people learning the craft for the pleasure of a hobby, rather than as a trade,[9] but there were certainly vocational students as well. Among the books still in Cranbrook House or the Cranbrook Library are some examples of student work, although it is not always possible to differentiate between them and the products of a teacher or assistant.[10]

Eschmann's bindings, which he always designed himself, are clean and spare. They retain nothing of the quaintness or elaborate decorative structure so typical of the Arts and Crafts period, relying rather on streamlined forms, bold color juxtapositions, and an elegant, curvilinear typography favored by leading designers in the 1920s. His cover for *The Odyssey of Homer* (pl. 28), consists of straight-line rules in gold tooling surrounding a rectangular inset of

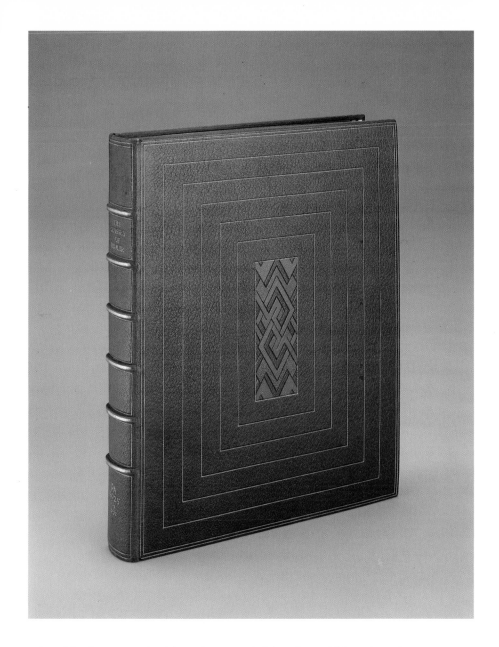

colored leather, organized in a sharp-angled interlace. Although such patterns are staples in the bookbinder's repertoire as far back as the sixteenth century, both the coloristic treatment and dense, zig-zag geometry of *The Odyssey's* decoration are assertively contemporary with the 1931 date of this binding. The sumptuous effect of Apuleius's *Cupid and Psyches* (fig. 119) is achieved through a similarly simple device of gilded parallel lines running horizontally across top and bottom, bracketing a distinctively Art Deco title which dominates the cover. This stylistic mode was basic to Eschmann's work although he was flexible enough to match the literary nature of a work when it suited, as in the binding created for William Morris' *Sir Galahad,* which is titled in English black-letter type.

The financial crisis of early 1933 forced the closure of several Cranbrook craft workshops, including Eschmann's. Moving for a short time to the Artisan Guild building—basically free space in downtown Detroit donated to Eschmann and a few other craftsmen, including Arthur Nevill Kirk and Ruth Ingvarson from Cranbrook—he continued to give classes, as before, both to amateurs and would-be professionals, principally from Wayne University. He was offered a position in Cleveland in 1935 and lived there until his death. Booth's reply to Mrs. Eschmann's inquiry giving reasons for the shut-down is sympathetic,[11] but, like the Cranbrook Press, the bookbinding workshop failed to make a reappearance after its initial run of activity.

Booth's deeper interest in metalwork, however, stemmed from his far more personal involvement in that medium. He was proud of his grandfather's having been a coppersmith, and made a point of emphasizing his own experience as a metalwork designer. (Before settling in Detroit and entering the newspaper world, Booth had been actively engaged in the metalwork business.) One of his sketchbooks, still in Cranbrook House, contains designs dating from his metalworking days, including a rough drawing for his last major project, an ornate railing of brass and steel constructed about 1887 (according to Booth's later note on the sheet) for the Bank of Toronto in Montreal (fig. 120). Other sketches are for various wrought iron gates placed on the Cranbrook estate as it developed.

120

GEORGE G. BOOTH. *Sketch for a Bank Railing.* c. 1887. Pencil on paper. 8 ¾ × 11 ½". Photo courtesy Cranbrook Educational Community

He also commissioned works from such outstanding craftsmen-designers of the period as Samuel Yellin, who fabricated the Cranbrook South Gate in 1917. Booth's letters indicate a highly critical attitude toward the work of these artisans, since he often sketched counter-proposals for them to incorporate in their designs.[12] In order to be able to create objects on his own terms, he established a workshop *in situ* where, as the campus took shape, most of the wrought iron gates, andirons, and other functional but decorative metal objects for Cranbrook were constructed, principally after the conceptions of Eliel Saarinen.

Despite his and his grandfather's background in the more commercial forms of fabricating metal, Booth's real passion seems to have been for fine metalwork—objects in gold and silver, embellished with other precious materials and enamel. Records show that he made significant purchases of works by George

121

ARTHUR NEVILL KIRK. *Triptych.* c. 1925.
Silver, ivory, enamel, and semiprecious
stones. 5 ½ × 3 ⅜ (wings open) × 3″.
Photo courtesy Cranbrook Archives. Collection Mrs. Austin E. Jones and Mrs. Arthur Nevill Kirk

Germer, Tiffany, Arthur Stone, and Georg Jensen. His reputation as a patron of fine metalwork was such that in 1922 and again in 1927 Jensen himself wrote Booth to ask advice about moving to the United States, possibly under his patronage. Booth's thoughtful and subtly discouraging response of October 13, 1927, seems to have settled the issue, and there is no testimony to any further correspondence between the two men.[13]

Booth's feelings about what he considered the higher levels of the decorative arts are summed up in a statement he prepared for the Detroit Society of Arts and Crafts, perhaps in 1926, but certainly sometime in the late twenties. As an active member of the Society, Booth had supported its programs and made many purchases from its exhibitions. "Can we now cease to concern ourselves with peasant Crafts of any kind—Linen, Pottery, Metal, etc. or with prim-

122

ARTHUR NEVILL KIRK. *Chalice.* c. 1933. Silver, crystal, and semiprecious stones. Photo courtesy Cranbrook Archives. Christ Church Cranbrook

123

ARTHUR NEVILL KIRK. *Study for Compote.* 1929. Ink and colored wash on paper. 10 ⅛ × 9 ¼″. Collection Mrs. Austin E. Jones and Mrs. Arthur Nevill Kirk

Colorplate 29

ARTHUR NEVILL KIRK. *Hand Mirror.* c. 1931. Silver, ivory, enamel, and semiprecious stones. 5 ¼ × 10″. Collection Carolyn Farr Booth

itive compromises such as Pewter, glassware, beads, leather work, etc.; nearly all of which is produced without any understanding of Art, but by trained fingers or machines?" he asked rhetorically.[14]

Fortunately, Booth was able to act on his own urging, and in 1927 he invited Arthur Nevill Kirk, a metalwork instructor at the Central School of Arts and Crafts, London, to come to the United States as a part-time instructor at the Society and also to provide ecclesiastical plate for Christ Church Cranbrook. Kirk accepted, and is found listed as an instructor for metalwork in the 1927–28 catalogue of the Society's Art School.

Kirk's father, like Eschmann's, ran a small business, in this case a jewelry shop in Lewes, Sussex, where he repaired watches. According to Kirk's wife, when her husband was only sixteen, Edward Perry Warren, a Bostonian who often visited Lewes, bought a pendant made by the young man and then commissioned other works.[15] Kirk graduated from and then taught for seven years at the Central School where traditional craftsmanship was dominant. In 1925 Kirk won a gold medal at the "Exposition Internationale des Arts Décoratifs et Industriels Modernes," Paris, for a triptych which remains today in the collection of the artist's family (fig. 121). This piece is a consummate expression of Kirk's impeccable workmanship, and Booth, who undoubtedly saw it on his visit to London in 1927, must have perceived correctly that it would harmonize perfectly with the simplified Gothic refinement of Bertram Grosvenor Goodhue's Christ Church design.

Kirk was a slow, careful worker who took justifiable pride in his enamel-working ability. The triptych is a shimmering example of his taste for combining hand-fashioned silver with colorful complementary materials: here, in

addition to the enameled surfaces of the central panel and inside wings, he has incorporated ivory, moonstones, carbuncles, and fire opals. Certain methods of silverworking seemed to Kirk antithetical to the handcraft tradition, and he rarely used a cast component (and if he did, it was always cast by someone else), nor did he employ any device as modern as a lathe.[16] Much of his work is ecclesiastical, even though Kirk did not share in the conventional piety of his fellow English revivalists and never attended church. While the triptych form itself is, of course, consciously archaic, and individual elements, such as the lobed foot, finials and wire decoration, are equally traditional, the completed piece reproduces no particular epoch or style. It is a unique, handcrafted object faithful to the ideals of the English Arts and Crafts movement but shows no corresponding debt to Art Nouveau. Kirk, a member of the Royal Society of Miniature Painters in London, also taught that subject in England and designed his own motifs for enamels. In style, the central panel's Madonna and Child recalls work by several English artists of this period—Eric Gill, for example—who abstracted figures and reduced their settings to create strong, uncomplicated patterns.

Mrs. Kirk joined her husband in Detroit a year after his arrival there; she recalls that most of the students of the Detroit Society of Arts and Crafts were then young high school graduates. When Kirk moved his family to Cranbrook and began to teach there, however, he took on more mature students from Wayne University and the community. His major projects continued to be furnishings for Christ Church, where the treasury remains today a glittering microcosm of Booth's concern for traditional values and includes some of Kirk's most spectacular pieces. The chalice he made about 1933 for Ellen Scripps Booth, who presented it to the Church in memory of her mother, is typical of this richly decorated work (fig. 122). In addition to variegated semiprecious stones, columns of crystals—a material Kirk used to great effect in his lavish processional cross of 1930—set off the ornate stem. This chalice and cross are certainly among his most ambitious and stylistically conservative pieces, complemented by many other chefs d'oeuvre: the altar cross (actually begun in England before he emigrated), a pastoral staff embodying an antique ivory, a silver, enamel and ivory book cover, and other objects for the main church and St. Dunstan's chapel there, which was essentially Booth's personal chapel. Kirk also fabricated an altar cross and candlesticks after drawings by O. H. Murray (the Church's principal designer) and reworked a Jensen ewer according to Booth's instructions. Kirk's accessories are stylistically compatible with other works in the Church treasury by Ralph Adams Cram, John Kirchmayer, Bertram Grosvenor Goodhue, Arthur Stone, and Omar Ramsden, as well as some antique objects.

In 1929 Kirk was appointed head of the silversmith workshop at Cranbrook and established himself in the new facilities with two assistants, Charles D. Price and Margaret Biggar. His brochure announced classes in jewelry and enameling, and he continued work on private commissions for Christ Church, George Booth, and others. His teaching methods revealed his artistic point of view: students were taught individually with little formal instruction and no lecturing. A shy man, Kirk preferred to talk with each member of the class in turn, discussing individual needs and goals. Since many of his students were businessmen, few went on to careers in the fine arts.

Kirk and his assistants were also expected to fabricate objects after Eliel Saarinen's designs. Although the two men's philosophies would seem to have been incompatible (Saarinen's work will be discussed below), once Kirk began working from Saarinen's drawings, new stylistic attitudes emerged in his own pieces. For instance, in 1930 Kirk made a cigarette box from a design by Saarinen (fig. 129), and shortly thereafter produced a tea service of his own, almost completely undecorated and bearing the geometry and straight sides associated with the Art Deco style.[17] This is probably the service which was shown in a contemporary handicrafts exhibition at the Architectural League in 1933 and was characterized by one critic as "giving an effect which, although contemporary in feeling, recalls an eighteenth century style."[18]

Those pieces are, however, unusual in Kirk's *oeuvre,* and his best works are highly ornamented. Like most artists, he began projects with sketches, which served the double purpose of working out ideas on paper and providing potential customers with visual material. A fine example of Kirk's technique from the many surviving drawings is a watercolor study for a compote made in 1929 (fig. 123).[19] This drawing clearly suggests the decorative intent of the piece, showing colored stones and enamel insets. It is, in fact, a valuable record because the small enamel pendants, also seen in early photographs, have now disappeared. While recalling a regal opulence of some former day—perhaps vaguely Byzantine or Renaissance—the compote's exact stylistic source in art history is not certain, nor was it probably intended to be.

Kirk fulfilled many ecclesiastical commissions during and after his years at Cranbrook, remaining one of a handful of American silversmiths with the considerable knowledge and inclination to furnish churches with their necessary accessories.[20] Booth, who occasionally requested a piece for his personal collection, considered Kirk the best maker of ecclesiastical objects in the United States.[21] He is, in fact, so closely identified with church furnishings that his secular pieces are often overlooked, when it was actually in that area that his work shows the greatest formal development.

Many of Kirk's early secular pieces *seem* ecclesiastical because of their uncompromisingly serious decorative vocabulary and form. His American style developed in several directions: a more elegant Art Deco dependence, a greater reliance on arabesques, and a penchant for more fantasy—even whimsy—in conception. The mirror commissioned by Henry S. Booth for his wife, Carolyn (pl. 29), typifies these new directions. A pair of mountain goats, heraldic in their abstraction and symmetry, lock horns in a chevron-shaped space suspended between a decorative device and some distant mountains. Wire and beading frame the enamel and define the edge of the mirror; a diaper pattern, punctuated with silver studs, enlivens the handle, which is completed by a rousing finial recalling the work of Jensen and central European designers in the early part of this century. It is both sophisticated and witty.

In 1933, Kirk's workshop also closed, another victim of Cranbrook's economic problems. After attempting to put the studios on an independent financial basis, the Foundation finally felt it could not afford even the small subsidies necessary to their survival. Kirk first moved to studios in the Artisan Guild and, when that shut down, to private quarters. He always had loyal students, including a group from Detroit Edison who studied with him for some years, and he taught classes at Wayne University. George Booth continued to commission work from him on a steady basis. Beginning around 1939, however, Kirk was handicapped by Parkinson's disease. His ability to work was seriously limited, and he increasingly required his wife's assistance until his death in 1958.

Kirk belonged to the last generation of silversmiths whose working procedures were restricted to the historically acceptable methods of pure handwork and stylistic vocabulary validated by the past. In this, he is more interesting to contemporary eyes than to those intervening generations which perceived historicism as uninspired and believed machine technology to be liberating. Kirk has remained a little-known figure except to specialists in this field, but such anonymity is probably in the nature of his craft; few silversmiths are well known.[22] But it is also true that the majority of Kirk's pieces rest in seldom-seen ecclesiastical treasuries, or in private collections. Equally, the Cranbrook workshop system, as initially established by Booth and the Foundation, was not designed to produce teachers and practicing artists in the crafts, so that Kirk had no immediate successor to sustain his reputation when the workshop closed.

It is significant that Booth, despite his admiration for Kirk, did not believe in a return to the medieval workshop but actually professed a more balanced viewpoint between handcrafts and the machine aesthetic. In 1930, M. W. Childs wrote an article in the *St. Louis Post-Dispatch* under the headline, "A Detroit Millionaire's Attempt to Restore the Hand Crafts."[23] Booth scribbled a note on the bottom of a letter from Childs: "Heads all wrong—Folly to think of *restor-*

124
ELIEL SAARINEN. *Study for a Hanging Lamp*. 1903. Ink and watercolor on paper. 19 ⅞ × 15 ½". Photo courtesy Suomen Rakennustaiteen Museo

ing Handicrafts—(i.e. to revert from machines to hand work). The perfection of art goes from brain to hand—and from the real artist to industrial uses or to the aesthetic enjoyment of cultured peoples. We aim to keep alive a high standard that our industrial products may reach the highest attainable level. . . ."[24] The first announcement of the Cranbrook Academy of Art, in 1932, included this statement of purpose: "To execute objects of art by hand as original pieces has its value and will always have, but it is, however, an important part of the Academy program to produce a design that can be multiplied by machine. The Academy has to be, therefore, in contact with various industries which will manufacture the design."[25] This idea, widespread in the early twentieth century, was seriously discussed at Cranbrook as a practical solution to its financial problems. In a letter dated only a few weeks before the silver and bookbinding workshops closed in 1933, Richard Raseman told the Foundation trustees: "We have felt that if less expensive objects could be made, the design being of the highest quality, people would be encouraged to patronize the shops at Cranbrook. . . . We are convinced that considerable work could be done in the field of metal objects which, being properly designed, would tend to influence contemporary design. This is a field in which Mr. Kirk is not interested. . . ."[26]

Eliel Saarinen, on the other hand, *was* keenly interested in the possibilities of commercial production and *not* involved in the process of metal handcrafting, precisely contrary to the practice of the school's instructor in that field, Kirk. Saarinen always recognized the value of decorative effects in his archi-

125
ELIEL SAARINEN. *Drawing for Andiron.* c. 1929. Pencil on paper. 3 ⅝ × 6 ⁷/₁₆″. Cranbrook Academy of Art/Museum

tecture, conceiving specially tailored metal fittings and accessories for even his earliest buildings. Renderings for his projects in Finland always include custom designed furniture, lamps, door hinges, and other details, intended to unify the total work of art. In these first buildings, he worked closely with Eric Ehrström who may have designed most of the decorative panels and undoubtedly fabricated the actual metal objects, but at least one drawing from Saarinen's hand survives, a study for a copper hanging lamp in the house known as Suur-Merijoki (fig. 124).

During Eliel Saarinen's Finnish period, at the beginning of the century, it was not uncommon for some artists to design objects intended for commercial manufacture, which were then marketed through the factory's sales catalogue.[27] Saarinen himself is known to have made at least one such design to be produced for mass consumption.[28]

At Cranbrook, Eliel Saarinen was intensely active in the field of metalwork. Basically, his work fell into one of two areas: the building and furnishing of Cranbrook, including his own residence, and the creation of prototypes or designs for commercial metalwork firms. Since Saarinen's own hand is to be seen only in drawings for these objects—although it is certain that, as a perfectionist, he attended closely while the work was being fabricated—it is interesting to note the steps followed in this part of the artistic process.

Eliel Saarinen's first design approach could almost be called a doodle; a very witty and perceptive summation of the budding idea. Each one of these very small sketches is drawn with the same considerable freedom as his study for an andiron (fig. 125). Translating these semi-fantasies into wrought iron would have been impossible, because dozens of such drawings[29] reveal more of Saarinen's taste for picturesque detail than his practical nature. The vocabulary, however, has been transformed from an early, and very Nordic, National Romanticism (see Clark) to a pared-down version of the motifs. This drawing, and others like it, probably date from the time Saarinen began to design furnishings for Cranbrook. It is certainly related by a combination of lively line and architectonic form to some andirons actually made for Cranbrook, which can be seen in an old photograph of the wrought iron workshop about 1930 (fig. 118).

Another large group of sketches for one of Saarinen's most extensive projects reveals similarities in style. The many wrought iron gates throughout Cranbrook, mostly fabricated by John C. Burnett and, later, Walter Nichols, are filled with the birds and leaping animals Saarinen favored as well as densely packed zig-zags, curlicues, and a telescoping motif which eventually appears on textiles, architectural forms, and every other aspect of his design (see De Long, Miller, and Thurman). Comparison of the andiron drawing with one of Saarinen's finished works, the main gate to Cranbrook School of 1928 (fig. 126), is striking because it demonstrates his ability to reduce the complex decorative scheme of his sketches to a simpler and more practical design without losing exuberance of detail. Although this gate is one of the wrought iron masterpieces at Cranbrook, it was not fabricated in the School's workshop. Instead, Saarinen's office provided full-size working drawings[30] for this gate to a well-known craftsman, Oscar Bach, who had already produced the handsome clockface found in the Cranbrook School Dining Hall. Despite the large amount of hand engraving necessary, Bach completed the gates in only three months. Booth was generally pleased with the result, but showed his expertise in technical matters of this sort by immediately spotting inadequacies in the hinges and pins, which Bach then rectified. A subsequent letter from Bach shows that Eliel Saarinen desired the birds on top to be gilded, making them an even more emphatic element.[31]

Perhaps the most spectacular wrought iron construction of Cranbrook is the Cupola, for which the working drawing of 1929 exists (pl. 30). Its decorative configuration is one that appears regularly in Eliel Saarinen's sketches and recalls an abstracted bird in flight, seen head on, or perhaps a pair of symmetrically opposed check marks. The technical problems of creating this motif in three dimensions are evident, but John Burnett, who oversaw the wrought iron workshop, and his assistant Francis Faus succeeded in doing so. Saarinen's drawing suggests that he intended a finial to surmount the summit of the domed shape, but

126

ELIEL SAARINEN (DESIGNER) AND OSCAR BACH (FABRICATOR). *Entrance Gate to Cranbrook School.* 1928. Wrought iron. 92 × 158″. Photo courtesy Cranbrook Archives. Cranbrook School

it seems not to have been made. The figure seen in the drawing recalls the work of Carl Milles, particularly the *Orpheus* presently installed atop a column in the Maija Grotell courtyard (fig. 186). Since Milles first visited Cranbrook only in 1929, it seems unlikely that there is any conscious reference here, but it does indicate the similarity of Milles' and Saarinen's taste. While the Cupola serves no particular function, it makes a strong architectural statement, acting as a visual counterweight for the tower on the quadrangle's opposite side (fig. 127).

For Kingswood, Eliel Saarinen designed another metal extravaganza, quite different in feeling, but completely in character with the festive quality of that school's architecture. In Kingswood's Dining Hall, one of Cranbrook's

Colorplate 30

ELIEL SAARINEN. *Drawing for Cranbrook School Cupola.* 1929. Ink, colored pencil, and pencil on paper. 27 ³⁄₈ × 20 ¹⁄₈″. Cranbrook Academy of Art/Museum

127

ELIEL SAARINEN. *Cranbrook School Cupola.* c. 1929–30. Photo: Askew. Courtesy Cranbrook Academy of Art/Museum

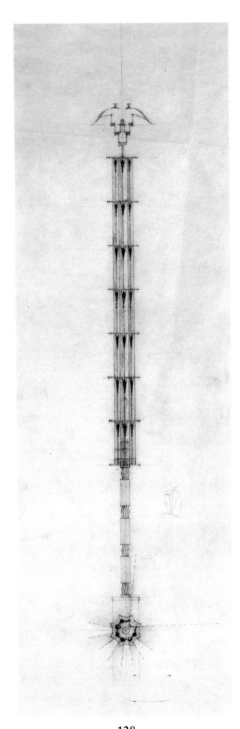

most gracious spaces, he placed a pair of elegant light standards, flanking the gigantic tapestry woven by his wife Loja (see Thurman). These fixtures are sixteen feet of silvery aluminum from base to top. The working drawing (fig. 128) is itself a masterpiece of invention which deftly indicates the striking qualities of the finished work. Saarinen intended the light standards to be meaningful visual accents as well as lighting devices, for their vertically repetitive motifs reiterate those found throughout the structure of the school as a whole. Standing floor lamps for Kingswood, which appear in old photographs of the Dining Hall (fig. 85),[32] are made of the same polished aluminum as the standards, and were manufactured by Nessen Studio, Inc. These lamps originally stood along the sides of the room. Their shades are formed by three inverted cones fitted together which echo the ascendant standards and direct the light upwards.

Eliel Saarinen's skill as a draftsman is proven in a number of exquisite drawings he prepared for smaller objects. In 1929, Kirk began work on a cigarette box designed by Saarinen (already mentioned), and still, today, in the collection of the Cranbrook Museum.[33] Saarinen's drawing, which has the precision and subtle shading of a late medieval silverpoint, stayed with Kirk and is still in his family's possession (fig. 129). The cigarette box and a candy box, also made by Kirk,[34] are wonderfully controlled designs, balancing clean surfaces lightly defined by a scalloped edge with the whimsy of a finial figure blowing soap bubbles. It is possible to make comparisons here with silverwork issuing from the Wiener Werkstätte, or possibly with Jensen's creations. Nevertheless, the effect is fresh and original.

The cigarette box has a history which reveals something of the relationship between Saarinen and Kirk, for problems could arise when collabo-

128

ELIEL SAARINEN. *Drawing for Kingswood Light Standard.* c. 1931. Pencil on paper. 22 ⅝ × 7 ³⁄₁₆″. Cranbrook Academy of Art/ Museum

129

ELIEL SAARINEN. *Drawing for a Cigarette Box.* 1929. Pencil on paper. 7 × 6 ⅝″. Collection Mrs. Austin E. Jones and Mrs. Arthur Nevill Kirk

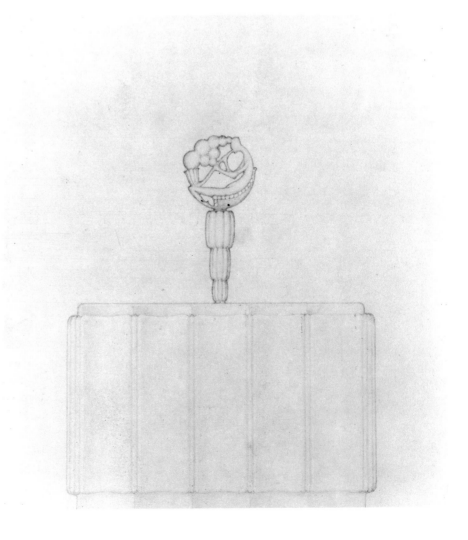

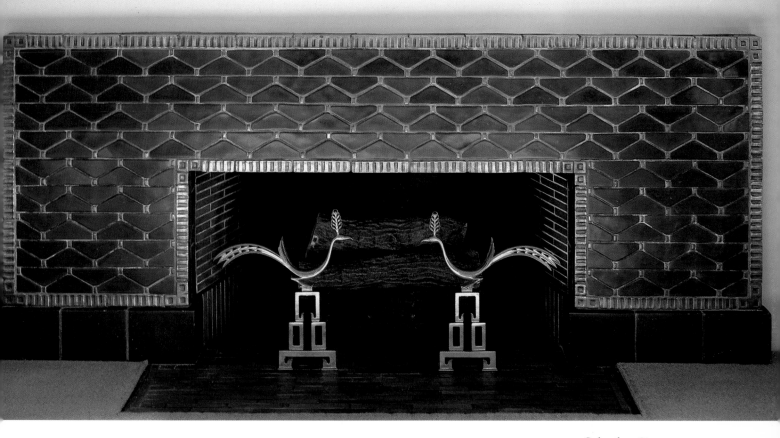

Colorplate 31

ELIEL SAARINEN. *Andirons.* 1929. Bronze.
22 ⅜ × 21 ¼ × 27 ¼". Collection Richard
Thomas and Cranbrook Academy of Art

ration was required between two talented men with different training and view-
points. Margaret Biggar, Kirk's assistant who also worked on the box, described
its fabrication:

> Mr. Saarinen . . . was a marvelous architect but he didn't know anything
> about designing silver to be handmade. And he had a cigarette box he wanted
> made. . . . It was all scalloped, and that had to be a piece of tooled steel, I
> think at least a half inch thick, and these scallops had to be filed in at least
> a quarter inch. And then we had to stamp it. You had to be careful to have
> it all rounded so when you cut the silver—it was a terrific job. . . . That could
> have been made commercially with no trouble. Or Mr. Kirk could have made
> it to look like on the same order but not that way, but Mr. Saarinen would
> have no part of it, Mr. Kirk telling him anything. So I had to file that piece
> of tooled steel and polish it so when Mr. Kirk stamped it, it wouldn't ruin
> the silver. We used up quite a bit of copper.[35]

At the same time that Eliel Saarinen was designing objects for
Cranbrook, he began work on a series of exhibition projects and continued to
produce prototypes for commercial manufacture. In many cases these three areas
overlapped.

The first important exhibition was held at The Metropolitan
Museum of Art in 1929, at the same time that Saarinen was working on his own
residence, and was titled "The Architect and the Industrial Arts: An Exhibition of
Contemporary American Design." Eliel Saarinen was one of several architects invited to design a room in collaboration with manufacturers, and he showed a dining room (fig. 89) which had much of the same character as his own house at
Cranbrook. In his short statement of intent, Saarinen stressed the necessity for
beginning "with simple forms, looking for truth and logic in regard both to con-

struction and to material," rejecting the use of historical styles.[36] Indeed, it was the simplicity of form, combined with a sensitive use of color and material, that gave this room its high elegance. The metal objects included a silver centerpiece, a flat bowl with a fluted foot executed by International Silver Co., similar to a model that International subsequently produced and marketed commercially.[37] Saarinen's later version of this bowl for International, which substituted a simple round foot without the fluting, was, in fact, the only Saarinen design that firm sold through its catalogues, although it fabricated a number of his prototypes. The bowl was sold in four sizes, ranging from a seven-inch-diameter compote to a fifteen-inch bowl, under the trade name Charter Sterling.[38]

The exhibition catalogue lists flatware manufactured by International; Reed and Barton; Rogers, Lunt and Bowlen; and Towle Manufacturing Company,[39] although it is not known which patterns were represented. Saarinen evidently saw flatware as a field with strong commercial possibilities, for drawings dated between 1928 and 1931 reproduce dozens of highly finished proposals, some

130

ELIEL SAARINEN. *Drawing for a Spoon.* 1928. Pencil on paper. Suomen Rakennustaiteen Museo

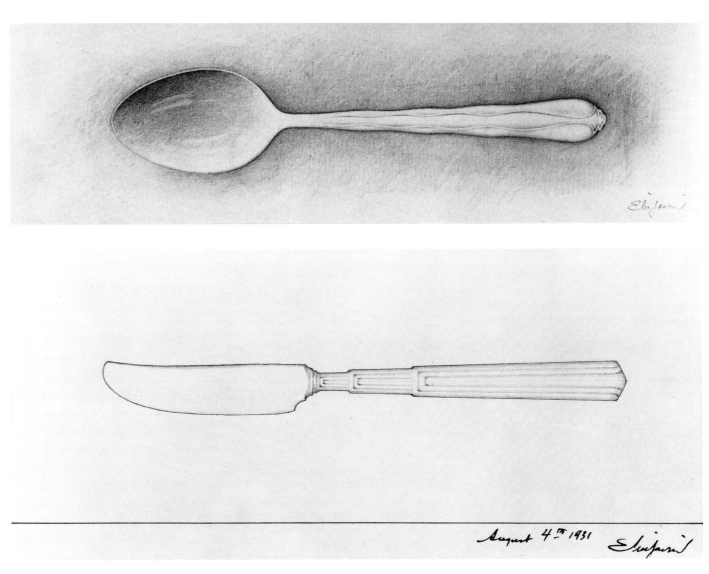

131

ELIEL SAARINEN. *Drawing for a Knife.* 1931. Pencil and ink on paper. Suomen Rakennustaiteen Museo

of them patented and at least one widely marketed.[40] Among the earliest dated studies is a spoon (fig. 130), the companion piece to a knife drawing that is inscribed 1928. A large group of drawings is dated 1931, including a handsome knife (fig. 131), which utilizes the familiar telescoping device in the design of the handle. In all cases, the studies are exquisitely drawn and finished, like the design for the cigarette box (fig. 129), suggesting that these are not first-idea sketches, but working plans for the silversmith. Saarinen also patented a number of designs in 1931 in agreements with International Silver, R. Wallace and Sons, Blackstone Silver Company, and others.[41] The differences among these designs were held to a narrow range and all are refined to the ultimate degree, so that the principal function of the decoration is to define shape rather than to disguise or dominate it.

Among the most striking objects in The Metropolitan Museum of Art room were two andirons (pl. 31), framed by brown and silver Pewabic Pottery fireplace tiles, very much as they were subsequently installed in Saarinen's living room at Cranbrook (see Eidelberg and Miller). For the major decorative motif, Saarinen used a cock with a splendid tail, set on a stepped base—motifs which appeared very close to those found in his contemporary wrought iron work and also in Loja Saarinen's weaving over the fireplace. The exhibition catalogue lists the manufacturer as the Sterling Bronze Company, Inc.,[42] although a newspaper article on the Cranbrook foundry shows the Cranbrook smith Francis Faus polishing an identical andiron.[43] A similar but less refined pair is in the view of the workshop illustrated above (fig. 118).

For his own dining room, Saarinen designed a hanging brass lamp (fig. 83) quite different from the straight-sided, flat-bottomed Metropolitan Museum piece (fig. 89) or those in his sketches[44] which harmonized with the geometry of the table and the strongly horizontal-vertical lines of the ensemble. The more sculptured forms of the Saarinen House lamp[45] gracefully complement the curved walls and ceiling of his Dining Room. A standing lamp from the Living Room (three were originally made) has a similar rounded and segmented shade (fig. 132);[46] these lamps must have been conceived as interacting units within the total design.

In 1931 Saarinen sent a large body of drawings of Cranbrook and some objects to an exhibition at the Architectural League in New York, as well as several pieces of silver executed by Kirk after Saarinen's designs. But the next major showplace for Saarinen's work (including metal) was the 1934 exhibition "Contemporary Industrial Art," again at The Metropolitan Museum of Art. His "Room for a Lady" (see Miller) featured a number of objects in silver manufactured by International Silver Company, including a spectacular urn which reveals a new formal ideal (pl. 32).[47] This room and additional pieces were then shown the next year at Cranbrook as an exhibition of home furnishings.[48] With the urn and other works made by International Silver, Saarinen exhibited a group of less expensive ware executed at Nessen Studio, Inc.[49] By this time, all trace of romanticism or whimsy had disappeared, replaced by a severe sense of geometry which eschewed the sculptured style of a few years earlier—a direction explicit in his architecture as well. The urn, although never publicly marketed, became renowned at Cranbrook social functions, as photographs indicate.[50]

From 1934, following Kirk's departure, and through much of 1937, the metal shop remained closed. Saarinen continued to design metalware during this period, although with less frequency after 1934—and he never taught the subject. In 1935 he announced a competition for the design of three wrought iron gates for a Mrs. Max Hoffman, and for a coffee set. Architecture student Harry Ormston's drawing for the coffee set (fig. 133) reveals an architect's taste for discipline and regularity, but lacks much feeling for the material (it was to have been executed in white metal or silver).[51] Beginning in 1935, Charles Price, who had been Kirk's assistant and who occasionally produced works after Saarinen's design, taught crafts in the Cranbrook School, and in 1936–37 he taught silver and metalwork in the Cranbrook Academy of Art Intermediate School. Otherwise, there seems to have been little activity during these years.

Then in 1937, the Academy admitted Harry Bertoia, who, as part of his scholarship duties, was to supervise the silver and metalworking studio, and to encourage participation by students.[52] Bertoia had graduated from Cass Technical High School in 1936 and the following year attended the school of the Society of Arts and Crafts, where some Cranbrook people undoubtedly noted his work. Shortly after his letter of admittance to Cranbrook had been sent in May, 1937, Mrs. Eliel Saarinen invited Bertoia to Cranbrook to show her some suggestions for a ring she wished to have made.[53] The following year he was appointed

132
ELIEL SAARINEN. *Standing Lamp for Saarinen House.* 1929. Bronze. 68 × 14″. Cranbrook Academy of Art/Museum

Colorplate 32

ELIEL SAARINEN. *Urn.* 1934. Silver. Urn: h.
14 ¼"; tray: diam. 18". Cranbrook Academy of Art/Museum

Metal Craftsman and began to teach full time, in addition to producing his own work. Like Kirk, Bertoia was a skilled artisan, but there is nothing retrograde about his choice of expressive form, and he eagerly experimented with technological advances in metalworking.[54]

Bertoia's work can be divided into two categories: beautifully imagined and completed metalware and playful jewelry, which was often improvised on his bench.[55] A small plated tea service made shortly after his arrival at Cranbrook is based on the geometry of a sphere resting on a right-angled base with high, squared finials on the teapot and sugar dish.[56] It derives, of course, from Eliel Saarinen's urn. A service made two years later indicates that Bertoia

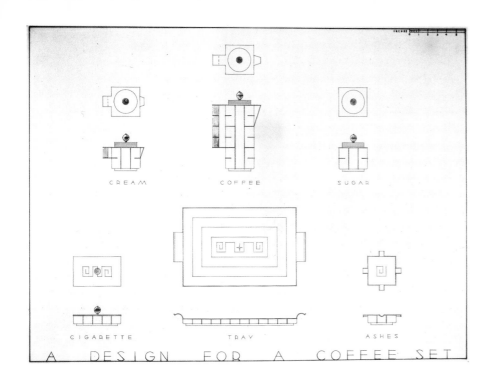

A DESIGN FOR A COFFEE SET

133
HARRY ORMSTON. *Competition Drawing for Coffee Service.* 1935. Photo courtesy Cranbrook Archives

134
HARRY BERTOIA. *Coffee and Tea Service.* 1940. Silver and cherrywood. Tray diam. 15 ½″; sugar 3 ⅛″; creamer 4 ⅝″; coffee 8″; tea 6 ⅝″; water pitcher 9 ¾″. Private Collection

had set his own course (fig. 134). It typifies Bertoia's cool and polished style: the jazzy "lean" of the forward surfaces and parabolic curves which are classic "forties modern." In this case he used cherrywood for the handles, but in similar projects, such as the Kamperman service in the collection of The Detroit Institute of Arts, the handles are lucite, a strikingly effective counterpoint to the plain silver surfaces. No drawings for these works survive, but he often made maquettes in baser metals to test the feel and clarify details before the final version was turned out in silver.

In addition to exploring all methods of working metal, Bertoia was interested in producing relatively inexpensive objects in non-precious materials. He was a frequent exhibitor at the Detroit Artists Market, and a newspaper photograph from 1939 reproduces a group of his pieces in brass and pewter.[57] A polished bronze vase of about 1940 reveals Bertoia using machine methods—specifically here, spinning—to create a flawlessly regular object where the only decoration arises in the play of reflections on the rich, golden surface (pl. 33).

By 1942, Bertoia was beginning to delve further into decorative possibilities, including rough and textured surfaces and irregular, sometimes biomorphic forms. This pioneering and formal inventiveness is particularly noticeable in his jewelry, for which he is perhaps best known in the years before becoming primarily a devotee of design and sculpture. One fine example is the Cranbrook *Centipede,* fashioned about 1942 (fig. 135). A sprouting ambiguity between animal and plant forms can be nothing but intentional—as is also the obvious relationship between biological shapes and artistic conventions, mingling humorous tension with playfulness. The wit and easy charm of his jewelry should not be confused with less than fine craftsmanship, however, for the means to produce these effects are sophisticated and the expertise required is extraordinary. In the forties, Bertoia exhibited his jewelry often both in Detroit and elsewhere. He was frequently paired in such exhibitions with Alexander Calder, who strikes a like attitude in his jewelry.[58] Both the formal and experimental devices of Bertoia's jewelry can be likened to those in his monoprints (pls. 58, 59, 60) and they have been exhibited together with reason.[59]

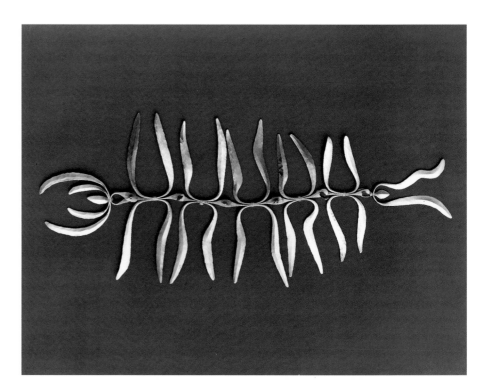

135
HARRY BERTOIA. *Centipede.* c. 1942. Brass. 19 3/4 × 8". Cranbrook Academy of Art/ Museum

Wartime problems began to affect the metal program at Cranbrook in 1942, when Bertoia also began teaching graphics because of a shortage of metal.[60] A few months later the Metalcraft department was suspended for the duration of the war.[61] Bertoia lived in Birmingham, Michigan, until he joined

Charles Eames on the West Coast in 1943. There, he continued to make jewelry, but stopped creating metalware after he left Cranbrook.

Bertoia not only revived the metal shop at Cranbrook, he pushed practice and design firmly into the twentieth century. His taste for modern technology—he says on his Cranbrook application form, "I can use any tool or machinery with dexterity"—coupled with a strong sense of form and craftsmanship provided an impetus that was interrupted by World War II but pointed to the direction of the future with great acumen.

Although there was no regular instructor in metalwork at the end of the war, in the fall of 1945, Educational Director Zoltan Sepeshy recommended that Hermann Gurfinkel (then a student enrolled as Herman Garfield, he has since taken back his original family name) serve as a part-time instructor for those who wished to use the metal shop.[62] Gurfinkel had just entered Cranbrook, but had had several years of practical experience as a machinist and had been apprenticed to a silversmith in Germany. Sepeshy wrote enthusiastically about the possibility of a collaboration between the artist and industry, the trained craftsman producing well-designed objects that could be reproduced *en masse* in order to elevate public taste. Despite Sepeshy's fervor, in 1947 the trustees once again cancelled the course in metalcraft.[63] Gurfinkel was a good teacher, according to those who studied with him, providing sound instruction in technique and a strong feeling for the craft.[64] A group of students petitioned to keep the shop open, but Gurfinkel decided to leave Cranbrook, and it was not until 1948 that metalworking classes resumed.

Among the students whom Gurfinkel had interested in metalworking was Richard Thomas, who kept the shop open the year after Gurfinkel left and was then appointed instructor following his own graduation in 1948. Thomas began instructing shortly after Cranbrook became an accredited degree-granting institution, although it still maintained (as it does today) its initial flexibility and dependence on individual work rather than formal classes. Before the war, Thomas had been a high school teacher and his awareness of the importance of the teaching process coupled with the creative ideal at Cranbrook produced an entire teaching department in metalwork—the first at Cranbrook, and one of the first in the United States.[65]

Thomas's educational methods, like his art, depend on a balance of discipline, understanding, and skill. He enumerates three concepts of equal value: a thorough knowledge of materials, the development of skills and technique, and a personal definition of the craftsman's limitations. These three mature, orderly processes will fuse with concept and evaluation to produce good work.[66] It is difficult to trace those who studied with earlier metalcraftsmen at Cranbrook, but Thomas has produced a great many students who have established themselves as teachers and metalsmiths of distinction.[67] His insistence on the primacy of technical skills has led him to codify them in publications that are now standard texts for the student.[68] Moreover, he has worked with students on a number of design projects in which they became equal partners throughout the creative process and shared in any financial remuneration.[69]

His collaboration with students and close attention to their development is, of course, an indication of the general educational change following World War II, as well as a factor representing his personal inclination. Although this point of view is quite different from that of Arthur Nevill Kirk, it is evident that Thomas admires Kirk (whom he never met) and, in addition, shares a number of the other's characteristics. Most obvious of these is the significant body of liturgical works both have produced. The majority of Thomas' commissions have been ecclesiastical, although, like Kirk, he is not a conventionally religious person. When the building boom after World War II raised churches as well as other structures, Thomas had the opportunity to design everything from unique silver objects to entire ensembles, such as a chapel complete with all its furnishings for the Sisters of Charity in Greensburg, Pennsylvania (not completed as planned), work for the Concordia Senior College in Fort Wayne, Indiana (building designed by Eero Saarinen), and the First Congregational Church in Port Huron, Michigan.

A chalice he designed in 1952 for Ascension of Christ Lutheran Church in Birmingham, Michigan, reveals his links with historical precedent as well as a postwar feeling for bold but graceful statements (fig. 136). The formal articulation of the base, stem with knop, and cup comes out of a tradition that Thomas says is founded in the continuity of symbols, materials, and function. His consistent use of such familiar symbols as the sheaf of wheat and grapes indicates respect for their evocative power. There is also an appreciation of quality in the perfection of the chalice's silver surface by the accent of complementary material, in this instance, the simple ivory knop. Decoration is, however, nearly eliminated in favor of stressing clarity through simple forms.

Thomas's ability to transpose traditional shapes into their modern equivalents is put to good use in his pastoral staff of 1962 (fig. 137). It is significant that the patron, the Rt. Rev. Herman R. Page, specifically requested

Colorplate 33

HARRY BERTOIA. *Vase.* c. 1940. Bronze. 11 ¼ × 5 ⁹/₁₆″. Cranbrook Academy of Art/ Museum

136
RICHARD THOMAS. *Chalice.* 1952. Silver and ivory. Ascension of Christ Lutheran Church, Birmingham

that Thomas first study a staff made earlier by Kirk.[70] Thomas' solution is completely consistent with historical antecedents, including the symbol of the crowned orb. Once again, he has eliminated ornamentation so that the essence of form is more perceptible than in examples by Kirk. The means to produce these forms often still follow those of Kirk's day, although Thomas insists on continual technical investigation. Metalsmiths, he believes, tend by their nature to be rather conservative: "Because we were a rather insular body of people it became necesssary for us to find our own solutions. In many of these instances, we found that we were simply rediscovering ancient techniques!"[71]

Thomas appreciates his place in the Cranbrook tradition. He has been active in saving examples of work by his predecessors when others considered them out of fashion. He has also produced major commissions for Cranbrook: a mace used for Cranbrook and Kingswood graduation ceremonies and Cranbrook's grand punch bowl (fig. 138). Both reinforce his position vis-à-vis symbols. The mace brings together four emblems that summarize all the major reli-

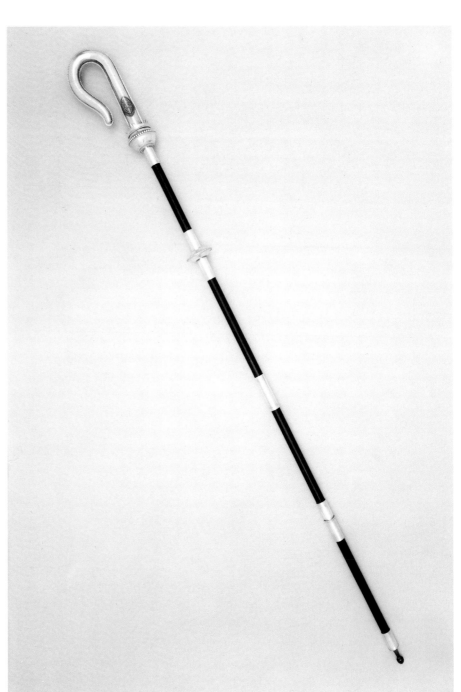

137
RICHARD THOMAS. *Pastoral Staff*. 1962. Silver and wood. H. 60″. Episcopal Archdiocese of Northern Michigan

138
RICHARD THOMAS. *Punch Bowl.* 1958. Sterling silver. 22 × 9″. Photo courtesy Cranbrook Archives. Cranbrook Educational Community

gions of the world, and the punch bowl is adorned with devices having local significance. Thomas' technical inventiveness was tested by the problems of creating the bowl, eventually requiring him to supervise spinning the form at Auto City Spinning. His wit is both original and to the point in the accessory he invented for Cranbrook parties; a pine block with two gold-plated spikes is floated in the bowl whenever it is filled with spiked punch.

Both as teacher and craftsman, Thomas has been in the vanguard of the revival of fine metalwork since World War II. The study and practice of silversmithing has, indeed, burgeoned in those decades, as a cursory look at exhibition catalogues and academic programs reveals. In this development, even through the hiatuses of the mid-thirties and mid-forties, Cranbrook is important as one of the few institutions that promoted the study of this craft in an educational environment. Cranbrook's practitioners have each pursued individual directions, from Kirk's personal and conservative work to Eliel Saarinen's conception of modern design, from Bertoia's technical experimentation to Thomas' disciplined craftsmanship and shared knowledge.

7 | TEXTILES

George G. Booth's concern with the Arts and Crafts in America did, as one would expect, include matters pertaining to the textile medium, as can be seen if one goes through his inventory[1] for Cranbrook House. As first President of the Detroit Society of Arts and Crafts,[2] it was natural for him to acquire pieces such as, for example, Deerfield blue and white embroidered runners.[3] Booth also corresponded with establishments such as Morris and Company, Decorators Ltd., in England (specifically, with H. C. Marrillier, its director),[4] and with Herter Looms of New York.[5] Many Herter-produced pieces are listed among Booth's own furnishings.[6] The Morris correspondence of 1911 and later, however, concerns itself with an order for a large tapestry[7] for the collections of The Detroit Museum of Art. Designed by Sir Edward Burne-Jones and titled *The Passing of Venus,*[8] the tapestry was woven by J. H. Dearle, initially a student of William Morris and eventually a partner, "doing the art work."[9]

In 1925 Booth wrote to Marillier in connection with two large tapestries (twelve by eighteen feet each) for Christ Church Cranbrook.[10] As their subject matter, Booth mentioned the possibility of the Old and New Dispensations. He hoped for a delivery date within two years. His closing paragraph includes a most amazing suggestion: "Perhaps the best thing to do would be to move the Merton Abbey weavers to America and to set up their looms here. I would not be surprised but what it might be a profitable and happy enterprise for them. But whether the atmosphere of America would be as favorable to their best work as England I suppose there might be much doubt."[11] Marillier, however, did not leap at this opportunity.[12] The diary of a local observer, Kate Thompson Bromley, elaborates upon this story: "he [Booth] seriously considered moving that indusry to Cranbrook, until he found that to be impractical on account of the difficulty in obtaining proper dyes in America."[13] However, the question of dyes could not have been so much of an issue, as they could have been sent to America.

Booth's orders for these two tapestries were a most important transaction which would keep the looms going for several more crucial years at a time that saw great unrest and the closing of many factories in England. Furthermore, Marillier saw an opportunity of training "another weaver or two for the job."[14] By October 1926 the designs and sketches for the hangings were completed and three years later, the panel illustrating the Old Dispensation reached Cranbrook.[15] However, it would not be until April 1932 that receipt of the second tapestry illustrating the New Dispensation was announced.[16] In a newspaper article the pair was described as belonging "among the world's largest."[17]

Albert Herter, founder of the Herter Looms,[18] shared Booth's outlook and concern in regard to the creation of truly American artistic expressions.[19] The 1918 correspondence between the two men speaks of a large tapestry to illustrate either the Arts and Crafts or the Great Crusade.[20] Once again, Booth's involvement with his initial order included a preliminary sketch and directives in regard to its gauge and the materials to be used.[21] Although the final tapestry, which depicted the Great Crusade, had originally been ordered for Booth's Cran-

139
ELIEL AND LOJA SAARINEN (DESIGNERS). *Sketch for Festival of the May Queen Hanging.* 1932. Paper, watercolor, gouache, and pencil. Image 26 ¾ × 23 ¾". Cranbrook Academy of Art/Museum

brook House library,[22] he changed his mind and gave it in 1920 to the Detroit Museum. In 1944 Booth reclaimed the piece and hung it at Cranbrook House.[23]

In an undated lecture to the Detroit Society of Arts and Crafts, Booth stated: "The Society should regard itself as the center of concern for the Department of Applied Arts in the new [Detroit] Museum [of Art], and might in time be officially recognized as such."[24] In the same address, under *Further Undertakings,* he listed future exhibitions including "Textiles, new and meritorious design and colors."[25] To be eliminated from the Society's stock on hand were "ordinary linen, dyed scarfs and batiks of ordinary class; needlework (not petit point) unless original and good design," and the general character of the new stock was to include: "Linen—superior design and workmanship and quality; Batiks—only good design as well as superior workmanship; Needlework—silk and wool embroidery of original and good design; Textiles—new and superior; Tapestry—wool and silk—foreign or domestic; Laces—original or highly artistic, new or old; Block printed fabrics—plates."[26] Thus it is clear that Booth's concern with the place of textiles in Arts and Crafts philosophy and practice was extremely serious.

In 1927, when the Cranbrook Foundation was created (see Taragin), Booth donated to it and to the Cranbrook museum his textile study collection of five hundred fragments, dating from the fourteenth through the eighteenth centuries. The collection included woven and embroidered fabrics of Euro-

140
Studio Loja Saarinen Logo. Photo courtesy Cranbrook Academy of Art/Museum

LOJA SAARINEN
CRANBROOK ACADEMY OF ART
BLOOMFIELD HILLS, MICHIGAN

pean origin that became the nucleus of the present-day Cranbrook Academy of Art/Museum textile collection. Booth added over the years to this collection, especially during the 1940s; his later acquisitions, including Peruvian, Coptic, Indian, and Persian examples, were made from well-known New York textile collectors and dealers.[27]

During these early years, Eliel Saarinen's wife, Loja, was to play a key role in regard to the textile medium. Trained as a sculptress, photographer, and model builder, she built most of Saarinen's models (see Clark and De Long). But she developed other interests at Cranbrook. An account by art critic Florence Davies records an exchange that apparently took place between Booth and Loja Saarinen while the entire Cranbrook complex was being discussed. Booth is quoted as having asked the following: "What are we going to do for rugs and textiles to go with these new buildings, and the contemporary furnishings which your husband is designing? Why don't you design some for us and let us send them to Finland where they do such beautiful weaving and have them woven on those looms." Loja replied: "Why not design them and weave them here?"[28] No sooner said than done. Studio Loja Saarinen was established in October 1928 (fig. 140). Closely associated to it but quite separate, a Weaving department was established in 1929 that included the weaving shops under the aegis of the Academy.

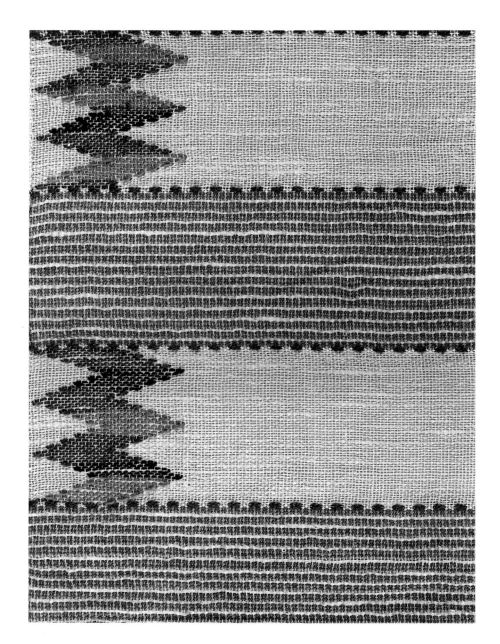

141
LOJA SAARINEN (DESIGNER) AND STUDIO LOJA SAARINEN (WEAVERS). *Valance for Saarinen House Studio.* 1929–30. Linen warp, linen and wool weft; plain weave with discontinuous wefts. 11 ¾ × 35″. Cranbrook Academy of Art/Museum

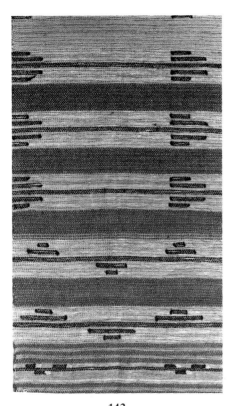

142

STUDIO LOJA SAARINEN (WEAVERS). *Curtain Material.* c. 1930. Linen warp, linen, wool, and silk weft; plain weave with discontinuous wefts. 44 × 14 ½″ (with fringe). Cranbrook Academy of Art/Museum

The concern at Cranbrook with textiles, carpets, or rugs (the terms were often used interchangeably) was not accidental. It was based on the belief that art should permeate the total environment. An attempt was made to create contemporary expressions rather than copying patterns which had become part of a generally accepted but stale vocabulary. Designs were created by unusually talented students under the direction of the head of the department. In addition, weaving was taught by an instructor in the Weaving department to students unfamiliar with the medium. Good design and sound techniques were taught in the shops. Studio Loja Saarinen concerned itself with outside commissions and orders for which Loja was paid as long as she was on the Academy's faculty.

After her return from Paris in 1903 to Hvitträsk where she joined her brother, Herman Gesellius, architect and partner of Eliel Saarinen and Armas Lindgren (see Clark and De Long), Loja had met Eliel Saarinen. She married him the following year. He, too, had been to Paris, although somewhat earlier than she.[29] In 1907, two years after their first child, Pipsan, was born and three years before the birth of their second child, Eero, the Saarinens travelled throughout Europe, especially in France, Switzerland, Austria, Germany, and The Netherlands. As the wife of a prominent architect, Loja knew many important artists and designers, and her role as hostess at Hvitträsk and Cranbrook provided much stimulation in spite of living in isolated communities. As part of her early training, Loja had gained knowledge about weaving and all the traditional textile arts. She learned as a sculptress to cope with masses and shapes, and her commissions in interior decoration (for example, at Hvitträsk in 1903) taught her about the interrelationships of colors and materials. A nephew's recollections about the furnishings at Hvitträsk after Loja's marriage to Eliel mentions a loom in the Morning Room and her making batiks on the small porch off the architectural studio.[30] Eliel's approval was always of prime concern for her. Their exposure to artistic movements in Europe, including the Deutsche Werkbund, the Wiener and Deutsche Werkstätten, and finally the Bauhaus, were important to both the Saarinens.[31]

Studio Loja Saarinen began with one loom and eventually expanded to a total of thirty.[32] According to a pamphlet issued by the Studio, its specialities were "handwoven art fabrics, rugs and window hangings by special commissions only." This entailed the creation of original designs; work was based on colors specifically selected for a particular environment. The use of the finest

143

STUDIO LOJA SAARINEN (WEAVERS). *Curtain Material.* c. 1931. Linen warp, linen and wool weft; plain weave with discontinuous wefts. 46 ½ × 10″. Cranbrook Academy of Art/Museum

materials—all-linen warps and wool, silk, cotton, and an occasional synthetic fiber in the weft—was guaranteed.

Among the first tasks the studio undertook was to provide the furnishing materials required for Saarinen House. Subtly colored, simply designed, technically accomplished, and intended to complement other accoutrements for

144

LOJA SAARINEN (DESIGNER) AND STUDIO LOJA SAARINEN (WEAVERS). *Table Runner.* 1942. Linen warp, linen, wool, and silk weft; plain weave with discontinuous wefts. 118 × 21 ¼″. Cranbrook Academy of Art/ Museum

Saarinen residences, a number of furnishing fabrics still survive. They include a valance (fig. 141), curtain and cushion materials (figs. 142 and 143), and a table runner (fig. 144). These pieces illustrate a traditional Swedish weaving technique known as H. V. technique, in which a pattern is introduced through discontinuous wefts; colored threads are introduced through inlay. This technique, which had been perfected at Handarbetets Vänner (also known as Foereningen Handarbetets Vänner) (The Friends of Handicrafts Association), where it was in use by 1905, was quicker and cheaper than tapestry weaving and also produced materials that could withstand heavy use.[33] All of these fabrics have a certain transparency, a reversibility which suited them especially well when used as curtain materials.

Prior to the existence of a weaving studio at Cranbrook, carpets like the one for the Saarinen House Dining Room (fig. 145) had to be made elsewhere. Eliel Saarinen provided the design for this rug, but its manufacture took place at the Barrymore Seamless Wiltons, Inc., in Philadelphia. Made of wool and cotton, the carpet was machine woven. In its design it repeated the octagonal shape of the table's base, and clearly defined rows of a repeated arched motif echo undulating shapes found in the wallpaper (fig. 83).

Loja frequently would design jointly with her husband; at other times Eliel would design a carpet (fig. 145) or hanging (fig. 139) by himself.[34] The so-called *Rug No. 2* was a joint venture (pl. 34). It is the only extant piece that carries Eliel Saarinen's initials as well as the Cranbrook monogram (an A within a C). Further identification is provided on a linen label attached to the reverse of the carpet and written in ink: "Cranbrook Academy, Rug *No. 2*; Designed by Loja Saarinen; Woven by Walborg Nordquist." This rug was the second item made in Studio Loja Saarinen. It introduces the peacock or bird—a common motif at Cran-

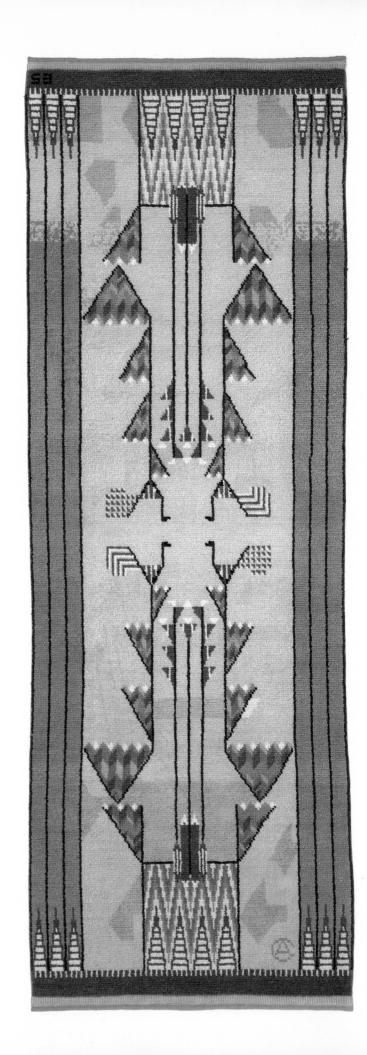

Colorplate 34
ELIEL AND LOJA SAARINEN (DESIGNERS) AND
LOJA SAARINEN AND WALBORG NORDQUIST
SMALLEY (WEAVERS). *Rug No. 2.* 1928–29.
Cotton warp, wool pile; plain weave with
ten picks of weft between each row of knots.
110 ½ × 39″. Cranbrook Academy of Art/
Museum

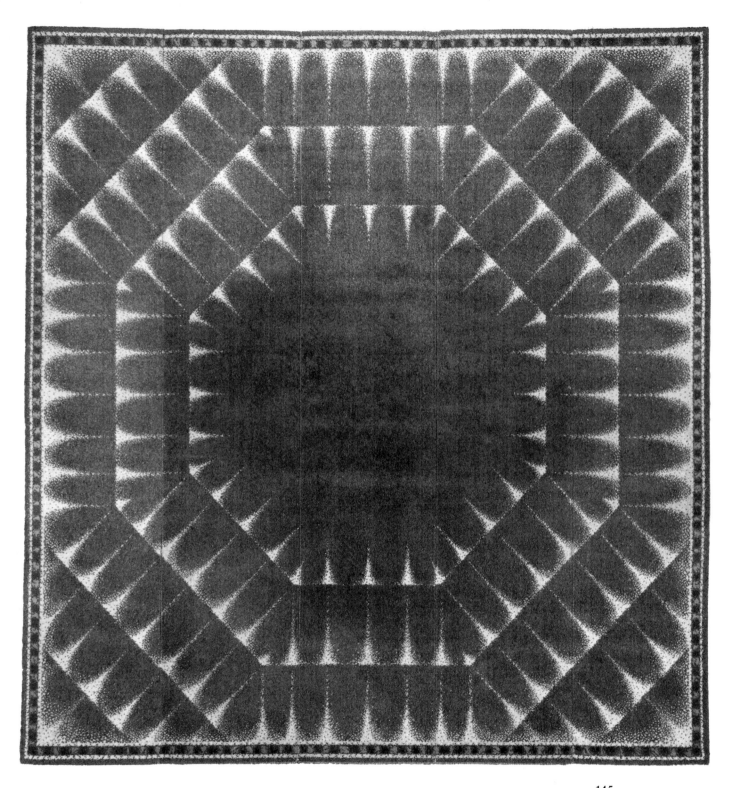

145

ELIEL SAARINEN (DESIGNER) AND BARRY-MORE SEAMLESS WILTONS, INC., PHILADEL-PHIA (WEAVER). *Carpet for Saarinen House Dining Room.* Wool warp, cotton weft, wool pile; machine woven in five sections. 11′ 2″ × 10′ 9″. Cranbrook Academy of Art/Museum

brook (figs. 125 and 126 and pl. 31) in the fiber medium, predating, for example, two other textiles featuring birds, the peacock hanging (fig. 146) and the sketch for the large *Festival of the May Queen Hanging* at Kingswood (fig. 139). Loja Saarinen provided overall guidance and made the selection of materials and colors.

On October 1, 1930, a one-year plan for the Weaving department was adopted. It stated that "Mrs. Saarinen was to take over the entire department and . . . to engage any help she may require." It continued: "Mrs. Saarinen [is] to take a few special students and [is] to receive the tuition paid, with the exception of 10% of such amount, which would be paid to the Foundation as a registration fee." The plan further assigned to Loja responsibility for purchasing all materials and keeping all accounts. It also mentioned that the possibility existed for Loja or her assistants to teach at Kingswood School in the future.[35]

To staff her studio Loja employed exclusively Swedish professional designers and weavers well versed in a form of artistic expression with an exceedingly long tradition in that country (fig. 147). First among those to join her was Maja Andersson Wirde, who left Stockholm on September 14, 1929.[36] She entered employment with the Cranbrook Foundation on October 1, 1929. Wirde was not a total stranger to America. Her work, part of the important "Swedish Contemporary Decorative Arts" exhibition, had preceded her in 1927.[37] In the accompanying catalogue Wirde was listed as one of the artists representing Foereningen Handarbetets Vänner, an association she had been connected with for years.[38] The choice to bring her to Michigan was indeed a wise one as her accomplishments were many. She was well known in Sweden as an extraordinarily talented artist.

Little is known about most of the other weavers and their backgrounds. A listing of 1930 provides their names, the specific jobs they had been assigned to, and their pay.[39] A newspaper account, also of 1930, speaks of "two weavers" (possibly Lillian Holm and Ruth Ingvarson), who apparently accompanied Maja Wirde from Stockholm to Cranbrook.[40] Ruth Ingvarson seems to have been at Cranbrook between 1930 and 1932, with returns in 1934 and 1941. She was born in 1902 in Glemminge, Sweden, and studied from 1922 to 1928 at

146

LOJA SAARINEN (DESIGNER) AND STUDIO LOJA SAARINEN (WEAVERS). *Peacock Hanging.* c. 1932. Linen and silk warp, silk weft; undulating point twill weave. 58 ½ (with fringe) × 47″. Cranbrook Academy of Art/ Museum

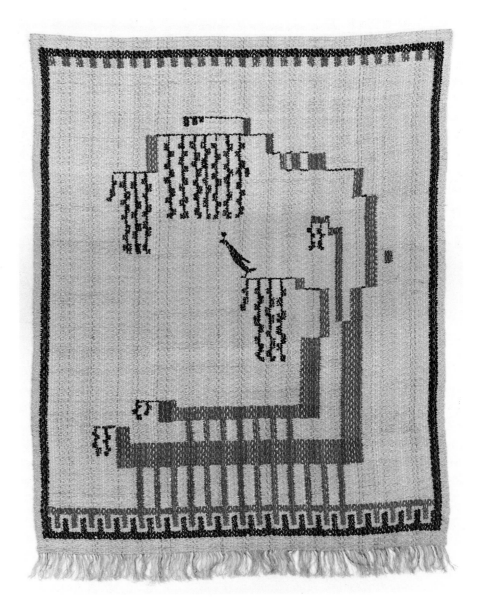

the studio of Märta Måås Fjetterström in Båstad. In 1932–33 she returned to Stockholm and completed further studies at Handarbetets Vänner there. The following year she returned to the United States. From 1951 to 1970 she taught part-time at Wayne State University as Instructor in Weaving,[41] although an association as far back as 1937 is possible.[42] One may ask why so many weavers were needed at Cranbrook in the early thirties. The answer is simple: they helped supply the furnishings for Kingswood School (see De Long and Miller).

Eliel Saarinen's architectural plan for the Kingswood corridors included carpeting (fig. 148). The incorporation of this detail in his drawing proves the importance functional materials had to this architect. Carpeting, curtains, furnishing materials, and hangings were also included in the initial stages of architectural planning and renderings.

Reminiscent of pavement and brick treatments at Cranbrook is a carpet originally designed by Loja Saarinen as part of the furnishings required for the Kingswood Headmistress' office (pl. 35). This carpet relates closely to a

Studio Loja Saarinen. Behind one of the twelve-foot looms can be seen (from left) weavers Elizabeth Edmark, Marie Bexell, Mrs. John Buckberrough, and Mrs. Gerda Nyberg. In the foreground is one of the Saarinen House carpets, which includes brick and pavement patterns. Photo courtesy Cranbrook Academy of Art/Museum

very sizeable carpet for the Saarinen House Living Room.[43] The outer border design of the Headmistress' carpet relates to radiator screen treatments throughout Kingswood and to the dado arrangement in the sketch for the *Festival of the May Queen Hanging* (fig. 139), the small sample weaving for this hanging (fig. 149), and the enormous hanging which still decorates the east wall of the Dining Hall at Kingswood (fig. 85). As an objet d'art the Headmistress' carpet belongs among the very best.[44]

In many cases, sketches, drawings, or cartoons for carpets, hangings, and textiles manufactured at Studio Loja Saarinen do not exist. One exception is the *Festival of the May Queen Hanging* at Kingswood; as we have seen, the sketch (fig. 139) and a small sample weaving showing the first figure off center to the left (fig. 149) have survived. Although unsigned and undated, the sketch has been attributed to Eliel and Loja Saarinen.[45] As with the Headmistress' carpet, the hanging's linear divisions introduce rectangular shapes of varying dimensions as a superimposed grid (this is also true of a sketch by both Saarinens for a hanging for the Tabernacle Church of Christ in Columbus [pl. 41] [see Miller and De Long]). The *May Queen Hanging*'s pattern was inserted in the discontinuous weft technique as the sample clearly shows.

In 1931 Maja Wirde designed an extraordinary carpet for the Kingswood Study Hall Lobby (figs. 150 and pl. 1). It was woven at Studio Loja Saarinen; stylistically, the carpet relates to work that Wirde had done while with Handarbetets Vänner in Stockholm.[46] It is divided into compartments balanced against asymmetrical, linear stepped motifs in the main field. The carpet fits well within the design vocabulary defined by Eliel Saarinen in the Study Hall and in the leaded windows, wooden paneling, and radiator screens at Kingswood. Its twelve medallions show architectural structures, representing various scenes from the Cranbrook campus. Several leaf forms appear to the lower right of each medallion throughout the carpet; undoubtedly one of them relates to the oak leaf, a symbol for Kingswood.[47] Of note is the complex border design. This treatment as well as the placement of isolated leaf shapes can already be seen in a watercolor, pen, and

Colorplate 35

LOJA SAARINEN (DESIGNER) AND STUDIO LOJA SAARINEN (WEAVERS). *Carpet for Headmistress' Office, Kingswood School Cranbrook*. 1931. Linen warp, wool weft, wool pile; plain weave with seven-eight picks of weft between each row of knots. 103 × 80 ½". Kingswood School Cranbrook

148

ELIEL SAARINEN (DESIGNER). *Hallway Carpet Layout for Kingswood School Cranbrook*. c. 1930–31. Tracing paper with ink and pencil underdrawing. Image 29 ⅞ × 51 ⁵⁄₁₆". Cranbrook Academy of Art/Museum

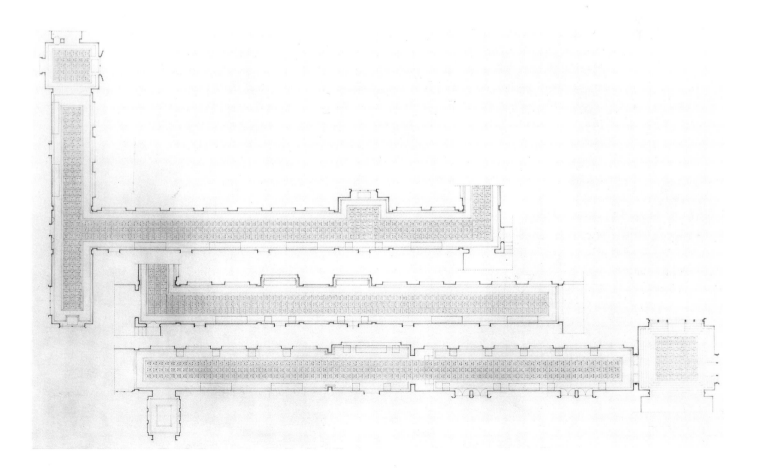

149
ELIEL AND LOJA SAARINEN (DESIGNERS) AND
STUDIO LOJA SAARINEN (WEAVERS). *Sample
for Festival of the May Queen Hanging.*
1932. Linen warp, linen, wool and silk weft;
plain weave with discontinuous wefts. 7′ 2″
× 3′ 9″. Cranbrook Academy of Art/Museum

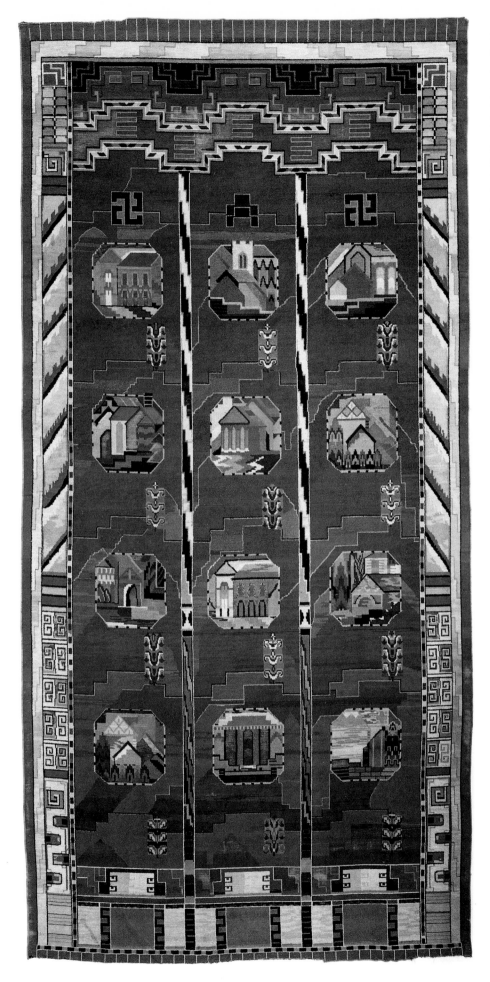

MAJA ANDERSSON WIRDE (DESIGNER) AND STUDIO LOJA SAARINEN (WEAVERS). *Study Hall Carpet for Kingswood School Cranbrook*. 1931. Linen warp, wool weft, wool pile; plain weave with eight picks of weft. 22′ 10″ × 11′ 3″. Kingswood School Cranbrook. The buildings represented are the following: Column 1, row 1, Cranbrook School Dormitory Pergola; row 2, Cranbrook School Dining Hall; row 3, Cranbrook Academy with Crafts Court Archway; row 4, Cranbrook School; column 2, row 1, Christ Church Cranbrook; row 2, Cranbrook Pavilion; row 3, Cranbrook School Dormitory Pergola; row 4, Greek Theater; column 3, row 1, Christ Church Cranbrook; row 2, Cranbrook School; row 3, Mill Race; row 4, Brookside School

ink sketch for a carpet layout design executed by Maja Wirde during her Handarbetets Vänner days in Stockholm.[48]

Another example of Wirde's astute design ability is the so-called *Animal Carpet* of 1932 (pl. 36), a further product of Studio Loja Saarinen. Wirde's abstract interpretations, juxtaposed with a most subtle color scheme, make this a pure Art Deco creation. The carpet carries the Cranbrook monogram. A watercolor, pen, and ink sketch still exists (fig. 151).[49]

Nothing illustrates the use of architectural motifs as a central design concept more splendidly than the hanging based on the 1925 master plan for Cranbrook, and made at Studio Loja Saarinen in 1935, probably by Lillian Holm and Ruth Ingvarson (Frontispiece and fig. 29). Woven in plain weave, the plan was inserted in the discontinuous weft technique in a subdued color scheme. One recognizes Cranbrook Academy of Art (center), Cranbrook School (left), Cranbrook Institute of Science (top center), and Kingswood School Cranbrook (top right). Also included are the Cranbrook Pavilion (bottom right), the Greek Theater (above the Pavilion at bottom right), and the faculty housing for Cranbrook School (top left). The buildings are shown in plan or elevation.[50] Border and frieze treatment relate to the *Festival of the May Queen Hanging,* its sketch, and the weaving sample for it, and to a design for another hanging of 1920 which was never executed.[51] A superimposed grid was introduced once more. Several sculptures by Carl Milles are included, and the two figures on top of the Pavilion may be no other than architect Eliel Saarinen, carrying a painter's palette and an architectural model, and possibly George G. Booth, the patron, personified by a black-booted bear wearing a tuxedo.[52]

It has been stated that the task of providing Kingswood with all its carpets and textiles took the work of twelve weavers under Loja Saarinen's supervision and that the job was completed within a year so that the school could open on time (fig. 152).[53] The looms were obviously of prime importance. Early records do not mention specific numbers of looms until June 1936 at which time five looms were added.[54] In 1939 sixteen looms are mentioned from twenty-eight to forty inches in width.[55] Early in 1941 a total of twenty-two looms are spoken of with two looms belonging to Loja Saarinen. They varied in size from twenty-eight inches to twelve feet.[56] The larger ones each required three to four weavers (fig. 147). By 1945 a total of thirty looms (including four harness looms) were in operation at the Academy, not to mention the many smaller ones being used at Kingswood. The type of loom used at Cranbrook was designed in 1936 by John P. Bexell, a talented cabinetmaker and the husband of one of Loja Saarinen's weavers. It was lightweight and could be operated easily. In 1945 at Loja's suggestion this loom was named the Cranbrook loom. It was patented and is still being manufactured today.

Material was purchased in this country or abroad. The order ledgers for 1929 provide numerous insights. "Zephyr" yarn, Craft yarn, Carpet Warp, and "Mudejara" skeins were purchased from Emile Bernat and Sons, Company, at that time located in Jamaica Plain, Massachusetts. Other supplies such as linen were ordered from C. O. Borgs, Lund, Sweden, and homespun came directly from Finland. Rayon thread was ordered by the color on small spools from Robinson Rayon Company, Inc., and "Rayon silk," a synthetic also called "Lustron," was also ordered.[57]

With the formal establishment of the Academy in 1932 and the first published announcements[58] regarding classes, Maja Wirde's teaching load must have been fairly light, for we find her teaching part-time (1932–33) at Kingswood School Cranbrook as well.[59] However, both engagements were short-lived; when the Depression finally hit Cranbrook in 1933, all craft studios were closed with the exception of Studio Loja Saarinen.[60] All craftsmen, among them Maja Wirde, were given notice. Their contracts expired at the end of June 1933.[61]

Maja Wirde left Cranbrook and went for the summer to Chicago, where she found employment at "A Century of Progress/1933 Chicago World's Fair." Thereafter, she returned to Algutsboda, Sweden, where she would live until her death in 1952.[62] Her colleague, Lillian Holm, would join her at the Swedish

Colorplate 36

MAJA ANDERSSON WIRDE (DESIGNER) AND STUDIO LOJA SAARINEN (WEAVERS). *Animal Carpet.* 1932. Linen warp, wool weft, wool pile; plain weave with four picks of weft between each row of knots. 152 × 108″. Cranbrook Academy of Art/Museum

151

MAJA ANDERSSON WIRDE. *Sketch for Animal Carpet.* c. 1932. Tracing paper, watercolor, and ink. Image 12 ¼ × 9 ¼″. Smålands Museum

152
*Kingswood School Cranbrook Library,
Showing Carpet, Curtain, and Upholstery
Materials.* The design vocabulary relates to
the window treatment. Maja Wirde de-
signed the ensemble for Studio Loja Saari-
nen in 1931. Photo courtesy Cranbrook
Academy of Art / Museum

Pavilion of the Chicago World's Fair.[63] It was Holm who, after Wirde's departure,
became weaving instructor at the Academy in 1934.[64] She also continued as a
weaving teacher at Kingswood in the Arts and Crafts department from 1933 to
1966.[65] In that year she retired and returned to Sweden.

Holm's weavings are stylistically quite distinct. Two hang in
the Auditorium Lobby at Kingswood. Photographs of seven additional weavings
have been found, all pictorial renderings, but the actual hangings have not been
located. Her *First Sight of New York* (pl. 40) combines architectural structures
with small, repeated rectangles which produce an enframement in the lower portion of the hanging and are carried into the upper half with a repeated triangular
shape. Abstracted human figures appear at right and left flanking the distant skyscrapers. Holm may have considered this piece one of her best. It was included in
an exhibition of contemporary art by local artisans at the Flint Institute of Arts in
1942.[66] In 1965, a year before Holm retired from Kingswood School Cranbrook
(and possibly from the Flint Institute where she also had taught for many years),
the hanging was given by her to the Flint Institute.[67]

Pipsan Saarinen Swanson was also involved in the creation of
Kingswood. As an interior decorator, she worked on the Auditorium—its stage
curtain, the ceiling with repeating large, circular lighting fixtures, and its wall
decorations (fig. 86).[68] She also was responsible for the Ballroom ceiling at Kingswood, an area today referred to as "Heaven."[69] Ceilings interested her; she had
done the Cranbrook School main lobby ceiling at the time when that building was

completed in 1927. Although Pipsan, together with her husband, Robert, had established a complete, contemporary interior design division in connection with his architectural firm, she continued her association with Cranbrook in that she taught "Costume Design" as well as "Batik Design Technique" from 1932 to 1933. She was provided with a "small, well equipped studio for the production of batiks the cost of the equipment being approximately $600.00,"[70] and appeared listed on the publicity folder announcing the Academy's 1932–33 curriculum. A contemporary described her as being "creative to her fingertips, with a marvelous sense of color and line, which her Mother also has . . ."[71] Although none of her batiks have survived, one of her dresses is still extant (fig. 153)[72] along with twenty-three fashion sketches (pls. 37, 38, 39) that date from this period.[73] The dress personifies the family's concern with the interrelationships of design elements so masterfully executed at Kingswood School Cranbrook, since its stepped pattern recalls the chimney and tower treatments seen there (figs. 36 and 38).

In 1935 Pipsan introduced another course at the Academy entitled "Contemporary Design of Interiors and Furnishings."[74] However, her teaching days soon drew to a close as interior design work within her husband's firm demanded more and more of her time. Along with all deeply involved architects and interior designers of that time, the Swansons realized that the contemporary interior required contemporary furnishings. As no such material was yet available it became the architect's and interior designer's task to design the needed furnishings. In 1939 the Swansons introduced through Johnson Furniture Company of Grand Rapids the first flexible furniture line, known as F.H.A., or Flexible Home Arrangements; this arrangement ultimately expanded to include sixteen manufacturers. Some of Pipsan's Cranbrook associates joined, including Marianne Strengell (fabrics and floor coverings), Charles Dusenbury (ceramics and sculpture), Ben Baldwin (interiors), and Lydia Winston (ceramics and dinnerware)[75] (see Miller and Eidelberg). In collaboration with her husband Pipsan designed furniture, as well as printed fabrics for Goodall Fabrics, metalware for Cray of Boston, lamps for Mutual Sunset Lamp Company, and glassware for U.S. Glass Company, as well as working as an interior designer for the Johnson showroom itself. She and her associates became known as the Saarinen-Swanson Group.[76]

From 1944 to 1947 Pipsan was a partner in the architectural firm of Saarinen, Swanson and Saarinen (see De Long and Miller), with her father, husband, and brother. She was responsible for the interiors. Among their projects were General Motors Technical Center, Milwaukee Cultural Center, the Des Moines Art Center, and Drake University.[77] In 1947 Pipsan and her husband formed a partnership, Swanson Associates. They worked on institutions, schools, hospitals, churches, and banks.[78] In the late 1950s Pipsan began to do private residences as well as business interiors.[79]

Several of Pipsan's carpets and textiles have survived. One example is *Spelunking* (pl. 42), a screenprinted textile which she designed for Edwin Raphael and Company. It shows her to have been an accomplished artist who knew how to interrelate patterns and colors most skillfully. The panel dates from the time when she received a first prize for printed textiles at the Michigan Artist-Craftsman's exhibition. Also from the sixties is a carpet (fig. 154) she designed which was manufactured by Suminoe Textile Company, Ltd., of Japan for E. T. Barwick Mills.

In addition to creating hangings and carpets for the Cranbrook campus, Studio Loja Saarinen also filled commissions. Among them were the carpets, curtains, and upholstery for the so-called "Frank Lloyd Wright Room," today part of the collection of the Victoria and Albert Museum in London.[80] This was originally an office that Wright designed for Edgar J. Kaufmann's department store in Pittsburgh. Wright designed the carpets and fabrics and had them woven at Studio Loja Saarinen under Loja's supervision. Wright knew she would be sympathetic to simplified designs and a controlled color scheme, since he had visited Cranbrook on several occasions during the 1930s (fig. 18) and had seen the furnishing materials at the residences and at Kingswood. Another commission, dating roughly to 1936–38, involved designs by Charles Eames for the John Philip Meyer

153

PIPSAN SAARINEN SWANSON (DESIGNER). *Dress.* c. 1933–35. Silk; plain weave with applied panels of silk, satin weave with leather, gold paint. 45 ¾ × approx. 35″ (at hip). Collection Ronald Saarinen Swanson

Colorplates 37, 38, 39

PIPSAN SAARINEN SWANSON. *Costume Designs.* c. 1932–33. Watercolor and pencil on paper. Plate 37: 14 ¼ × 5 ¾"; plate 38: 12 ¾ × 5 ⅞"; plate 39: 14 ⅛ × 5 ½". Cranbrook Academy of Art/Museum, Gift of Pipsan Saarinen Swanson

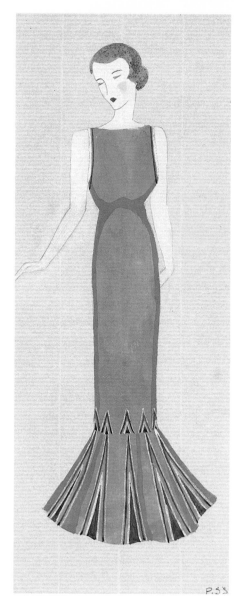

Colorplate 40

LILLIAN HOLM (DESIGNER AND WEAVER). *First Sight of New York.* 1930s. Linen, wool, and cotton; plain weave with discontinuous wefts (initialed *LH*). 82 × 64 ⅛". Flint Institute of Arts, Gift of Lillian Holm in memory of Ralph T. Sayles

House in St. Louis (see De Long and Miller). In a 1976 interview,[81] Eames talked about the carpets for this house and the great hesitation he initially had in approaching Loja Saarinen about having them woven at her studio. However, in the end he did ask her. One of the carpets is still in private hands in St. Louis.

Another commission of prime importance for Studio Loja Saarinen was the hanging ordered in connection with the building of the Tabernacle Church of Christ in Columbus, Indiana (today the First Christian Church). Both the sketch (pl. 41) and the large hanging (fig. 155) are still in existence. The subject is the Sermon on the Mount; this is the only known surviving textile with a religious subject that came out of the Saarinen studio. The church records describe the Sermon on the Mount as "the ideal for human conduct" and the hanging is said to suggest "worship as well as obedience."[82] The sketch, a colored pencil and gouache drawing, has been attributed to Eliel Saarinen; it is unsigned and undated. The hanging itself is signed in ink on a piece of appliquéd fabric attached to the lower left-hand corner on the reverse: "TAPESTRY was DESIGNED by ELIEL AND LOJA SAARINEN WOVEN on CRANBROOK LOOMS 1941 by: LILLIAN HOLM and RUTH INGVARSON SUPERVISED by LOJA SAARINEN."[83] A contemporary description states:

It had been months in the weaving . . . and had been woven by Lillian Holm and Ruth Ingvarson. One of the biggest tapestries woven in this country, and

probably as beautiful as any, for the colors are soft and rich. The large studio [Carl Milles' Cranbrook studio] was the only place with a high enough ceiling at Cranbrook to hang it. At the end of that huge room it was decorative and glowing. It must have been a great happiness to the weavers to see it in place, for as they could only judge the section, on which they were working. The subject of the tapestry was the Sermon on the Mount and it had as a whole a religious feeling, to my surprise for Mr. Saarinen had seemed to me something of a cynic.

From this description one also learns the following:

Pipsan (Loja's daughter) said her mother had worked on the tapestry for weeks after it was finished, accentuating the color here and there. She had worked on it on a large table, unrolling it and re-rolling as she finished a section. The whole tapestry had been woven in a large room in the big studio building; and the two weavers had woven steadily for months. I didn't see their names, but understood that Mrs. Holm's at least had been woven into it, to be sure of it being credited to her in time to come.[84]

To accentuate certain areas was indeed possible after the panel had been woven in the discontinuous weft technique. Additional threads could be inserted with a needle and the design emphasized where more visual attention was required.

Other commissions which entailed the making of textiles and carpets by Studio Loja Saarinen were for the Richard Hudnut Salon (1929–30) (see Miller) and the Yardley Shop (n.d.), both on Fifth Avenue in New York, and the Chrysler Showroom on Jefferson Avenue, Detroit (possibly 1934).[85]

In a letter to Loja Saarinen dated July 30, 1942, George Booth expressed his concern about the future of the Weaving department at Cranbrook: "For myself I am only very anxious to see that the Weaving department shall have a good number of students who leave Cranbrook with enthusiasm thus insuring us more students—we must try to have some very good rugs to exhibit—and be sure that the Cranbrook Looms have the reputation of being the best in the country—and our school the best place to learn how . . ." A month later Loja Saarinen answered him:

Concerning the students' [sic] Weaving Department and your wish to have "some very good rugs for exhibit," I would like to stress a few points to avoid some disappointments in the future. The students are, of course, eager to get as much as possible out of the Weaving course, wherefore they spend most of their time in doing samples of different weaves, which will be of use to them later on. Very few of them have either time, means nor opportunity to make larger pieces or rugs or other textiles. Exhibitions like Cranbrook Pavilion in 1935 (which you liked so much), and at the Detroit Art Institute 1932 [sic], cannot be expected anymore because all textiles came from my studio and not from the students' department. The good reputation and influence our Weaving Department has had throughout the country is, to the greatest part due to the large and durable things from my studio.

In this same letter she listed the reasons for the retirement she was being "forced into." "I am now to give up my work. Because of the War I have not got any orders and have no means to do things for exhibition or to keep them in stock. I enjoyed doing the work and I knew that my work was the best advertising for the Weaving Department which after all was my baby and simultaneously it has been a source of inspiration for the students."[86] In 1945 Booth's concern about "some very good rugs for exhibit" was addressed in that a special fund was established "for the purpose of designing and producing an exhibition of superior Cranbrook workmanship in the weaving of rugs."[87] A total of twenty pieces was created to travel the country after an initial Cranbrook showing.

A number of textile artists and technicians came to Cranbrook during and after Loja's tenure who carried on the traditions of excellence and innovation she established.

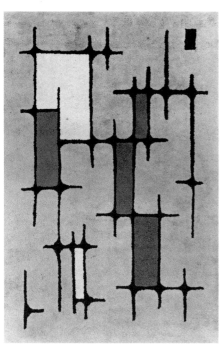

154

PIPSAN SAARINEN SWANSON (DESIGNER) AND E. T. BARWICK MILLS/SUMINOE TEXTILE CO., LTD. (MANUFACTURER). *Carpet.* c. 1961. Wool pile; hand-hooked. 9′ 2″ × 6′ 1″. Collection Ronald Saarinen Swanson

When Marianne Strengell arrived in February 1937 she was no stranger for she had known the Saarinen and Milles families for years. Her mother, Anna, was an accomplished interior designer. Her father, Gustaf, was a well-known architect and author. It was he who had accompanied Eliel Saarinen to Chicago in 1923, the year of the Chicago Tribune competition (see De Long), and it was he who had acted as Saarinen's interpreter while in the States. Marianne Strengell recalled that when she was a teenager, Saarinen, on one of his summer trips, made the suggestion that she come to America one day.[88] By the time she was twenty-eight years of age, this suggestion had become a reality.

Strengell received her basic education and artistic training in Helsinki, where she studied with Elsa Gullberg, the renowned Swedish textile artist. Young though she was, her accomplishments were many, including participation in international exhibitions in Barcelona (1929), Antwerp (1932), Milan (1933), and Paris (1937). Information contained in a letter requesting permission for her to enter the United States with the status of professional artist is noteworthy: "Capable instructors are extremely scarce in the United States. The Art of Handweaving has almost died out except in a few centers. The Government is attempting to revive the art in some of its resettlement projects."[89] Strengell's visa was granted and she was employed at Cranbrook as "permanent resident artist giving instruction in the design and weaving of modern textiles."[90] From 1937 until

155

LOJA AND ELIEL SAARINEN (DESIGNERS) AND LILLIAN HOLM AND RUTH INGVARSON OF STUDIO LOJA SAARINEN (WEAVERS). *The Sermon on the Mount.* 1941. First Christian Church, Columbus, Indiana

156

DAVID FREDENTHAL (DESIGNER). *Sketch for a Hanging.* 1937. Pastel on paper. 8 × 10″. Photo courtesy Geoffrey Locklin. Collection Miriam Kellogg Fredenthal

Colorplate 41

ELIEL SAARINEN. *Sketch for The Sermon on the Mount.* 1941. Pencil, colored pencil, and gouache on paper. Image 26 ⅞ × 11 ⅞″. Collection Robert Saarinen Swanson

157

DAVID FREDENTHAL (DESIGNER) AND MIRIAM KELLOGG (FREDENTHAL) (WEAVER). *Hanging.* 1937. Linen, wool, silk, and cotton; plain weave with discontinuous wefts, fringed. 28 × 42 ½″. Photo courtesy Geoffrey Locklin. Collection Miriam Kellogg Fredenthal

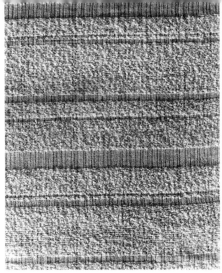

158

MARIANNE STRENGELL (DESIGNER) AND
GERDA NYBERG (WEAVER). *Curtain Material.* c. 1945. Cotton and rayon warp, looped
mohair, linen, rayon, and metal thread weft;
plain weave with supplementary wefts. 115
× 37 ¾″. Cranbrook Academy of Art/Museum

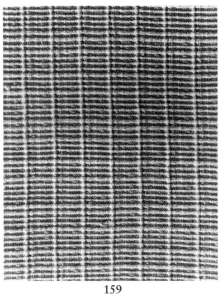

159

MARIANNE STRENGELL (DESIGNER) AND
GERDA NYBERG (WEAVER). *Upholstery Material.* c. 1945. Wool, cotton, and rayon
warp, cotton and jute weft; plain weave
(dyed). 107 ½ × 31 ½″. Cranbrook Academy of Art/Museum

1942 she was Instructor of Weaving under Loja Saarinen; she actually took over the department in 1942, the year Loja retired.[91]

Strengell's contributions were many and she was acknowledged early on for her splendid accomplishments.[92] She enjoyed complete freedom in her teaching even though the department remained for the first five years under Loja's supervision.[93] The instruction Strengell provided was directed toward the creation of designs and their execution, including "rugs, drapery fabrics, dress materials, etc.," until 1942, the year the Academy was acknowledged as an institution of higher learning with the power to grant degrees by the State of Michigan. From then on, graduate students enrolled in weaving for a two-year program. They were first introduced to the designing of samples and large pieces on a 4–10 harness loom. They also were taught designing for the power loom; the study of and experimentation with new materials; and analysis and research work which included dyeing, spinning, yarn performance, dress design, and merchandising. Courses for beginning students introduced "construction, possibilities and limitations of a loom, warpwinding, setting up warp, counting of materials. Experiments in textures and techniques on a 2–4 harness loom and the use and analysis of different materials."[94]

One can clearly discern Strengell's ability and technical knowledge in these course announcements, as all of these topics were of prime importance to her. Of great interest also is a 1942 teaching outline signed and submitted by her. In detail it described her approach, including handspinning and extensive study in regard to powerloom weaving.[95] During the first graduate year a course in dyeing is listed; during the second graduate year, work on the powerloom, trips to factories, study of Jacquard looms [sic], block printing, and silkscreen-printing are mentioned. To read this report today is most interesting in that the plan was indeed implemented in nearly all aspects, including the addition of a teaching assistant (Robert D. Sailors) in June 1944, and the acquisition of a powerloom (installed January 1945).[96]

One aspect not addressed in Strengell's course listings is pictorial weaving. Studio Loja Saarinen had executed abstract, yet representational, weavings and the subject was most certainly included in the Kingswood curriculum over the years. However, at the Academy pictorial weaving was not taught. The only exception known to have been made was in 1937.

Curiously enough, the student involved was not a weaving student. It was Miriam Kellogg (Fredenthal) (Sculpture, 1937), who enrolled with Carl Milles in the fall of 1937, but who learned when she arrived that Milles had unexpectedly returned to Sweden. According to her recollections, at Strengell's suggestion Kellogg tried weaving and liked what she was doing. Eventually, one of her closest friends, David Fredenthal (Painting, 1936–37), did a sketch (fig. 156) for her which she intended to translate into a wall hanging (fig. 157). Little did she realize the objections that would arise. The matter was brought to the attention of the faculty by Eliel Saarinen and his final decision was paraphrased by her as follows: "It is not our intention to encourage the textile medium to be used to express fine art concepts, but since your project combines the effort of two students we will permit you to execute it. You must promise to complete the hanging by the end of the semester."[97] The technique to be used was a plain weave with the pattern to be inserted with discontinuous wefts, a favored technique that Studio Loja Saarinen had used ever since its inception, as we have seen.[98]

Strengell's style of teaching was advanced for her time; it was informal and emphasized working within a framework of limitations. Aside from experimentation with design, fibers, and colors, she required her students to consider seven criteria while planning projects: materials, price, climate, labor, equipment, architectural placement, and personalities.[99] Her teaching was forward-looking.

In 1944 a policy was established at Strengell's suggestion in regard to her students. As she said:

I feel, and Mr. Saarinen agrees with me fully, that it is of utmost importance for the student of weaving and textile design to be able to execute work for orders or sale. Learning to handle the client, analyze the problem as to environment, personality, price, etc., learning to present a sketch that will give a layman an exact picture of the goods he will receive and carrying out the order is of great educational value to a student. If the student feels that there already now is a market for him this fact will stimulate greater efforts and he will also be able to execute many more pieces, as there would be a rotation and money to place in materials, which the average student does not have available.

This policy was approved with the stipulation that the faculty would provide guidance as long as the student was at the Academy. It was further felt that the materials turned out had to be of a "quality and standard which the Academy could approve without reservation."[100]

The first ten years Strengell spent at Cranbrook were governed by limited availability of materials and a day-to-day "waste not, want not" philosophy. They were also years of tremendous accomplishments in the field of manmade fibers and in the development of mass production. Detroit and the automobile industry flourished and needed good-looking, durable fabrics. It was in these areas that Strengell fulfilled her responsibility as an "active member of [her] profession, enjoying national recognition,"[101] as George G. Booth had anticipated when the Trust Indenture for the Academy was written.

It is understandable that during the war years practical issues were considered to be of foremost importance in the field of textile production and that pictorial weaving was felt to constitute an unnecessary luxury. Artists focused their talents on products which (through mass production) would reach more than a select few. Lower prices no longer had to mean poor quality. High quality was available but only through people like Strengell who could translate the artistic quality of the handmade object into a mass-produced object in her medium and for her manufacturers. Strengell produced hand-woven samples as prototypes for mass-produced fabrics. She employed Gerda Nyberg of Pontiac, Michigan, as her weaver. Nyberg had been born in 1903 near Ramsberg, Sweden, and had come to Michigan in 1928. Her association with the Academy began in 1930, when she joined the staff of Studio Loja Saarinen.[102] Representative of Strengell's designs and Nyberg's weaving from the years 1945–60 are five woven fabric lengths (figs. 158, 159, 160, 161, 162). Panels were created by combining natural and synthetic fibers in a most skillful way. These pieces are inventive in their combinations and the foremost earth tones introduce a wealth of colors unheard of a century before.

During these years printed fabrics were also reintroduced. Commercially woven fabric bolts could be decorated through silkscreen printing, a process which eliminated the time-consuming weaving process. Silkscreen on fabric had been introduced in 1938 by a group led by Anthony Velonis, who began a project through the WPA in New York.[103] The concept of screen printing is ancient and has been used in the Orient for centuries; in its American application it became a product of the war and postwar years. Artists like Angelo Testa, Noemi Raymond, and Dan Cooper provided the industry with striking, simplified patterns. In the 1940 all-American competition of furniture and fabric design at The Museum of Modern Art, New York, a category of printed fabrics was included.[104] In 1944, the "International Textile Exhibition" at Greensboro, North Carolina, included a printed textile category among its divisions.[105] In 1946, Testa and Raymond were included in the "First Biennial Exhibition of Contemporary American Fabrics and Ceramics" at the Cranbrook Academy of Art/Museum.[106] At the Academy, Strengell included in her 1942 plan of study the study of "Blockprinting, silkscreen, etc."[107] In 1947 she herself designed *Shooting Stars* (fig. 163), her first printed fabric and, incidentally, the first printed fabric Knoll Associates would carry in their textile collections.[108] Other printed fabrics followed, among them three now at Cranbrook (pl. 43 and figs. 164 and 165). Plate 43 and figure 164 were produced by double-printing the screen. Clear and precise lines form shapes juxtaposed through color combinations. Abstract in their designs, these fabrics could easily be used for curtain or upholstery materials. It is of interest to note that

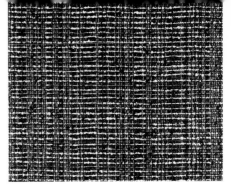

160
MARIANNE STRENGELL (DESIGNER) AND GERDA NYBERG (WEAVER). *Wall-Covering Material.* c. 1950. Nylon and rayon warp, mohair, metal thread, and cellophane weft; plain weave. 8′ 3½″ × 3′ 4½″. Cranbrook Academy of Art/Museum

161
MARIANNE STRENGELL (DESIGNER) AND GERDA NYBERG (WEAVER). *Curtain Material.* c. 1956. Cotton warp, looped mohair, rayon, and metal thread weft; plain weave with supplementary wefts. 129 × 38″. Cranbrook Academy of Art/Museum

162
MARIANNE STRENGELL (DESIGNER) AND GERDA NYBERG (WEAVER). *Upholstery Material.* c. 1955–60. Cotton, rayon, and metal thread warp, synthetic fiber weft; plain weave. 108½ × 37″. Cranbrook Academy of Art/Museum

Colorplate 42

PIPSAN SAARINEN SWANSON (DESIGNER) AND EDWIN RAPHAEL CO. (PRINTER). *Spelunking*. 1952–62. Screen-printed silk; satin weave. 105 × 52″. Cranbrook Academy of Art/Museum, Gift of J. Robert F. Swanson

painting and design students at the Academy would address the question of printed textile design over the years.[109]

Strengell worked with numerous industrial designers, including Raymond Loewy (United Airlines Jets), Russel Wright (coordinated home furnishings), the Saarinen-Swanson Group (fabrics), and General Motors ("Motorama" in 1958 and 1960). In the United States she designed fabrics, carpets, printed

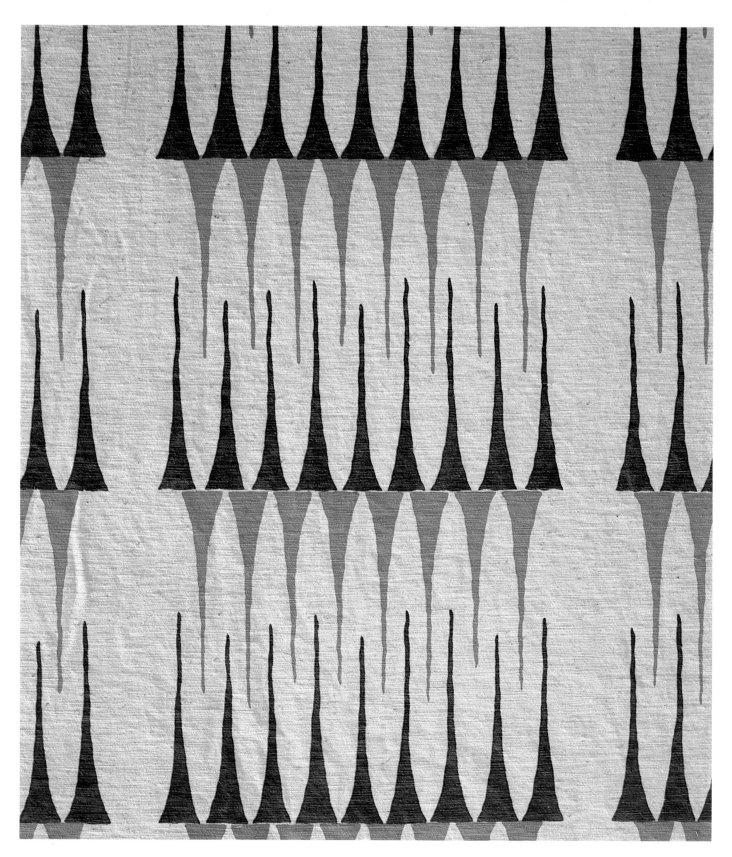

textiles, screens, blankets, bedspreads, table mats, and so on for many companies including Knoll Associates, Cabin Crafts, Horner Woolen Mills, Owens Corning Fiberglas Co., V'Soske, Alcoa, Pacific Weavers, Tai Ping, Fieldcrest, and Karastan. Abroad she worked with and designed printed fabrics for Artek in Helsinki and for Finska Bomulls in Aktiebolaget; automobile fabrics for Happich in Germany; and printed fabrics, woven materials, carpets, automobile fabrics, upholstery and

Colorplate 43

MARIANNE STRENGELL (DESIGNER). *Curtain Material.* c. 1954. Screen-printed cotton; plain weave. 70 ½ × 38 ½". Cranbrook Academy of Art/Museum, Gift of Mrs. Walter P. Hickey

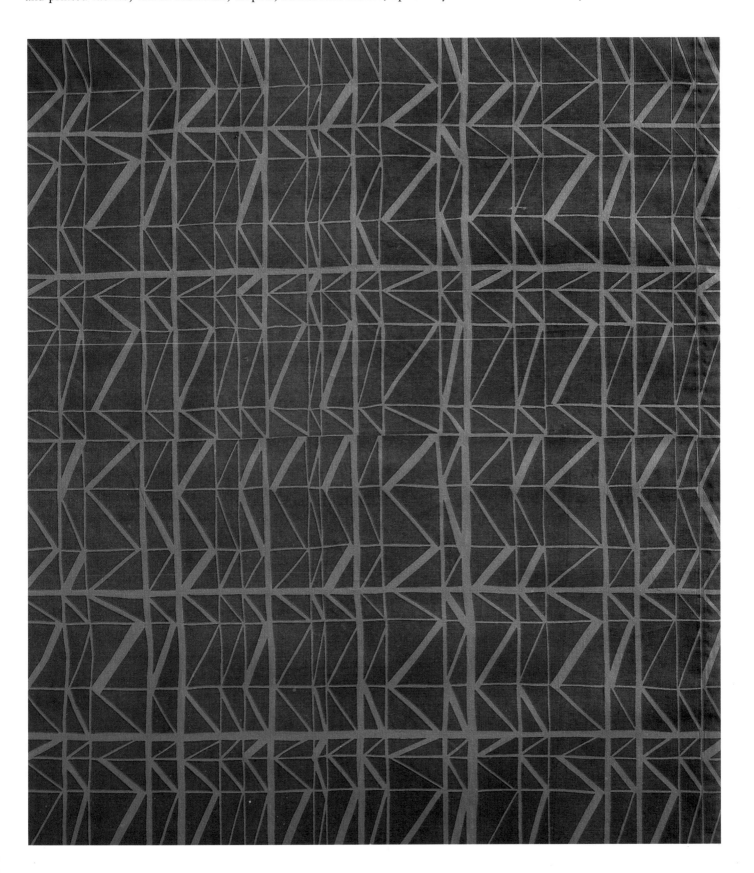

dress materials, table mats, and other fabrics for companies in South America and Asia. She worked with Eero Saarinen and Associates on the General Motors Technical Center, designing handwoven carpets for all lobbies as well as additional handwoven carpets and powerloomed floor coverings and fabrics for the Research Building; all fabrics and carpets for the Main Restaurant; and all fabrics for the major offices in the Styling Building (see De Long and Miller). Strengell also worked with Skidmore, Owings and Merrill, Edward Durrell Stone, Henry Hebbeln, Harold H. Fisher and Associates, and Olav Hammarstrom, and has shown in over seventy exhibitions since 1937.

In 1951 Strengell traveled to Japan and the Philippines as advisor on weaving and textile design for cottage industry under the International Cooperation Administration. Aided by Hammarstrom, her husband, who had been appointed furniture advisor for the project, Strengell devised a loom which became known as the Strengell Loom. It was designed so that it could be operated with or without a fly shuttle and was sturdy enough that carpets and heavy materials as well as very fine and thin cloths could be woven on it. In width the loom measured forty-two inches.[110]

Five years after retiring from Cranbrook in 1961, Strengell was invited by the government of Jamaica to start a weaving program, analyze natural resources and fibers, select equipment, set up a studio, and train fifteen weavers, who would thereafter take over and lead the project, developing a line of Jamaican

163

MARIANNE STRENGELL (DESIGNER). *Curtain Material for Knoll Associates, Inc., entitled "Shooting Stars."* 1947. Rayon; plain weave; screen-printed. 110 × 45". Collection Marianne Strengell

designs. The following year she returned to Jamaica to lecture, plan a new studio, train more weavers, and expand the original design collection. Travel, commissions, exhibitions, and experimentation with color, texture, and fibers as well as photography, painting and textile collage continue to occupy Marianne Strengell today.[111]

In 1945 Cranbrook Academy had introduced its first annual student exhibition and in the following year, the first of its biennial exhibitions of contemporary American fabrics and ceramics was held. These exhibitions were of prime importance for they exposed faculty and students alike to the very latest accomplishments within the two disciplines. The exhibitions were invitational and lasted until 1954. In addition to Cranbrook faculty and alumni, they included key professionals in the field.[112] In 1949 the second biennial took place.[113] The third biennial was held in 1951.[114] The fourth and final exhibition in 1953 did not include Cranbrook alumni and faculty.[115] The work of many accomplished and competent alumni of the Weaving department at Cranbrook Academy were included in these and other exhibitions. Unfortunately, their achievements could not be covered here nor could they all be identified and listed.[116] However, two graduates who were students in the forties deserve special mention. They are Robert D. Sailors and Charles Edmund (Ed) Rossbach.

Sailors' first contact with Cranbrook occurred during the summer of 1941; he received his M.F.A. in May 1943. Due to his "outstanding ability,"

164

MARIANNE STRENGELL (DESIGNER). *Curtain Material.* c. 1947. Linen; plain weave; screen-printed (one screen double-printed). 9' 8 ½" × 4' 2 ½". Cranbrook Academy of Art / Museum

Colorplate 44

ROBERT D. SAILORS (DESIGNER AND WEAVER). *Curtain Material.* 1940s. Mohair and metallic thread; plain weave. 36 ½ × 11″. Collection Robert D. Sailors

Colorplate 45

ROBERT D. SAILORS (DESIGNER AND WEAVER). *Curtain Material.* 1953. Rayon warp, rayon and lurex weft; plain weave. 151 × 36″. Cranbrook Academy of Art/ Museum

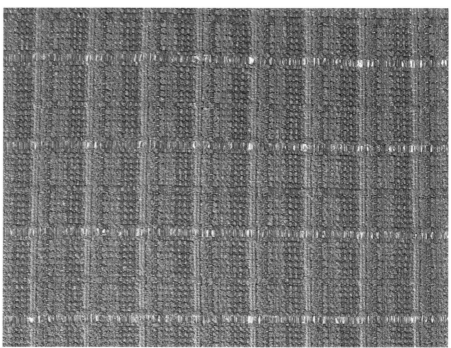

a straight-A record, and high recommendations,[117] he was granted a full fellowship for the academic year 1943–44. In June 1944 he became the first Weaving department graduate to teach in the capacity of "Assistant Director and Instructor at the Weaving Department" under Marianne Strengell. In 1944 he was sent to the Rhode Island School of Design to familiarize himself with the functions of a powerloom, since the Cranbrook Trustees were considering the purchase of one.[118] Urgent letters reached Cranbrook from Rhode Island in regard to motor, transformer, and voltage information needed in his study and analysis.[119] A powerloom, Model S1, was finally acquired from Crompton and Knowels Corporation of Worcester, Massachusetts, and installed in the Academy's Weaving department in January 1945. It was a silk weaving loom with small bobbins (these proved difficult to use for handweavers due to their size). It wove fabric sixty-four inches wide. Teaching on the powerloom became Sailors' responsibility.[120] To integrate powerloom weaving into the curriculum was not difficult, for since the early 1940s the subject had been included from a theoretical point of view.[121] Now it was possible for a student during his second year of study to design samples specifically for the powerloom, and research was carried out addressing questions such as designing for a specific price bracket and merchandising. It was indeed a rare possibility to be able to study hand weaving and powerloom weaving together and the Cranbrook powerloom venture was of great interest to other institutions that taught weaving during the forties, including The Art Institute of Chicago[122] and Black Mountain College, North Carolina.[123]

Sailors enjoyed teaching and must have been good at it.[124] His thesis was entitled "Contemporary Instruction for Contemporary Weaving." How marvelous to have been able to explore some of his theories in practice! Sailors had studied with Strengell and had been exposed to her experiments with man-made fibers, colors, and textures during the early forties. Like her, he dealt strictly with non-pictorial creations. He experimented with everything, including "burlap, awning canvas, floor mops and corn husks."[125] In his recollections of his early days at Cranbrook he describes how he would go to the Five-and-Dime Store to search for anything that could be utilized in weaving. There he found the "chore boy," a pot scrubber made of copper wire. He unravelled it and used it in his weaving.[126]

Sailors' inventiveness is well documented in his own collection of six-by-six inch sample weavings. Torn cotton strips were inserted as wefts; exposed warps were introduced, and leather, sisal, jute, Naugahyde, and wooden sticks were arranged in clever combinations. The use of Lurex, rayon, and other synthetics in combination with natural fibers has continued to intrigue him (pls. 44 and 45 and fig. 166).

In 1946 Sailors nearly left Cranbrook to join the Puerto Rico Industrial Development Company as Head of their Weaving Division. However, he was reluctant to accept a position unless he could get a one year's leave of absence from the Academy. The company, on the other hand, was interested in having a longer commitment from him. In the end, the position was filled by another talented Cranbrook weaving student, Geraldine Funk (Alvarez), who after graduating in 1944 had joined Dorothy W. Liebes' studio in San Francisco. Sailors continued to teach at Cranbrook, participated in competitions such as the "1945 La France Industries," Philadelphia, and did commission work which included curtain material for George G. Booth, woven on the powerloom,[127] carpets for Zoltan Sepeshy's residence, and bolts of fabric in a "herringbone" weave for Frank Lloyd Wright's Albert Adelman house in Fox Point, Wisconsin.[128] He stayed at Cranbrook until the end of 1947, when—due to financial difficulties—the position of Instructor in Weaving was eliminated.[129] Sailors had a contract with the Celanese Corporation of America in his pocket when he left; it involved designing yarns from their fibers and weaving fabrics "to be used in dress goods for Lord and Taylor in New York."[130] He set up his own company in a small town at Bitely, Michigan, and advertised "Handwoven and Power Loomed Fabrics," an unusual combination as it was common practice to specialize in either one or the other technique. He eventually employed twenty-three individuals and was represented in showrooms in Chicago (Richard Muller), Detroit (Edward Tomalka), Grand Rapids (Arthur

Colorplate 46

ED ROSSBACH (DESIGNER AND PRINTER). *Curtain or Upholstery Material.* 1952–53. Stenciled Mexican cotton; plain weave. 123 × 34 ¾″. Collection Ed Rossbach

165

MARIANNE STRENGELL (DESIGNER). *Curtain Material.* c. 1955. Linen, plain weave; screen-printed (one screen double-printed). 9′ 9″ × 4′. Cranbrook Academy of Art/Museum

166

ROBERT D. SAILORS (DESIGNER AND WEAVER). *Upholstery Material.* 1950s. Lurex; plain weave. 67 ¼ × 22 ¾″. Collection Robert D. Sailors

L. Shera), Miami (Otto Lagus), Los Angeles (Norman Hans), as well as New York, Minneapolis, and Dallas.

The textiles included in this exhibition illustrate his approach. They are outspoken statements and include metallic warps or wefts in conjunction with traditional fibers, or are woven entirely of synthetics. They are examples of hand weaving which could, however, be reproduced in powerloom weaving, and were created after the selected fibers had been fully studied, including their limitations.

Sailors has participated in numerous exhibitions since his years at Cranbrook, among them the "Annual International Textile Exhibition" at the University of North Carolina, Greensboro. In a revealing letter written in 1947 to Noma Hardin, Jury Chairman, Sailors emphasized the special importance of those shows:

I am certain that if [the exhibitions] had been started ten years ago the fabrics available to the public today would be in better taste. Until recently there has been no reference or standard that the weavers, designers or manufacturers could utilize. The handweavers had no goal and could only copy the colonial patterns handed down or diagrammed in many books and thereby lost the greatest joy in weaving, namely, that of creating. The designers were in a similar predicament in that few were able to experiment on handlooms to discover new possibilities with new and old materials. Most of their work was done on paper and the materials used were usually the same year after year designing the same type of fabric which the company was known for. The manufacturers were content to let the designers continue this monotonous designing for after all, the company was making money. The purpose of these exhibitions was of great and far reaching importance. For the first time in history of art exhibitions, the textile designer has the opportunity to show and see contemporary work in all its phases, with every section of the United States represented and as many foreign countries as conditions will permit. The demand for creative designers has never been as great as it is today and in the near and expanding future, when so much machinery stands in need of cultural direction. Textile design and production are making history.[131]

Another star student of the forties was Charles Edmund (Ed) Rossbach. He had an M.A. in Art Education from Columbia University, New York and had taught before the War interrupted his life. He spent the years from 1942 to 1945 in the Signal Corps, Alaska Communication System. As a recipient of the G.I. Bill, he came to Cranbrook Academy in the spring of 1946, graduating in August 1947. His interest was clearly defined in a statement accompanying his application form: "After almost four years in the Army, I feel the need to participate as a student in a group which regards art as significant in Society. I selected Cranbrook as offering the most stimulating environment—of teachers and students earnestly absorbed in their art. At present I have the opportunity to teach art at a State University; however, before returning to the teaching profession I wish again to be a student doing creative work of my own." He was not alone—a great many men reached Cranbrook as a result of the G.I. Bill and the student enrollment changed considerably (see Clark and Taragin). Rossbach elected to major in ceramics with a minor in weaving. It was, however, in the field of design—and textile design in particular—that he would make a career. He took courses with Strengell, Sailors, and (during the summer session of 1947) with Antoinette Prestini.[132] At the Honors Convocation in May 1947, his accomplishments were well recognized for he received not only an award in ceramics, but also Acquisitions Honors and Honorable Mentions in Weaving. After graduation he taught for three years at the University of Washington and then joined the faculty at the University of California, Berkeley, where his field of expertise became design and textile design.

Rossbach has acknowledged the strong influence Sailors had on him.[133] He has become one of the top design professors in America, carrying the Cranbrook vision to the university and in so doing inspiring hundreds of students during his long and productive career in the fiber medium. This was exactly what George G. Booth had hoped for.[134] Rossbach's accomplishments as a practicing artist included in exhibitions began during his student days at Cranbrook. He has also authored books on marionettes, basketry, and—most recently—the art of paisley.[135]

Textiles by Rossbach included here illustrate his skill not only as a weaver but also as a designer who is not opposed to occasionally introducing pattern in a functional fabric intended for upholstery (pl. 46) or, for that matter, into carpets. The occasional inclusion of synthetic fibers (fig. 167 and pls. 48 and 49) shows him to be a conservative designer and weaver, well aware of what is technically possible and available, but still equally concerned with natural fibers (fig. 168 and pl. 47) and their inherent qualities.

It was through Ed Rossbach that Jack Lenor Larsen found his way to the Academy. Larsen met Rossbach when Larsen returned to the University of Washington in 1948. As one of Rossbach's students, Larsen assisted him in teaching weaving classes. Although Larsen had originally selected furniture design as his professional field, by 1947, and after his initial introduction to weaving, he had found his true metier. He worked in Los Angeles with Dorthea Hulse, an accomplished handweaver and teacher. He was her student, wove for her, and subsequently became her design assistant. In 1947 he met Dorothy W. Liebes, who encouraged him and invited him to her townhouse showroom. This visit was of great importance to the young Larsen. "Disillusioned by the array," he has said,

167

ED ROSSBACH (DESIGNER AND WEAVER). *Casement Material.* 1946–47. Cotton and cellophane; open plain weave. 100 ¼ × 32″. Collection Ed Rossbach

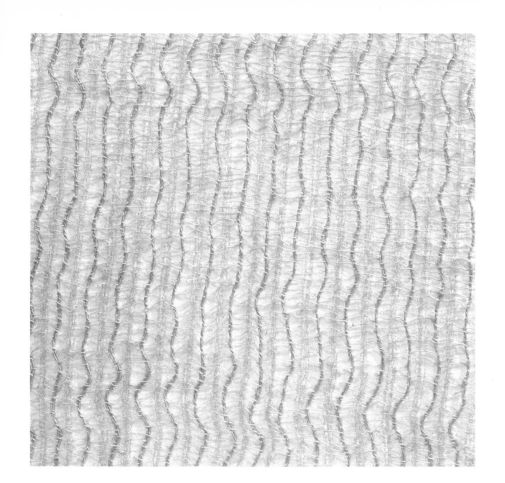

"I decided upon resuming work at the University of Washington."[136] There he majored in art and textiles. His thesis was entitled "Some Contemporary Implications of Ancient Peruvian Textiles"; he had had firsthand exposure to the latter through a friend, Chan Khan, who had moved to Seattle from Lima with a fine collection of Peruvian textiles and other artifacts. Larsen had a small studio, his own looms, and began to work professionally on commissions from Arthur Morgan Design Associates and Del Teet, Seattle.

Thus Larsen came to Cranbrook as a weaver and craftsman-designer who knew exactly what he wanted. There was no other institution in America that could have taught him to understand materials and techniques as well as giving him exposure to faculty and students who were interested in his own as well as related fields. His major became weaving, his minor metalsmithing, and he was accepted as a full scholarship student under Marianne Strengell.[137] Aside from the faculty's supervision and critiquing, of equal importance was the interchange with one's peers.[138] What seems important is the fact that in spite of this communal closeness, diversity was ever present and the seemingly easy temptation to copy one's colleagues' work somehow never surfaced.

By the spring of 1951 Larsen had his M.F.A.; his thesis was entitled "Notes on Textile Designing for Mass Production." Although he had initially intended to become a teacher at either an art school or at a university, teaching was not going to become part of his career. After graduation from the Academy, Larsen moved to New York, started his studio there, formed Jack Lenor Larsen, incorporated in 1953, and initiated Larsen Design Studio by 1958 with Win A. Anderson as President.

Aspects of production preoccupied Larsen; handweaving versus powerloom weaving became an issue of immense importance to him. The exposure to powerloom weaving at Cranbrook proved most helpful for he had been taught to look upon the powerloom as "a handloom with motor."[139] It gave him a confidence which most handweavers did not have; to them the handloom and the powerloom had nothing in common. Larsen's success would manifest itself in the ability to translate handwoven characteristics into mass-produced textiles using "the many yarns and random repeat that became a Larsen style and a widespread market influence."[140] Larsen recognized the importance of aesthetics and functional requirements, the relationship of the designer to stylists, and the necessity of having a thorough knowledge of all processes, of being a practicing weaver (who does not just work on graph paper), of being willing to acquaint oneself with the mills that produce goods, and of having a complete knowledge of weaves, fibers, and yarns—natural or synthetic.

Within ten years, Jack Lenor Larsen, incorporated had soared to international recognition with branches in Zurich, Stuttgart, and Paris. In the fifties, sixties, and seventies Larsen travelled extensively throughout the world. He also participated in numerous exhibitions including shows that focused on his work and its widespread influence on other textile artists. Larsen has published widely[141] and has executed countless commissions and received awards internationally over the years. His textiles are represented among the holdings of major museum textile collections such as those of The Art Institute of Chicago; Cooper-Hewitt Museum of Design; the Metropolitan Museum of Art; The Museum of Modern Art; Philadelphia Museum of Art; The Detroit Institute of Arts; Archives of American Art, Washington, D.C.; Kunstindustrimuseet, Copenhagen; Victoria and Albert Museum, London; Jerusalem Museum; Royal Scottish Museum, Edinburgh; and Museum Bellerive, Zurich.[142]

Jack Larsen's accomplishments are phenomenal and speak for themselves. Known generally as the most publicized Cranbrook graduate, he has carried the Cranbrook vision around the world. One is reminded of a statement he made in his Cranbrook application papers: ". . . should I be accepted at Cranbrook Academy of Art I will do my best to be worthy of its name and its faculty . . ."[143] He has kept his word. His influence upon American design has been tremendous and continues to be so. His corporation today includes Thaibok Fabrics, Ltd., Larsen Carpet and Leather Divisions, as well as a furniture division

168

ED ROSSBACH (DESIGNER AND WEAVER). *Upholstery Material.* 1952. Silk; four-harness variation; plain weave. 101 × 38″. Collection Ed Rossbach

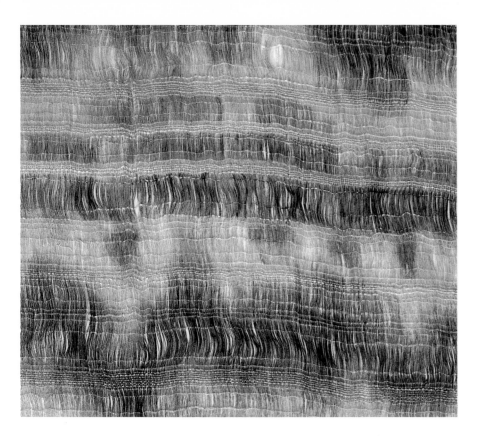

Colorplate 50

JACK LENOR LARSEN (DESIGNER) AND JACK LENOR LARSEN, INC. (MANUFACTURER). *Painted Linen.* 1953. Warp-painted linen, open plain weave. 105 × 39″. Jack Lenor Larsen, inc.

Colorplate 51

JACK LENOR LARSEN (DESIGNER) AND JACK LENOR LARSEN, INC. (MANUFACTURER). *Remoulade.* 1956. Twenty-seven fibers including wool, cotton, linen, silk, jute, rayon, metallic thread, etc.; plain weave with supplementary warp floats. 50 ½ × 43 ¾″. Jack Lenor Larsen, inc.

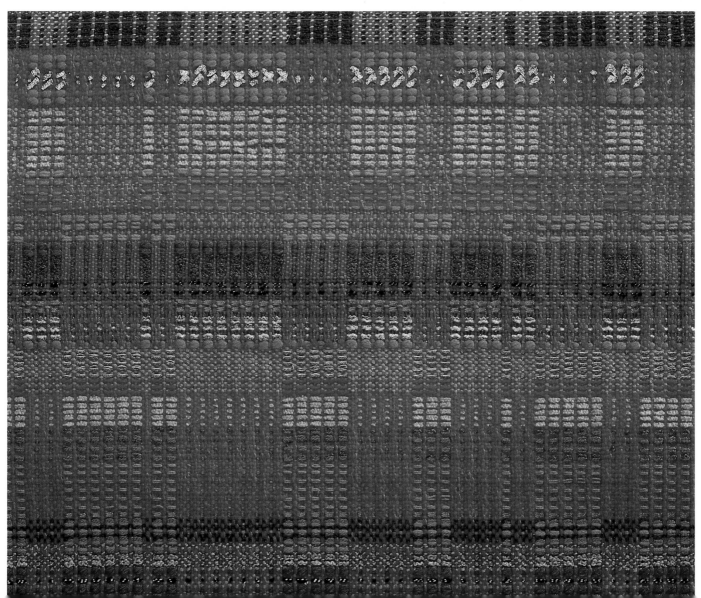

169

JACK LENOR LARSEN (DESIGNER) AND JACK
LENOR LARSEN, INC. (MANUFACTURER). *Interplay*. 1960. Saran monofilament; warp
knot construction. Jack Lenor Larsen inc.

established in 1976. His international empire includes thirty production centers
and an equal number of showrooms around the world. Larsen is the epitome of
Cranbrook talent that knows no limitation and, once attuned to the process of
creating, can translate this ability into other disciplines.

Larsen's textiles in this exhibition date from 1953–60. *Painted
Linen* (pl. 50) shows him juxtaposing a painted warp with an open plain weave.
It exemplifies the so-called "exhibition length," which—in addition to six-inch-by-
six-inch samples—was the routine means by which textiles were executed by students while at Cranbrook. *Painted Linen* came out of Larsen's first New York
studio, and its combination of an open plain weave with additional patternization
in the painted warp was fairly unique at that time. (The technique was, of course,
an ancient, non-European, one which found French interpretation during the eighteenth and nineteenth centuries in warp-printed silks.) *Remoulade* (pl. 51) of 1956
introduces Larsen as a designer free of all color restrictions. In this he followed in
the footsteps of his instructor, Marianne Strengell, and also of Dorothy W. Liebes.
Somber tones are replaced by a primary color palette, introducing materials which
would be used in interiors and would revolutionize interior decoration. *Interplay*
(fig. 169), manufactured in 1960 and still available in several colors, presents Larsen as a designer unafraid of experiments, this time with a warp knit casement of
saran monofilament. Finally, *Bamako* (pl. 47), designed in 1960 by Rossbach and
produced by Larsen in 1962–63, represents a joint venture of Jack Lenor Larsen,

incorporated, for Larsen frequently purchases designs from artists or employs them as needed.

In the discipline of weaving, Cranbrook introduced Swedish traditions to America in that it employed craftsmen who had either studied at Hand-arbetets Vänner in Stockholm or at the Märta Måås Fjetterstrom Studio in Båstad. With Loja Saarinen, Pipsan Saarinen Swanson, and Marianne Strengell, Finnish and European Arts and Crafts training reached Cranbrook. Weaving was never looked upon as folk art. Along with all the other decorative or applied arts it was seen in direct relationship to architecture. With the Saarinens this concept included the idea of the interconnection between a specific environment and everything that was to furnish it. Design became the means by which this theory could be achieved. Carpets, hangings, and furnishing materials carried motifs found in floor, ceiling, window, or wall treatments executed in stone, brick, wood, or metal. If pictorial images were used in weaving, as with the branching tree or the peacock motifs, their use was integrated to comply with the overall decorative vocabulary as seen throughout the architectural complex at Cranbrook.

Truth to material, its possibilities and limitations, was another axiom clearly defined and followed at Cranbrook. The results in the weaving field were far-reaching, culminating in the transposition of handweaving characteristics into industrially produced textiles. Powerloom production received cultural direction from Marianne Strengell and, later, from her students, Robert Sailors and Jack Lenor Larsen. Individual expression was also a concept encouraged at Cranbrook. The students had learned their lessons well from Strengell, who wanted "above all textures instead of pattern and an intermingling of various fibers brilliantly glossy, dull mat finishes, flat yarns and novelty spun yarns. I have absolutely no conscience when it comes to mixing organic and inorganic fibers providing it 'works'. Fabrics must provide a background rather than a stage setting for people."[144] They had also learned that Strengell looked upon fabrics and rugs as architectural building materials, not to be confused with paintings, since textiles, or for that matter carpets, were never intended to hang on walls. And finally, they had been educated to understand that architect, designer, and manufacturer had to be able to communicate and work together.

The textiles and carpets produced at Cranbrook speak for themselves and have always been acknowledged as unique and advanced statements. The roots of the Cranbrook weaving vision can be traced to Finland and Sweden. With Ed Rossbach and Jack Larsen, the circle has been closed and weaving has returned to Europe with as American a spirit as it could ever possess. America, in turn, would have been the poorer had it not been for this extraordinary isolated happening in Bloomfield Hills, Michigan.

8

CERAMICS

For those acquainted with the history of twentieth-century American ceramics, the name of Cranbrook Academy has certain positive resonances. It summons to mind Maija Grotell, who for many decades created her magisterial vases there and who taught some of the most celebrated contemporary potters in this country: Toshiko Takaezu, Richard DeVore, and John Parker Glick to name but a few of Cranbrook's illustrious graduates.

Yet the beginnings and development of the Cranbrook ceramics program prove to be a curious chronicle. Nowadays we can see that it was inevitable that there would be such a program. Certainly there was a growing tendency to include ceramics in American art school curricula. Also, Eliel Saarinen and George Booth, the two chief protagonists in the development of Cranbrook Academy, were interested in the medium. On the other hand, there was no concerted effort to create a strong ceramics department, at least not at the beginning. Except for some elusive first moments, the ceramics program at Cranbrook as we know it today commenced only in 1938 and did not gain full momentum until after World War II, that is, not until almost the very end of the period under discussion.

Booth's generous patronage of the American Arts and Crafts movement frequently extended to ceramics but his taste in the late teens and early twenties was essentially conservative. Just as his own house and furnishings did not reflect most important developments in modern design, so too his interest in ceramics centered around traditional values. For example, he was one of the leading patrons of Adelaide Alsop Robineau's exquisite porcelains and he purchased richly glazed wares from Leon Volkmar's Durant Kilns and from Mary Chase Perry Stratton's Pewabic Pottery in Detroit.[1] The work of these ceramists represents a restrained imitation of Oriental glazes and forms, and did not then offer the challenge of an avant-garde idiom. Likewise, Booth's purchases of intentionally rustic-style tiles from the Moravian Pottery and archaicizing tiles from the Pewabic Pottery are consistent with the taste of someone patronizing Neo-Gothic and Neo-Tudor architects.[2]

It was not until the latter portion of the 1920s that Booth began to collect ceramics representative of an avant-garde European style. The turning point seems to have been his visit in 1926 to a showing at the Metropolitan Museum of Art of French decorative arts from the 1925 Paris Exposition. The conjunction of this exhibition so soon after his meeting Saarinen and the decision to create the Academy and Museum was certainly fortuitous. Booth made a number of purchases *in situ*[3] and then, through the next few years, substantially increased his collection. Although his purchases of European ceramics were surprisingly limited to either traveling exhibitions or local American representatives, it is revealing to consider what he purchased and how markedly his taste had changed. Among the *moderne* French ceramists whom he patronized were Jean Mayodon, André Metthey, Emile Lenoble, René Buthaud, Jean Luce, Raoul Lachenal, George Serre, and Madelaine Sougez; he also bought Scandinavian examples from the Gustafsberg, Royal Copenhagen, and Herman Kahler factories.[4]

Colorplate 52
MAIJA GROTELL. *Vase.* 1951. Stoneware. 13 × 11 ¼ × 11 ¼". Cranbrook Academy of Art/Museum

Interestingly, Booth's patronage of modern American ceramists did not become extensive. He bought some pieces from the Cowan Pottery of Cleveland, tiles from the American Encaustic Company, and masks from Vally Wieselthier, the Viennese artist who had recently settled in New York.[5] But Booth was diverted by the creation of Cranbrook just as American ceramics in a modern mode were beginning to flourish.

Eliel Saarinen's interest in ceramics was very differently centered. As can be seen in photographs of the architect's early interiors, be they in Finland or even at Cranbrook, rarely was a vase visible.[6] Saarinen had a very sparse sense of interior accessorization. On the other hand, Saarinen made use of ceramic tiling in many of the projects he undertook. Continuing a practice he had begun early in the century in Finland, he made the hearth a focal point of the room through the use of strongly colored glazed tiles. A justly celebrated example is the fireplace surround in the Living Room of Saarinen House at Cranbrook (pl. 31). It is composed of alternately posed, dark brown glazed polygonal tiles punctuated by and encased in borders of silvered tiles. Interestingly enough, the tiles were executed at the Pewabic Pottery in Detroit, an operation which Booth had long patronized. But whereas the Pewabic Pottery normally favored an uneven, handcrafted appearance, the effect here is of sharp precision, with a *moderne* color combination.

We might also consider the entrance hall to Kingswood. Here too Saarinen created a stunning effect of color and texture through the overall use of green tiles from the Pewabic Pottery. Son Eero sculpted in clay a lighting fixture to adorn the crest of the staircase (fig. 170). Conceived in the form of a lion supporting a cornucopia—a modernized, comic version of a classical theme—it too was fired and glazed in the same Pewabic green. The union of ceramic sculpture and architecture, though never an officially promulgated doctrine, was frequently

170

EERO SAARINEN. *Lighting Fixture.* c. 1930–31. Glazed ceramic. 25 ¼ × 16 × 25″. Kingswood School Cranbrook

employed by the Saarinens.[7] Later on, as we shall see, Eero frequently had his wife, Lilian, sculpt ceramic embellishments for his architectural projects.

On a few occasions Eliel Saarinen even tried his hand at designing ceramic dinnerware. For The Metropolitan Museum of Art's 1929 exhibition, "The Architect and the Industrial Arts," he designed a porcelain service which was then executed by Lenox (fig. 171).[8] The angled forms and the manner in which the crisply defined edges have been strengthened in a dark color (presumably black) suggest Viennese antecedents, especially a porcelain service Josef Hoffmann designed some two decades earlier.[9] Correspondences between Eliel Saarinen's designs and work emanating from the Austrian capital are, of course, something which has already been noted before in his oeuvre (see Clark). Although the elder Saarinen also designed the dishes for the dining halls of the Cranbrook schools, the concept of teaching ceramic design in a Bauhaus manner, with an eye to industrial production, never developed at the Cranbrook Academy.[10]

Booth had evidently intended from the very start that ceramics be one of the media taught at the Craft Studios. In mid-1929 he asked an associate formerly with the Detroit Arts and Crafts Society to suggest candidates for the position of resident ceramist.[11] She proposed Arthur Baggs, the noted ceramist who then headed the prestigious ceramics program at Ohio State University in Columbus. Her second suggestion was Charles Binns of Alfred University, the dean of ceramic instructors in America, and lastly she proposed Vally Wieselthier as a possible candidate. We do not know if Booth contacted any of these ceramists. All that can be said is that nothing materialized for some time.

A small and humble ceramic program commenced finally after mid-1931, under the direction of Ruth Erikson Allen, wife of the Supervisor of Art Education at Cranbrook.[12] She had worked at the famous Grueby Pottery in Boston at the turn of the century and, more recently, had taught ceramics at the Pratt

171

ELIEL SAARINEN (DESIGNER) AND LENOX (FABRICATOR). *Dinner Service.* 1928–29. Porcelain. Photo courtesy Suomen Rakennustaiteen Museo. Location unknown

Institute in New York. Typical of the non-professional nature of the classes held at the Craft Studios in its early years, the pottery course was frequented by "matrons of [Bloomfield] Hills Society." Instruction was limited to two consecutive weekday mornings. The curriculum consisted of learning to construct tiles and vessels with slabs and coils of clay—rudimentary modes that Mrs. Allen had taught at Pratt. She also gave instruction in various forms of decoration which amateurs could easily learn. A description of actual student work—a "lamp base . . . encircled by Cherubic babies of the South Sea Isles against a background of palm trees"— suggests just what might have been expected from such a class.[13] In any event, Mrs. Allen's venture was short-lived and may have come to an end well before the Allens left Cranbrook in June 1932.

All this time—from the autumn of 1930 until the end of 1931— Waylande Gregory tried to secure, and was ultimately successful in obtaining, a position as ceramic sculptor at Cranbrook.[14] It was under his direction that a serious ceramic program first developed. Gregory had trained with the famed American sculptor Laredo Taft, and was then working at the Cowan Pottery in Cleveland, primarily as a designer of small, serially cast figures. He had even begun to receive public recognition, winning a first prize in The Cleveland Museum of Art's 1931 "May Show." But, due to the impending closure of the Cowan Pottery and lured by the potential of Booth's great financial resources, Gregory aggressively pursued a position at Cranbrook. Through the mediation of a friend he established communication, first with Frank Allen, then with Saarinen, and finally with Booth himself. Booth may have been predisposed to the artist because he had already purchased some of Gregory's statuettes from Cowan.[15] Eliel Saarinen liked his work[16] and he also may have been thinking how Gregory's large ceramic sculpture could be used in architectural projects as part of the Cranbrook idea of the unification of the arts.[17]

Gregory arrived on January 31, 1932 and, as arranged, was given a workshop in the Craft Studios.[18] He had the small kiln renovated and persuaded Booth to invest in an electric Globar kiln for the firing of large ceramics at high, stoneware temperatures.[19] Although the installation of Gregory's expanded facilities proved more costly and time-consuming than had been anticipated, still, the first successful firing of the kiln took place that spring.

Gregory was soon actively at work, fulfilling his contract which stipulated that "All art work . . . must be of high standard and principally original and individual pieces."[20] Among the first works that the artist created during these months was the *Girl with Olive* (fig. 172).[21] The sleek, elongated head, columnar neck, and especially the parallelism of head and hand have strong links to Brancusi's *Mademoiselle Pogani*, but there are also indications that Gregory was not immune to the elegiac charms of Carl Milles' sculpture (fig. 188). (Indeed, Gregory's contemporary *Girl with Braids* is strikingly close to Milles' work.)[22]

The stylistic and thematic range of Gregory's ceramic sculptures is surprising. Some were roughly textured terracottas, such as his *Ichabod Crane, Kansas Madonna* (a horse and foal), and *Horse and Dragon*.[23] Others were conceived with smoother surfaces and stylized, angular rhythms of a type associated with the Art Deco style. One was *Radio,* a pair of reliefs of sleek, tautly posed women;[24] another was a large *Europa and the Bull*.[25]

Always basking in the light of publicity, Gregory took advantage of every opportunity at Cranbrook in those busy days. His new work and some from his Cowan Pottery period was included in an exhibition of Cranbrook crafts that was held at Kingswood School in May 1932, and he also participated in a summer group show held in the Cranbrook Museum.[26]

In accord with the then prevalent practice at Cranbrook, Gregory received no official salary; he had what was at first called a "fellowship," although more frequently he called himself a "resident artist." Like the other craftsmen there, his income was to depend upon the sale of his ceramic sculpture and tuition money from students whom he had to seek himself. Gregory had small brochures printed at the Cranbrook shop, one advertising his sculpture, the other his classes (fig. 173).[27] He succeeded in assembling a small coterie of students who,

172
WAYLANDE GREGORY. *Girl with Olive.* 1932. Stoneware. 14 ³⁄₈ × 8 × 6 ³⁄₄". Yolande and Waylande Gregory Foundation

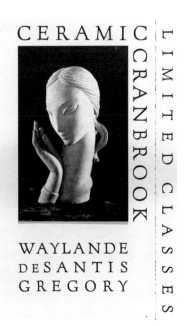

CERAMIC
CRANBROOK
LIMITED CLASSES

WAYLANDE
DESANTIS
GREGORY

173
Brochure Advertising Waylande Gregory's Ceramic Classes. 1932. Cranbrook Archives

while possibly more serious than the society matrons studying with Mrs. Allen, still were generally not intent on ceramics as a career.[28] To alleviate the artist's constant financial woes Booth arranged that he could teach two classes at Kingswood School, thus inaugurating a position that would help sustain other Cranbrook ceramists for several more decades.[29]

Gregory's stay at Cranbrook was never as ideal as he had first envisioned it.[30] He and his wife registered constant complaints. They felt Cranbrook was too distant from Detroit, and thus isolated from potential patrons. They complained that the faculty house assigned to them was too small. There were problems regarding money; prices were too high and who was to be responsible for which bills was always an issue. There were petty annoyances and disputes with other faculty members—all of which caused a great deal of friction between Gregory and the powerbrokers of Cranbrook: Booth, Saarinen, and the Executive Secretary, Richard Raseman.

In January 1933, at the end of the first year at Cranbrook, Gregory's contract was renegotiated, although not without additional haggling and complaints. Matters came to a head on March 4, 1933, when due to the so-called "National Bank Holiday" Booth closed all the Craft Shops and cut off their electricity and heat. Undeterred by official declarations, Gregory loaded his kiln, turned the power back on, and started to fire. This was soon discovered and the power was cut off again, but not without Gregory bewailing the damage done to pieces within the kiln.[31] When a cold snap froze some of the green ware in his unheated studio there were further outcries. Like Eschmann, Kirk, and Wirde, Gregory made plans to leave (see Farmer and Thurman). On March 6 he removed all his works from the Museum in protest.[32] Within the next weeks he successfully applied for a teaching position at Cooper Union in New York City.[33] Although he remained at Cranbrook until the end of June, there was no reconciliation. Quite the contrary, hostilities increased until ultimately Gregory brought a lawsuit against Booth, one which would not be settled until two years later.

The ceramic sculptures he created at Cranbrook helped the artist attain national prominence. In May 1933, a large one-man exhibition of his works (many of which stemmed from his stay at Cranbrook) opened at The Detroit Institute of Arts and then circulated in the Middle West and East;[34] a separate one-man exhibition was held in the Montclair Art Museum.[35] It may have been with some bitterness that his former employers noted in the fall of 1933 that Gregory's *Girl with Olive* had won the first prize for ceramic sculpture at the Syracuse Museum's prestigious "National Ceramic Exhibition."[36] And throughout the remainder of the decade he continued to exhibit the sculpture he had created at Cranbrook. *Horse and Dragon* won honorable mention in 1933 at the Chicago Art Institute.[37] *Girl with Braids* won a prize at the 1934 Syracuse Ceramic National.[38] *Kansas Madonna* won an honorable mention at the 1934 Syracuse Ceramic National.[39] *Girl with Olive, Girl with Braids,* and *Kansas Madonna* were all included in an important exhibition of American ceramics that toured Scandinavia in 1937.[40] Even his celebrated *Europa and the Bull* (pl. 53), exhibited as late as 1938 at the Syracuse Ceramic National and at the San Francisco Golden Gate Exposition, was but a minor reworking of one of his Cranbrook pieces. Through these many exhibitions and prizes, as well as major W.P.A. commissions, Gregory gained recognition as one of America's foremost ceramic sculptors. He and his works were constantly in the limelight but, significantly, the publicity almost never mentioned his stay at Cranbrook.

Gregory's position and old studio were soon filled by the sculptor Marshall Fredericks. First hired to teach art courses at the school for boys and Kingswood School,[41] he also began teaching at the Academy in the summer of 1934.[42] Although he had learned the craft of ceramics in Cleveland, his major concern remained sculpture (see Marter). He taught pottery and modeling in clay to those interested but between 1934 and 1938 there was no real ceramic program at the Academy.[43]

In the summer of 1934, just when Fredericks joined the Academy faculty, the Finnish-born ceramist Maija Grotell visited Cranbrook and

MAIJA GROTELL. *Vase.* c. 1935. Earthenware. 5 ½ × 5 ¾ × 5 ¾". Private Collection

Colorplate 53
WAYLANDE GREGORY. *Europa and the Bull.*
c. 1937–38. Stoneware. 23 ¾ × 27 × 8 ½″.
Everson Museum of Art

brought with her some of her recent vases.[44] At this point in her career she had been in the United States for less than a decade and had achieved some distinction: a certificate of excellence in Cleveland in 1931 and an honorable mention at the "National Ceramic Exhibition" in Syracuse in 1933. We do not know how Grotell and Eliel Saarinen first came to know each other but it may well have come through the frequent interchanges among members of the Finnish-American community.

Saarinen evidently approved sufficiently of Grotell's work to arrange that she should have an exhibition and sale of her wares at the Cranbrook Museum.[45] The exhibition opened just before Christmas 1934 and continued into the first month of the new year. The exhibition was favorably received and a few pieces were purchased, some by Saarinen, Zoltan Sepeshy, and the Cranbrook Museum.[46] Her work at this time was a low fired ware decorated with vivid pictorial images: violinists, picnickers, horses, scenes of urban New York. They were rendered either as simplified forms bounded by fluent, Matisse-like contours, or as decorative, cubistic schemes. Her palette was noted for its brilliance, with striking combinations such as turquoise and black, or lemon yellow and silver. One can readily understand why Saarinen would have admired her ceramics. Matters of nationality aside, many of Grotell's *moderne* designs approach those then being executed at Cranbrook. The silver and white design of skyscrapers and smokestacks on one of her vases (fig. 174) suggests analogies with Lillian Holm's *First Sight of New York* (pl. 40). A similar correspondence can be noted between Grotell's vases with patterns of abstract deer (one of which was bought by Saarinen) and gates with the same type of animal motif and playful, cubistic design that the architect designed for the school for boys.

Yet despite Grotell's 1934 exhibition, little else was done during these years to further a ceramics program at Cranbrook. Marshall Fredericks remained nominally in charge, but his concern was still with sculpture. Leon Volkmar came to speak about his pottery in November 1935,[47] but not until a year and a half later were there any indications of a search to find someone to head a ceramics program. In May 1937 the Academy sent out an inquiry seeking the nomination of "a young potter and ceramist . . . [with] strong creative ability."[48] Grotell received such a letter and asked that she be considered for the position but Raseman's reply was negative.[49] (Among other reasons, he wrote that the Academy preferred a man for the position.) Undaunted, Maija forwarded photographs of her latest work and, with good grace, also suggested that they turn to Arthur Baggs at Ohio State University, not only because he was "a person of exceptional talent" but also because he "produces very fine pupils, both men and women."[50]

We do not know whether the Academy actually tried to hire a ceramist at this point. Certainly nothing conclusive occurred. In January 1938 they once again approached Grotell, this time offering her the position.[51] After a brief

175

ELIEL SAARINEN. *Entrance to the Library, Cranbrook Academy, c. 1942.* At left of doorway, CARL MILLES, *St. Paul.* c. 1926–27. Bronze. H. 38 ½″. Photo courtesy Cranbrook Academy of Art/Museum

exchange of correspondence, she visited the school in March and accepted the position.[52] Upon her official arrival in September an exhibition of her pottery helped introduce her to the students and the community.[53]

Although much of her time was taken up by instructional duties, Grotell devoted evenings and weekends to her own work; little mattered to her beyond her ceramics, and she was already accustomed to the hardships of a demanding schedule. The physical facilities and the artistic environment of Cranbrook helped propel Grotell toward artistic maturity. Previously initiated aspects of her work now could be fully realized. She had already begun to work with high fire glazes and stoneware bodies, and now had the opportunity to further her experiments unhampered. Also, as is true of any ceramist, a major portion of her work consisted of experimentation with new glazes. Grotell loved to try different formulas and continued to do so for the next three decades. As she herself explained, she was never curious about her neighbors or their activities, but she was always curious about materials and intrigued by the challenges they offered. Lastly, the great size of the Cranbrook kiln allowed her to work on a physical scale far greater than ever before.

Quite naturally, some of Grotell's first works at Cranbrook were adaptations of previous ones. For example, she made another version of the

176
CHARLES DUSENBURY. *Europa and the Bull.*
c. 1940. Stoneware. 14 × 12 ⅝ × 7 ¾".
Cranbrook Academy of Art/Museum

previously cited vase with a cityscape (fig. 174) but she hardened its geometric pattern, tightened the cylindrical form of the vessel, and, most importantly, trebled its height.[54] Gradually, though, she began to rely entirely on geometric patterns, a trend which had begun just prior to her arrival at Cranbrook. A splendid example from these years is an impressively large vase with a checkerboard pattern on the cylindrical neck and emphatic throwing rings around the spherical body (pl. 54).[55] The contrasting patterns boldly emphasize the adjacent, yet distinctly separate volumes. This vase's architectonic formality and scale give it a strong sense of sculptural presence which helps it escape the confines of "minor" art.

An equally large vase from this time suggests a slight but ultimately important shift of direction (pl. 55). It too has an impressive sense of scale and geometry, but now the decoration—a brilliant platinum set against a matte blue surface—is built up in low relief and rhythmically staggered. This type of decoration can be understood within Grotell's Cranbrook context. Its stepped arrangement and sculpted effect suggest analogies with Eliel Saarinen's treatment of ornament on the exterior walls of the Cranbrook Academy Library (fig. 175).[56] From this moment on, Grotell frequently built up her decoration, either by adding strips of clay or by painting on slip in an adaptation of the traditional *pâte-sur-pâte* method, to create what, at least in the world of ceramics, seemed a unique idiom.

Whereas it is all too easy to dwell upon the beauty of Grotell's vases, we must remember that the greater part of her time was devoted to teaching. Indeed, she always presumed that teaching, not the sale of her pottery, would be the mainstay of her existence.[57] Following her arrival in the United States she had held a variety of positions, but primarily in settlement houses and summer camps.[58] Her new post at Cranbrook must have seemed splendid, not only because of the beauty of the site and the kinship of her Scandinavian colleagues, but also because she was now associated with an established program wholly committed to art. On the other hand, we should be wary of overestimating her new position. As before, she was a master potter in a nonprofessional ceramics program. Many of her students were from other disciplines and took ceramics only as a leisure activity.

Moreover, a major portion of the Cranbrook ceramics program in the late thirties and forties was still devoted to ceramic sculpture. Still, Grotell was well suited for her position because she had taught clay modeling in her previous posts and was thus sympathetic.[59] As the student records and photographs of contemporary exhibitions reveal, many of the students in Grotell's classes produced the sort of small ceramic sculpture so popular at the time: figurines of cowboys, barnyard animals, etc. Grotell was known for her solicitousness in providing the students with instruction in clay bodies, for providing glaze formulas, and for offering encouragement wherever possible.

A good example of the type of work done under her supervision is Charles Dusenbury's *Europa and the Bull* (fig. 176). Dusenbury had studied intermittently at Cranbrook since 1935, first with Sepeshy, then with Fredericks, and finally with Milles. In the spring 1940 term he studied with Grotell and from then on devoted much of his activity to ceramic sculpture. Not surprisingly, this *Europa* suggests analogies with Milles' work, recalling in theme the master's by-now-familiar opus (fig. 189 and pl. 57) and, in its roughly modeled surface, Milles' more contemporary work like the *St. Paul* (fig. 175). However, Dusenbury's comic treatment of the sensual myth is more in accord with the general tenor of American ceramic sculpture than with anything specific to Cranbrook.

One of the interesting subcurrents at Cranbrook was the idea of using ceramic sculpture in an architectural context. As we have already seen, the Saarinens, father and son, worked on such collaborative projects and this family tradition continued. Eero asked his then-fiancée, Lilian Swann (a sculpture student at the Academy), to create a series of ceramic plaques for the exterior walls of the Crow Island School (figs. 42, 43, 177).[60] Conceived as humorous animals to be placed at the eye level of children, they provide a colorful accent to the building. Later Lilian Swann collaborated with Eero on several other architectural projects; she also began making ceramic sculptures using a technique of curved slabs

reminiscent of the architect's molded plywood shells. Although Grotell provided technical help, information on glazes, kiln space, and even student assistants, still the work (aside from firing) was done in Lilian Swann's own studio. On other occasions, ceramic and architecture students joined forces but the concept of ceramic architectural sculpture remained little more than a sporadic subcurrent at the Academy.

Indeed, Grotell's presence and work gradually changed the Cranbrook ceramic program to one committed to a "vessel aesthetic." The ceramic shop became a center of friendly activity with the teacher, always referred to as "Maija," in constant supervision (fig. 178). Since few students came with professional knowledge of the medium, much less mastery, Grotell began slowly with fundamentals—although there was no fixed curriculum. Demonstrating in a relatively traditional way, she introduced the students to wedging and throwing. Many students have recalled how inspirational it was to see her throwing, transforming a mass of shapeless clay into one of her powerfully large vessels.[61]

Serious students were introduced to the fundamentals of glaze science, and were taught to grind with mortar and pestle in a traditional and laborious way. The standard ceramic texts used in America, such as those by Binns and Parmelee, were suggested for reference; the 1940 publication of Leach's *A Potter's Book,* with its formulae for ash glazes, added a new and significant dimension to the students' work—it could also result in a fun-filled search through Cranbrook's forest and many fireplaces for raw material.[62] Students were constantly encouraged to experiment with clays and glazes on their own[63] but if dedicated work was blocked by an unforeseen technical obstacle, Grotell was always ready to step in and share her knowledge; she disdained the idea of secrets just as much as she encouraged independence.[64]

The closeness with which she supervised and encouraged her students is attested to by the work of William Watson, the student whom at that time she considered "the best student" she ever had.[65] Although he had entered the Academy to study sculpture, producing Milles-like figures under Marshall Fredericks, his interest in modeling led him to Grotell's classes and there he was so stimulated that he changed his major. An early vase of his reveals her close tutelage (fig. 179).[66] Indeed, it might well be mistaken for a work of hers due to its clear-cut volumetric forms, its sense of geometric decoration, and its brilliant contrast of turquoise and black glazes.

177

LILIAN SWANN SAARINEN. *Anteater and Child.* c. 1939. Terra cotta. 5 ⅞ × 8 ⅜ × 1 ⅝". Collection Lilian Swann Saarinen

Grotell encouraged her students to submit their work not only to Academy and local exhibitions but also to major competitions like the Syracuse Ceramic National. At these exhibitions one was likely to see Grotell's vases alongside those of her students like William Watson or Edna Vogel. But, at the same time, it must be remembered that the ceramics program, as was true of the other programs at Cranbrook, was not an accredited professional one. For example, when William Watson left the Academy in 1941 he had no degree and thus went to study under Arthur Baggs at Ohio State University in an official Master's program.

The war years had their effect on the ceramics program just as they had on everything else at Cranbrook.[67] The tempo changed as the men went to war and the number of students dropped considerably. Nonetheless, there were students—helped by the restructuring of the curriculum for accreditation—and

178
Maija Grotell in the Ceramic Studio. c. 1938–40. Photo courtesy Cranbrook Archives

Grotell inspired friendships and deep respect which made her a firmly entrenched member of the Cranbrook Academy community.

Grotell's style showed a gradual shift of direction in the late forties and fifties. Her endless experiments with glazes produced some very interesting effects and, not surprisingly, the exhibition of her work held at the Cranbrook Academy Museum in 1957 was presented in terms of glaze classifications.[68] When governmental rules during the War restricted the use of uranium, a key ingredient in producing an orange glaze, she was sufficiently intrigued to find a substitute through the use of chrome and iron. She also spent over a decade in the creation of a brilliant blue.

One avenue of research which particularly fascinated the artist was a bubbled effect obtained by applying a Bristol-type glaze over an Albany slip

179
WILLIAM WATSON. *Vase.* c. 1939–40. Stoneware. 19 × 19 ¼ × 9 ¼″. Cranbrook Academy of Art / Museum

(pl. 52). The pocked surface, like the crater glazes used by the Natzlers of California, shows a new appreciation for the accidents of the kiln fire and yet also reveals an overriding sense of firm command. Grotell learned how to control the size of the burst bubbles and how to use this surface in conjunction with applied decoration by cutting through the glaze with surgeon-like skill.[69] Indeed, while many of these later works show interesting effects of bleeding glazes, there is always a sense of precision which separates her work from that of younger postwar ceramists who more fully submitted to the element of chance found in Oriental practice.

Grotell's sense of design also showed new directions. Her predilection for strong spherical and cylindrical forms remained constant, and even some of her favorite angular motifs were retained, although generally in new combinations. But she also introduced organic and curvilinear motifs. Beginning in the mid-1940s she initiated a series of large globular vases decorated with joined, looped segments (fig. 180); in the 1950s the loops became flattened arcs. These vases demonstrate both the sense of continuity and change within her work. Their scale and shape, their staggered rhythms, and the manner in which the slip decoration is built up in relief recall her vase of the early forties (pl. 55), but now the decoration is curved and the colors muted. Some of her ceramics from the postwar years have motifs resembling flowers (pl. 52) and bursting stars; others have calligraphy recalling the artist's own script monogram or fluttering ribbons. Perhaps most

229

striking of all are the bold, amoeboid forms on a series of bowls (fig. 181). While this fascination with organic forms was an international postwar phenomenon, it is not necessary to search beyond Cranbrook's boundaries. To find parallels—if not sources of inspiration—we need only consider the furniture of Charles Eames (fig. 106 and pl. 17) (whom Grotell admired and who, in turn, photographed her and her work) and also the jewelry of her good friend and colleague Harry Bertoia (fig. 135).

While Grotell was clearly affected by the artistic milieu of Cranbrook, we must be wary of placing undue emphasis upon her participation in cooperative projects.[70] She fiercely protected her independence and the indepen-

180

MAIJA GROTELL. *Vase.* c. 1952–53. Stone-ware. 12 × 12 × 12". The Detroit Institute of Arts

dence of her shop. For example, her involvement in the General Motors complex should not be overexaggerated (figs. 48 and 98). While it is true that she helped develop the low fire glazes that give the buildings such colorful brilliance, she did so somewhat unwillingly. This is not to say that she disapproved of joining ceramics to commercial purposes; it just did not interest her.[71] She encouraged students in their commercial ventures, but she followed her own goals.

Certainly the ceramics shop was busy in the years after the war. As elsewhere at Cranbrook, there was an upsurge in student enrollment.

However, there were changes in Grotell and her pedagogy. She became increasingly withdrawn, both in her personal life and in her manner of teaching. She worked in private in her studio downstairs and she became increasingly less verbal. All this created a barrier which many students could not penetrate; on the other hand, those that did found a teacher of great warmth and inspiration.

Also, more and more of the enrolling students were serious ceramic majors who had had previous training and who intended to pursue a professional career. They knew how to throw and had the fundamentals of glaze chemistry. Thus less was required in terms of basic instruction. Grotell still remained omnipresent in the studio, patiently observing and waiting for students to ask ques-

181

MAIJA GROTELL. *Bowl.* c. 1951. Stoneware. 6 ¼ × 12 × 12″. Cranbrook Academy of Art/Museum, Gift of Dr. French McCain

tions. She seems to have had an uncanny ability to understand her pupils' needs and tailored her response to the individual student. Most frequently the important critiques were held at a quiet moment over a cup of coffee or downstairs in her studio but, inevitably, they were private encounters.

Grotell's ceramics, arranged on shelves around her private studio or brought up into the general students' shop to illustrate a point, exerted their force and charm on many students who, consciously or not, imitated her repertoire of forms, glazes and decorative motifs. Even if Grotell was not articulate, still, she had certain ways of explaining her work to the students. Generally it was in terms of analogies with phenomena in natural science. Her double glazing was compared with the multiple layers of cells in a blade of grass, or the layers of feathers on a bird's wing. The decorative motifs on her ceramics were likened to birds' wings, tree branches, rocks, etc. Effects of texture and color found parallels in rocks and shells in the Cranbrook Institute of Science.

Many of her students came not only with previous training and experience but also with a sense of the artistic direction they personally wished to pursue. Grotell's intent was to help encourage them to find it, not to mold them in her own image. Grotell herself recounted how during a critique she told a student that she personally did not like the forms of certain vessels because they were, as she put it, like "women in high-heeled shoes." Grotell described her own vases as "women in low-heeled shoes" and thus expressive of her own, stolid stature.[72] However, and this is the point which needs to be stressed, Grotell felt that the "high-heeled" vases were appropriate for that student and encouraged her in that direction.

Given Grotell's conduct of her classes it is not surprising that much of the pottery that came out of the Academy in the late forties and fifties seems more like a cross section of American ceramics than work produced under one teacher. As is often the case in student work, there are correspondences between the various styles represented and the work which could be seen at the Syracuse Ceramic National or at Wichita, Miami, and the other leading ceramic exhibitions, or in the pages of *Craft Horizons, Ceramics Monthly* and other periodicals. Important stimuli were also close at hand—at the various exhibitions held at Cranbrook and at The Detroit Institute of Arts. The ceramists chosen for these exhibitions included not only the older, prewar guard, some of whom were working in updated styles, but also many newcomers who were exploring bold, avant-garde idioms. Included were such luminaries as Karen Karnes, Charles Lakofsky, Carlton Ball, and Peter Voulkos. Most striking is the fact that Grotell evidently helped in the selection of these participants and, as we know from students' reports, praised their works in her classes.

One of the important ceramists to emerge among Grotell's students in the early 1950s was Harvey Littleton. He had entered Cranbrook in 1941 to study sculpture but, like most of the male students, had to withdraw at the outbreak of World War II. Then in the fall of 1949 he re-entered the Academy (now as a ceramics major). Like many of his peers, he had advanced and even professional standing. Right after the war, while still in England, he studied ceramics with Nora Braden, a pupil of Bernard Leach's, at the Brighton School of Art. On his return to the United States he gained a bachelor's degree in design at the University of Michigan, became a partner in a design firm in Ann Arbor, Michigan and taught pottery at the Ann Arbor Potters' Guild. While he attended Cranbrook, the mid portion of each week was devoted to teaching ceramics at the Toledo Museum of Art.

One of the vases Littleton made while at Cranbrook, and a prize-winner at the 1951 Michigan Artist-Craftsmen exhibition, suggests his accomplished level of work (fig. 182).[73] Like most ceramic work being done at the Academy, its symmetrical form and taut, thin walls are a direct reflection of the throwing process.[74] The stripes of muted color at rigid perpendicular angles to each other, a design harking back to prewar geometry, are softened by the irregularities of the flowing glazes. The importance of form and fitting decoration was frequently emphasized by Grotell and her students. After two years of study at Cranbrook, Littleton was awarded his M.F.A. degree and began teaching at the University of Wisconsin at Madison. (Indeed, an increasing number of Grotell's students found teaching positions, as ceramics was added to more and more university curricula.)

The direction of Littleton's career changed dramatically, beginning in 1959 with a conference discussion on glassmaking and continuing in 1962 at a workshop at the Toledo Museum of Art where, together with Dominick Labino, he developed a technology for producing glass in a small workshop.[75] Littleton soon was one of the premier glassblowers in America and a leader in what

182
HARVEY LITTLETON. *Vase.* c. 1950. Stoneware. 13 ¼ × 6 × 6″. The Detroit Institute of Arts

became a national movement. His success with glass caused him to abandon ceramics but there will always be a reminder of his Cranbrook training in the way that he borrowed the title of Eliel Saarinen's 1948 book, *Search for Form,* to use for his own seminal work, *Glassblowing: A Search for Form,* published in 1971.

Another ceramist at the Academy during this period, with a far more radical style, was Leza McVey. Wife of William McVey, an instructor of sculpture, she worked in Grotell's studio and, in fact, was selected by Grotell to teach the summer course in 1948. Bored by the symmetry of thrown shapes, McVey sought more interesting silhouettes by relying on hand built forms (fig. 183).[76] Often the elongated neck is capped by a stopper which not only completes the zoomorphic metaphor but also denies the vessel its function as a vase, as a receiver of flowers.[77] Although these daring organic shapes are at a far remove from Grotell's classic sense of form, it should be remembered that during these years Grotell herself was experimenting with biomorphic decoration in a two-dimensional manner and, in any event, she appreciated a wide latitude of styles; her criterion was the seriousness of the work. McVey's asymmetrical pieces were also appreciated by Eero Saarinen and offer provocative parallels with Lilian Swann Saarinen's contemporary ceramic sculpture.

McVey's ceramics received much recognition; the vase illustrated here was winner of the first prize at the Syracuse Ceramic National in 1951. However, McVey did not like the role of teacher and preferred to work unobtru-

183
LEZA MCVEY. *Stoppered Bottle*. 1951. Stoneware. 16 × 6 × 5″. Everson Museum of Art

sively in private, gradually removing herself from the ceramic shop and firing her work at Kingswood or in the kiln her husband installed for the Sculpture department. Thus, while her ceramics were not as integral to the Academy's ceramic program nor as influential as they might have been, still they suggest something of the emergence of progressive styles at Cranbrook in the postwar period.

Toshiko Takaezu was the student who could well be described as Grotell's spiritual and artistic heir. She had studied ceramics with Claude Horan in her native Honolulu, and had begun to teach and exhibit nationally.[78] But, after seeing illustrations of Grotell's work in a magazine, she was drawn to Cranbrook. Like so many students she worked relatively alone at first, too timid to speak to her new mentor, until, encouraged by one of the other students, she asked for a critique. Delivered privately, as was Grotell's way, it opened the way to what gradually became a close working relationship that lasted well beyond Takaezu's three years of study at the Academy. Takaezu's comments about her teacher illuminate what many of the students felt and also suggest something of the difficulty in trying to define Grotell's pedagogy.

Hawaii was where I learned technique; Cranbrook was where I found myself.
The critique would sometimes fall into place for me months later but it was

always true. Maija doesn't say very much and what she doesn't say is as important as what she does say, once you realize that she is thoroughly aware of everything you do.[79]

Takaezu had brought Hawaiian volcanic sand to use in her ceramics and, perhaps less consciously, she had also brought an Eastern tradition of calligraphy for decoration, a palette of muted ash glazes, and a preference for small bowls, teapots, and similar forms. Such Orientalizing tendencies, though, were as much in favor in the West. Gradually a sense of artistic independence emerged. In the mid 1950s she upended a teapot and created a spouted vase, the first in a long series.[80] Though often initiated on the wheel, her vessels were manipulated into highly organic shapes brought together by attenuated bridges or joined in clusters, each portion capped by its separate spout (fig. 184). While this evolution was natural and self-contained, there are also clear parallels with other ceramists of the time who favored spouted, biomorphic forms.[81] By the end of the fifties Takaezu was creating simpler, rounded forms terminated with diminutive spouts (pl. 56).[82] There was also a shift in coloration. While many of the muted browns and blacks were continued, they were now complemented by a bravura display of brilliant colors: strong cobalt blues, magentas, and greens. Rightly compared with painted landscapes, the overlapping and glowing fields of color set against pure, placid forms brought this ceramist national acclaim and prominence.

There were changes of venue as well. After graduation in the spring of 1954, Takaezu taught with Harvey Littleton at the University of Wisconsin and then, through the help of the McVeys, went to The Cleveland Institute of Art where she headed the ceramics department for the next six years. In the beginning she taught summer sessions at the Academy[83] and there was the idea that she should remain in the Cranbrook area to take her teacher's place when Grotell retired. Although this did not happen, it could be argued that Takaezu indirectly fulfilled this role, inheriting and maintaining many of Grotell's principles. Takaezu's selfless dedication to her art, spread by her role as an active participant in seminars throughout this country, has been, like her mentor's, an inspirational force. There is also a great artistic bond, for as disparate as the works of these two generations may seem, there is an underlying unity. Takaezu's return to basic, simple forms—enormous cylinders ranging up to almost eight feet in height and spheres almost three feet in diameter—suggest the maturation of her teacher's ideas, just as the intense coloration does. Also, the sense of monumental presence in both artists' works proclaims their mutually held belief that ceramics are as valid and noble as painting or sculpture.

As we have seen, the 1950s and sixties witnessed a great increase in student activity and a correspondingly wide variety of artistic expression. Through Grotell's untiring devotion to her department until 1966, the year of her retirement, it became a leading educational force. Howard Kottler, John and Susanne Stephenson, Katherine Choy, Marie Woo, Richard DeVore, and John Parker Glick are but a few of the many additional graduates' names that could be mentioned. The diversity of these artists suggests something of the nature of the Academy and the ceramics program. It is proof, if proof still be needed, that the ceramics program became one of encouraging individual expression.[84] Despite the initial importance of architecture and design, no unified approach to style emerged. But what did emerge was a sense of dedication and creativity which greatly contributed to the vitality of modern American ceramics.

184

TOSHIKO TAKAEZU. *Vase.* c. 1953–54. Stoneware. 10 × 8 × 5″. Photo courtesy American Crafts Council. Collection Toshiko Takaezu

9 | SCULPTURE AND PAINTING

Works produced by Cranbrook sculptors and painters, both for the academic facility and elsewhere, reflect the aesthetic concepts espoused by the two principal artists-in-residence there, Eliel Saarinen and Carl Milles. Sculpture was viewed as a necessary corollary to architectural design; functional and artistic valuations were considered of equal importance. The Cranbrook experience was validated both by faculty and students. Not only was the environment a stimulating one, both professionally and personally, but the solitude of Bloomfield Hills encouraged the formation of close friendships which would result in successful collaborative projects in architectural design for many years afterward. Under the leadership of Saarinen and his Scandinavian colleague Milles, and with the cooperation of painter Zoltan Sepeshy and other instructors, Cranbrook developed as an academy of art where the exchange of ideas and proposals among students was the basis for the development of a certain "vision" of modern design. Although the contribution of Cranbrook artists to the "mainstream" of twentieth-century art may seem limited, their sensitive integration of fine arts with design continues to have an impact. Cranbrook was experimental, both in physical layout and in educational theory. Now, more than fifty years after the founding of the Cranbrook Academy of Art, the artistic achievements of faculty and students are beginning to be evaluated.

For twenty-five years of Cranbrook's history the Sculpture department was identified solely with Swedish sculptor Carl Milles. Having achieved international acclaim before his arrival in the United States, Milles was in mid-career when he took up residence at Bloomfield Hills, Michigan, in 1931.[1] His subsequent work on large-scale sculpture commissions for public spaces in American cities, as well as frequent exhibitions of his works, provided him with opportunities for recognition in this country. Milles' friendship with Saarinen and the financial support of George Booth were essential ingredients for his professional success during the Cranbrook years.

In addition, Milles' prodigious artistic production was a source of inspiration to his students. Marshall Fredericks and Tony Rosenthal, among others, show their indebtedness to the Swedish master, albeit in different sculptural styles. Milles' sensitive collaboration with architects such as Eliel Saarinen ultimately led to similar practices by a second generation of Cranbrook artists. For example, Harry Bertoia, who was originally an instructor in metalwork at Cranbrook (see Farmer), later joined with his colleague Eero Saarinen to produce innovative abstract constructions for architectural interiors.

From the inception of plans for the Cranbrook community, sculpture was intended to complement architectural design, both in the physical appearance of the grounds, and in the educational philosophy for the Academy of Art. Painting, although included in the curriculum of the school, never assumed major importance in the architectural design of Cranbrook. Woven wall hangings, created by Loja Saarinen and others, or sculptural reliefs were preferred to paintings in the decoration of interiors. Even in later works by some Cranbrook architects and designers such as Eero Saarinen, Harry Weese, Ralph Rapson, and oth-

185
GEZA MAROTI. *Door of Knowledge.* 1927–28. Photo courtesy Cranbrook Academy of Art/Museum. Cranbrook School

237

ers, painting had a negligible role while sculpture was frequently integrated with architecture.

The appearance of sculpture at Cranbrook dates back to the earliest stages of development of the educational complex. When Eliel Saarinen commenced work on the school for boys, he asked George Booth to engage his colleague and friend Geza Maroti to design the sculptural embellishments for the structures. The Hungarian, who had been a frequent visitor at Saarinen's home, Hvitträsk, in Finland, had taught sculpture and produced public commissions for twenty years in Budapest. Booth had no personal knowledge of Maroti, but on Saarinen's recommendation he agreed to pay the sculptor a monthly salary, and guaranteed round-trip transportation for his journey from Budapest to the United States. The sculptor arrived at Cranbrook in January 1927, and lived there for two years.[2] Maroti prepared models for the stone carvings intended to ornament the school for boys. His qualifications for this task included many previous architectural commissions in his native country. The sculptor had designed the Hungarian contributions to International Expositions and had been Professor of Sculpture in the Hungarian National Royal School of Arts and a member of the National Hungarian Society of Arts and Crafts.[3]

Geza Maroti's view that architecture was the basic or fundamental art, and that the work of the sculptor is best when architecturally conceived, made him an appropriate collaborator with Eliel Saarinen. He shared the conviction of the Finnish architect that sculpture served to humanize a building and ought to function as an integral part of it. The Hungarian sculptor's ideas about expressing figural compositions and ornament architecturally rather than pictorially were given full realization at Cranbrook. In keeping with the Arts and Crafts traditional concern for métier, and with recognition of the purpose of this educational facility, Maroti designed decorative motifs for doorways, niches, and pillars, many of these details with symbolic allusions (fig. 185). Ornamental motifs and small figures are attributes of fields of study, historical personages, or personifications of famous cities of the past. The stylized reliefs of flora and fauna combine with the archaicized figural types to create iconographic schemes harking back to the sculptural decorations of the ancient and medieval periods. One of the most "learned" examples is the bas-relief which Maroti designed for the library at Cranbrook School. Intended to represent the "Gift of Knowledge," the panel depicts the history of the human race from Adam and Eve to the voyage of Columbus. The figural style appears indebted to both Egyptian and early classical sources.[4]

Maroti's traditional designs found acceptance with George Booth who had a growing collection of medieval and Renaissance objects, and who was dedicated to the Arts and Crafts movement in England (see Harris and Clark). By November 1927, Booth was praising Maroti for his "extraordinary artistic abilities" and was interested in extending the Hungarian artist's residence in the United States in order to employ him for the Art department of the school for boys, which had opened in September of that year.[5] At the same time the Detroit Society of Arts and Crafts was considering Maroti for a position as critic and lecturer in their art school. Maroti continued to live at Cranbrook through the following year. In addition to his work there, he designed sculptural embellishments for the main entrance and vaulted passages in Albert Kahn's Fisher Building in Detroit.[6]

In January 1929, Maroti asked Booth to release him from their earlier financial arrangement since all models for ornamental and figurative details for the existing structures at Cranbrook had been completed. Mentioning that his studio was too far from Detroit, Maroti stated that he and his wife felt too isolated in the country.[7]

After the departure of Maroti early in 1929, Booth searched for another sculptor for the craft studios. By mid-summer he had engaged David Evans, a young Englishman whose ceramic sculpture Booth had seen and purchased from an international exhibition of ceramic art held at The Metropolitan Museum of Art in 1928. The artist was hired by the Cranbrook Foundation as Professor of Sculpture and Life Drawing in October 1929. Born in Manchester, England, where he studied initially at the School of Art, Evans had also been enrolled at the Royal College of Art. In 1923 he won the Prix de Rome for *Labor,* two struggling male figures dressed as workmen.[8] Having spent several years in Rome as a result of this award, he returned to London where he received commissions for portrait busts and church memorials. Evans' solid academic training and conservative style must have appealed to Booth.

It was intended that Evans would execute works for various buildings under construction at Cranbrook. In May 1930 he did complete a relief panel in bronze which immortalized the football team of the school for boys. The shallow relief filled with interior rhythms and archaicized figural types shows the impact of the *moderne* style which was practiced by many of Evans' contemporaries.[9] Although Evans taught life classes at the Academy, he became dissatisfied with the conditions of his employment. Booth had intended his resident sculptor to develop his own workshop, to find commissions in addition to those offered by the Cranbrook Foundation, and to attract students. A portion of the student fees was to be returned to the instructor as income so that the combination of these ventures could assure that each of the "craftsmen" would be self-sufficient (see Farmer and Eidelberg).

186
CARL MILLES. *Sketch for Orpheus.* c. 1926, installed 1930. Bronze. 87 × 21 × 16″. Cranbrook Academy of Art/Museum

In November 1929, Carl Milles had visited Cranbrook and negotiations were underway to bring the Swedish master to the Academy as resident sculptor. When Milles was appointed in 1931, Evans left for New York, and returned to England the following year.[10]

Milles' arrival at Cranbrook in 1931 was preceded by many letters from George Booth concerning the terms of the sculptor's appointment and details about his new studio and residence. Booth wrote:

> We are looking forward to your coming to Cranbrook this fall, and are doing everything possible to complete the house and studio by that time. I notice what you say about people writing you about teaching at Cranbrook. Of course you know that we understand that you did not undertake to be a "teacher" but would act as a critic and be helpful in any other way you could. After all, I rather think this is the very best way of teaching.[11]

Milles' bronze *Orpheus* (fig. 186) was purchased in August 1930 and installed in the courtyard of the Academy within months of its purchase.[12]

For two decades after his initial appointment, Carl Milles was a major luminary and guiding force at the Cranbrook Academy of Art. His bronzes enhanced the grounds of the educational community, and his large studio was constantly filled with major sculpture commissions. Thus, his presence and activity at Cranbrook infused his students with a seriousness of purpose for their own works. At the time of his arrival in America, Milles was considered one of the leading sculptors of the period. His public commissions in Sweden had been installed in major cities, and he was beginning to receive recognition for his achievements internationally.[13]

When Eliel Saarinen, with the approval of George Booth, asked Milles to come to Cranbrook, many factors contributed to the choice of the Swedish sculptor. Saarinen had known Milles for a number of years, and undoubtedly their shared Scandinavian roots, and the considerable artistic practice each had had in his homeland, would contribute to a successful working relationship. The Finnish architect was already committed to the sculptural decoration of his structures, but his plans for the Cranbrook community also included freestanding sculptures to be installed in the gardens, particularly to enhance certain vistas. Knowing of Milles' many years of experience creating sculptural groups for public settings, as well as his skills in creating fountains, Saarinen recognized in the Swedish artist a perfect collaborator in his long-range plans for Cranbrook. In addition, Milles seemed ideal as a colleague and advisor for the architect's other commissions which required a union of sculpture with architectural design.

Milles, who had previous experience working closely with such architects as Ivan Tengbom, must also have recognized the advantages offered by this proximity to Saarinen. The sculptor was actively seeking American commissions, and wished to increase his creative activity and augment his recognition abroad. Events of subsequent years show how successfully their mutual purposes were fulfilled, for Milles did indeed consult with Saarinen on his major commissions for public sculpture, and Saarinen encouraged Booth to purchase an impressive selection of Milles bronzes which were subsequently installed in various locations at Cranbrook.

For Booth there were several considerations that were satisfied by the appointment of Milles. Most importantly Booth was interested in finding a leading artist with an international reputation to be sculptor-in-residence at Cranbrook. He had envisioned the relationship of master to student at the Academy as functioning similarly to that at the American Academy in Rome which he had visited in 1922 (see Clark and Taragin). Milles was also familiar with the American Academy, and shared Booth's interest in this educational model. Clearly Booth was also influenced by Saarinen's recommendation, by the international acclaim which Milles had already received, and by the traditional approaches to sculpture which Milles espoused.

Considering the literature which already existed on Milles,

187
Cranbrook Residence of Carl Milles, Collection of Greek and Roman Marbles, 1941. Photo courtesy Cranbrook Archives

Booth must have been well aware of the Swedish sculptor's many accomplished fountain designs and his major sculpture commissions. An English writer compared Milles to Bernini, with his skill in combining fountains and figural groupings,[14] and Milles' ideas about the relationship of sculpture to landscape architecture must have appealed enormously to Booth. Moreover, by supporting a sculptor who was committed to traditional methods and materials, Booth, imbued as he was with the aesthetics of the Arts and Crafts movement, was dedicating Cranbrook to the belief in the survival of age-old approaches to sculpture.

It is understandable that Milles' archaicizing classicism combined with Northern mysticism should have appealed to George Booth. Milles' eclecticism—his fusion of Gothic angularities with a more delicate romantic classicism as practiced in France, and acknowledgment of other sources—was greatly admired, and matched Booth's own eclectic tastes as a collector. Like Booth, who was a businessman and patron of the arts, Milles also had considerable personal ambition. Therefore, their relationship was based on mutual respect for their individual achievements.

Milles planned on a grandiose, Baroque scale with extended compositions of figures. In his fountains at Halmstad, Linköping, and Göteborg, Sweden, he successfully integrated arching streams of water with his sculptural motives. By fusing static and dynamic elements and successfully exploring linear and liquid forms to create overall patterns, he encompassed large spatial areas with his monumental works. Yet Milles did not deny that he was a sculptor of the twentieth century. For Milles and Saarinen the approach to modernism was similar: restrained, simplified forms and figure types with the linear stylizations and archaicisms associated with Art Deco.

When Carl Milles and his wife Olga settled at Cranbrook in 1931, a studio and his residence, which was adjacent to Saarinen's, had already been completed. Almost immediately work was begun on another, large studio which the sculptor could use for the preparation of the twenty-six-foot figure of Orpheus intended for a fountain in front of the new Concert Hall in Stockholm. This studio, which was ninety feet long, was completed the following year. Milles' position as director of the Sculpture department and sculptor-in-residence did not require his offering formal instruction, nor did it entail administrative responsibilities. Regularly, he would circulate among the advanced students and offer suggestions for the improvement of their work.[15] Modeling, casting, and other technical skills were actually taught by other members of the staff. In 1934 Marshall Fredericks was hired for this purpose, and when he left Cranbrook for military service during World War II, other instructors presented the basic courses in sculpture.[16]

Many of his students.later recalled that Milles invited them to his home where he regaled them with his personal experiences as an artist, and lectured on his collection of ancient sculpture. During his early years at Cranbrook the Swedish sculptor continued to buy Greek and Roman marbles, which he referred to as his "library," and kept on view in the living room of his home (fig. 187). These antique works were available reference material for Milles' personal development of certain figural types, but he would also use this collection to demonstrate certain ideas about sculpture. Holding a flashlight which he directed on the pieces to reveal certain details, Milles would expound on the contributions of the ancients to sculpture.

Milles' antique collection, some of which was questionably attributed, did include several original Greek marbles.[17] At one time it was presumably Milles' intention that this collection be purchased by the Cranbrook Museum, but the artist retained the works until they were acquired by the Swedish government and permanently installed at Millesgården.[18] After his initial appointment as director of the Sculpture department at Cranbrook in 1931, Milles' residence at the Academy was sporadic. His arrangement with Booth had stipulated that he would remain there for a minimum of three months every year, but in 1933, for example, he spent most of his time in Rome and Sweden.[19]

Both Saarinen and Booth seemed eager to assure Milles' continued association with Cranbrook, and the purchase of a substantial number of the sculptor's bronzes became an item for negotiation. In January 1933, Milles wrote to Saarinen of his willingness to sell a collection of fifty of his works which were currently on view at the Brooklyn Museum to Cranbrook. Later he wrote to George Booth:

> I am anxious to have your decision regarding my collection before sailing, since all my future plans depend upon this transaction. May I suggest that you discuss this matter with the trustees, leaving details to be settled upon my return. With my collection at Cranbrook, I should feel more at home here and be able to continue my work with more satisfaction and security and I would feel that from now on Cranbrook would be my center of activities.[20]

In July 1934, an agreement was made between Milles and the Cranbrook Foundation for the purchase of more than sixty works in bronze which were to be installed on the grounds at Cranbrook, placed in the schools or in the Museum.[21] This purchase resulted in the largest collection of Carl Milles' works to be found anywhere in the world, other than at the artist's home in Lidingö, Sweden.

Even before this major acquisition of Milles' bronzes, certain works had already been installed on the campus of the Academy. The *Jonah Foun-*

188

CARL MILLES. *Orpheus Fountain*. 1934–37, installed 1938. Bronze. H. each figure approx. 96″. Cranbrook Academy of Art/Museum

tain, for example, was completed in 1932, and the figure of Orpheus (fig. 186) was already in place in 1930.[22] Mounted on a column in the manner of the ancients (a practice which was also favored by Milles' mentor, Rodin) the muscular figure of the god of music plucks at his lyre which symbolizes his mystic dominion over the world. Silhouetted against the sky, and perched above the rooftops of some of the original craft workshops, the figure's upthrust arms bearing aloft his musical instrument suggest the power of music to elevate the spirit of man.

Milles had won the preliminary competition for the sculpture to be placed outside the new Concert Hall of Stockholm in 1926. However, the commission was delayed and was not officially awarded to the sculptor until after he had taken up residence at Cranbrook. In the Stockholm *Orpheus Fountain* the powerful and expressive image of the god of music awakens the consciousness of eight surrounding figures, all of whom respond individually to his sweet music. The overwhelming emotional effect produced in each of these figures is suggested by the disposition of the bodies, the conscious and agitated rhythms of the forms in space. In Orpheus' call for the release of these humans from materialism and their baser natures, Milles expresses the spiritualist philosophy which was central to his life and art.[23]

There is only one cast of the twenty-six-foot statue of Orpheus which was created at Cranbrook, and sent to Stockholm, but bronze castings of the surrounding nudes from the *Orpheus Fountain* were acquired as part of Cranbrook's purchase of Milles' work (see Front Cover and fig. 188). Installed in their current location in 1938, these figures seem suspended in space as they respond with various emotions to the music of the lyre (even though in this version Orpheus is absent). The figure type is unmistakably Northern: angular, with carefully defined facial features. Although the effect of the original sculptural group has been lost because of the absence of the main figure, the *Orpheus Fountain* at Cranbrook still makes an imposing visual statement.

Other major works by Milles were also given positions of prominence on the grounds at Cranbrook. Among the most impressive installations is *Europa and the Bull* (fig. 189; model, pl. 57), positioned at the head of a series of terraced pools where bronze tritons are arranged along two diagonals (pl. 61). This *Triton Pool* is the best example at Cranbrook of Milles' use of water to enliven a static composition. Arching streams continue the internal rhythms of the sculptural forms into space.

A profile view of *Europa and the Bull* shows Milles' mastery of both pictorial and sculptural effects. The female nude is positioned precariously atop the large, muscular bull. The animal is not shown leaping forward, as in versions of this subject by other artists. Rather, the short front legs have collapsed beneath the animal, and the massive body rests on the ground. The hind legs,

189

CARL MILLES. *Europa and the Bull.* c. 1926, installed 1935. Bronze. H. 112″. Cranbrook Academy of Art/Museum

although upright, are firmly planted. Thus the position of the bull forms a stabilizing contrast to the dynamic figure above. Milles was conscious of the interplay of mass and void in his creation of Europa. Bold muscular forms juxtaposed with smooth surfaces, curving lines in space, and the overall sense of design harken back to Greek sculpture of the early fifth century B.C.[24] The linear rhythms of *Europa and the Bull* are echoed in the tritons which "lead" us visually from the main group down the slope of the hill and are given playful accompaniment by the lively fountains (pl. 61).

During the 1930s and in the following decade, despite periodic absences, Carl Milles was occupied with various commissions in the United States. His proximity to Saarinen, with whom he developed a personal as well as a professional association, contributed to the new directions evident in his architectural sculptures. New themes, materials, and figural types appear in his work. Among the many projects which were initiated at Cranbrook, the *Peace Memorial* for St. Paul, Minnesota, the Aloe Plaza fountain, St. Louis, Missouri (figs. 190 and 191) and the *Fountain of Faith,* Falls Church, Virginia, are of particular interest.[25]

The gigantic figure of an American Indian [26] as the Great Spirit represents Milles' initial response to his residence in this country. Made of Mexican onyx, the *Peace Memorial* was commissioned for the City Hall in St. Paul which had been designed by Holabird and Root. To compensate for the confined space reserved for the thirty-six-foot image of the Great Spirit, Milles ingeniously mounted

190

CARL MILLES. *The Meeting of the Waters.* 1939–40. Bronze. H. each figure approx. 96". Photo courtesy Missouri Historical Society. Aloe Plaza, St. Louis

his curved work on a turntable which made a complete rotation every two hours. Initially the Swedish sculptor considered making the work in glass, but when this proved impractical, the figure was carved in onyx. The *Peace Memorial* was made even more dynamic by the interior and exterior lighting of the piece.

191
CARL MILLES. *The Meeting of the Waters* (detail). 1939–40. Photo courtesy Missouri Historical Society

Among the most successful projects to be initiated by Milles during the first decade of his residence at Cranbrook was the design of a fountain for a public plaza in St. Louis, Missouri. Milles' *Meeting of the Waters* (figs. 190 and 191) was commissioned for Aloe Plaza as part of an urban renewal program for the city of St. Louis. Under the sponsorship of the Works Progress Administration, city architects and engineers improved the area adjacent to the main entrance of Union Station by demolishing a group of dilapidated buildings.

192

Carl Milles in his Studio with his Assistant, Svea Klein, and Models for the Fountain of Faith. 1949. Photo courtesy Svea Klein

193

CARL MILLES. *Pegasus and Bellerophon.* 1949. Bronze. H. 138″. Photo courtesy Des Moines Art Center

Mrs. Louis B. Aloe, widow of a highly regarded city official, wanted a fountain to be installed on the new plaza which had been dedicated to her husband. As early as 1931, she contacted Carl Milles for this purpose after seeing an exhibition of his work in St. Louis.[27] Through Mrs. Aloe's unfailing determination and financial support, the *Meeting of the Waters* was finally dedicated in May 1940.

Controversies arose concerning the design of the fountain and the sculptures installed there. A public outcry was caused by the nudity of the figures, and Milles was also criticized for using imagery of the sea rather than

freshwater creatures and river gods. The sculptor's use of tritons and naiads is related to his earlier works, but here the allegory alludes specifically to the city of St. Louis. The *Meeting of the Waters* symbolized the joining of the Mississippi and Missouri Rivers, which actually takes place a few miles north of the city. In Milles' fountain the Mississippi River is represented by a youthful male figure carrying a single flower which he offers to a demure female nude who personifies the Missouri. The two principal figures are followed by a retinue of tritons and naiads, respectively, who present gifts of fish and shells. These exuberant sculptural groups are also intended to represent the tributaries of the two main waterways.

This fountain is the unique example of a fully developed program by Milles which was designed for a public plaza in an American city. The sculptor consulted with Eliel Saarinen and employed the young architect Charles Eames for assistance in designing the basin for the fountain and preparing the scale model for the site.[28] Although the completed work did not meet Milles' specifications for the size of the basin, the improvement of the adjacent industrial buildings, or the landscaping—and despite the initial controversies—the fountain was generally well received by both the public and critics.[29]

One of the most interesting aspects of this ensemble is not the bronze sculptures per se, but the intervals between them. Milles has consciously incorporated spatial volumes into his scheme, and ninety jets of water help to create a complex and dynamic interplay between voids and solids. Early sketches for the work show how deliberately Milles had planned the composition of the water jets to complement the rhythmic interrelationship of figures and fish. While the jets of water form parabolic curves which unify all of the elements in this grandiose scheme, the expressive poses of the individual figures (fig. 191) warrant special attention.

For the Aloe Plaza work there was some attempt to relate the fountain to its urban location and Milles was conscious of designing a sculptural grouping combined with water which would make an impressive visual impact from a distance. In recent decades, the city has razed the buildings running parallel to Aloe Plaza to form a series of malls which may eventually extend to the Mississippi River. Thus, Milles' *Meeting of the Waters* represented an early attempt to use sculpture to revitalize a depressed area of the inner city.[30]

In the years immediately preceding his departure from Cranbrook in 1951, Milles was occupied with other major commissions in the United States. Most notable was his design for the *Fountain of Faith* in the National Memorial Park, Falls Church, Virginia.[31] In this cemetery Milles was offered a site near the main entrance for the construction of his fountain celebrating the reuniting of loved ones after death. Milles included images of individuals whom he had known personally. Examples of various age groups from toddlers to the elderly were depicted (fig. 192), while an angel presided over the joyous meeting of family members in the afterlife. In this sculptural ensemble the artist had no need to relate to an architectural setting because the fountain was installed in a park. Thus, the creation of a composition to satisfy several different perspectives was unnecessary. In this fountain, however, what was disregarded in overall unity is compensated for by the rich variety of figures intended to be viewed at close range. Here Milles summarized his vast knowledge of sculptural types, including works by the ancients, Mannerists, and German Romantics. For example, the attenuated proportions of some of the smooth-limbed female nudes positioned atop branches relate them to similar figures found in the paintings of Philip Otto Runge,[32] and suggest Milles' affinity with his Northern heritage. In the final decade of his own life, Milles produced this sculptural program on death and immortality in which the figures dominate the composition while the streams of water are secondary in importance.

In 1949 Milles sold his *Pegasus and Bellerophon* (fig. 193) to the Des Moines Art Center. Ten years earlier the same sculpture had been included in the model for the Smithsonian Gallery of Art, Washington, D.C., created by Eliel and Eero Saarinen with Robert Swanson (see De Long).[33] Although this museum was never built, the simple masses of the low-slung construction were re-

194

MARSHALL FREDERICKS. *War Memorial Fountain, Cleveland.* 1964. Bronze. H. 35′
Photo courtesy Marshall Fredericks

peated in Eliel Saarinen's design for the art museum at Des Moines, Iowa. As in the original scale model for the Smithsonian project, Milles' sculptural group was installed in a reflecting pool adjacent to the main structure. The image of a hefty winged horse hurtling through space with a nude male figure is a fitting complement for Saarinen's serene, unornamented architectural design. Milles' dynamic composition was inspired by the Greek myth of the mortal Bellerophon who angered Zeus by attempting to reach the heavens on his winged steed, Pegasus. The god sent a hornet to sting the horse and cause the rider to plummet towards the earth. Milles' comments on this work are consistent with the spiritualist philosophy found in his earlier sculptures: "Greek and other artists always depicted Pegasus with the rider on his back, while I visualize the poet flying independently . . . both animal and man having expressions of longing for something, we don't know what."[34]

Carl Milles left Cranbrook in 1951 and returned to his home in Sweden. Between 1951 and his death in 1955, Milles divided his time between the American Academy in Rome and Millesgården. Despite his departure from Cranbrook, the legacy of his interest in traditional sculptural methods and materials was assured by the impressive display of the sculptor's production on the grounds. However, with the continuing interest in abstract sculpture, Milles has received little critical attention in recent years.

Milles' students were overwhelmed by the magnitude of his achievement, and did not deviate from his approach to the creation of sculpture —nor did he encourage them to do so. Since those who sought counsel from the master were required to be advanced students, most had already settled on a personal direction for their work. Therefore, the choice to come to Cranbrook was made only by those who were already sympathetic to the sculptural style of Milles, and hoped to benefit from his supervision.

Among Milles' students during his years at Cranbrook were Frances Rich—who pursued a lifelong career as a sculptor after her initial success with a figure for the New York Worlds's Fair, 1939—Carroll Barnes, a California sculptor, and Lilian Swann (later Lilian Saarinen) who came to Cranbrook with previous artistic training, and produced a bronze panther for the New York World's Fair, 1939 (see Eidelberg).[35]

Typical of Milles' effect on his students is the production of Marshall Fredericks, who had studied briefly with the master in Sweden, and who came to Cranbrook in 1933 and in 1934 became Instructor of Sculpture and Modeling, remaining for nine years. In his mature work Fredericks adhered to the sculptural principles espoused by Milles. During his artistic career this American sculptor of Scandinavian heritage won many competitions, and executed works for public sites. Among his earliest commissions was the Barbour Memorial Fountain for Belle Isle Park, Detroit, Michigan. This ensemble, created while the artist was still teaching at Cranbrook, featured a leaping gazelle surrounded by four animals native to the area.[36]

One of Fredericks' finest achievements, the *War Memorial Fountain,* Cleveland, Ohio (fig. 194), required nineteen years to complete before its dedication in 1964. The monument honors Clevelanders who sacrificed their lives in World War II and the Korean War and was initiated with a campaign for private donations by the *Cleveland Press.* By the late 1940s the sculptor had produced the plaster model which was approved by city officials (fig. 195), but the installation of the work was delayed. Fredericks worked closely with local architects in resolving problems related to the siting of the fountain.[37]

The completed work includes a thirty-six-foot bronze figure which is intended to symbolize man's immortal spirit rising above the flames of war and tribulation, and reaching upward in search of eternal life and peace. Beneath this male nude is a filigreed sphere which includes symbols of Eternal Life, Spirit, and Dominion taken from ancient myths and legends. Surrounding the central ensemble are four polished granite carvings depicting civilizations of different parts of the world. Set into the rim of the basin were the names of more than five thousand Clevelanders who died in World War II and the Korean War.

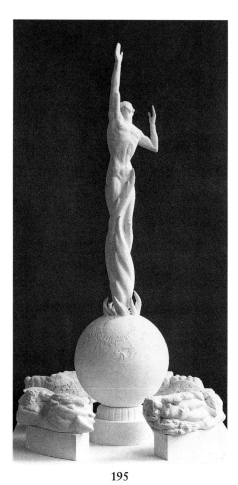

195

MARSHALL FREDERICKS. *War Memorial Fountain, Cleveland* (original scale model). 1947. Plaster. H. 52 ½". Photo courtesy Marshall Fredericks. Collection Marshall Fredericks

Fredericks explained his symbolic intentions in a written description of the memorial. According to the artist, the central figure is "the noble spirit of Mankind . . . a living thing, exalted and purified, freed of early limitations, rising above the physical into Eternal Life."[38] This emphasis on the figure escaping his earthly bonds parallels the spiritualist philosophy of Fredericks' mentor, Carl Milles. Both sculptors consciously used water for symbolic and visual effects. In Fredericks' *War Memorial Fountain,* the continuous spray of water from the basin alludes to the constant hope for peace in the world, and keeps alive the memory of those who died. In his choice of bronze and polished granite for this work, Fredericks also continued the traditional approach to the creation of public monuments which Milles himself helped to extend into the middle of the twentieth century.

Only one year later, a very different piece of sculpture by a student of Milles was installed in a public square of another American city. Tony Rosenthal's *Cube* (fig. 196) (also known as *Alamo*), fabricated of cor-ten steel, is related to the reductivist sculpture which was characteristic of the 1960s. This work, however far removed from the style of his teacher, also shows Rosenthal's indebtedness to his association with other Cranbrook artists. Rosenthal, who worked initially with Archipenko, and attended Cranbrook in the late 1930s, credited Milles with instilling in him a sensitivity and respect for materials.[39] Milles' productivity, his professionalism, and his active collaboration with architects and engineers in the designing of public monuments had also been an inspiration to the young artist.

After serving in the military, Rosenthal moved to California in 1946 where he continued his association with Charles Eames and Eero Saarinen, friends from the Cranbrook years. Thus, it is with the second generation of Cranbrook artists that Rosenthal shares his strongest affinity. While in California the sculptor began to experiment with various metals, and inevitably his work became more abstract. Architectural commissions were offered to him during these years and after his move to New York in 1960.

The *Cube* was related to Rosenthal's working of solid metals in the early 1960s. The artist wrote, "This piece is the result of many varying studies first sketched in wood, and then in small size in solid brass chunks and bolted together. The simplicity and bold forms have resulted from the direct cutting and thinking in this material."[40]

Installed at Astor Place in New York City, the *Cube* provides a focal point for an open plaza. The presence of this work has encouraged pedestrian traffic and activity in the vicinity. By positioning the work on a single point, Rosenthal has suggested the dynamic character of the piece. In addition, a bearing below the *Cube* assures that the work will rotate when pushed. Originally the sculpture was a temporary installation for the New York Cultural Festival Showcase, but it became so popular that a private collector and the artist donated the work for the Astor Place site. Petitions circulated by students in the nearby Cooper Union for the Advancement of Science and Arts supported this decision, and the *Cube* became the first piece of nonobjective sculpture to be acquired by the City of New York for permanent installation.[41] This work is truly environmental: related to its surroundings, and constantly changing in character as a result of the varying activities taking place beneath and around it.

Rosenthal's sensitivity to principles of modern design in architecture was shared by some of his contemporaries at Cranbrook. Harry Bertoia was among those who were also of the generation of Eero Saarinen and Charles Eames. Having come to Cranbrook in 1937 after excellent training in metalcraft at the Cass Technical High School, and art instruction at the school of the Detroit Society of Arts and Crafts, Bertoia was soon teaching metalworking at the Academy (see Farmer). In addition to his work in this medium, Bertoia also studied drawing with Wallace Mitchell, and produced some competent watercolor studies in the manner of Zoltan Sepeshy. At Cranbrook he also produced some woodcuts which have the crudeness and angularities of German Expressionist prints.

TONY ROSENTHAL. *Cube/Alamo.* 1966.
Cor-ten steel. H. 15′. Photo courtesy Tony
Rosenthal. Astor Place, New York City

Bertoia's change to an abstract style probably resulted from his
friendship with William Valentiner, father of Brigitta whom he married in 1943.
Valentiner, then Director of The Detroit Institute of Arts, had a private collection
with works by Kandinsky and Klee, and also purchased works by the German
Expressionists for the museum. He often talked to the young artist about contemporary abstraction.[42] Bertoia shows an indebtedness to Paul Klee particularly in
his early monoprints made with printer's ink (pl. 58). The artist began to experiment with pieces of metal and small blocks of wood coated with ink and pressed
on paper to produce geometric compositions related to late works by Kandinsky

197

HARRY BERTOIA. *Sculpture Screen*. 1954. Welded metal. 16 × 72 × 2′. Photo courtesy Manufacturers Hanover Trust Bank, New York City

(pl. 59). Other drawings were created by rolling printer's ink on a table top and laying rice paper over this surface, on which the artist "drew" with pencils or his fingers. In some works the surface was covered with ink, and after the colors were dry, black paint was applied and later scraped away to reveal the colors beneath (pl. 60). Works were also produced by cutting wooden blocks into geometric solids, and using them to form abstract shapes on a previously shaded surface. These monoprints of the 1940s are direct antecedents for the geometric metal screens Bertoia fabricated during the following decade.

During the 1950s Bertoia began his active collaboration with architects on designs for interior spaces that continued until his death in 1978. After living in California for seven years, Bertoia and his family moved in 1950 to Barto, Pennsylvania, where he designed chairs for Knoll Associates, and began to experiment with freestanding metal sculptures (see Miller and Farmer). As in his earlier monoprints, Bertoia repeated geometric units, positioning them at regular intervals to form spatial constructions. Often the artist achieved unusual effects by coating the metal plates and connecting rods with molten metals. The planar ele-

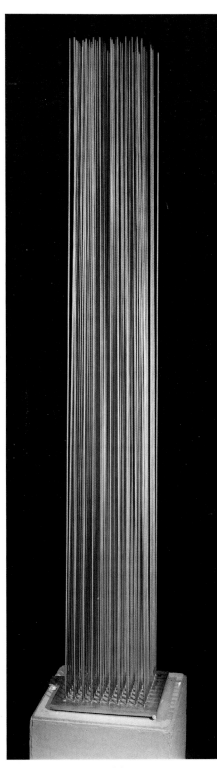

198
HARRY BERTOIA. *Tonal.* 1967. Copper,
nickel, and brass. H. 72″. Photo courtesy
The Pennsylvania Academy of the Fine Arts

ments respond to the play of light on the surfaces, and seem capable of gliding through space. Shortly after Bertoia began to experiment with these metal screens, Eero Saarinen came to his studio and examined one of the recently completed examples (pl. 19).[43] At the time Saarinen was designing the General Motors Technical Center in Warren, Michigan, and he recognized the possibilities in Bertoia's design for embellishing an architectural interior. The sculptor subsequently fabricated a metal screen measuring thirty-six feet in length and ten feet in height which served the functional purpose of providing a formal entrance for the staff cafeteria. The work makes a strong sculptural statement in the interior, and the components respond to daylight which streams through the large plate glass windows parallel to the screen.

In 1954 Bertoia designed an even more successful welded metal screen for Manufacturers Hanover Bank in New York (fig. 197), an office building constructed by Skidmore, Owings and Merrill. This screen, which measures seventy-two feet long and sixteen feet high, is more than two feet deep. Thus, the plastic effects of the geometric and organic forms attached to connecting rods are fully explored here. In this design for an architectural interior, which is among the finest of his career, the sculptor combines rectangular elements with smaller biomorphic forms to suggest the playful irregularities of nature. The ceiling of panels provides an even distribution of light over the surface of the work, and encourages reflections. Installed on the second floor of the bank adjacent to Fifth Avenue, the sculpture is a focal point of the architectural interior, while serving to divide the public banking area from private offices.

In the early 1950s Bertoia also experimented with cloudlike "floating" sculptures which are related to some of the paintings from his Cranbrook years.[44] Bertoia recalled:

I used to make paintings on the most transparent paper I could find—paint just a shape here, leave a lot of space around it, and then another shape and color them. Then I would stretch the paper on a frame, and hang it up against the light. The colors would float in the air, some closer, some farther back. I started to get interested in all these space experiments long ago—at Cranbrook after I had been there for a little while.[45]

The delicate, ethereal effect found in this new work was used to great advantage as the basis for his next architectural commission, the reredos for the Chapel at the Massachusetts Institute of Technology (fig. 66). This nondenominational chapel designed by Eero Saarinen needed a focal point above the altar that could also partition off a staircase to the sacristy from the nave. Saarinen's interest in a dramatic visual effect for his dark interior was satisfied by Bertoia's thin metal elements which seem to float freely in space. A shaft of light which enters the interior through an oculus directly above the altar creates a sense of mystery as the reflecting metal forms shimmer in space.

During the following decade Bertoia explored another interest—the use of sound and motion in sculpture. His early work had indicated an indebtedness to Alexander Calder, a pioneer in the development of kinetic sculpture.[46] By 1960 Bertoia's experimentation with various metals also resulted in sculptures which moved and made sounds. During the final years of his life, the artist produced many sounding works (fig. 198), fabricated of long rods which reverberated when touched. The "music" produced approximated many natural sounds: wind blowing through trees or waves crashing against rocks, for example. The sculptor's study of the properties of metal led to the discovery of a full repertoire of sounds made possible by using this material. This interest in sound-producing sculpture was related by the artist to a memory from his early childhood. He recalled that a band of gypsies came to his village, San Lorenzo, with shiny metal cooking utensils which they hoped to sell. By beating these metal objects with small implements, the gypsies produced a variety of sounds, and the memory of these "concerts" remained with Bertoia for the rest of his life.[47] In his last years the sculptor was so involved with his sounding sculptures that he made

199

ZOLTAN SEPESHY. *Marine Still Life.* 1946. Tempera on masonite. 30 × 38″. The Detroit Institute of Arts

tape recordings and phonograph records of performances with the works installed in his barn.[48]

Bertoia's work is indicative of the diversity of responses to sculptural experimentation by a younger generation of Cranbrook artists. In their own individual styles, Lyman Kipp, Gabriel Kohn, and Duane Hanson, among others, continued to reflect the Cranbrook experience of professional stimulation and personal innovation.

For Booth and Saarinen a painting department at Cranbrook was considered necessary to the formation of a respectable art academy. Since there was little attempt to incorporate paintings, drawings, or prints into the design for interiors of the educational community, Saarinen's preference for textiles as wall decoration allowed more independence for the development of the painting program. Although some painting students were approached by those in the architectural program to create murals for collaborative competitions, most painters were not actively involved in the integration of this medium into architectural design.

In the Painting department there was no prevailing style or artistic approach. The distinguished painters who have attended Cranbrook include abstractionists and realists, those concerned with traditional methods, as well as innovators in mixed media. From the beginning the Cranbrook Academy of Art offered painting students a stimulating professional environment, but little formal instruction. Zoltan Sepeshy and John Cunningham were the initial faculty members in this department.[49] Wallace Mitchell was appointed to offer basic instruction in painting and drawing in 1936.

  Zoltan Sepeshy was a successful realist painter in the Middle West at the time of his appointment to the Cranbrook staff in 1931. Having come to the United States from Hungary in 1921, Sepeshy worked for Detroit architect Albert Kahn, and was also an instructor in painting at the art school of the Detroit Society of Arts and Crafts. Saarinen heard about Sepeshy through Geza Maroti, who advised the Finnish architect to employ a Hungarian painter at Cranbrook

200

because they were well trained.[50] Throughout his years as head of the Painting department, Sepeshy was recognized for his mastery of technical skills. His works were exhibited regularly at the Midtown and the Newhouse Galleries in New York, and he won many awards. Recalling the early years at Cranbrook, Sepeshy later commented: "it was not set up as an educational institution, it was only an idea . . . . It was not structured . . . . Well, at any rate, this vaguely suggests a certain type of guild system, does it not? There were masters and there were disciples who came to get whatever wisdom they could get out of the place."[51] Sepeshy, who came to Cranbrook with the more authoritative approach to art instruction which had been instilled in him during his academic training abroad, credited Saarinen with the teaching philosophy of the Academy: "Cranbrook was unique for its 'freedom'—freedom that those who attended the Academy at this point had in studying, posing their own problems, for instance, and trying to find solutions—more according to their own ideas of solutions rather than a solution superimposed by the master."[52] Like Milles, Sepeshy gave no formal instruction, but would circulate among the advanced students to offer suggestions and review their progress. Once a year he would give a lecture on tempera painting, which was also the subject of one of his publications.[53]

  In his own work, Sepeshy preferred industrial scenes, landscapes and still life subjects, and his meticulous craftmanship presented these to full advantage. Not interested in the social commentary which was to be found in the paintings of many realists of the 1930s, Sepeshy emphasized geometric forms, and eliminated the accidental or ephemeral in the interest of a direct and harmonious arrangement of forms in space. *Marine Still Life* (fig. 199) was awarded first prize at the Carnegie Institute in 1947, and is exemplary of his formalist approach to a harbor view. The juxtaposition of a colorful array of angular, simplified shapes creates light and movement in the composition. Sepeshy's skills as a draftsman in rendering "picturesque" subjects, and his accomplished use of tempera to extend the chromatic range in his paintings, account for the recognition he received during his years at Cranbrook. Like his colleagues Saarinen and Milles, he remained in-

Colorplate 59
HARRY BERTOIA. *Untitled.* 1941. Printer's ink on paper. 18 3/8 × 26″. Collection Mrs. Brigitta Bertoia

debted to his classical academic training, while acknowledging twentieth-century modernism. Cézanne and the Cubist painters were undoubtedly of interest to him, but his elaborated technique often resulted in a more traditional appearance for his paintings. Yet Sepeshy's synthesis of abstraction and realism in his own work may account for his support of a diversity of approaches in the paintings of his students.[54] In 1946 Sepeshy became Director of the Cranbrook Academy of Art, and in 1959 he was made President, a post he held until his retirement in 1966.

Wallace Mitchell had a long career at Cranbrook. Initially employed to teach basic courses in painting and drawing at the Academy, he also taught at Kingswood School and Cranbrook School for boys. In 1944 he became Registrar, and in 1955 Director of the Museum. From 1970 until his death in 1977, Mitchell was President of Cranbrook. During the 1930s the artist worked realistically, and he often produced watercolors of rustic scenes. By the mid-1940s Mitchell had become a nonobjective painter, creating small works in casein which featured a disciplined organization of geometric elements and dynamic color relationships. In January 1950, Mitchell was given his first solo exhibition in New York, and his tightly structured abstractions were compared to works by I. Rice Pereira.[55] Mitchell's paintings were purchased by Hilla Rebay, who gave financial support to American abstractionists. As a result of Rebay's interest in his work, Mitchell's abstractions were shown in Paris in the "Réalités Nouvelles" exhibition of 1947.[56] In an untitled work of that year (fig. 200), Mitchell used casein to create a spatial interplay of geometric shapes attached to vertical rods. The arrangement of elements results in spatial illusionism with a pattern of interlocking shapes and

Colorplate 60
HARRY BERTOIA. *Untitled*. 1950. Printer's ink on masonite. 30 × 41″. Collection Mrs. Brigitta Bertoia

colors. Mitchell's paintings of the 1940s often parallel Bertoia's experiments with geometric abstraction in the same decade, and suggest that the friendship of these two artists might have encouraged the direction of their work during these years.

Cranbrook was a supportive environment for those in residence, and the level of professional activity of both faculty and students was impressive. Typical of the students' incentive to achieve personal recognition was their active participation in collaborative competitions. Architecture students would find sculptors and painters to join with them in preparing drawings and models for a specific project. One of the most popular was the Rome Collaborative Competition, which was organized by the Alumni Association of the American Academy in Rome and held annually. The alumni awarded cash prizes to teams of students in architecture, painting and sculpture, and landscape architecture, for the best proposals and models for a selected problem (figs. 201 and 202). Cranbrook students frequently were winners in this competition, and the projects were a prime

example of the fulfillment of Eliel Saarinen's intentions for the Cranbrook Academy of Art. Addressing the American Institute of Architects in 1931, Saarinen declared: ". . . if the teacher is a living artist, and if the student has natural gifts to become a living artist, it is very easy. You hardly need to teach him. He will find his path himself."[57] Cranbrook Academy of Art, which continues to produce distinguished artists today, is a validation of Saarinen's educational approach.

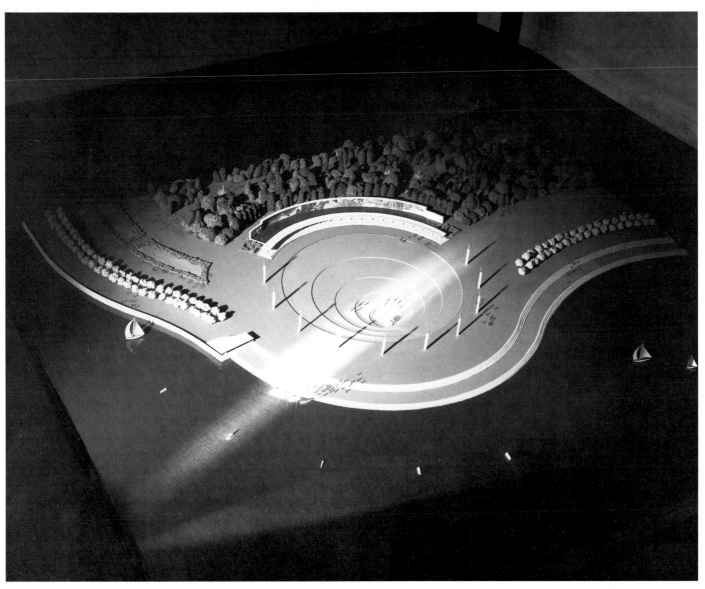

201 and 202

EDWARD ELLIOTT, THEODORE LUDEROWSKI, BERTHOLD SCHIWETZ, AND MARGARET GARCEAU. *Rome Collaborative Competition* (drawing and model). 1940. Photos courtesy Cranbrook Archives

AFTERWORD

A towering structure of wood and metal reached upwards to the ceiling of the Museum. From the dizzying heights of the tower, reached by three sets of stairs, a huge ramp over one hundred feet long descended into the main gallery. On the ramp was a trolley which, operated by wire and winches, went slowly downwards to a revolving platform, turning through a system of pulleys and cogs attached to a bicycle. To the side of the ramp, halfway down, was a large metal structure with a suspended chair which was slowly lowered through a trap door, out of sight. Slowly descending the ramp, using trolley, trap door, or turntable, students modeled their creations and costumes of fabric, fur, and flesh. Performance, ritual, fun, fashion, and spectacle were enhanced with slide projections, flashing lights, neon sculptures, wind tunnels, music, sound, smoke, and fire. Such was the structure and setting for a spectacular event staged in the spring of 1982 to celebrate Cranbrook Academy's fiftieth anniversary.

Today, one hundred and fifty graduate students from throughout the world work and study together at Cranbrook in nine major disciplines: architecture, ceramics, design, fiber, metalsmithing, painting, photography, printmaking, and sculpture. Each department is headed by an artist-in-residence and these nine individuals make up the faculty. Like the President and Dean, the faculty are practicing artists whose continuing involvement and commitment help stimulate and guide the students. The emphasis is on learning. Hard work and personal effort nurture individuality, flexibility, inquiry, innovation, potential, and excellence.

Critical to the learning process is individual work within the studio. Each student at Cranbrook has an individual working space. The importance of this cannot be overemphasized. The painter Nancy Brett has said, "Cranbrook was the genesis of my developing a serious commitment to my work. The situation there was not unlike working in my studio space today. There you were in your own space, faced with yourself and your problems and with your own decisions."[1]

As in the past, collaborative activity and interdisciplinary creativity continue among the students of Cranbrook and complement the intensity of individual involvement within the studio. The student who originally thought of the fiftieth-anniversary fashion show and performance said that her inspiration was early photographs showing dance performances in the Greek Theater built by George G. Booth in 1915. Indeed, in 1916 the "Cranbrook Masque" was presented, its central theme being Poetry's struggle against Materialism. The cast of 134 people had 300 costume changes.[2] The activity and excitement of the 1916 performance were repeated more than six decades later with students working together at a high level of energy and enthusiasm, creating a memorable event. Tradition lives on at Cranbrook, as does achievement.

The author Martin Filler recently wrote that "Behind all the designs at Cranbrook was the belief that every activity of daily life is an opportunity for ceremony and celebration, creativity and pleasure."[3] Pleasure has always

Colorplate 61

CARL MILLES. *Triton Pool.* c. 1926, installed 1938. Bronze. H. each figure approx. 63". Cranbrook Academy of Art/Museum

been part of Academy life. Students from the early days recall games and parties, along with the intensity of work in the studio. Florence Knoll recalls, "We used to work from early morning . . . til ten o'clock" and talks of taking time off for a late-afternoon touch football game.[4] Now the hours and games are different because students work later, often into the early hours of the morning, and play soccer or softball. Nevertheless, the sense of fun and pleasure complements the hard work and commitment within the studio.

When entertaining at home, Eliel Saarinen is said to have mixed a memorable martini for his guests, who often included famous artists and entertainers. Visiting artists continue to come to the Academy; this program has grown considerably in the past few years, bringing in many distinguished individuals for the enlightenment and education of the students. Parties, dances, receptions at Saarinen House, museum previews, exhibitions, films, lectures, and seminars are among the social and cultural activities that add further excitement and enrichment.

Within this setting, the Museum remains an invaluable resource, as does the Library. The Museum organizes and offers changing exhibitions of contemporary art in its spacious upper galleries. The Cranbrook collection, shown in the lower galleries, presents the work of notable Cranbrook artists, designers, and architects. The building, designed by Eliel Saarinen, also houses the bookstore and lecture hall. The Museum affords students and faculty the opportunity to look at and learn from original works of art, to exhibit their work, and to cooperate with artists and curators on exhibitions and installations.

Finally, the grounds of Cranbrook, "one of the most enchanted and enchanting settings in America,"[5] are another source of pleasure and inspiration, as is the architecture of Eliel Saarinen, "an encyclopedia of design."[6] In this unique setting, two years of graduate study allow a luxurious and rare moment for contemplation and creativity. Unlike many institutions, the Academy has always sought to remain small in size. Within its intimate environment, artists and students live and work together, sharing each other's special struggle for growth. In the words of sculptor Susan Smyly, "Cranbrook [is] a place where people from all over the country—all over the world, for that matter—come to work. The impact of different thoughts, different people from different places [makes] it the most exciting and challenging of environments."[7]

The Academy remains on the cutting edge of art, architecture, and design. Past achievements act as a stimulus and challenge to present students who continue to extend and expand the influence and vision of Cranbrook as we enter our second half-century.

George G. Booth stated that "there is a spirit of fertility which through imaginative treatment and prophetic experiment will bring art forth to interpret itself and seed again . . . art belongs to each age anew . . . there is something for this day to create as its record, monument and inspiration to another generation."[8] A recent Cranbrook student has said, "Hopefully, we will all leave here realizing that the Cranbrook experience was planned. Now we are on our own. To experience the best means we have to give our best. It is really only the beginning."[9]

APPENDICES

BIOGRAPHIES OF
THE ARTISTS

EDMUND NORWOOD BACON

Born May 2, 1910, Philadelphia, Pennsylvania. Attended Cornell University, 1927–32; B. Arch., 1932. Traveled in Europe, Middle East, and Africa, 1932–33. Worked for Henry Killam Murphy, Shanghai, 1933–34, and for W. Pope Barney, Philadelphia, 1934–35. Graduate study with Eliel Saarinen at Cranbrook, 1935–36. Associated with Institute of Research and Planning, Flint, 1936–39. Traveled in Europe and Middle East, 1939–40. Associated with Philadelphia Housing Association beginning in 1940 and later with Philadelphia City Planning Commission. Executive Director, Philadelphia City Planning Commission, 1949–70. Taught at University of Pennsylvania beginning in 1950. Associated with Mondev International and in private practice, 1970 to present.

BENJAMIN JAMES BALDWIN

Born March 29, 1913, Montgomery, Alabama. Studied in Department of Architecture, Princeton University, 1931–35. Studied painting with Hans Hofmann in New York and Provincetown, 1935–36. Attended Graduate School of Architecture, Princeton University, 1936–38. Studied at Fontainebleau, summer 1937. Attended Cranbrook Academy of Art, fall 1938–spring 1939. Worked for Saarinen and Saarinen, Bloomfield Hills, 1939–40. Partnership with Harry Weese, Kenilworth, Illinois, 1940–41. Served in U.S. Navy, 1942–45. Worked for Skidmore, Owings, and Merrill, New York, 1945–46. Opened independent practice in New York, 1947. Partnership with William Machado, c. 1948–56. Practiced in Montgomery, 1948–55. Practiced in Chicago, 1956–63. Practiced in New York, July 1963–73. Opened practice in East Hampton, Long Island, and Sarasota, Florida, 1973 to present.

HARRY (ARIETO) BERTOIA

Born 1915, San Lorenzo, Udine, Italy. Graduated from Cass Technical High School, Detroit, 1936. Attended Art School of the Society of Arts and Crafts, Detroit, 1936–37. Accepted as a student at Cranbrook Academy of Art, 1937, where he also reopened the metal shop. Taught metalwork at Cranbrook from 1938 to 1943, when the metal shop was closed. Taught graphic art, 1942–43. Moved to California to work with Charles and Ray Eames as furniture designer, 1943. Received citizenship, 1946. Postwar work in Point Loma Naval Electronics Laboratory. Set up studio in Bally, Pennsylvania, in 1950, producing designs for Knoll Associates, Inc., and major sculptural projects. Died 1978.

CHARLES YERKES DUSENBURY

Born April 30, 1915, Detroit, Michigan. Studied at Cranbrook Academy, 1935–36 (painting); spring 1937–spring 1938 (sculpture); assistant to Milles, September 1938–August 1939; spring 1940 (ceramics); 1947–48 (sculpture). Studied at Wayne University, Detroit, 1940–41. Married Marianne Strengell, September 20, 1940. Wartime employment (personnel director in aircraft factory), 1941–45. Taught art at Cranbrook School for boys, 1946–47. Member of Saarinen-Swanson Design Group. Divorced 1949. Established ceramic studio in Tryon, North Carolina, 1948–55; married Gertrude Paul, 1954; moved to Pompano Beach, Florida, 1955–75; returned to Tryon; only part-time career as sculptor and painter.

CHARLES EAMES

Born June 17, 1907, St. Louis, Missouri. Studied architecture, Washington University, St. Louis, fall 1925–spring 1928. Worked for Trueblood and Graf, St. Louis, 1927, 1929–31. Traveled in Europe, 1929. Partner in Gray and Eames, St. Louis, 1932. Partner in Gray, Eames and Pauley, St. Louis, 1933. Lived in Mexico, c. 1933–34. Partner in Eames and Walsh, 1935–36. Received scholarship to Cranbrook Academy of Art, September 1938–June 1939. Taught design at Cranbrook Academy of Art, September 1939–June 1941. Worked for Eliel and Eero Saarinen, Bloomfield Hills, 1939–40. Married Ray Kaiser, June 20, 1941. Moved to Los Angeles, 1941. Developed molded plywood techniques and founded Molded Plywood Division, Evans Products Co., 1941–45. Furniture designs produced by Herman Miller Furniture Co., 1946 ff.; consulting designer, 1946–78. Died August 21, 1978, St. Louis.

RAY KAISER EAMES

Born Sacramento, California. Attended May Friend Bennett School, Millbrook, New York, 1931–33. Studied painting with Hans Hofmann in Gloucester, New York and Provincetown, c. 1933–c. 1939. Attended Cranbrook Academy of Art, September 1940–January 1941. Married Charles Eames, June 20, 1941. Partnership with Charles Eames, 1941–78. Office of Charles and Ray Eames, 1978 to present.

JEAN ESCHMANN

Born 1896, Basel, Switzerland. Apprenticed for three years to G. Wolfensburger, a Zurich bookbinder; also studied at the Züricher Kunstgewerbeschule. Worked in Vaduz, Halle, Rankweil, Austria, and then held short-term jobs in various cities on a *Wanderjahr*. Emigrated to the United States, 1919, and, after several general positions, began work for Riverside Press in Cambridge as a bookbinder. Appointed Director of the bookbinding workshop at Cranbrook in 1929 until the closing of that facility in 1933. Headed studio at the National Library Bindery in Cleveland beginning 1935. Became head of the bookbinding studio at the Army Medical Library, Cleveland, 1943. Died 1961.

MARSHALL FREDERICKS

Born 1908, Rock Island, Illinois, to parents of Scandinavian ancestry. Attended John Huntington Polytechnic Institute for one year, and Cleveland School of Art, 1926–30. Awarded Matzen Travelling European Fellowship. Studied and traveled in Scandinavia, Germany, France, and Italy, 1930–31. Worked in Carl Milles' studio, Stockholm. Instructor in Sculpture, Cleveland School of Art, 1931–33. Received scholarship for study with Carl Milles at Cranbrook Academy, 1933. Appointed to teach at Cranbrook School, fall term 1933. Instructor of Ceramics and Modeling, Cranbrook Academy, 1934–38. Thereafter taught basic courses in Sculpture department until 1942. Early commissions included *Barbour Memorial Fountain,* Michigan, 1937, and *Baboon Fountain* for New York World's Fair, 1939. Served in U.S. Army, 1942–45. Many public commissions after War, including Rotunda, Ford Motor Company, Dearborn, 1953; *Spirit of Detroit,* 1959; Cleveland *War Memorial Fountain,* 1964. Produced more than 500 sculptures. Awarded six commissions by the U.S. government. Received gold medal from the American Institute of Architects, 1952. Lives in Birmingham, Michigan.

WAYLANDE DE SANTIS GREGORY

Born June 13, 1905, Baxter Springs, Kansas. Studied at Kansas State Teachers College, Kansas City Art Institute, and with Loredo Taft in Chicago. Sculptor of architectural ornament in the Middle West. Designer at the Cowan Pottery, Rocky River, Ohio, 1928–31. Sculpture studio in Cleveland. Resident ceramic sculptor at Cranbrook, February 1, 1932–June 1933. Maintained studios in Metuchen, New Jersey, and New York City. Known for monumental ceramic sculpture (*Light Dispelling Darkness* fountain in Edison, N.J.; *Fountain of the Atoms* at New York World's Fair, 1939; eighty-one-foot frieze on the Municipal Center, Washington, D.C.); also serially cast vessels and figurines; portraitist. Exhibited nationally, principally 1930–50; many prizes: Cleveland (1929, 1931); Syracuse (1933, 1937, 1940); Architectural League of New York (1936); Paris (1937). Established studio in Bound Brook, New Jersey, c. 1940. Also worked in wire and sheet metal in latter part of career. Died August 18, 1971.

MAJLIS ("MAIJA") GROTELL

Born August 19, 1899, Helsinki, Finland. Studied at Central School of Arts and Crafts, Helsinki, with A. W. Finch; graduated c. 1920–21. Worked as textile designer at Finska Handarbetets Vänner and produced ceramics at Ateneum. Arrived in United States, October 1927. Various positions as ceramics instructor: Inwood Pottery, New York City, 1927–28; Union Settlement, New York City, 1928–29; Luther Gulick Camps, South Casco, Maine, 1928–31; Henry Street Settlement, New York City, 1928–38; School of Ceramic Engineering, Rutgers University, New Brunswick, New Jersey, 1936–38. Became naturalized citizen, 1934. Head of Ceramic department, Cranbrook Academy of Art, 1938–66. Exhibited widely, 1930–50; many awards: Barcelona (1929); Syracuse (1933, 1934, 1936, 1941, 1946, 1949); Paris (1937); Wichita (1947, 1951, 1954); Detroit (1949, 1950, 1951, 1953, 1955); Cannes (1955). Died December 6, 1973.

LILLIAN HOLM

Born October 20, 1896, Båstad, Sweden. Received early education at Oestraby Bjaersjoelagaerd, Sweden. Prior to coming to America, worked as weaver at Märta Måås Fjetterström's Studio at Båstad. Employed by Cranbrook Foundation as weaver, December 3, 1929. May have known Maja Andersson Wirde, who apparently came to Cranbrook with two weavers in 1929. Listed as Instructor of Weaving at Studio Loja Saarinen, 1934–37. Listed as Instructor of Weaving and Textiles in the Intermediate School, Loja Saarinen in charge of department, 1937. Taught weaving at Kingswood School Cranbrook within the Department of Arts and Crafts, 1933–66. Replaced Marianne Strengell at time of birth of Charles (Chris) Yerkes Dusenbury, spring 1943. While at Cranbrook also taught at Flint Institute of Arts; her name appears under staff as Instructor of Weaving from 1941 on. Gave Flint Institute of Arts her hanging entitled *First Sight of New York,* 1965. Returned to Båstad, 1966. Died March 4, 1979, Båstad.

ARTHUR NEVILL KIRK

Born 1881, Lewes, Sussex, England. Worked with his father, a jeweler and watch repairman. Attended Brighton School and then the Central School of Arts and Crafts, London, 1916–20. Faculty member there in metalwork and miniature painting, 1920–27. Also Director of the Chalice Well Crafts School, Glastonbury, summers 1924–27. Emigrated to the United States in 1927 at the invitation of George G. Booth to instruct in the Art School of the Detroit Society of Arts and Crafts, and to design and execute metalwork for Christ Church Cranbrook. Taught at Cranbrook School, 1927–29. Appointed Director of the metal workshop at Cranbrook Academy of Art, 1929. Workshop closed in 1933. Taught classes at the Artisan Guild and then at Wayne University until ill health forced his retirement in 1947. Died 1958.

FLORENCE MARGARET SCHUST KNOLL BASSETT

Born May 24, 1917, Saginaw, Michigan. Attended Kingswood School, Cranbrook, 1932–34. Attended Cranbrook Academy of Art, September 1934–June 1935. Attended School of Architecture, Columbia University, fall 1935. Attended Cranbrook Academy of Art, fall 1936–August 1937. Traveled in U.S., fall 1937. Attended Cranbrook Academy of Art, August, September, and December 1939. Studied architecture at the Architectural Association, London, September 1938–July 1939. Worked for Walter Gropius and Marcel Breuer, Cambridge, Massachusetts, winter 1940. Studied architecture at Illinois Institute of Technology, Chicago, September 1940–June 1941.

Moved to New York, c. 1941. Worked for Harrison and Abramovitz, New York, c. 1941–42. Joined Hans G. Knoll Furniture Co. as head of Knoll Planning Unit, c. 1943. Knoll Associates, Inc., formed, c. 1946. Married Hans Knoll, August 1946. H. G. Knoll International formed, c. 1951. Hans Knoll died and Florence Knoll named President of company, 1955. Knoll International, Ltd., formed, c. 1955. Married Harry Hood Bassett, 1958. Resigned as President and became design consultant to company, 1959. Severed ties with company, 1965. Private design practice, 1965 to present.

DONALD ROBERT KNORR

Born December 25, 1922, Chicago, Illinois. Studied architecture at University of Illinois at Urbana-Champaign, 1941–43, summer 1946, 1947. Served in U.S. Navy, 1943–46. Attended Cranbrook Academy of Art, summer 1947–summer 1948. Worked for Saarinen, Saarinen and Associates, Bloomfield Hills, 1948–49. Moved to San Francisco, 1949. Worked for Skidmore, Owings, and Merrill, San Francisco, 1949–51. Partner in Don Knorr and Associates, San Francisco, 1951–57. Partner in Knorr-Elliott Associates, San Francisco, 1957–76. Partner in Lane-Knorr-Plunkett, Anchorage, Alaska, c. 1970 to present. Partner in Don Knorr and Associates, San Francisco, 1976 to present.

JACK LENOR LARSEN

Born August 5, 1927, Seattle, Washington. Bremerton High School, Bremerton, Washington, 1940–45. School of Architecture, University of Washington, Seattle, 1945; studied furniture design, 1946–48. Started weaving; attended University of Southern California, Los Angeles; Los Angeles City College; and Chouinard, Los Angeles. Returned to University of Washington, Seattle, 1948. Received B.A.; opened Studio, Seattle, 1949. Cranbrook Academy of Art, M.F.A., 1950–51. Established studio in New York, 1951. Formed Jack Lenor Larsen, incorporated, 1953. Initiated Larsen Design Studio with Win A. Anderson as President, 1958. Consultant to U.S. State Department for Grass Weaving in Taiwan and Vietnam, 1957–59. Co-director of Fabric Design Department at Philadelphia College of Art, Philadelphia, 1959–60. Opened Jack Lenor Larsen International in Zurich, Stuttgart, and Paris; also introduced in collaboration with Coral Stephens his African collection at Piggs Peak, Swaziland, World's Craft Council, 1963. Jack Lenor Larsen, incorporated purchased Thaibok Fabrics, Ltd., 1972. Established Larsen Carpet and Larsen Leather Division, 1973. Designed

Visiona IV exhibition for Bayer AG in Frankfurt, Germany, 1974. Artist-in-Residence, Royal College of Art, London, England, 1975. With James Jereb, President of Jack Lenor Larsen, incorporated, founded Larsen Furniture division, 1976. Appointed Affiliate Professor, University of Washington, Seattle, 1980. Exhibitions and Awards: Solo show, Portland, Oregon, 1949. Participant, International Textile Exhibitions, Greensboro, North Carolina, 1950, 1952, 1954. Good Design shows, The Museum of Modern Art, New York City, 1951, 1955. Fellow, Royal Society of Art, London, 1959–60. Associate and Honorary Fellow, American Institute of Interior Designers; past chairmanship, Haystack Mountain School for Crafts. Vice-Chairman and Fellow, American Crafts Council. Member, Advisory Committee, The Museum of Modern Art. Associate, Cranbrook Academy of Art. Overseer, Parsons School of Design. Director, Pilchuck Glass Center, Seattle. Lecturer, Royal College of Art, London, Advisory board member, American National Color Association. Exhibited at Cranbrook Academy of Art, 1963. Gold medal, 13th Milan Triennale, 1964 (had been Design Director and Commissioner for the U.S. Pavilion). Gold medal, American Institute of Architects, 1968. Elsie DeWolfe Award as well as American Print Designer Award, 1971. *House Beautiful* Pace Setter Award, 1973. Honorary Fellow, ASID; Elliot Noyes Fellow, Aspen International Design Conference; and Fellow, American Craft Council, 1978. Received three honorary doctoral degrees of fine arts (Parsons School of Design, New School for Social Research, New York City; Philadelphia College of Art; and Rhode Island School of Design), 1981–82. Retrospectives include: Stedelijk Museum, Amsterdam; Museum of Fine Arts, Boston; and Renwick Gallery, Washington, D.C., 1968–72. Museum Bellerive, Zurich, 1970. Kunstindustriet Museum, Copenhagen, 1976. "The Larsen Influence, The First 25 Years," Fashion Institute of Technology, New York City, 1978. "Jack Lenor Larsen: 30 ans de création textile," Pavilion de Marsan, Palais du Louvre, Paris, 1981. Commissions: Drapery material for Lever House, New York City, through Arundell Clarke, 1952. Designed and produced for Pan-American airlines the first fabrics for jet airliners, 1958. With Edward Larabee Barnes, worked on campus designs for Haystack School, Deer Isle, Maine, 1959. Designed a Fine Arts Collection of towels, sheets, and blankets for J. P. Stevens, 1965. Designed further fabrics for 747 jets for both Pan-American and Braniff, 1968. Worked with architect Louis Kahn and designed a series of wall panels for the First Unitarian Church of Rochester, New York, 1966. Further architectural work included an act curtain for Filene Center (destroyed by fire, spring 1982), Wolf Trap Farm, near Washington, D.C.; a theater curtain for Phoenix Civic Plaza; twenty-two silk hangings for Sears Bank and Trust Company, Chicago; a theater curtain for St. Charles Cultural Center, Illinois; designs for porcelain dinnerware for Dansk International; and upholstery collections for Cassina and Vescom.

HARVEY KLINE LITTLETON

Born June 14, 1922, Corning, New York. Studied at University of Michigan, Ann Arbor, 1939–42. Studied at Cranbrook Academy, spring term 1941. Service in U.S. Army, September 1942–December 1945. Studied at Brighton School of Art, Brighton, England, with Nora Braden. Studied at University of Michigan, Ann Arbor, 1946–47 (Bachelor of Design). Partner in Corporate Designers, Ann Arbor; taught at Ann Arbor Potters' Guild, 1947–49. Studied at Cranbrook Academy, 1949–51 (M.F.A. ceramics). Taught ceramics at Toledo Museum of Art, 1949–51. Taught at University of Wisconsin, Madison, 1951–77. Exhibited ceramics widely; awards include Detroit (1951, 1954); Syracuse (1954); Milwaukee (1951, 1954). Workshops with Dominick Labino as consultant at Toledo Museum of Art, 1962; developed technology for studio glass production; left ceramics. Leading glassmaker; extensive solo and two-person exhibits throughout U.S. and Europe. Published *Glassblowing: A Search for Form,* 1971. Established studio in Spruce Pine, North Carolina, 1977.

LEZA MARIE SULLIVAN MCVEY

Born May 1, 1907, Cleveland, Ohio. Studied at Cleveland Institute of Art, 1927–32. Married sculptor William McVey, March 31, 1932. Worked as ceramist and clay sculptor in Houston, Texas, 1935–37; Austin, Texas, 1939–42; San Antonio, Texas, 1943–44. Studied at Colorado Springs Fine Arts Center, 1944–45. Worked in Austin, Texas, 1946–47. At Cranbrook Academy, 1947–53; taught summer session 1948. Moved to Cleveland, 1953; established studio in Pepper Pike, Ohio, 1955. Exhibited ceramics primarily between 1947–55; awards include Syracuse (1950, 1951); Detroit (1951); Cleveland (1953, 1954, 1955). Solo exhibition at Cleveland Institute of Art, February 1–March 5, 1965.

CARL MILLES

Born 1875, Lagga, near Uppsala, Sweden. Attended Jacobskola in Stockholm. At age 17 was apprenticed to a cabinetmaker. Studied at School of Technology, Stockholm,

271

1895–97 (woodworking, carving, and modeling). Lived in Paris, 1897–1904, working for cabinetmakers. First sculpture accepted at Salon, 1899. Worked in Rodin's studio. Awarded commission for Sten Sture monument in Uppsala, 1902. Travel in Holland, Belgium, Germany, Austria, Italy before settling in Sweden, 1906. Built villa and studio at Lidingö, near Stockholm. Professor of Royal Academy of Fine Arts in Stockholm, 1920–31. Major fountain commissions for cities in Sweden, 1920s, and *Orpheus Fountain* for Concert Hall, Stockholm, 1936. Solo exhibition at Tate Gallery, London, 1927–28, followed by first trip to U.S., 1929. Returned to Cranbrook Academy of Art, 1931; Director of Sculpture department until 1951. Major commissions in these years for American cities: St. Paul, Minnesota; Wilmington, Delaware; St. Louis, Missouri; and Falls Church, Virginia. Honorary degree, Yale University, 1935. Awarded gold medal by American Institute of Architects, 1938. Elected to Royal Academy, London, 1940. Left Cranbrook, 1951, and returned to Lidingö. Winters at American Academy in Rome. Died 1955, Millesgården.

WALLACE MITCHELL

Born 1911, Detroit, Michigan. Studied at Olivet College and Hamilton College, 1930–33. Graduated from Northwestern University, 1934. Studied with Zoltan Sepeshy at Cranbrook Academy of Art, 1934–35. Received Master's degree from Columbia University, 1936. Appointed Instructor in Drawing and Painting, Cranbrook Academy, 1936–54. Served as Secretary and Registrar, 1944–63. Director of Museum, 1955–70. President of Cranbrook Academy of Art, 1970–77. Included in group exhibitions in U.S. and abroad, 1936–76. Twelve solo exhibitions in New York, Chicago, Minneapolis, and Michigan. Participated in "Réalités Nouvelles" exhibitions circulated to Paris and throughout Germany by Solomon R. Guggenheim Foundation, 1947–48. Died 1977, Bloomfield Hills.

RALPH EARL RAPSON

Born September 13, 1914, Alma, Michigan. Attended Alma College, 1933–35, and University of Michigan, Ann Arbor, 1935–38; B. Arch., 1938. Graduate study with Eliel Saarinen at Cranbrook, 1938–40. Worked in Saarinen office, Bloomfield Hills, 1940–43. Head, Department of Architecture, Institute of Design, Chicago, 1943–46. Assistant Professor, School of Architecture, Massachusetts Institute of Technology, 1946–51, 1953–54. Designer for Department of State's Foreign Building Office, Paris, 1951–53. Head, Department of Architecture,

University of Minnesota, Minneapolis, 1954 to present.

BERNARD (TONY) ROSENTHAL

Born 1914, Highland Park, Illinois. Graduated from University of Michigan, Ann Arbor, 1936. Studio in Chicago, 1936–39. Studied with Carl Milles, Cranbrook Academy of Art, 1939–40. Work selected for annual exhibitions, The Art Institute of Chicago. Served in U.S. Army in England and Paris, 1942–46. Met Henry Moore, Le Corbusier, Braque, and Dérain. Frequent visits to Brancusi's studio. Moved to Malibu, California, 1946–60. Solo exhibitions in Chicago and California, including San Francisco Museum of Art, 1950; Santa Barbara and Long Beach Museums, 1952. First participated in Whitney Annual Exhibitions, 1953, and annuals at Pennsylvania Academy of the Fine Arts, 1954. Solo exhibition at Carnegie Institute, Pittsburgh, and Honor Award, American Institute of Architects, 1959. Moved to New York, 1960. Solo shows at Kootz Gallery and Knoedler Gallery. Participated in city-wide "Sculpture in Environment" show from which *Cube (Alamo)* was acquired by New York City, 1967. Participated in many shows of large-scale sculpture in America, 1969 to present. *Steel Park* commissioned by New York, 1980. Lives and works in New York, with another studio in East Hampton, Long Island.

CHARLES EDMUND (ED) ROSSBACH

Born January 2, 1914, Chicago, Illinois. Lyons Township High School, LaGrange, Illinois, 1927–31. University of Washington, Seattle, 1936–40; received B.A. in painting and design. Columbia University Teachers College, New York City, 1940–41; received M.A. in art education. Teacher for seventh grade, Puyallup, Washington, 1941–42. U.S. Army, 1942–45. Cranbrook Academy of Art, 1946–47; received M.F.A. in ceramics and weaving. Taught design, painting, drawing, and weaving at University of Washington, Seattle, 1947–50. Married artist Katherine Westphal, 1950. Professor of Design, teaching design and textile design, University of California, Berkeley, 1950–79. Retired and appointed Professor Emeritus by University of California, Berkeley, 1979. Exhibitions and Awards: Won prizes at the International Textile Exhibitions sponsored by the Women's College of the University of North Carolina at Greensboro, 1946, 1947. Won further prizes, San Francisco Museum Decorative Arts Competition; "International Textile Exhibition," University of Washington, Seattle; California State Fair; and International Textile Exhibitions at Greensboro, 1950, 1951, 1952,

1954. Won prizes at "Sixth Annual Decorative Arts Exhibition," Richmond, California, and was included in opening exhibition, Museum of Contemporary Crafts, New York, 1957. Further exhibitions followed in California (San Francisco, Richmond). Included in Museum of Contemporary Crafts, New York, shows ("Design for Contemporary Interiors," "Visual Communications in the Crafts," and "Designer—Craftsmen USA"), 1958, 1960; won woven and printed textile awards at Richmond, California, 1960. Further group showings included exhibitions at The Pasadena Art Gallery and Grand Rapids ("Seventeen Textile Designers") and Smithsonian Traveling Exhibition, "Fibers, Tools and Weaves." Exhibited in "The Object as Poet," Renwick Gallery, Washington, D.C., 1976; at The Museum of Modern Art, New York City, in "The New Classicism," 1977. International exhibitions over the years included participation at the Brussels World's Fair, 1958; the U.S. State Department Traveling Exhibition to Europe and the Far East, 1960; "Structures in Textiles," Stedelijk Museum, Amsterdam, 1976; and "Fiber Works—The Americas and Japan," National Museum of Modern Art, Kyoto, 1977. Solo shows at Oakland Art Gallery; University of Florida, Gainesville; Museum of Contemporary Crafts, New York; Nordness Gallery, New York; Museum West, San Francisco; Ohio State University at Columbus; and Henry Art Gallery in Seattle, 1952. Represented in collections of The Museum of Modern Art; Stedelijk Museum, Amsterdam; Museum of Contemporary Crafts; Trondheim Museum, Norway; University of Illinois, Urbana; University of Nebraska, Lincoln; University of Indiana, Bloomington.

DAVID LINCOLN ROWLAND

Born February 12, 1924, Los Angeles, California. Attended session given by László Moholy-Nagy at Mills College, Oakland, summer 1940. Attended Stockton (California) Junior College, 1942. Served in U.S. Army Air Corps, 1943–45. Attended Principia College, Elsah, Illinois, 1945–49. Attended University of Southern California, Los Angeles, fall 1949. Attended Cranbrook Academy of Art, spring 1950–summer 1951. Worked for Norman Bel Geddes, New York, c. 1951–c. 1956. Opened independent practice in New York, 1956 to present.

DAVID BENTON RUNNELLS

Born March 10, 1913, Baker, Oregon. Attended University of Illinois, 1931–38; B. Arch., 1938. Attended University of Stockholm on traveling fellowship, 1938. Graduate study with Eliel Saarinen at Cranbrook, 1940. Worked in Saarinen office, Bloomfield Hills. Practiced in Kansas City beginning in 1946, first in association with James I. Clark, Edward W. Waugh (studied with Eliel Saarinen at Cranbrook, 1944–45), and George Matsumoto (studied with Eliel Saarinen at Cranbrook, 1945), and later independently. Head, Industrial Design Department, Kansas City Art Institute. Began teaching at University of Kansas, Lawrence, 1959. Died November 21, 1973, Bournemouth, England.

EERO SAARINEN

Born August 20, 1910, Kirkkonummi, Finland. Moved with family to United States, 1923. Studied sculpture at Académie de la Grande Chaumière, Paris, 1929–30. Attended Yale University, 1931–34; B.F.A., 1934. Traveled in Europe, Middle East, and Africa, and worked for Karl Eklund in Helsinki, 1934–36. Began practice with Eliel Saarinen in Bloomfield Hills, 1936; J. Robert F. Swanson a frequent associate. Office known officially as Saarinen, Swanson, and Saarinen, 1944–47; as Saarinen, Saarinen, and Associates, 1947–50; afterwards as Eero Saarinen and Associates. Taught at Cranbrook, 1939–41. Worked for Office of Strategic Services, Washington, D.C., 1942–45. Returned to Bloomfield Hills, 1945. Office moved to New Haven, 1961. Died September 1, 1961, Ann Arbor, Michigan, as last arrangements for move were being completed.

EVA LISA (PIPSAN) SAARINEN SWANSON

Born March 31, 1905, Kirkkonummi, Finland. After elementary schooling, attended Atheneum, Helsinki, and University of Helsinki, 1921–23. Studied weaving, fabric design, ceramics, metalwork, etc. Immigrated to Evanston, Illinois, and then to Ann Arbor with her family, 1923. Moved to Cranbrook, 1925. Married J. Robert F. Swanson, 1926. Prior to and during the building of Kingswood School Cranbrook, worked on designs for Kingswood. Taught costume design as well as batik design and technique at Cranbrook Academy, 1932–33. Introduced course in contemporary design of interiors and furnishings as Instructor at Cranbrook Academy, 1935. Robert Saarinen Swanson born, 1928. Established Interior Design department under aegis of husband's architectural office; with husband became associated with Johnson Furniture Company, Grand Rapids, and F.H.A. (Flexible Home Arrangements), 1929. Designed furniture, printed textiles (Goodall Fabrics), lamps (Mutual Sunset Lamp Company), metalware (Croy of Boston), glassware (U.S. Glass Company). Project inactive during War years. Retained by Truscon Paint Company as color consultant for Hamtramck, Michigan, schools, 1935. Ronald Saarinen Swanson born, 1939. F.H.A. project resumed and expanded to include sixteen manufacturers, 1946. Became partner in charge of interior design for Saarinen, Swanson, Saarinen, 1944–47. Established Swanson Associates with her husband, 1947. Firm was incorporated, 1954, and operated from then on as Swanson Associates, Inc. Began to work on private and office interiors. Exhibitions and Awards: Exhibited widely with other members of her family, 1925–45; two AID recognitions, 1947, one for printed fabric for Goodall Fabrics, the other for a lamp manufactured by Mutual Sunset Lamp Manufacturing Company. Received third AID award for metal candelabra, 1948 (manufactured by Cray of Boston). Printed fabrics included in "Fourth Biennial Exhibition of Textiles and Ceramics," Cranbrook Academy of Art/ Museum, and thereafter selected by the Smithsonian Institution, Washington, D.C., for traveling exhibition, 1953. Textile shown in major exhibition, J.L. Hudson Company, Detroit, with roundtable discussion. First prize for printed textiles at "Michigan Artist-Craftsmen's Exhibition," The Detroit Institute of Arts; showed at House and Garden Display, Merchandise Mart, Chicago, 1954. *Tundra,* a curtain material, won an award at "Western Michigan Artists Exhibition," Grand Rapids; award for custom furniture design, exhibition at Museum of Science and Industry, Chicago, from Hardwoods Industry; designed a "dream house" for Pittsburgh Plate Glass Company of Detroit (for national advertising purposes), 1956. Received Louise Bolander Award for outstanding contributions in home furnishing industry, 1957. Exhibited textiles at World's Fair, Brussels, 1958. Fourth AID award, V'Soske Rug Competition, 1961. Designed silkscreen-printed curtain fabrics for Edwin Raphael Company and area rugs for E.T. Barwick Mills; exhibited them both at January market, Chicago, 1962. Retained by E.T. Barwick Mills as color consultant and designer for rugs, 1957–76. Honorary member, American Institute of Architects, 1972. Died October 23, 1979, Bloomfield Hills.

GOTTLIEB ELIEL SAARINEN

Born August 20, 1873, Rautasalmi, Finland. Studied painting and architecture, Helsinki, 1893–97. Private practice in Helsinki and Kirkkonummi with Herman Gesellius and Armas Lindgren, 1896–1905; with Gesellius, 1905–07; independently, 1907–23. Second marriage to Loja Gesellius, 1904. Traveled to United States and began limited practice in Evanston, Illinois, 1923. Traveled with family to Finland, summers, 1923 to 1939. Taught at University of Michigan, Ann Arbor, 1923–24. Continued independent practice in Ann Arbor, 1924–25. Moved practice to Bloomfield Hills, 1925. President of Cranbrook Academy, 1932–46; continued as Director of the Department of Architecture and Urban Design, 1946–50. Died July 1, 1950, Cranbrook.

LILIAN LOUISA SWANN SAARINEN

Born April 17, 1912, New York City. Studied with Albert Stewart, 1932–34; Heinz Warnecke, 1935–36; Brenda Putnam, 1937. Studied at Cranbrook Academy, summers 1937, 1938(?), 1938–39, and at irregular periods through the summers of 1952, 1954. Awarded third prize for sculpture, exhibition of National Association of Women Sculptors and Painters, 1937. Exhibited N.Y. World's Fair, 1939. On prize-winning team for theater design in Rome Collaborative Competition, 1939. Married Eero Saarinen, June 10, 1939. Commissions for ceramic sculpture for Crow Island School, Winnetka, Illinois; Post Office, Carlisle, Kentucky; Toffaneti Restaurant, Chicago; Hudson's Northland Shopping Center; Jefferson National Expansion Memorial, St. Louis, Missouri. Divorced 1952. Studio in Cambridge, Massachusetts.

LOUISE (LOJA) GESELLIUS SAARINEN

Born March 16, 1879, Helsinki, Finland. Basic education, Konstforeningen Art School, Helsinki. Studied at Taideteollinen Keskuskoulu, 1898–99. Studied at Suomen Taideyhdistyksen Piirustuskoulu, 1899–1902. Went to Paris where she studied sculpture at Académie Colarossi under Jean-Antoine Injalbert. Returned to Helsinki, 1903, joined brother Herman Gesellius, architect and partner to Eliel Saarinen and Armas Lindgren, and worked on commissions for interiors, photography, and sculpture. Married Eliel Saarinen, March 6, 1904. Eva Lisa (Pipsan) Saarinen born, 1905. Eero Saarinen born, 1910. Immigrated to Evanston, Illinois, with her family. Joined husband with family at Ann Arbor, Michigan, 1923. Moved with family to Cranbrook, 1925. Established Studio Loja Saarinen, 1928. Prior to and during the building of Kingswood School Cranbrook, worked on all textile and carpet designs for complex, 1929–31. Employed Maja Andersson Wirde as textile designer and weaver at studio, 1929. Other weavers who are recorded as having been connected with the studio in 1930 were: Kerstein Berglund, Mrs. Marie Bexell, Lilly Bjerkin, Esther Broberg, Anna Danielson, Elizabeth Edmark, Hilda Franzen, Lillian Holm, Ruth Ingvarson, Ragnhild Johnson, Gerda Nyberg, Walborg Nordquist Smalley, and Peggy Buckberrough. Retired as Head of Department of Weaving and Textile Design, 1942. Exhibitions and Awards: Gold medal, Académie Colarossi. Cross of Liberty, bestowed upon her by the Government of Finland, 1918. "Batiks" (with Pipsan), Evanston, Illinois, 1923. With Eliel, Architectural League in New York, 1923. "Cranbrook Artists Exhibition," The Detroit Institute of Arts, late 1931. "Arts and Crafts Exhibition," Cranbrook Academy of Art, summer 1932. With Pipsan, exhibited textiles at the Academy; participated with husband, daughter, and son-in-law in exhibition of group arrangements of home furnishings, Cranbrook Pavilion, 1935. With Eliel, designed "Room for a Lady." With Pipsan, showed textiles, The Metropolitan Museum of Art, 1935. With Pipsan, exhibited rugs and carpets, international exhibition, The Metropolitan Museum of Art; displayed carpets and rugs, American Pavilion, World Exposition, Paris and received silver medal; (with Eliel) at Norfolk Museum of Art and Science, Virginia; also included in traveling exhibition, The American Federation of Arts, New York, 1937. Exhibited at Toledo Museum and Cincinnati Art Museum (same exhibition) as well as Cleveland Museum of Art; included in an exhibition at Northwestern University, Evanston, Illinois, 1938. Decorative arts exhibition, "Golden Gate International Exposition," in San Francisco, 1939. Society of Arts and Crafts, Boston; Philadelphia Art Alliance; The Metropolitan Museum of Art, New York ("Contemporary Industrial Art" exhibition), 1940. Participated in Industrial Design Competitions for Home Furnishings, The Museum of Modern Art, 1940–42. Other exhibitions in Berea, Kentucky, Washington, D.C., and Ann Arbor. Her name appears for last time in an exhibition of handwoven textiles and rugs by Cranbrook faculty and students, The Art Institute of Chicago and The Royal Ontario Museum, Toronto, 1945. Died April 21, 1968, Bloomfield Hills. (See Albert Christ-Janer, *Eliel Saarinen, Finnish-American Architect and Educator,* Chicago, 1948, revised ed., 1979, p. 139; early résumé, property of Ronald S. Swanson; Cranbrook Archives, Cranbrook Academy of Art Papers, Loja Saarinen to R. P. Raseman, June 2, 1939; Cranbrook Academy of Art, Administration Records 1931–1966, Loja Saarinen to R. P. Raseman and to Dorothy W. Liebes, Mar. and Apr. 1938; *Chicago Tribune,* Mar. 25, 1945.)

ROBERT DAVID SAILORS

Born May 23, 1913, Grand Rapids, Michigan. Attended primary and high school, Grand Rapids, 1920–32. Attended Olivet College, 1932–35. School of The Art Institute of Chicago, 1935–38; received B.A. in art education. Taught art at Evanston High School, Evanston, Illinois, fall 1938–1939. Cartoonist, *Detroit Free Press,* 1939–41. Instructor, Grand Rapids Art Gallery School, 1941–1942. Cranbrook Academy of Art, summer 1941. Scholarship student, Cranbrook Academy of Art, September 1942–spring 1943. Received M.A., spring 1943. Full Fellowship, 1943–1944. Assistant Director and Instructor, Department of Weaving, Cranbrook Academy, June 1944–winter 1947. Opened own Contemporary Textiles Weaving Company, Bitely, Michigan, winter 1947; operated with twenty-three employees until 1962. Taught at Central Michigan College, summer 1956. Moved company to Grand Rapids, winter 1962; operated there until December 1974. During that time taught weaving at University of Michigan, Extension Department, Kalamazoo Art Institute. Moved studio to Cortez, Florida, 1974, where it continues to operate as Robert D. Sailors Fabrics producing handwoven textiles, shades and rugs. Exhibitions and Awards: American Federation of Arts Traveling Show, September 1943–44. Further exhibitions, together with Loja Saarinen and Marianne Strengell, in Denton, Texas, and with Eliel and Loja Saarinen at Berea, Kentucky. Tied for first prize, "The First Annual International Textile Exhibition," Weatherspoon Art Gallery, The Women's College of the University of North Carolina in Greensboro, 1944. "Modern Textile Design," The Museum of Modern Art, New York; exhibition of handwoven textiles and rugs created by Cranbrook faculty and students, The Art Institute of Chicago and the Royal Ontario Museum in Toronto, 1945. Exhibitions throughout the U.S.

ZOLTAN SEPESHY

Born 1898, Kassa, Hungary (now Kosice, Czechoslovakia). Attended Royal Academy of Art in Budapest. Continued studies in Vienna and Paris. Traveled through Germany, Italy, and France. Came to United States, 1921. Exhibited with Michigan artists in Detroit, 1922, and won prize. Traveled to Mexico and Canada. Worked for Michigan architect Albert Kahn doing architectural perspectives; met Eliel Saarinen; painting instructor at Art School of Detroit Society of Arts and Crafts, 1924; at Wayne University, 1926. Appointed to faculty in Painting and Drawing, Cranbrook Academy of Art, 1931. Became Educational Director, 1944–46, and Director, 1946–59. Served as President, 1959–66. Thirty-six solo exhibitions in art galleries, museums, and universities. Murals at General Motors Technical Center and various public buildings. Awarded first prize, Carnegie Institute, 1947; Morse Gold Medal, National Academy of Design, 1952. Died 1974.

MARIANNE STRENGELL (DUSENBURY) HAMMARSTROM

Born May 24, 1909, Helsinki, Finland. Graduated from Atheneum, Helsinki. Svenska Sloejdforeningen, part of staff working on International Exhibition of Stockholm, Sweden, 1929–30. With Ab Hemflit-Kotiahkeruus O.Y., Helsinki, as Art Director, 1930–36. Executive Assistant for Finnish Exhibition at Triennale, Milan, Italy, 1933. Co-owner and designer of Koti-Hemmet, Helsinki, 1934–36. Designer of two collections for Bo Aktieselskab, Copenhagen, Denmark. Designed for powerloom production in Finland and Sweden. Arrived Cranbrook, February 1937. Married Charles Yerkes Dusenbury, 1940. Sandra Yerkes Dusenbury born, 1941. Charles (Chris) Yerkes Dusenbury II born, 1943. Divorced 1949. Cranbrook Academy of Art, Instructor of Weaving, Costume and Textile Design, 1937–42. Head of Department of Weaving and Textile Design, 1942–61. Married Olav Hammarstrom, August 1949. Sent by International Cooperation Administration to Japan and Philippines as Technical Advisor on weaving and textile design for cottage industry, 1951. Volunteered for UNESCO Technical Assistance Administration, New York, concerning weaving and cottage industry, 1951–52. Retired from Cranbrook Academy; moved first to Camden, Connecticut, then to New York, 1961. Designed fabrics for New York textile firms.

Employed by U.N. in Kingston, Jamaica, to establish cottage weaving industry, 1966. Returned to Cranbrook Academy as visiting professor and critic in weaving and textiles, 1967–68. Lived in Cambridge, Massachusetts, 1968–74. Lived on Cape Cod, Massachusetts, 1974 to present. Worked extensively with architects (Eero Saarinen and Associates; Skidmore, Owings and Merrill; Edward D. Stone); with industry (Knoll Associates, Inc.; V'Soske; Owens Corning Fiberglas Co.; Alcoa; Karastan; Fieldcrest; Chatham Manufacturing Company); and design studios (Ford Motor Company, General Motors Corporation, Chrysler Corporation, American Motors Corporation). Exhibitions and Awards: Silver medal, Antwerp and Milan exhibitions. Bronze medals, Barcelona and Brussels exhibitions. Included in exhibitions in Stockholm and Göteborg prior to departure to America. Participated in New York World's Fair; "International Rug and Carpet Exhibition," The Metropolitan Museum of Art, New York; "Decorative Arts Exhibition," Golden Gate International Exposition; again at The Metropolitan Museum of Art in the "Contemporary American Industrial Art Exhibition," 1939. Participated in Industrial Design Competition for Home Furnishings, The Museum of Modern Art, New York, 1940–42. Her fabrics were included in American Federation of Arts Traveling Show and "Modern Textile Design," The Museum of Modern Art, 1943–45. Cranbrook faculty and student exhibition of handwoven textiles and rugs, Cranbrook, The Art Institute of Chicago, and the Royal Ontario Museum, Toronto, 1945. Frequently included in International Textile Exhibitions, Women's College of the University of North Carolina, 1944–54. Included in Museum of Contemporary Crafts exhibition of wall hangings and rugs, 1957. Cranbrook Academy of Art, exhibitions from 1938 on. Included in first three Biennial Exhibitions of Contemporary Textiles and Ceramics there, 1946, 1949, 1951. Last Cranbrook exhibition, 1968 (hand- and powerloomed rugs as well as photo murals). Close to seventy solo exhibitions. Extensive travel throughout career, especially to Turkey, Iran and Iraq, India, Indonesia, Java, Thailand, Hong Kong, Japan, the Philippines and Hawaii.

TOSHIKO TAKAEZU

Born June 17, 1922, Pepeeko, Hawaii. Worked at Hawaiian Potters' Guild and Honolulu Planning Mill. Taught at Honolulu YWCA Adult Education program and in elementary school. Studied at Honolulu Academy of Art and with Claude Horan at University of Hawaii. Studied at Cranbrook Academy, 1951–54 (M.F.A. ceramics; weaving and sculpture as minors). Traveled to Japan, 1955–56. Many teaching positions: Flint Institute of Art, 1952–53; teaching assistant at Cranbrook Academy, 1953–54; University of Wisconsin, Madison, 1954–55; Cranbrook Academy summer school, 1954, 1955, 1956; Cleveland Institute of Art, 1956–64; Honolulu Academy of Arts, 1958, 1959; Haystack School of Crafts, Deere Island, Maine, 1958–60; University of Hawaii, 1964; Penland School of Crafts, North Carolina, 1964–70; Princeton University, Creative Arts Program, 1966–present. Has exhibited widely throughout the country, including many solo exhibitions. Studio in Quakertown, New Jersey, since 1975.

RICHARD C. THOMAS

Born April 6, 1917, Marion Center, Pennsylvania. Attended State Teachers College, Indiana, Pennsylvania, 1936–40; received B.S. 1940. U.S. Army service in reproduction (visual arts) section. Accepted as student at Cranbrook Academy of Art, 1946. Metal shop reopened under his direction, 1947. Received M.F.A. from Cranbrook, 1948; appointed Instructor of Metalwork and Head of department same year. Lives at Cranbrook.

WILLIAM WATSON

Born March 14, 1914, Wilson, North Carolina. Studied at University of North Carolina, Chapel Hill, 1932–33, 1935–36; received B.A. Studied at Cranbrook Academy, spring 1938–spring 1941; at Ohio State University, Columbus, 1941–42, 1946–47; M.F.A. ceramics, 1947. Service in U.S. Air Force, 1942–46. Studied with Marguerite Wildenhain at Pond Farm, Guerneville, California, after World War II. Taught at University of Georgia, Athens, 1948–49, and Florida State University, Tallahassee, 1949–70. Exhibited Syracuse (1940, 1942 with honorable mention, 1946, 1954, 1956, 1958); Wichita (1948); Miami (1954, 1956); Cranbrook (1954). Died September 10, 1976.

HARRY MOHR WEESE

Born June 30, 1915, Evanston, Illinois. Attended Massachusetts Institute of Technology, 1933–36; transferred to Yale University, 1936–37; returned to M.I.T., 1937–38; received B. Arch., 1938. Graduate study with Eliel Saarinen at Cranbrook, 1938–39. Research assistant, Bemis Housing Foundation, M.I.T., 1939–40. Designer, Skidmore, Owings, and Merrill, Chicago, 1940–41. Private practice with Benjamin Baldwin, Chicago, 1941–42. U.S. Navy, 1942–46. Married Kate Baldwin, 1945. Designer, SOM, Chicago, 1946–47. Independent practice, Chicago, 1947 to present.

MAJA ANDERSSON WIRDE

(also Sigrid Maria Andersson, Maja Andersson, Maja Wirde, M. Andersson, M. Wirde)
Born November 14, 1873, Ramkvilla, Sweden. Received basic education at Karlskrona, Tekniska and Högre Konstindustriella Skolan, Stockholm, 1897–1901. Taught drawing at Tekniska Skolan, Stockholm. Joined staff of Handarbetets Vänner, Stockholm, as designer and artistic leader, 1907. Traveled extensively in Italy, Germany, France, Belgium, Denmark, and England, 1910–24. Included in major exhibitions: Malmö, 1914; Göteborg, 1923; Stockholm, 1930. Left Stockholm for Cranbrook Foundation, September 1929. Employed by Cranbrook Foundation as Instructor of Weaving, October 1929. Taught courses in textile designing and weaving at Studio Loja Saarinen, and weaving and textiles for Cranbrook Academy of Art. Taught half-time at Kingswood School Cranbrook while continuing teaching at Studio Loja Saarinen, 1932–33. Given notice, February 1933. Contract expired June 30, 1933. Spent summer 1933 in Chicago at A Century of Progress, 1933 Chicago World's Fair as part of staff of Swedish Pavilion. Returned to Sweden; settled at Algutsboda; established studio; carried out commissions. Joined partnership with Sigrid and Helga Synnergren of Soedra Sveriges Kyrkliga Textil (Southern Swedish Church Textiles), Lund, 1939, but remained and worked in Algutsboda; her association with the atelier continued until her death in 1952. With Sigrid Synnergren, wove samples required for fabrics and designed patterns to be embroidered on them by her own or the Synnergren studio. Died February 11, 1952, Algutsboda, Småland, Sweden. (See *Svenskt Konstnars Lexikon,* Malmö, 1967, vol. V, p. 704; Enrollment Records, Tekniska Skolan, Stockholm, Sept. 22, 1897; Oct. 3, 1898; Oct. 5, 1899; Oct. 5, 1900; Obituaries from Swedish newspapers; Cranbrook Archives, Cranbrook Foundation Employment Record Card [inactive file—reference]; Föreningen Handarbetets Vänner, *Arsberattelser* [Annual Reports], 1904–30; Cranbrook Archives, Miscellaneous Cranbrook Academy of Art Correspondence, Box 15, List of staff at Cranbrook compiled by John Gerard; 1930 Cranbrook Foundation Publication, p. 31; Cranbrook Academy of Art Papers, Announcement of Classes, 1932–33; Cranbrook Foundation, Series 1, Box 6, Katherine Rogers Adams to Cecil Billington, Feb. 2, 1932; Cranbrook Academy of Art Correspondence, Reports, 1930–49, Series 1, Box 3, Richard P. Raseman to Cranbrook Foundation Trustees, Feb. 24, 1933; Notebooks with samples of varying sizes, Kulturen, Lund, Sweden.)

CHRONOLOGY

1904

George G. Booth purchases a portion of his estate, to be named Cranbrook, in Bloomfield Township, a suburb of Detroit, Michigan.

1908

George G. and Ellen S. Booth move from Detroit into Cranbrook House, their new home designed by Albert Kahn.

1912

The farm group is built on the Cranbrook estate, designed by local architect Marcus R. Burrowes.

1916

The dedication of the Greek Theater, designed in 1915 by Marcus R. Burrowes, presages the eventual dedication of Cranbrook to cultural and public uses.

1918

The Meeting House, designed by George G. Booth with his son Henry S. Booth, is built at Cranbrook for religious services and other community activities.

1922

Bloomfield Hills School (now called Brookside School Cranbrook) opens its doors to elementary students.
In February, George G. and Ellen S. Booth visit the American Academy in Rome.
Eliel Saarinen enters the international competition for the Chicago Tribune Tower and wins second prize.

1923

In April the Saarinen family arrives in Evanston, Illinois, where Eliel Saarinen works on plans for the development of the Chicago lakefront. In November, the Saarinens move to Ann Arbor, where Eliel is Visiting Professor in Architectural Design at the University of Michigan.
George G. Booth is introduced to Eliel Saarinen through his son Henry, a student of Saarinen's at the University of Michigan. Henry S. Booth works on his student project: a design for an academy at Cranbrook.

1924

Eliel Saarinen is asked by George G. Booth to develop the Cranbrook Educational Community; Saarinen begins plans for Cranbrook Academy of Art.

1925

Construction begins on Christ Church Cranbrook as designed by Bertram Grosvenor Goodhue Associates.
Eliel Saarinen plans Cranbrook School for boys to be built on the site of the 1912 farm group.
The Saarinens move from Ann Arbor to Bloomfield Hills.
Henry S. Booth and J. Robert F. Swanson are engaged by George G. Booth to design the first of the Academy buildings to be used as an architectural office, library, and museum. Eliel Saarinen assists with the design; construction begins.

1926

Construction begins on Cranbrook School.

1927

At the request of Eliel Saarinen, Hungarian sculptor Geza Maroti arrives at Cranbrook in January to assist with architectural details at Cranbrook School.
The Cranbrook Foundation is established by Trust Indenture through the generosity of George G. Booth, Chairman, Board of Trustees; Henry S. Booth, Vice-Chairman; and Warren S. Booth, Treasurer. Other Trustees include James S. Booth, Henry S. Hulbert, Dr. Samuel S. Marquis, and Gustavus D. Pope. Cecil Billington is Secretary and James L. Oliver is appointed Assistant Secretary-Treasurer.
George G. Booth authorizes the Foundation Trustees to establish an academy and an arts

and crafts school at Cranbrook. The academy, when fully developed, is seen as including departments of architecture, design, decoration, drawing, painting, sculpture, drama, landscape design, music and artistic craftsmanship, a library, and a museum.

George G. Booth donates his art library and art objects to the Foundation.

Eliel Saarinen continues to be engaged as chief architectural advisor for Cranbrook Architectural Office, which is operated by the newly formed Foundation.

Cranbrook School for boys opens on September 19, with Dr. William O. Stevens as Headmaster.

Ellen S. and George G. Booth propose to Cranbrook Foundation Trustees consideration of a school for girls at Cranbrook.

Arthur Nevill Kirk of London is engaged by George G. Booth to create silver objects for Christ Church Cranbrook; Kirk also works part-time as Instructor of Arts and Crafts at Cranbrook School.

1928

Eliel Saarinen begins designs for Residence #1 (Saarinen House) and Residence #2 at the Academy, to be completed in 1930.

The Cranbrook School Headmaster's Residence is designed on Academy Way; this residence will be used for a variety of purposes in the coming years.

Construction begins on the First Arts and Crafts studio building at the Academy and on an addition to the Architectural Office.

Discussions are held by the Trustees of The Cranbrook Foundation to employ artists and craftsmen for the Art Department although buildings are not yet completed.

Geza Maroti carves bas relief in Cranbrook School library.

Henry P. Macomber of Boston Society of Arts and Crafts is engaged as Secretary of the Foundation's Art Department.

Loja Saarinen founds her weaving studio to produce rugs and textiles for Cranbrook buildings.

1929

George G. Booth proposes that the Academy operate in a fashion similar to the American Academy in Rome, and that the arts and crafts school become an integral part of the Academy rather than being separated from architecture, painting, and sculpture.

The following artists are appointed to the craft studios: Tor Berglund (cabinetmaker), John C. Burnett (ironworker), Jean Eschmann (bookbinder), David Evans (sculptor), Arthur Nevill Kirk (silversmith), Henry P. Roberts (printer), and Maja Andersson Wirde (weaver).

Geza Maroti leaves Cranbrook permanently.

Carl Milles first visits Cranbrook; Eliel Saarinen asks him to become resident sculptor and Director of the Department of Sculpture. Milles consents and, before leaving for Europe, promises to return to the Academy.

The north wing addition to the original Academy building and the addition to the First Arts and Crafts studio building are completed.

The Saarinen family (Eliel, Loja, Pipsan, Eero) begins designs for a girls' school, Kingswood School Cranbrook.

Eliel Saarinen designs a dining room for the exhibition "The Architect and the Industrial Arts: An Exhibition of Contemporary American Design" at The Metropolitan Museum of Art, New York.

1930

George G. Booth proposes that fellowships be established for future Academy students.

David Evans exhibits his sculpture at the Academy in January, completes the bronze *Football Group* relief, and leaves Cranbrook in June.

Edward Alonzo Miller is appointed head of the Printing department in February, replacing Henry P. Roberts.

With the death of blacksmith John C. Burnett, the iron shop closes on September 17.

Henry P. Macomber's services to the Academy end in November. Also during this month, Frank L. Allen is employed as Supervisor of Art Education for all Cranbrook schools.

The weaving and silver shops, under Loja Saarinen and Arthur N. Kirk respectively, are reorganized to establish their own markets and pay their operating expenses rather than working under the direct patronage of George G. Booth.

Construction begins on Kingswood School Cranbrook.

Studio #3 is constructed parallel to Residence #2 along Academy Way.

Construction begins in the summer on the first Cranbrook Institute of Science building, designed by George G. Booth.

1931

Carl Milles is appointed resident sculptor; he brings with him Verner Lindstrom as his plaster caster and pointer. Milles donates *Triton with Shell* to The Cranbrook Foundation.

At Milles' request, arrangements are made to construct a large sculpture studio for him as designed by Eliel Saarinen.

Loja Saarinen designs rugs and textiles for Milles' residence at the Academy.

Zoltan Sepeshy works at the Academy as Instructor in Painting.

As a result of Frank L. Allen's proposals, art

classes are formed in the other Cranbrook schools; he also instructs in painting.

Allen exhibits his watercolors at Cranbrook Academy of Art in February.

Ruth Eriksson Allen (Mrs. Frank Allen) teaches pottery at the Academy.

The cabinet shop, directed by Tor Berglund, is placed under the same fiscal policy as the weaving and silver shops.

Kingswood School Cranbrook opens in the fall with Dr. Katherine Rogers Adams as Headmistress.

"Cranbrook Exhibition" is held at The Detroit Institute of Arts in December. Art and craft works by all artists then at Cranbrook are included.

1932

The creation of an arts council, made up of resident artists and craftsmen, with Eliel Saarinen as Chairman, is authorized by The Cranbrook Foundation Trustees in April.

The Academy is formally established under the aegis of The Cranbrook Foundation in June; George G. Booth proposes that the presidency be offered to Eliel Saarinen, who accepts; that the office of Executive Secretary be created to handle routine matters (Richard Raseman assumes these duties); and that one Foundation Trustee be designated to cooperate with Academy officers (Henry S. Booth is appointed).

Cranbrook Institute of Science is established as an institution separate from The Cranbrook Foundation by formal Trust Indenture.

The large studio (#4) for Carl Milles is completed; another additional studio wing for sculpture (Studio #5) is planned and construction begins. Milles finishes his first major work at Cranbrook, *Jonah Fountain.*

Waylande Gregory comes to Cranbrook from Cleveland and establishes the ceramic sculpture and modeling facility.

Frank L. Allen's services end at the Academy in June.

Tor Berglund leaves Cranbrook in August.

Classes at the Academy are announced. These include a postgraduate course in architecture (Eliel Saarinen), an advanced course in sculpture (Carl Milles), drawing and painting (Zoltan Sepeshy and John Cunningham), ceramic sculpture (Waylande Gregory), weaving and textiles (Maja Wirde), bookbinding (Jean Eschmann), jewelry and enameling (Arthur N. Kirk), and costume design and batiks (Pipsan Saarinen Swanson).

A summer exhibition of art and craft works by Academy faculty is held at Cranbrook.

In December, Zoltan Sepeshy exhibits his paintings and drawings at the Academy.

1933

Eliel Saarinen is re-elected President of the Academy.

The operation of the Academy, as well as essential equipment and furnishings, are turned over by the Trustees to the President and Executive Secretary.

Because of the poor financial situation, all craftsmen are notified that contracts will expire at the end of June and will not be renewed.

The museum and all the arts and crafts shops are closed with the exception of the weaving studio under Loja Saarinen. Waylande Gregory, Jean Eschmann, Arthur N. Kirk, Maja Wirde, and Edward A. Miller leave the Academy.

Marshall Fredericks receives a scholarship to study sculpture at the Academy in February. He teaches crafts at Cranbrook School in the fall.

Summer classes in painting are held by John Cunningham at the Academy; he leaves Cranbrook in the fall.

A joint exhibition of the textiles of Loja Saarinen and her daughter Pipsan Saarinen Swanson is held at the Academy.

Lake Jonah is completed at the foot of Academy Way.

Studio #5 is completed.

1934

A significant collection of sculpture by Carl Milles is purchased by The Cranbrook Foundation.

Loja and Eliel Saarinen design "Room for a Lady," which is included in the exhibition "Contemporary Industrial Art" at The Metropolitan Museum of Art, New York.

Lillian Holm teaches weaving under Loja Saarinen at the Academy.

Rachel DeWolfe Raseman instructs in interior design.

Summer school is held at the Academy. Reginald Bennett instructs in painting. Marshall Fredericks teaches modeling and ceramics and continues as an instructor until 1942.

Wallace Mitchell enters the Academy as a student.

Zoltan Sepeshy exhibits his paintings at the Academy in May.

Maija Grotell of the Henry Street Settlement House, New York, exhibits her ceramics at the Academy in December.

The Cranbrook Pavilion, built in 1924, is remodeled as a lecture hall and exhibition space for use by the Academy and others within the community; the formal opening in December features an exhibition of sculpture by Carl Milles and paintings by Zoltan Sepeshy.

1935

Eliel and Loja Saarinen and J. Robert F. and Pipsan Saarinen Swanson hold an exhibition of home furnishings at the Cranbrook Pavilion in May.

Pipsan Saarinen Swanson teaches a course, "Contemporary Design of Interiors and Furnishings," in the spring. Her course and Rachel Raseman's in interior design are not continued in the fall.

Summer school is held in painting and in modeling and ceramics with Reginald Bennett and Marshall Fredericks as instructors.

Loja Saarinen and her daughter Pipsan Saarinen Swanson exhibit textiles at The Metropolitan Museum of Art, New York.

Special lectures at the Academy are given by Ely Jacques Kahn, Frank Lloyd Wright, and Le Corbusier.

1936

In January, Frank Lloyd Wright speaks again at the Academy.

The Intermediate School is established within the Academy for less advanced students in the arts.

Wallace Mitchell joins the Academy as Instructor of Drawing and Painting under Zoltan Sepeshy.

Charles D. Price works for one year as an instructor in the silver and metal shop.

William W. Comstock joins the Academy as Instructor of Design.

Construction begins on a twenty-room dormitory north of Carl Milles' studio; it opens the following year.

Ground is broken for the new building of the Cranbrook Institute of Science, designed by Eliel Saarinen.

Eero Saarinen joins his father's architectural firm.

Zoltan Sepeshy exhibits his paintings at the Academy.

1937

Ellen S. and George G. Booth propose to The Cranbrook Foundation Trustees in June that a new museum be designed by Eliel Saarinen to house the Academy's art collections.

Marianne Strengell is appointed Instructor of Weaving and Costume Design, replacing Lillian Holm, who continues to teach weaving at Kingswood School.

Harry Bertoia receives a scholarship to the Academy.

Frank Lloyd Wright speaks at the Academy on April 29.

1938

Maija Grotell is appointed head of the Ceramics department, a position she will hold until her retirement in 1966. An exhibition of her ceramics is held at the Academy.

Harry Bertoia reopens the metal shop at the Academy and begins teaching.

Charles Eames receives a fellowship to study with Eliel Saarinen at Cranbrook.

Marianne Strengell exhibits her textiles at the Academy in the fall.

Construction begins on four additional faculty residences, a dormitory, and studios at the Academy, all designed by Eliel Saarinen.

Plans for the new art museum are well underway by June; the new building will house the art collection and art library.

1939

Eero Saarinen works as an assistant in the Department of Architecture under his father.

Charles Eames teaches design, replacing William Comstock.

The course in costume design is discontinued.

Summer session is re-established with workshops in drawing and painting, modeling and sculpture, pottery and ceramics, metal crafts, weaving and textiles. Classes are taught by the regular staff of the Intermediate School: Wallace Mitchell, Marshall Fredericks, Maija Grotell, Harry Bertoia, and Marianne Strengell.

A faculty exhibition is held in December in the Cranbrook Pavilion; the installation is designed by Eero Saarinen and Charles Eames.

First prize is awarded to Eliel and Eero Saarinen, architects, and J. Robert F. Swanson, associate, for their design for the Smithsonian Art Gallery, Washington, D.C.; because of the War this project is not built, however.

1940

Construction begins, according to Eliel Saarinen's revised designs, on the Museum and Library for Cranbrook Academy of Art.

Life magazine sponsors an exhibition of contemporary American art in May in the new studio building (built 1938).

The Intermediate School staff again teaches classes during the summer session.

Marianne Strengell exhibits her textiles at the Academy.

1941

Charles Eames and Eero Saarinen win first prize for seating in "Organic Design in Home Furnishings," a competition at The Museum of Modern Art, New York.

Charles Eames leaves the Academy and moves to California to continue experimentation with molded plywood designs.

Walter Baermann comes to the Academy from the California School of Design in Pasadena as Instructor of Industrial Design.

Richard Davis is appointed Curator of the

new Museum in January.

Summer session is held by the staff of the Intermediate School. Mary Lean replaces Marianne Strengell in weaving for the summer session only.

1942

Eliel and Eero Saarinen remove their architectural office from the Cranbrook grounds. Eero leaves his teaching position at Cranbrook in February to devote full time to his architectural work.

Eliel Saarinen conducts classes in urban design at the Academy for a group of forty Detroit architects called Architects Civic Design Group.

Loja Saarinen closes her weaving studio; Marianne Strengell takes charge of the Department of Weaving.

A Trust Indenture for the establishment of Cranbrook Academy of Art as a separate entity from The Cranbrook Foundation empowered to grant degrees is ratified and adopted by the Trustees on May 21.

The Trustees of the Foundation become the first Trustees of the Academy. They are: Gustavus D. Pope, Chairman; George G. Booth, Vice-Chairman; Cecil Billington, Secretary-Treasurer; Henry S. Booth; James S. Booth; Warren S. Booth; Henry S. Hulbert; Samuel S. Marquis; and Ralph Stone.

Harry Bertoia takes on additional classes in graphic arts.

Walter Baermann leaves the Academy for the armed forces; Frank Greer assumes his design courses.

Marshall Fredericks joins the armed forces and is replaced by Janet DeCoux as Instructor of Modeling and Sculpture.

The use of the term "Intermediate School" is discontinued.

Summer session is held in drawing and painting, modeling and sculpture, design and crafts.

Curator Richard Davis leaves Cranbrook for the armed forces in September; George G. Booth volunteers to be Acting Director of the Museum to prepare for its opening.

1943

Eliel Saarinen's *The City: Its Growth, Its Decay, Its Future* is published by Reinhold Publishing Corporation, New York.

In April, Eliel Saarinen requests of the Trustees that a search be initiated to replace him as President of the Academy.

The first degrees are granted by Cranbrook Academy of Art.

Richard Raseman leaves the Academy for the armed services in May. Henry S. Booth fills in as Executive Secretary until his resignation on December 1 because of illness.

Zoltan Sepeshy is then appointed Registrar ad interim, assuming administrative duties.

Ernst Scheyer is appointed Instructor of the History of Art and Civilization.

Verner Lindstrom, who had been working in Carl Milles' studio as his plaster caster, instructs students in plaster mold construction and plaster casting.

Lillian Holm substitutes in the spring for weaver Marianne Strengell.

Instructors for the summer session include Maija Grotell, Wallace Mitchell, Ernst Scheyer, Zoltan Sepeshy, and Marianne Strengell.

Because of the War and lack of students, the Design department is temporarily suspended; Frank Greer enters the Army in April.

Harry Bertoia's metal craft classes are cancelled due to the difficulty of obtaining metals; he continues instruction in graphic arts until his departure in September to do war plant work and to assist Charles and Ray Eames with their molded plywood chair designs.

Clifford B. West is appointed to assist Sepeshy with his drawing class.

J. Davidson Stephen is appointed Assistant Instructor in the Architecture department for five months (beginning December 1) to help Saarinen with an urban planning group of Detroit architects.

1944

Henry S. Booth succeeds Gustavus D. Pope as Chairman of the Academy Board of Trustees.

The architectural firm of Saarinen, Swanson & Saarinen is formed.

In July, Eliel Saarinen states that he is willing to continue on as President of the Academy. Also in that month, Zoltan Sepeshy is appointed Educational Director of the Academy.

Robert Sailors is appointed Instructor of Weaving under Marianne Strengell.

Svend Steen, previously part-time at the Academy, works as supervisor of the wood shop.

Janet DeCoux leaves the Academy.

In addition to the regular faculty, Jon Jonson teaches sculpture for the summer session.

The Design department is re-established; Howard Dearstyne becomes the instructor in November.

First student under the Servicemen's Readjustment Act (G.I. Bill) studies at the Academy.

1945

Jon Jonson is invited back as Instructor of Modeling and Sculpture beginning January 1.

A power loom, presented to the Weaving department by The Cranbrook Foundation, is installed in January.

The metal shop is reopened on a part-time basis under the direction of Herman Garfield, an advanced design student.

Nancy Leitch is appointed to assist in ceramics under Maija Grotell.

Ernst Scheyer leaves the Academy.

In June, Albert Christ-Janer comes to Cranbrook as Director of the Museum; he also teaches a survey course in art history.

Harriet Dyer Adams works as Curator of the Museum.

A summer session is held at the Academy. The staff includes Maija Grotell, Robert Sailors, Jon Jonson, Howard Dearstyne, Wallace Mitchell, Albert Christ-Janer.

Eliel and Loja Saarinen and Carl Milles become American citizens.

1946

George G. Booth resigns as Chairman of The Cranbrook Foundation and is succeeded by his son Henry on February 7.

Eliel Saarinen becomes President Emeritus of Cranbrook Academy of Art on July 1 and continues as Director of the Department of Architecture and Urban Design. Zoltan Sepeshy is appointed Director of the Academy beginning July 1.

A summer session is held at the Academy; a survey of modern art is taught by Harriet Dyer Adams. Other faculty includes Howard Dearstyne, Maija Grotell, Jon Jonson, Nancy Leitch, Wallace Mitchell, and Robert Sailors.

Norman Nagle teaches design, replacing Howard Dearstyne.

First biennial exhibition of contemporary textiles and ceramics is held at the Museum.

Zoltan Sepeshy's *Tempera Painting* is published by American Studio Books in New York.

1947

The architectural firm of Saarinen, Swanson & Saarinen is dissolved; father and son continue to work together as Saarinen, Saarinen & Associates.

Maija Grotell shows her ceramics at the Museum in February.

In February, after his death at Cranbrook, a memorial exhibition of the work of Jon Jonson is held in the Museum.

The following instructors leave the Academy: Robert Sailors, Herman Garfield, and Nancy Leitch.

Mary B. Coulter is appointed as an assistant in ceramics under Maija Grotell.

An exhibition of abstract paintings by Wallace Mitchell is held in April in the Museum.

Summer session instructors include Harriet Dyer Adams, Maija Grotell and Martha Middleton (ceramics), David Mitchell and Kyle Morris (drawing and painting), Norman Nagle, Antoinette Prestini (weaving), Cecil Richards (sculpture).

Albert Christ-Janer leaves the Academy in September for the University of Chicago.

William McVey is appointed Instructor of Sculpture under Carl Milles in September.

1948

Ellen Scripps Booth dies at Cranbrook House on January 24.

Harriet Dyer Adams leaves her position as Curator of the Museum in February.

Esther Sperry is appointed Museum Curator in April.

Richard Thomas is appointed Instructor of Metalsmithing; he also works as Assistant Instructor in the Design department.

Berthold "Tex" Schiwetz takes over from Verner Lindstrom in plaster casting in Carl Milles' studio.

Ernst Scheyer resumes lectures in art history at the Academy until 1951.

William Sparr is appointed to teach weaving on the power loom under Marianne Strengell.

Summer session is held at the Academy. The instructors are Maija Grotell and Leza McVey (ceramics), Norman Nagle, Clifford West and Frederick Meyer (drawing and painting), Richard Thomas, William McVey, Ernst Scheyer, and Estelle Heller (weaving).

Norman Nagle leaves the Academy in the fall.

Ralph Steen helps his father, Svend, in the wood shop.

Search for Form. A Fundamental Approach to Art by Eliel Saarinen is published by Reinhold Publishing Corporation, New York.

Eliel Saarinen, a biography by Albert Christ-Janer, is published by University of Chicago Press.

1949

Theodore Luderowski becomes Instructor of Design on January 1.

George G. Booth dies in Detroit on April 11.

Esther Sperry resigns as Curator of the Museum in May.

The faculty for the summer session is Maija Grotell and Martha Middleton Lauritzen (ceramics), Theodore Luderowski, Wallace Mitchell and Clifford West, Richard Thomas, Paul Frazier (sculpture), Ernst Scheyer, and William Sparr (weaving).

Eva Ingersoll Gatling works as Curator of the Museum beginning September 1.

1950

An exhibition of paintings by Zoltan Sepeshy is held in the Museum in April.

Eliel Saarinen dies at Cranbrook on July 1.
Summer session instructors include Martha M. Lauritzen and J. T. Abernathy (ceramics), Theodore Luderowski, Wallace Mitchell and Clifford West, Richard Thomas, Cecil Richards (sculpture), Paul Wescher (survey of modern art), and William Sparr.

The fabrics of Marianne Strengell are exhibited at the Museum in September.

John Risley works for the year as an assistant in the Sculpture department.

J. T. Abernathy works as an assistant in ceramics under Maija Grotell.

Robert H. Snyder is engaged as Instructor of Architecture in the fall.

With the death of Eliel Saarinen, the teaching of urban design is discontinued.

1951

Milles retires to the American Academy in Rome and his estate, Millesgården, in Sweden. Berthold "Tex" Schiwetz accompanies Milles to Italy, where he takes charge of the latter's studio.

"Eliel Saarinen Memorial Exhibition" is held at the Museum in April.

Joseph Bulone works as an assistant in the Sculpture department under William McVey.

Clifford West teaches anatomy at the Academy through 1962.

Dale Huffman works as ceramics assistant under Maija Grotell.

Summer session is held at the Academy. The staff are Martha M. Lauritzen and Barbara Carmel (ceramics), Theodore Luderowski, Kyle Morris and Wallace Mitchell (painting), Richard Thomas, William McVey, Eva Gatling (survey of modern art), and William Sparr.

Three scholarships for advanced study are established in memory of George G. Booth, Ellen S. Booth, and Eliel Saarinen.

1952

Gustavus D. Pope, former Chairman of the Academy Board of Trustees, dies on March 2.

Richard Gale is hired to work in the wood shop for the year.

James Black works as an assistant to William McVey in sculpture.

Stephen Polchert is appointed as an assistant in ceramics under Maija Grotell.

The faculty for the summer session includes Robert Snyder, Martha M. Lauritzen and Barbara Carmel, Theodore Luderowski, Wallace Mitchell, Harold Milbrath (metalsmithing), Cecil Richards (sculpture), Eva Gatling, and William Sparr.

Ceramics by Maija Grotell are exhibited at the Museum in February and March.

1953

Svend Steen, Instructor of Woodworking, dies in March.

Nils Jorgensen works in the wood shop through 1955.

William McVey resigns his position as Instructor of Sculpture.

Paul Granlund and Lyman Kipp work as assistants in the Sculpture department.

Summer session courses are staffed by the following: Robert Snyder (architecture), Marietta Hipple and Robert Kline (ceramics), Theodore Luderowski, Michael Waskowsky (painting), Richard Thomas, Gabriel Kohn (sculpture), Azalea Thorpe and William Sparr (weaving).

Wallace Mitchell exhibits his paintings at the Museum in April.

Toshiko Takaezu is an assistant to Maija Grotell in the Ceramics department.

1954

The Academy Trustees consider working toward accreditation by the North Central Association of Colleges and Schools.

Glen Chamberlain becomes Instructor in the Sculpture department; Morris Brose works as his assistant through 1957.

Robert Kline assists Maija Grotell in the Ceramics department.

Summer session faculty are Robert Snyder, Toshiko Takaezu (ceramics), Theodore Luderowski, Wallace Mitchell, Richard Thomas, Paul Granlund (sculpture), Azalea Thorpe and William Sparr, and Hugh C. Acton (wood shop).

Museum exhibitions include the designs of Theodore Luderowski and sculpture by Glen Chamberlain.

John DeMartelly conducts workshops in graphic arts through 1960.

1955

Wallace Mitchell takes charge of the Museum, replacing Eva I. Gatling.

Madison Fred Mitchell becomes Instructor of Painting under Zoltan Sepeshy.

In honor of his eightieth birthday on June 23, an exhibition of the work of Carl Milles is held in the Museum.

Carl Milles dies on September 19 at Millesgården.

Summer session is held at the Academy. The staff are Toshiko Takaezu and Robert Kline, Theodore Luderowski, Louis Hafermehl (painting), E. Dane Purdo (metalsmithing), Morris Brose (sculpture), Azalea Thorpe, William Sparr and Twila Alber (weaving).

LeMaxie Glover supervises the wood shop, replacing Nils Jorgensen.

1956

Berthold "Tex" Schiwetz returns to the Academy to teach sculpture until 1962, replacing Glen Chamberlain.

The large Milles studio is divided into two floors to provide additional space for students.

Kenneth Isaacs arrives in the fall to work as Instructor of Design, replacing Theodore Luderowski.

Stanislav O'Jack takes charge of the wood shop.

Summer session faculty includes Toshiko Takaezu and Robert Kline, Theodore Luderowski, Louis Hafermehl, Vernon MacNeil (metalsmithing), Morris Brose, Twila Alber and William Sparr (weaving), and LeMaxie Glover (wood shop).

1957

Charles McGee replaces Kenneth Isaacs as Instructor of Design.

Richard DeVore works as assistant in the Ceramics department under Maija Grotell.

One gallery in the Museum is converted for use as an auditorium, to be completed in 1959.

Summer session faculty includes Richard DeVore and Robert Kline (ceramics), Leon Mead (design), M. Fred Mitchell, Morris Brose, Anna Kang and William Sparr (weaving).

Recent work by Harry Bertoia is shown in the Museum.

Robert Rothman gives lectures in art history.

1958

Irving Stollman works as assistant to Charles McGee in the Design department.

Jon Rush works as assistant in the Sculpture department.

Summer session faculty includes Richard DeVore and Robert Kline, Charles McGee, Victor Candell (painting), William Sparr and H. Theodore Hallman, Jr. (weaving).

A scholarship is established in memory of Carl Milles.

John Collinson and A. Franklin Page begin their lectures in art history and aesthetics.

1959

Jack Madson replaces M. Fred Mitchell as Instructor of Painting under Zoltan Sepeshy.

Zoltan Sepeshy assumes the title of President of Cranbrook Academy of Art.

Ernest Toth assists Richard Thomas in the Metalsmithing department in the spring.

Summer sessions are discontinued.

1960

Cranbrook Academy of Art is accredited by the North Central Association of Colleges and Schools.

John W. Blanchard succeeds Henry S. Booth as Chairman of the Trustees for the Academy.

Laurence Barker becomes Instructor of Graphic Arts, establishing graphic arts as a full department.

Howard Brown comes in the fall to teach design, replacing Charles McGee.

Richard Thomas' *Metalsmithing for the Artist-Craftsman* is published by the Chilton Book Company, Radnor.

1961

Marianne Strengell leaves the Academy and is replaced by Glen Kaufman as Instructor of Weaving.

Eero Saarinen dies on September 1.

NOTES

In references to exhibition catalogues published by museums rather than by commercial publishers, the museum's name is included following the city of publication.

1. NORTH BY MIDWEST
Neil Harris

1. For some insights into American Communitarianism, and its relationship to the West, see Arthur E. Bestor, *Backwoods Utopias. The Sectarian and Owenite Phases of Communitarian Socialism in America, 1663–1829,* Philadelphia, 1950; *idem,* "Patent Office Models of the Good Society: Some Relationships between Social Reform and Westward Expansion," *American Historical Review* 58 (1953), pp. 505–26; Whitney R. Cross, *The Burned-Over District. The Social and Intellectual History of Enthusiastic Religion in Western New York, 1800–1850,* Ithaca, 1950; J. F. C. Harrison, *Quest for the New Moral World. Robert Owen and the Owenites in England and America,* New York, 1969; and John Humphrey Noyes, *History of American Socialisms,* Philadelphia, 1870. Henry Nash Smith, *Virgin Land: The American West as Symbol and Myth,* Cambridge, Mass., 1950, remains indispensable as a guide to the Western idea.

2. For the American Arts and Crafts movement, particularly for its Middle West variants, see Robert Judson Clark, ed., *The Arts and Crafts Movement in America, 1876–1916,* Princeton, 1972, chap. 2; David A. Hanks, *The Decorative Designs of Frank Lloyd Wright,* New York, 1929; *Prairie School Architecture in Minnesota, Iowa and Wisconsin,* St. Paul: Minnesota Museum of Art, 1982; Ralph Fletcher Seymour, *Some Went This Way. A Forty Year Pilgrimage Among Artists, Bookmen and Printers,* Chicago, 1945; Brian A. Spencer, ed., *The Prairie School Tradition. The Prairie Archives of the Milwaukee Art Center,* New York, 1979; and Susan Otis Thompson, *American Book Design and William Morris,* New York, 1977. T. J. Jackson Lears, *No Place of Grace. Anti-Modernism and the Transformation of American Culture, 1880–1920,* New York, 1981, chap. 2, offers a critical and contextual analysis of Arts and Crafts ideology. The Middle West's influence extended far beyond its borders. Thus the architects Greene and Greene, at the center of California Arts and Crafts, were born in Ohio, and studied at Calvin Woodward's Manual Training High School in St. Louis.

3. I have found helpful here Leonard K. Eaton, *American Architecture Comes of Age. European Reaction to H. H. Richardson and Louis Sullivan,* Cambridge, Mass., 1972; John Boulton Smith, "Art Nouveau and National Romanticism in Finland," *Apollo* 115 (May, 1982), pp. 380–87; and Ritva Tuomi, "On the Search for a National Style," *Abacus* 1 (1979), pp. 57–96. Smith goes into the debates about Swedish Art Nouveau, involving the critiques of Gustaf Strengell, Sigurd Frosterus, and William Finch, as well as the contributions of Louis Sparre, Hugo Simberg, Gallén-Kallela, and the architectural firm of Gesellius, Lindgren & Saarinen. Elisabet Stavenow-Hidemark, "Viking Revival and Art Nouveau: Traditions of Excellence," in David Revere McFadden, ed., *Scandinavian Modern Design 1880–1980,* New York, 1982, pp. 47–85, appeared after this essay was completed.

4. Information about these institutions can be found in Smith, *op. cit.;* Joy Hakanson Colby, *Art and a City,* Detroit, 1956; and *Arts and Crafts in Detroit 1906–1976. The Movement, The Society, The School,* Detroit: The Detroit Institute of Arts, 1976.

5. For more on the Prairie School see H. Allen Brooks, *The Prairie School. Frank Lloyd Wright and His Midwest Contemporaries,* Toronto, 1972. A detailed discussion of Nature, architecture, and romanticism, as they involved one great Midwestern admirer of Saarinen, can be found in Narciso G. Menocal, *Architecture As Nature: The Transcendentalist Idea of Louis Sullivan,* Madison, 1981.

6. Meredith Nicholson, *The Valley of Democracy,* New York, 1919, p. 16.

7. Julian Street, *Abroad At Home: American Ramblings, Observations, and Adventures of Julian Street,* New York, [1914], 1920, pp. 65–66. Another interesting view of the region at this time can be found in Arthur E. Bostwick, *The Different West: As Seen By a Transplanted Easterner,* Chicago, 1913.

8. For Midwestern cultural pretensions in the late nineteenth and early twentieth centuries see Helen L. Horowitz, *Culture & The City: Cultural Philanthropy in Chicago from the 1880s to 1917,* Lexington, 1976; Edward Hungerford,

The Personality of American Cities, New York, 1913; and Thomas S. Hines, *Burnham of Chicago. Architect and Planner,* New York, 1978, especially chapter 8 which discusses the Cleveland civic plan. For Midwestern attitudes to the city see Don S. Kirschner, *City and Country. Rural Responses to Urbanization in the 1920s,* Westport, 1970.

9. A. MacCallum Scott, *Through Finland to St. Petersburgh,* London, 1908, pp. 69–70, 82. Scott was particularly impressed by two structures designed by Gesellius, Lindgren & Saarinen: the Nordiska Bank and the Pohjola Insurance Company. He also admired the work of Lars Sonck, and noted the Finnish affinity for granite, and the massive, rugged strength of many commercial buildings. This is the quality which has led some to see H. H. Richardson's influence prevalent in Scandinavia.

10. Leonard Eaton, *op. cit., passim,* discusses European interest in Sullivan and Richardson. For Midwestern interest in Darmstadt and Vienna, there is growing evidence. See, for example, *The Domestic Scene (1897–1927): George M. Niedecken, Interior Architect,* Milwaukee: Milwaukee Art Museum, 1981.

11. The Kaiser took particular interest in Burnham's Chicago Plan. See Hines, *op. cit.,* pp. 343–44. For more on American city planning in this era see Robert Bruegmann, Sally Chappell, and John Zukowsky, *The Plan of Chicago: 1909–1970,* Chicago: The Art Institute of Chicago, 1979; Joan E. Draper, *Edward H. Bennett. Architect and City Planner, 1874–1954,* Chicago: The Art Institute of Chicago, 1982; J. L. Hancock, "Planners in the Changing American City, 1900–1940," *American Institute of Planners Journal* 33 (Sept. 1967), pp. 290–304; and Mel Scott, *American City Planning Since 1890,* Berkeley, 1971. The Burnham Plan was exhibited also in Dusseldorf and London.

12. Henry Goddard Leach, "Concerning Scandinavian Art," *Independent* 72 (Dec. 26, 1912), p. 1494. See also "Scandinavian Art," *Outlook* 102 (Dec. 21, 1912), pp. 836–37; and Clare Ruge, "Arts and Crafts in Europe," *Independent* 59 (Sept. 7, 1905), pp. 563–73, this last a survey which was prompted by the Scandinavian art display in St. Louis for the Louisiana Purchase Exposition. It is worth noting the appearance at this time of The Society for the Advancement of Scandinavian Study (1911), dominated by Midwestern scholars, and meeting, almost exclusively in these first years, in Illinois and Minnesota. The society's objective was to promote research in "the languages, literature and culture of the Scandinavian North. . ." Obviously, Scandinavian immigration to the Middle West was another source of mutual interest. See, among the many works devoted to the subject, Lars Ljungmark, *Swedish Exodus,* Carbondale, 1979; and Ingrid Semmingsen, *Norway to America: A History of the Migration,* Minneapolis, 1978.

13. *The International Competition For A New Administration Building For the Chicago Tribune MCMXXII,* Chicago, 1923. Of this total, thirty-seven came from Germany. While Denmark, Finland, and Norway were represented, Sweden was not.

14. See, for example, the comment of W. L. George, that the Middle West had "material wealth" which made it "so splendid an exhibition. . . . America has wealth in hand, which Europe has not; only work is wanted" (W. L. George, "Hail, Columbia! America In The Making," *Harper's* 142 [Jan. 1921], p. 142). George, a British visitor, goes on to note the region's self-consciousness and search for culture. "The Middle West wants things, everything, everything that man can get, whether it is gold, or love, or knowledge; it wants even aestheticism" (p. 151).

15. For Midwestern literature see Robert C. Bray, "In Pursuit of a Distinctive Utterance: Realistic Novels in the Midwest, 1871–1914," unpublished Ph.D. dissertation, University of Chicago, September, 1971; Hugh Dalziel Duncan, *Culture and Democracy: The Struggle for Form in Society and Architecture in Chicago and the Middle West During the Life and Times of Louis H. Sullivan,* Totowa, 1965; John T. Flanagan, "The Reality of Midwestern Literature," in Thomas T. McAvoy, ed., *The Midwest: Myth Or Reality?,* South Bend, 1961, pp. 75–91; and Gerald Nemanic, ed., *A Bibliographic Guide to Midwestern Literature,* Iowa City, 1981.

16. These texts include Edgar Lee Masters, *Spoon River Anthology* (1915); Sherwood Anderson, *Winesburg, Ohio* (1919); and four novels by Sinclair Lewis, *Main Street* (1921); *Babbitt* (1922); *Elmer Gantry* (1927); and *Dodsworth* (1929). Also in this literature of Middle West denigration might be included essays by H. L. Mencken, Marquis W. Childs, Waldo Frank, and a number of others, writing for the *New Republic,* the *American Mercury,* and *Harper's.*

17. Leonard Lanson Cline, "The Fordizing of a Pleasant Peninsula," in Ernest Gruening, ed., *These United States. A Symposium,* New York, 1923, pp. 180, 187. These essays originally appeared in the *Nation.* H. L. Mencken wrote on Maryland, Zona Gale on Wisconsin, and Edmund Wilson on New Jersey.

18. Sherwood Anderson, "I'll Say We've Done Well," in Gruening, *op. cit.,* p. 110. "I claim that we Ohio men have taken as lovely a land as ever lay outdoors and that we have, in our towns and cities, put the old stamp of ourselves on it for keeps," Anderson added.

19. William Alan White, "A Puritan Survival," in Gruening, *op. cit.,* p. 12.

20. Sinclair Lewis, "The Norse State," in Ernest Gruening, ed., *These United States, A Symposium,* second series, New York, 1924, p. 30.

21. A few artist colonies were established in the late nineteenth century, such as those in Cornish, New Hampshire, and Woodstock, New York, but more elaborate developments did not take place until somewhat later. The MacDowell Memorial,

a colony established in Petersborough, New Hampshire, with a legacy from the American composer, Edward MacDowell, was an important influence. Summer colonies were created, more informally, at Gloucester, Massachusetts, Ogunquit, Maine, and Provincetown, on Cape Cod. At the turn of the century a group of artists began to build studios at Taos, New Mexico; by the 1920s this had become an important colony, in part because of the notoriety of Mabel Dodge Luhan. Santa Fe also had developed its own artist group by then, and in 1929 a well endowed artist community was created in Saratoga Springs, New York, at Yaddo, the mansion and estate left by Katrina Trask. More is needed on the history of artist colonies in America, but this was, in effect, one of the powerful functions served by Cranbrook, whose largely European art faculty created, in its own way, a model artist community. For more on the subject see "Rural and Summer Colonies of the Arts and Crafts," *International Studio* 34 (June 1908), supplement, pp. 151–52; Rose Henderson, "Art That Blooms At the Desert's Rim," *Outlook* 134 (Aug. 1, 1923), pp. 504–07; "Free Air for Art," *Independent* 117 (Sept. 11, 1926), pp. 288–91; and Sally Saunders, "Santa Fe's New Conquistadores," *Outlook* 155 (Aug. 20, 1930), pp. 607–09, 635. A complete story would also have to include Elbert Hubbard's Roycroft, at East Aurora, New York, near Buffalo.

22. Anne Morrow Lindbergh's comments when she lived near Cranbrook for a time during World War II are particularly interesting. See *War Within and Without. Diaries and Letters of Anne Morrow Lindbergh, 1939–1944,* New York and London, 1980, pp. 299–307, 375, 393, 413–14, 444. She called Cranbrook the "Ivory Tower sitting on the outside of the volcano of Detroit" (p. 299).

23. Cranbrook Archives, Papers of George G. Booth, Box 5, Talks 1902-17 Folder, Address delivered at the Detroit Museum of Art during the "Second Annual Exhibition of Arts and Crafts," Dec. 7, 1905.

2. CRANBROOK AND THE SEARCH FOR TWENTIETH-CENTURY FORM
Robert Judson Clark

1. Detroit Public Library, Burton Historical Collection, Diary of Kate Thompson Bromley, Jan. 2, 1944.

2. The best visual parallel is the frontispiece of Peter Behrens, *Feste des Lebens und der Kunst,* Leipzig, 1900. Regarding the themes of crystals, grails, and transformations, see Stanford Anderson, "Behrens' Changing Concept," *Architectural Design* 39 (Feb. 1969), pp. 72–78; Rosemarie Haag Bletter, "The Interpretation of the Glass Dream—Expressionist Architecture and the History of the Crystal Metaphor," *Journal of the Society of Architectural Historians,* 40 (Mar. 1981), pp. 20–43; Wolfgang Pehnt, *Die Architektur des Expressionismus,* Stuttgart, 1973, esp. pp. 37–41; Elisabeth Krimmel, "In Schönheit sterben; Über das Religiöse im Jugendstil," in Gerhard Bott, ed., *Von Morris zum Bauhaus,* Hanau, 1977, pp. 69–89.

3. See abstract of my paper, "The German Return to Classicism after Jugendstil," *Journal of the Society of Architectural Historians,* 29 (Oct. 1970), p. 273.

4. Marika Hausen, "Gesellius—Lindgren—Saarinen viå sekelskiftet," *Arkitekten* 9 (1967), pp. 6–12.

5. Wilhelm Schäfer, "Die Gehäuse der Ausstellung des Verbandes zu Köln," *Die Reinlande* (June 1906), 201–04. Saarinen traveled in Germany in 1904 and 1907; on the second trip he met Olbrich in Darmstadt and Behrens in Düsseldorf: Albert Christ-Janer, *Eliel Saarinen,* Chicago, 1948, p. 127.

6. Kenneth Reid, "Eliel Saarinen—Master of Design," *Pencil Points* 17 (Sept. 1936), p. 465.

7. J. S. Sirén, "A Discourse at the Opening of Eliel Saarinen's Memorial Exhibition in Helsinki, Finland, on June 1st 1955," unpublished typescript, Cranbrook Academy of Art/Library, p. 11.

8. Christopher Grant LaFarge, *History of the American Academy in Rome* (New York, 1915), pp. 10, 12.

9. "This is an American Academy," *Detroit News,* October 1, 1922, p. 20. See also R. J. McLaughlin, "Roman School has Great Work," in the same issue.

10. The Detroit Institute of Arts, Registrar's Department, Donor Files, Correspondence 1923–24; "Handicraft from the Wiener Werkstaette," *Bulletin of the Detroit Institute of Arts* 5 (Mar. 1924), pp. 46–47.

11. Charles R. Richards, ed., *Art in Industry,* New York, 1922, p. 473.

12. *Ibid.,* p. 316.

13. Eliel Saarinen, "The Story of Cranbrook," unpublished manuscript, 1950, Cranbrook Archives, n.p. The Saarinen text exists in its original manuscript form in the collection of Margueritte Kimball, Cambridge, Massachusetts, and in a transcription at Cranbrook.

14. Henry-Russell Hitchcock, *Architecture: Nineteenth and Twentieth Centuries,* Baltimore, 1958, p. 361.

15. Paul Goldberger, "Eliel and Eero Saarinen," in Joseph J. Thorndike, Jr., ed., *Three Centuries of Notable American Architects,* New York, 1981, p. 311.

16. Andrew Fleming West, *The Proposed Graduate College of Princeton University,* Princeton, 1903, p. 15.

17. Suomen Rakennustaiteen Museo, Eliel Saarinen, Unpublished manuscript, c. 1925, pp. 227–28.

18. Booth later ordered the 1925 model de-

stroyed because, it is said, "he felt that people might accuse him of having delusions of grandeur" (John Gerard to R. J. Clark, Feb. 5, 1981).

19. Paul Joseph Cremers, *Peter Behrens,* Essen, 1928, pl. 16.

20. Gert Reising, *Das Museum als Öffentlichkeitsform und Bildungsträger bürgerlicher Kultur,* Darmstadt, n.d., *passim.*

21. Gottfried Semper, *Wissenschaft, Industrie und Kunst,* Braunschweig, 1852, *passim;* Nikolaus Pevsner, *Academies of Art,* Cambridge, 1940, pp. 251–253.

22. Alfred Roller, "Fünfzig Jahre Wiener Kunstgewerbeschule," *Kunst und Kunsthandwerk* 21 (1918), pp. 336–49. See also Rupert Feuchtmüller and Wilhelm Mrazek, *Kunst in Österreich, 1860–1918,* Vienna, 1964, *passim.*

23. James P. Haney, "Industrial Art Education in Germany," in Richards, *op. cit.,* pp. 396–419.

24. Henry van de Velde, *Geschichte meines Lebens,* Munich, 1962, p. 291.

25. Hans Maria Wingler, *The Bauhaus,* Cambridge, 1969, p. 31.

26. The first American, apparently, to study at the Bauhaus was Edward Fisher from Philadelphia, who spent most of the year 1927 in Dessau. Howard Dearstyne, who later taught briefly at Cranbrook, studied at the Bauhaus in 1928–1933.

27. Gerhard Wietek, ed., *Deutsche Künstlerkolonien und Künstlerorte,* Munich, 1976, *passim.*

28. Alexander Koch, ed., *Grossherzog Ernst Ludwig und die Darmstädter Künstlerkolonie,* Darmstadt, 1901, *passim; Ein Dokument Deutscher Kunst, 1901–1976,* Darmstadt: Hessisches Landesmuseum *et al.,* 1976, 5 vols.

29. Hans-Günther Sperlich, *Versuch über Joseph Maria Olbrich,* Darmstadt, 1965, p. 18.

30. Joseph Maria Olbrich, "Unsere nächste Arbeit," *Deutsche Kunst und Dekoration* 6 (May 1900), p. 366.

31. "Das Programm der Grossherzoglichen Lehr-Ateliers für angewandte Kunst zu Darmstadt," *Deutsche Kunst und Dekoration* 19 (Jan. 1907), pp. 379–82.

32. Cranbrook Archives, Indenture of the Cranbrook Foundation, November 28, 1927, p. 7.

33. Cranbrook Archives, Papers of George G. Booth, George G. Booth to Eliel Saarinen, August 12, 1930.

34. Cranbrook Archives, *The Cranbrook Development,* Address by Eliel Saarinen, AIA, given at the American Institute of Architects' Convention in San Antonio, Texas, April 1931, pp. 3–4, 6–7. See also *idem,* "The Cranbrook Development," *Architectural Progress* 5 (July 1931), pp. 10–12, 21.

35. Eliel Saarinen, "The Story of Cranbrook," *op. cit.,* n.p.

36. Carl Feiss, "Out of School," *Progressive Architecture,* 34 (Jan. 1953), pp. 128, 131, 133–134. Feiss later taught at Columbia University and practiced in Washington, D.C., as well as serving as consultant to the Historic Savannah Foundation.

37. Cranbrook Archives, Henry P. Macomber to George G. Booth, July 4, 1944.

38. Paul David Pearson, *Alvar Aalto and the International Style,* New York, 1978, pp. 191–92.

39. The *Academy News* of May 1939 mentioned recent visits by Lewis Mumford, Frank Lloyd Wright, Malvina Hoffman, Osvald Sirén, Gunnar Asplund, Mr. and Mrs. Alvar Aalto, Robert Kelso, and Walter Curt Behrendt. Also see Taragin.

40. Letters between Gordon M. Buehrig and Richard P. Raseman, Oct. 31, 1940; Mar. 21, 1941 (Cranbrook Archives).

41. Cranbrook Archives, Cranbrook Foundation, Trustees Records, Series I, Box 3, Cranbrook Academy of Art (Correspondence, Reports) 1930–1949 Folder, "Report on the Present and Future of the Cranbrook Academy of Art" by Walter Baermann, Oct. 13, 1941, p. 2.

42. *Cranbrook Academy of Art Announcement, 1942–1943,* n.p.

43. J. S. Sirén, *op. cit.,* 13.

44. See photograph in David Gebhard and Harriette Von Breton, *Architecture in California, 1868–1968,* Santa Barbara: Art Galleries of the University of California, 1968, pl. 77.

45. The New York World's Fair of 1939 featured works by Carl Milles, Marshall Fredericks, David Fredenthal, Zoltan Sepeshy, and others. Objects by Maija Grotell, Marianne Strengell, Cecilia Bancroft Graham, and Sepeshy were to be seen at the San Francisco exposition. See *Academy News* 1 (May 1939), n.p.; Golden Gate International Exposition, Department of Fine Arts, *Contemporary Art,* San Francisco, 1939, no. 333; Eugen Neuhaus, *The Art of Treasure Island,* Berkeley, 1939, p. 143.

46. *Organic Design in Home Furnishings,* New York: The Museum of Modern Art, 1941.

47. There was great enthusiasm for them from the side of the Anthroposophists, some of whom saw Eero Saarinen as the heir to the forms of their founder, Rudolf Steiner. See Wolfgang Gessner, *Baukunst in der Wende unserer Zeit,* Stuttgart, 1959, pp. 153–54. The younger Saarinen has also been cited for his part in hastening the end of orthodox modernism; see Robin Boyd, "The Counter-Revolution in Architecture," *Harper's Magazine* 219 (Sept. 1959), pp. 40–48.

3. THE HISTORY OF THE CRANBROOK COMMUNITY
Davira S. Taragin

1. Cranbrook Archives, Minutes of the Cranbrook Foundation, vol. 1, pp. 4–5; Papers of George G. Booth, Box 6, Writings on "The Cranbrook Idea" 1924–39 Folder, George G. Booth, "Memoranda for Consideration by Board on Estate of Cranbrook as an Educational Center," Jan. 15, 1927; Eliel Saarinen, "The Story of Cranbrook," unpublished manuscript, Collection of Margueritte Kimball, Cambridge, Mass., 1950, pp. 1–19, *passim*.

2. Interview with Henry Scripps Booth, Dec. 1981.

3. George G. Booth, *The Cranbrook Press, Something about the Cranbrook Press and on Books and Bookmaking; Also a List of Cranbrook Publications, with Some Fac-simile Pages from the Same,* Detroit, 1902, pp. 8–9.

4. Archives of American Art, Interview with Henry Booth by Dennis Barrie, Jan. 13, 1977, pp. 1, 8.

5. For the most comprehensive biography of George G. Booth, see Arthur Pound, *The Only Thing Worth Finding,* Detroit, 1964, pp. 19–241, *passim;* see also *Detroit News,* Apr. 11, 1949, pp. 1, 3; "George G. Booth Creates Great Cultural Foundation as Gift to Posterity," *Editor and Publisher and the Fourth Estate* 60/33 (Jan. 7, 1928), pp. 1, 4.

6. Two publications dealing with Detroit at the turn of the century and Booth's extensive activities in the Arts and Crafts movement in America are *Arts and Crafts in Detroit 1906–1976: The Movement, The Society, The School,* Detroit: The Detroit Institute of Arts, 1976, pp. 21–35, 48–51, 59–72, 213–16; and Joy Hakanson Colby, *Art and a City: A History of the Detroit Society of Arts and Crafts,* Detroit, 1956, pp. 3–17, *passim.* I would like to thank Dennis Barrie for making available that portion of his unpublished notes and working manuscript for *Artists in Michigan 1900–1976* dealing with Booth and his relationship with Detroit's cultural institutions.

7. Archives of American Art, Papers of George G. Booth, Roll 664, frame 923, George G. Booth to J. J. Crowley, July 23, 1918.

8. Cranbrook Archives, Papers of George G. Booth, Box 5, Talks 1902–1917 Folder, Address delivered at the Detroit Museum of Art during the "Second Annual Exhibition of Arts and Crafts," Dec. 7, 1905.

9. Archives of American Art, Scrapbook of Society of Arts and Crafts, Roll D 280, frames 160, 163–64, *Society of Arts and Crafts Fourth Annual Report, Officers and Members,* 1911.

10. Cranbrook Archives, Papers of George G. Booth, Box 12, Folder D—Correspondence—Business, George G. Booth to Board of Directors, The Detroit School of Design, Sept. 8, 1913.

11. Barrie, *Artists in Michigan . . . , op. cit.;* The Detroit Institute of Arts, Registrar's Department, Donor Files—George G. Booth, George G. Booth to Trustees of The Detroit Museum of Art, Oct. 6, 1915; Jan 21, 1916; Clyde Burroughs to Booth, Jan. 29, 1916; June 28, 1919; George G. Booth to Dr. W. R. Valentiner and Members of the Arts Commission of The Detroit Institute of Arts, July 10, 1944.

12. Cranbrook Archives, Papers of George G. Booth, Box 14, Society of Arts and Crafts I Correspondence—Business Folder, George G. Booth to Gustavus Pope, Feb. 24, 1926; Archives of American Art, Interview with Henry Booth by Barrie, *op. cit.,* pp. 14–15; The Detroit Institute of Arts, Museum Archives, Minutes of the Board of Trustees, Jan. 11, 1918, p. 262.

13. Barrie, *Artists in Michigan . . . , op. cit.;* The Detroit Institute of Arts, Registrar's Department, George G. Booth Donor File, George G. Booth to Dr. W. R. Valentiner and Members of The Arts Commission of The Detroit Institute of Arts, July 10, 1944; Booth to Valentiner, Oct. 30, 1944; Valentiner to Booth, Oct. 24, 1944; Clyde Burroughs to The Common Council City of Detroit, Dec. 6, 1944.

14. Cranbrook Archives, Henry S. Booth Letters, Harry Booth to Ellen Scripps Booth, Nov. 9, 1921; Harry Booth to the Booth Family, Nov. 20, 1921; George G. Booth to Harry Booth, Feb. 1922.

15. In spite of Booth's efforts, the department's association with engineering was not dissolved until 1931 when the College of Architecture was established as a separate division under the leadership of Emil Lorch. Wilfred B. Shaw, *A Short History of the University of Michigan,* Ann Arbor, 1934, pp. 82, 106; The University of Michigan, Bentley Historical Library, Michigan Historical Collections, Papers of Emil Lorch, Box 3, Folder 3–15, corr. 1920, Notes from meeting held in the office of President M. L. Burton, Dec. 2, 1920; Lorch Papers, Box 4, Folder No. 4–15, Draft of letter from Emil Lorch to President Alexander Grant Ruthven, Aug. 16, 1932.

16. The George G. Booth Traveling Fellowship was instituted to provide funds for recent graduates of the University of Michigan's architectural program to travel abroad to study. First awarded in 1924, it was an outgrowth of Booth's visit to the American Academy in Rome in 1922 (see below). Archives of American Art, Papers of George G. Booth, Roll 665, frames 1083–084; George G. Booth to Emil Lorch, Jan. 17, 1923; frame 1102, George G. Booth to President M. L. Burton, Apr. 30, 1923; Roll 664, frame 990, George G. Booth to Emil Lorch, Oct. 23, 1922; Cranbrook Archives, Henry S. Booth Letters, Harry Booth to George G. Booth and Ellen S. Booth, Mar. 25, 1924.

17. Booth was warned by officials at the Detroit Museum that such a center for the arts could only survive if located downtown. Fortunately, his desire to pursue the idea was not affected by the initially negative response to his inquiries. The Detroit Institute of Arts, Museum Archives, The

Clyde H. Burroughs Records, Box 13, Folder 1, William Tyler Miller to Clyde Burroughs, Oct. 18, 1919; Burroughs to Miller, Nov. 3, 1919.

18. Cranbrook Archives, Henry S. Booth Letters, Harry Booth to Ellen Booth, Apr. 1, 1921; Apr. 8, 1921; George G. Booth to Harry Booth, Dec. 6, 1921; Joseph Breck, *The Cloisters: A Brief Guide,* New York: The Metropolitan Museum of Art, 1926, pp. 3–4.

19. Interestingly, in 1923 George Booth and his son, Henry, donated a car for the American Academy's use. Both men had noticed during their individual visits to the institution the difficulties in transportation experienced by the faculty and students. Cranbrook Archives, Papers of George G. Booth, Box 11, "A" Correspondence—Business Folder, George G. Booth to Gorham Phillips Stevens, June 23, 1923.

20. "In the Beginning," *Cranbrook Bulletin,* Spring-Summer 1944, [p. 3]; Cranbrook Archives, Papers of George G. Booth, Box 13, "Mc" Folder—Correspondence—Business, Draft of letter from George G. Booth to Lilly McClelland, June 29, 1918.

21. The younger Booth was so impressed with Saarinen that in December 1923—when the Architectural Society of the University of Michigan in conjunction with the Michigan Chapter of AIA and the Michigan Society of Architects held a reception for the Finnish master—he wrote and directed "A Pageant of Arts and Crafts" that was the main event of the evening. George Booth was one of the speakers at the dinner. Cranbrook Archives, Papers of George G. Booth, Box 9, Albert Kahn II Correspondence—House and Property, Albert Kahn to George G. Booth, Aug. 27, 1942; Archives of American Art, Papers of George G. Booth, Roll 665, frame 1101, Emil Lorch to George G. Booth, Apr. 28, 1923; Interview with Henry Booth by Barrie, *op. cit.,* p. 18; Cranbrook Academy of Art/Museum, Henry S. Booth, ed., Conversations with Henry S. Booth, Mary Riordan, Davira Taragin, and John Gerard, Sept. 10, 1979, pp. 1–5; Saarinen, "Story of Cranbrook," *op. cit.,* pp. 3–10, 15–25, *passim;* City of Detroit, Journal of the Common Council, Jan. 8, 1924–Jan. 6, 1925, July 1, 1924, pp. 1557–1561.

22. Archives of American Art, Interview with Henry Booth by Barrie, *op. cit.,* p. 15; Papers of George G. Booth, Roll 664, frames 1254–256, "Memorandum on the Founding of Cranbrook School," Jan. 12, 1937; Cranbrook Archives, Trustees Minutes, vol. 1, pp. 44–48, Sept. 10, 1928; vol. 1, pp. 79–80, May 13, 1930; Saarinen, "Story of Cranbrook," *op. cit.,* pp. 30–34.

23. Cranbrook Archives, Cranbrook Foundation, Trustees Records, Series I, Box 3, Cranbrook Academy of Art—Annual Reports 1933–1942 Folder, The Cranbrook Academy of Art Annual Report for Fiscal Year ending June 30th, 1935; Henry S. Booth Letters, George G. Booth to Harry Booth, Feb. 16, 1936; Cranbrook Foundation, Trustees Records, Series I, Box 1, George

G. Booth Chairman Folder 1937–45, Notes from Mr. Booth to the Trustees of the Cranbrook Foundation, June 21, 1938.

24. Cranbrook Archives, Papers of George G. Booth, Box 15, Eliel Saarinen I—Correspondence—CAA Folder, George G. Booth to Eliel Saarinen, Aug. 12, 1930; Papers of George G. Booth, Box 6, Writings on "The Cranbrook Idea 1924–1939" Folder, "An Academy of Art at Cranbrook," by G.G.B., n.d. [c. 1925].

25. Cranbrook Archives, Papers of George G. Booth, Box 6, Writings on "The Cranbrook Idea 1924–1939" Folder, "An Academy of Art at Cranbrook" by George G. Booth with later penciled editing by G.G.B., n.d. [c. 1927]; interview with Howard Preston, Aug. 1981.

26. Arthur Nevill Kirk was the first of these craftsmen to serve as a part-time instructor of arts and crafts at the school for boys. Cranbrook Archives, Trustees Minutes, vol. 1, pp. 44–48, Sept. 10, 1928; Papers of George G. Booth, Box 14, Society of Arts and Crafts I Correspondence—Business, George G. Booth to Helen Plumb, Feb. 1, 1927; A. N. Kirk to Helen Plumb, Jan. 5, 1927; Papers of George G. Booth, Box 15, Geza Maroti Correspondence—CAA Folder, George G. Booth to Immigration Secretary, Aug. 5, 1927; Henry S. Booth Letters, George G. Booth to Harry Booth, Mar. 10, 1930; Cranbrook Foundation, Trustees Records, Series I, Box 3, Cranbrook Academy of Art (Correspondence, Reports) 1930–1949 Folder, George G. Booth to Cranbrook Foundation Trustees, Sept. 29, 1930; interview with Henry S. Booth, Dec. 1981.

27. Cranbrook Archives, Papers of George G. Booth, Box 15, Eliel Saarinen I Correspondence—CAA Folder, George G. Booth to Eliel Saarinen, Aug. 12, 1930; Cranbrook Foundation, Trustees Records, Series I, Box 3, Cranbrook Academy of Art (Correspondence, Reports) 1930–1949 Folder, Notes by George G. Booth, July 1930; Henry S. Booth Letters, George G. Booth to Harry Booth, Feb. 17, 1930; Mar. 10, 1930; Trustees Minutes, vol. 1, pp. 132–33, June 16, 1932; Archives of American Art, Papers of George G. Booth, Roll 665, frame 557, George G. Booth to Henry P. Macomber, Oct. 1, 1930; Roll 664, frames 171–72, Charles Harris Whitaker to George G. Booth, Jan. 16, 1929; frame 207, George G. Booth to Charles Harris Whitaker, Sept. 4, 1929.

28. It is difficult to determine the nature of the financial arrangements made with Gin D. Su, probably the first architecture student. From 1932 to 1933 two full scholarships including tuition, room, and board were awarded to Carl Feiss and Marshall Fredericks. The economic climate in the country, however, made it impossible to continue this policy. Cranbrook Archives, Cranbrook Foundation, Trustees Records, Series I, Box 3, Cranbrook Academy of Art—Annual Reports 1933–1942 Folder, Richard P. Raseman to George G. Booth, June 5, 1934.

29. Archives of American Art, Papers of George

G. Booth, Roll 666, frame 252, Cecil Billington to Eliel Saarinen, June 30, 1932; interview with Mrs. Rachel D. Black, June 1982.

30. Saarinen, "Story of Cranbrook", *op. cit.,* [p. 68].

31. *Ibid.,* [p. 69].

32. Suomen Rakennustaiteen Museo, Eliel Saarinen, Unpublished manuscript, c. 1925, [pp. 217–31]; Barrie, *Artists in Michigan . . ., op. cit.;* Joy Hakanson, "Cranbrook," *Craft Horizons* 19 (May-June 1959), p. 18.

33. Cranbrook Archives, Papers of George G. Booth, Box 15, Eliel Saarinen I Correspondence—CAA Folder, Eliel Saarinen to Cranbrook Foundation, Sept. 25, 1935.

34. See Eliel Saarinen, *Search for Form: A Fundamental Approach to Art,* New York, 1948, pp. 326–47, *passim.*

35. Cranbrook Archives, Cranbrook Foundation, Trustees Records, Series I, Box 3, Cranbrook Academy of Art (Correspondence, Reports) 1930–1949 Folder, Richard P. Raseman to Board of Trustees, Jan. 18, 1933; Feb. 24, 1933.

36. Cranbrook Archives, Cranbrook Academy of Art, Administration Records 1931–66, Series I, Box 1, Henry S. Booth 1942–1956 Folder, Unsigned statement, Dec. 2, 1946; Art Academy Announcements 1932–1953 Box, *Cranbrook Academy of Art Announcement of Department of Architecture and Design for Post Graduate Work 1933; Cranbrook Academy of Art Announcement 1934–1935;* Cranbrook Foundation, Trustees Records, Series I, Box 3, Cranbrook Academy of Art (Correspondence Reports) 1930–1949, "Memorandum for the General Information and Guidance of the Offices of the Academy, July 1, 1933."

37. Cranbrook Academy of Art/Library, Vertical Files, Eliel Saarinen Folder, George G. Booth to Emil Lorch, Mar. 10, 1932; *Arts and Crafts, op. cit.,* pp. 213–16.

38. Cranbrook Archives, Cranbrook Foundation, Trustees Records, Series I, Box 3, Cranbrook Academy of Art—Annual Reports 1933–1942 Folder, Cranbrook Academy of Art Annual Reports 1933–34, 1934–35; *Cranbrook Academy of Art Announcement of Department of Architecture 1933,* p. 5; interview with Joy Hakanson Colby, June 1982.

39. University of Michigan, Michigan Historical Collections, Bentley Historical Library, Papers of Emil Lorch, Box 4, Folder 4–8, Conference with President Alexander Grant Ruthven, Oct. 8, 1931; *Arts and Crafts, op. cit.,* pp. 213–16.

40. Cranbrook Archives, Cranbrook Foundation, Records of William Frayer, Box 1, George G. Booth Folder, "Memorandum of the Informal Meeting at the Foundation Office," Feb. 11, 1936; Papers of George G. Booth, Box 13, William Frayer Folder—Correspondence—Business, William Frayer to George G. Booth, Dec. 4, 1936; Lee A White to William Frayer, Oct. 5, 1935; Henry S. Booth Letters, George G. Booth to Harry Booth, Feb. 16, 1936.

41. Cranbrook Archives, Cranbrook Foundation, Trustees Records, Series I, Box 3, Cranbrook Academy of Art—Annual Reports 1933–1942 Folder, The Cranbrook Academy of Art Annual Reports for Fiscal Years ending June 30th, 1935, and June 30th, 1936; Henry S. Booth Letters, George G. Booth to Harry Booth, Feb. 16, 1936.

42. Cranbrook Archives, Henry S. Booth Letters, Harry Booth to George G. Booth and Ellen Scripps Booth, Sept. 25, 1941.

43. Cranbrook Archives, Cranbrook Foundation, Trustees Records, Series I, Box 3, Cranbrook Academy of Art—Annual Reports 1933–1942 Folder, The Cranbrook Academy of Art Annual Reports 1936–37, 1938–39; Henry S. Booth Letters, George G. Booth to Harry Booth, Feb. 16, 1936.

44. Dennis Barrie, "Cranbrook Academy of Art Painting and Sculpture," in *Cranbrook U.S.A.,* Bloomfield Hills: Cranbrook Academy of Art, 1982, [pp. 3–4]; interview with Dorothy Sepeshy, Dec. 1981; interview with William Whitney, Dec. 1981; Cranbrook Academy of Art/Museum, "Jill Mitchell Speaks with Barbara Price," Apr. 1982, pp. 1–2, 13–18; questionnaires prepared by Davira S. Taragin and sent to random Academy alumni, response from Bradford S. Tilney; Hakanson, "Cranbrook," *op. cit.,* pp. 18–20; Saarinen, "Story of Cranbrook," *op. cit.,* [p. 101].

45. Cranbrook Archives, Cranbrook Foundation, Trustees Records, Series I, Box 3, Cranbrook Academy of Art—Annual Reports 1931–1942 Folder, Cranbrook Academy of Art Annual Report, 1935–1936.

46. Interview with Colby, *op. cit.; Cranbrook U.S.A.; op. cit.,* [pp. 3–4].

47. Cranbrook Archives, Cranbrook Foundation, Trustees Records, Series I, Box 3, Cranbrook Academy of Art (Correspondence, Reports) 1930–1949 Folder, "Report on the Present and Future of the Cranbrook Academy of Art" by Walter Baermann, Oct. 13, 1941; "Memorandum Concerning the Meeting of the Academy of Art Faculty held Nov. 3, 1941"; Series I, Box 1, Walter Baermann Folder, George G. Booth to the Trustees of the Cranbrook Foundation, Nov. 19, 1941; Papers of George G. Booth, Box 15, Eliel Saarinen I—Correspondence—CAA Folder, "Analysis of Past and Future Educational Policies of the Cranbrook Academy of Art," by Eliel Saarinen, Jan. 12, 1942; Papers of George G. Booth, Box 15, Richard P. Raseman Correspondence—CAA Folder, Richard Raseman on the Academy, Jan. 24, 1942; interview with Dorothy Sepeshy, Dec. 1981.

48. Conversation with Richard Thomas, May 1982; Cranbrook Archives, Art Academy Announcements (Catalogues) 1932–1953 Box, *Cranbrook Art Academy Announcement 1943–1944;* Cranbrook Academy of Art, Miscellaneous Alumni Records.

49. Interview with Margueritte Kimball, May 1982; Cranbrook Archives, Cranbrook Academy of Art, Alumni Records, Frederick R. Meyer Folder, Wallace Mitchell to Veterans Administration, Aug. 23, 1944; Administration Records, 1931–66, Series I, Box 4, Zoltan Sepeshy 1942–1946 Folder, Zoltan Sepeshy to Cranbrook Academy of Art Board of Trustees, Apr. 24, 1945; Apr. 5, 1946; Oct. 24, 1946; June 3, 1948; May 25, 1950.

50. Saarinen considered the Finnish architect Alvar Aalto and his own son, Eero, as the two most worthy candidates. Cranbrook Academy of Art, Cranbrook Academy of Art Board of Trustees Minutes, vol. 1, p. 53, Mar. 4, 1943; vol. 1., pp. 59–60, Apr. 29, 1943; Cranbrook Archives, Papers of Kate Thompson Bromley, Aug. 9, 1948, pp. 99–101.

51. Saarinen, "Story of Cranbrook," *op. cit.,* p. 54.

4. ELIEL SAARINEN AND THE CRANBROOK TRADITION IN ARCHITECTURE AND URBAN DESIGN
David G. De Long

1. Among exceptions to this viewpoint, and essential to a balanced understanding of the evolution of modern architecture, is Henry-Russell Hitchcock, *Architecture: Nineteenth and Twentieth Centuries,* Baltimore, 1958; 4th ed., 1977. The International Style as perceived in America was defined by Hitchcock and Philip Johnson, in *The International Style,* New York, 1932. I use the word "style" in its broad sense, trace modern style as an achieved phenomenon to late nineteenth-century Chicago, and mean the term to refer to the fundamental architectural qualities of space and form that underlie an entire period. I regard the International Style, the Prairie School, and "post-Modernism" as modes or manners of expression that are component parts of modern architecture. For a general definition of style, see Meyer Schapiro, "Style," *Anthropology Today,* Chicago, 1958, pp. 287–312.

2. The competition was announced in June 1922; 204 submissions were accepted by December 1, and 59 were received after the closing date. The conditions of the competition are described and 260 of the entries illustrated in *The International Competition for a New Administration Building for the Chicago Tribune,* Chicago, 1923.

3. Their design was recently discussed by Carl W. Condit, in *Chicago, 1910–29,* Chicago, 1973, pp. 108–114. See also Robert A. M. Stern (with Thomas P. Catalano), "Raymond Hood: Pragmatism and Poetics in the Waning of the Metropolitan Era," in *Raymond M. Hood* (Catalogue 15, Institute for Architecture and Urban Studies), New York, 1982, esp. pp. 7–8.

4. Louis H. Sullivan, "The Chicago Tribune Competition," *Architectural Record* 53 (Feb. 1923), pp. 151–57.

5. Thomas E. Tallmadge, "A Critique of the Chicago Tribune Building Competition," *Western Architect* 32 (Jan. 1923), pp. 7–8; Sheldon Cheney, *The New World Architecture,* New York, 1930, p. 29. Tallmadge also cites Saarinen's design as an important example of a modern skyscraper in Thomas E. Tallmadge, *The Story of Architecture in America,* New York, 1927, pp. 290–95. The general perception of the design as modern is further discussed in Cervin Robinson and Rosemarie Haag Bletter, *Skyscraper Style: Art Deco, New York,* New York, 1975, pp. 44–48.

6. The location of the submission drawings is not known.

7. Sullivan's skyscrapers are discussed in Hugh Morrison, *Louis Sullivan,* New York, 1935: chap. 5.

8. The influence of Saarinen's design is discussed in Vincent Scully, *American Architecture and Urbanism,* New York, 1969, pp. 151–54. Obvious precedents include the Woolworth Building, New York, completed 1913, by Cass Gilbert (1859–1934); and the Richardsonian project of 1887–88 for a twenty-eight-story office building by Leroy Buffington (1847–1931) with Harvey Ellis (1852–1904).

9. The most comprehensive survey in English of Saarinen's work remains Albert Christ-Janer, *Eliel Saarinen,* rev. ed., Chicago, 1979. The history of the Helsinki Railway Station is discussed in Marika Hausen, "The Helsinki Railway Station," *Taidehistoriallisia Tutkimuksia* 3 (1977), pp. 57–114. Sources underlying Saarinen's Tribune design are discussed in Walter L. Creese, "Saarinen's Tribune Design," *Society of Architectural Historians Journal* 6 (July-Dec. 1947), pp. 1–5. Relationships between Saarinen's project and imagery developed by Claude Bragdon, in *The Frozen Fountain,* New York, 1932, are being studied by Tom Van Leeuwan.

10. The period encompassing National Romanticism, with forms derived partly from medieval Finnish architecture and partly from such outside sources as H. H. Richardson's American work, is discussed in Nils Erik Wickberg, *Finnish Architecture,* Helsinki, 1962, pp. 80–85. See also, James M. Richards, *A Guide to Finnish Architecture,* New York, 1966. Relationships between Finnish and American architecture are discussed in Leonard K. Eaton, *American Architecture Comes of Age; European Reaction to H. H. Richardson and Louis Sullivan,* Cambridge, Mass., 1972. Saarinen and his partners, Herman Gesellius (1874–1916) and A. E. Lindgren (1874–1929), began practicing in 1896 and were acknowledged within a few years as leading proponents of National Romanticism in Finland.

11. Suomen Rakennustaiteen Museo, Eliel Saarinen, Unpublished and untitled manuscript, 1925, pp. 52–53. Saarinen's theories of design are later more fully developed in Eliel Saarinen,

Search for Form, New York, 1948. For a bibliography of Saarinen's writings, Christ-Janer, *op. cit.,* p. 161.

12. For instance, Eliel Saarinen, "Address of Eliel Saarinen," *Octagon* 3 (Apr. 1931), pp. 6–13. The anti-Beaux-Arts stance of this position is confirmed by later writings, as in Eliel Saarinen, "The Story of Cranbrook," unpublished manuscript, Cranbrook Archives, 1950, n.p. Bertram Goodhue, writing to congratulate Saarinen on his Tribune prize, claimed to be allied with Saarinen in design philosophy and said he was "cordially hating the *Ecole des Beaux-Arts* and all its manifestations" (Suomen Rakennustaiteen Museo, Saarinen Scrapbooks, Bertram Goodhue to Eliel Saarinen, Dec. 9, 1922).

13. Suomen Rakennustaiteen Museo, Saarinen Scrapbooks, Holmes Onderdonk to Eliel Saarinen, Dec. 8, 1922. Onderdonk referred to Saarinen's design as "Finnish Renaissance."

14. Christ-Janer, *op. cit.,* p. 136.

15. Saarinen spoke of his interest in the skyscraper as being awakened by the Tribune Competition, and of his wish to develop "a whole city picture" based on its form, in Eliel Saarinen, "A New Architectural Language for America," *Western Architect* 32 (Feb. 1923), p. 13.

16. Howard Cheney, the advisory architect to the Tribune Competition, wrote, ". . . many of us sincerely hope that at some future date an opportunity will present itself to make possible the execution of your design here in Chicago, and on our rapidly developing upper Michigan Boulevard, which is becoming one of the most notable and distinctive Boulevards in the world" (Suomen Rakennustaiteen Museo, Saarinen Scrapbooks, Howard L. Cheney to Eliel Saarinen, Dec. 12, 1922).

17. This project, illustrated with Saarinen's drawings, is fully described in Eliel Saarinen, "Project for Lake Front Development of the City of Chicago," *American Architect and Architectural Review* 124 (Dec. 5, 1923), pp. 487–514. In this article, Saarinen speaks of his prior knowledge of Burnham's plan, and of his belief that it should form "a foundation for a rational recreation of Chicago." Burnham's plan had been published in Daniel H. Burnham and Edward H. Bennett, *Plan of Chicago,* Chicago, 1909.

18. The efficiency of ramps in large, multi-level parking garages was detailed in an article featuring Chicago designs by Holabird and Roche: Harold F. Blanchard, "Ramp Design in Public Garages," *Architectural Forum* 35 (Nov. 1921), pp. 169–175.

19. While the project had no immediate effect in terms of actual building, subsequent development in the area is not totally at odds with Saarinen's proposal. Also, the Terminal Park project for Chicago (1929) by Raymond Hood, Ralph Walter, Holabird and Root, and others, seems influenced by Saarinen's; it is illustrated and briefly discussed in Carol Herselle Krinsky, *Rockefeller Center,* New York, 1978, pp. 20–21. Also, Stern, *op. cit.,* pp. 76–77, 116.

20. Camillo Sitte's seminal book, *Der Städtebau nach seinen künstlerischen Grundsätzen,* Vienna, 1889, is analyzed in George R. Collins and Christiane Crasemann Collins, *Camillo Sitte and the Birth of Modern City Planning,* New York, 1965; for Saarinen's tie, pp. 91–92. Saarinen's achievements as a planner in Finland, and his reliance on Sitte, Raymond Unwin, and others are analyzed in Marc Treib, "Urban Fabric by the Bolt: Eliel Saarinen at Munkkiniemi-Haaga," *Architectural Association Quarterly* 13 (Jan.-June, 1982), pp. 43–58. I am grateful to Mr. Treib for discussing aspects of this article with me.

21. Saarinen's theories are developed in Eliel Saarinen, *The City; Its Growth, Its Decay, Its Future,* New York, 1943. For his analysis and appreciation of Sitte, see pp. 115–128. For his criticism of formal planning, see pp. 128–133. For an acknowledgment of the importance of Sitte to his work beginning in 1896, see Eliel Saarinen, "A Note on Camillo Sitte," in Camillo Sitte, *The Art of Building Cities,* trans. Charles T. Stewart, New York, 1945, pp. iii–iv.

22. Cranbrook Archives, Cranbrook Academy of Art, Administration Records, Eliel Saarinen to the President, American Institute of Architects, Nov. 23, 1934.

23. Cranbrook Archives, Papers of George G. Booth, Emil Lorch to George G. Booth, Apr. 28, 1923.

24. Saarinen taught at the University of Michigan, Ann Arbor, from November 1923 through March 1924. Henry Scripps Booth as well as J. Robert F. Swanson, Saarinen's future son-in-law, were both students there at the time. University of Michigan Records, Jeanelle Richardson, College Recorder, to Chiyo Ishikawa, Cranbrook, Aug. 21, 1981. Henry Booth has identified surviving studies in the Cranbrook Academy of Art/Museum as his student projects for Cranbrook (interview, June 2, 1981).

25. Cranbrook Archives, Papers of George G. Booth, Remarks by George G. Booth on receipt of an AIA citation, June 25, 1942.

26. Albert Kahn later claimed that he had been instrumental in bringing Saarinen to Booth's attention, as he had recommended Saarinen for the Detroit commission when he (Kahn) was too busy to accept himself; Cranbrook Archives, Papers of George G. Booth, Albert Kahn to George G. Booth, Aug. 27, 1942.

27. Saarinen's Detroit Riverfront project is published in Donald Tilghman, "Eliel Saarinen," *Architectural Record* 63 (May 1928), pp. 393–402; Robert W. Adams, "Shall Detroit Have A New Civic Center?" *Detroiter* 15 (July 7, 1924), pp. 5–8; and *American Architect* 129 (Apr. 20, 1926), pp. 481–82. Saarinen may have begun work on this or a related Detroit project late in 1923 and in conjunction with his teaching at the University of Michigan, as is suggested by a 1923 clipping in the Saarinen Scrapbooks, Suomen Rakennustaiteen Museo.

28. Östberg's work is discussed in Elias Cornell, *Ragnar Östberg, Svensk Arkitekt,* Stockholm, 1965.

29. Östberg had been a member of the jury for the Finnish House of Parliament, and Saarinen had visited Nyrop in 1910; Christ-Janer, *op. cit.,* pp. 35, 136.

30. Cranbrook Archives, Eliel Saarinen Correspondence, George G. Booth to Eliel Saarinen, Oct. 6, 1924. Other letters in this file confirm continued progress during succeeding months. A model mentioned as received by Booth on May 25, 1925, is presumably the monumental one built by Loja Saarinen (fig. 5).

31. Eliel Saarinen continued to develop the master plan during later years, but with less intensity. A site plan dated 1945 and showing proposed additions to the Academy is presumably the last in the sequence; it is in the Cranbrook Academy of Art/Museum. Saarinen's focus on the school for boys is referred to in Cranbrook Archives, Papers of George G. Booth, George G. Booth to Frank E. Robbins, Sept. 30, 1925.

32. The dates of construction are summarized in Cranbrook Archives, Cranbrook School Records, unprocessed material.

33. John Gerard, Curator of Collections, Cranbrook Academy of Art/Museum, has compiled an unpublished report on the development of the site plans and related drawings that suggests a chronological sequence and explains component parts.

34. Cranbrook Archives, Papers of George G. Booth, George G. Booth, "An Academy of Art at Cranbrook," 1925.

35. Tapering, trapezoidal courtyards, often defined partly by colonnades, as in the Cranbrook site plan, can be found in such contemporary Scandinavian work as Östberg's Town Hall and Asplund and Lewerentz's 1915 Woodland Cemetery plan, among others; both are illustrated in Stuart Wrede, *The Architecture of Erik Gunnar Asplund,* Cambridge, Mass., 1980, figs. 7, 19. See also Alvar Aalto's 1925 church competition entry, Jämsa, illustrated in Paul David Pearson, *Alvar Aalto and the International Style,* New York, 1978, fig. 54.

36. As described elsewhere in this volume (see Marter and Thurman), Eliel Saarinen collaborated with Geza Maroti and Pipsan and Eero Saarinen on certain aspects of the building.

37. Goodhue received the commission in 1923, construction began in 1925, the cornerstone was laid in 1926, and the church was consecrated in 1928 according to Florence Davies, "Christ Church, Cranbrook," *American Magazine of Art* 20 (June 1929), pp. 311–25.

38. Eero Saarinen later claimed that his father had been influenced by Östberg and by buildings at Oxford; Cranbrook Archives, Cranbrook Academy of Art/Museum Records, Memorandum from Eero Saarinen to Loja Saarinen and Eva Gatling regarding the Saarinen exhibition, Nov. 1, 1950.

39. The general fascination of Scandinavian architects with medieval and Early Christian architecture in Italy is discussed in Pearson, *op. cit.,* p. 19.

40. Among others who have described this process is Carl Feiss (interview, May 21, 1982).

41. This is discussed and the building illustrated in "Cranbrook School," *Architectural Record* 64 (Dec. 1928), pp. 452–60, 475–506, 525–28.

42. The overlapping dates of the buildings at Cranbrook have been summarized by John Gerard in the legend to the 1982 site plan (fig. 28) on p. 351.

43. Saarinen House is described as an example of modern architecture in Henry P. Macomber, "The Michigan Home of Eliel Saarinen," *House Beautiful* 74 (Oct. 1933), pp. 133–36; also in Anson Bailey, "The Home of Eliel Saarinen," *Master Builder* (Aug. 1934), pp. 231–36. For a more recent discussion, see Peter C. Papademetriou, "Eliel Saarinen Residence," *Global Architecture: Houses* no. 9 (1981), pp. 8–19.

44. In addition to the exhibited exterior perspective (signed 1926), an earlier perspective (signed 1925) is in the drawing archives of the Suomen Rakennustaiteen Museo. The plan of the church is published together with other drawings in Tilghman, *op. cit.,* pp. 400–02.

45. An open competition for a building to house a secretariat, large assembly hall, and other facilities was announced in 1926; 377 projects were received by the time of the first judging in 1927; nine top designs were selected, and at a second judging held in December 1927, the top four competing firms were asked to collaborate on a new design. Eliel Saarinen's entry did not place, though that by Le Corbusier and P. Jeanneret did. Most of the published entries are more traditional than Saarinen's, and many were meant to recall some historic style. For a discussion of the competition, see John Ritter, "World Parliament/ The League of Nations Competition, 1926," *Architectural Review* 136 (July 1964), pp. 17–23. Contemporary accounts included Charles Girault, "Concours d'Architecture pour l'édification d'un Palais de la Société des Nations à Genève," *L'Architecture* 40 (1927), pp. 369–88; and F. M. Osswald, "The Acoustics of the Large Assembly Hall of the League of Nations," *American Architect* 134 (Dec. 20, 1928), pp. 833–42.

46. These unsigned and undated sketches in Saarinen's hand are identified as "architectural fantasies" by the Suomen Rakennustaiteen Museo. In addition to the formal perspective, the SRM has a preliminary perspective of the project. Another perspective showing a lower drum is in the library of the School of Architecture at the University of Michigan, Ann Arbor.

47. Cranbrook Archives, Cranbrook Foundation, Trustees Minutes, Nov. 28, 1927; Apr. 23, 1928; Sept. 10, 1928.

48. A watercolor perspective now in the Headmistress' office is signed by Saarinen and dated 1929. Design and construction progress is noted

in Cranbrook Archives, Cranbrook Foundation, Trustees Minutes, May 13, 1930, among other entries.

49. Saarinen's production of these drawings is described by one of his assistants at the time, L. M. Wetzel, in an interview with John Gerard (Cranbrook Academy of Art/Museum).

50. The first major publication of Wright's work that included these houses was Frank Lloyd Wright, "In the Cause of Architecture," *Architectural Record* 23 (March, 1908), pp. 155–221.

51. Eliel Saarinen, "Story of Cranbrook," *op. cit.*, n.p.

52. Original drawings for the Memorial are in the Burnham Library, Art Institute of Chicago. They include plans of a third variation with a slightly altered platform arrangement; these are signed and dated 1937. Photographs of the model with the Kingswood columns, dated August 1933, are in the Cranbrook Archives. The project was supported by Kate Buckingham, and was to have been in Chicago's Lincoln Park. Models and working drawings had been completed by the end of the 1933–34 academic year according to Cranbrook Archives, Cranbrook Academy of Art, Administration Records, "Report of the Cranbrook Academy of Art, 1933–34." Saarinen proposed a somewhat similar, but more classical pavilion for the Chicago War Memorial competition, 1929-30; his entry is published in "The Chicago War Memorial," *Western Architect* 39 (Jan. 1930), pl. 5; the original elevation is in the National Academy of Design, New York City.

53. Interview with Carl Feiss, May 21, 1982. Feiss was a student of Saarinen's when the Hamilton Memorial was first designed.

54. Published in "The Hudnut Building," *Architectural Forum* 55 (Oct. 1931), pp. 415–22. The building does not survive.

55. Alumni records at the Academy list Gin D. Su as the first student in architecture.

56. Cranbrook Archives, Cranbrook Foundation, Trustees Minutes, June 16, 1933. Saarinen's position as Chief Architectural Advisor to Cranbrook is also discussed in the minutes (Nov. 28, 1927).

57. As summarized by Booth (Cranbrook Archives, Papers of George G. Booth, George G. Booth to Emil Lorch, Mar. 10, 1932).

58. John Pratt, a doctoral candidate at Cornell University, is currently writing a dissertation on the effect of Saarinen's teaching at Cranbrook, and has interviewed many of the alumni about their experiences and impressions. He has kindly allowed me access to his research notes.

59. Christ-Janer, *op. cit.*, p. 20. Eero's ability as a delineator was described by Donal McLaughlin, a Yale classmate who later invited Eero to join him in working for the O.S.S. in Washington during World War II (interview with McLaughlin, Apr. 1982).

60. Eliel Saarinen's support is documented by correspondence with Everett V. Meeks, then Dean of Yale's School of Fine Arts. Letters as well as student records confirming prizes and dates of attendance are kept in the files of the School of Architecture at Yale University.

61. Yale's reliance on Beaux-Arts methods is discussed in "Arbiter of the Arts," *Architectural Forum* 86 (June 1947), pp. 74–76, 152, 154. Competition problems issued by the Beaux-Arts Institute of Design in New York were used in conjunction with studio courses by several schools, including Yale. Winners were mentioned and their designs sometimes illustrated in the *Bulletin of the Beaux-Arts Institute of Design* (hereafter *BAID*). Published designs by Eero Saarinen include a police station, *BAID* 8 (June 1932), p. 8; a memorial tunnel entrance, *BAID* 8 (Aug. 1932), p. 15; a palace for an exiled monarch, *BAID* 8 (Oct. 1932), p. 11 (now in the Avery Architectural Library, Columbia University); a synagogue, *BAID* 9 (Nov. 1932), p. 25; a city residence, *BAID* 9 (Jan. 1933), p. 13; an American academy in Florence, *BAID* 9 (May 1933), p. 13 (Avery); a monument to J. S. Bach, *BAID* 9 (Aug. 1933), p. 13 (now in the R.I.B.A., London); a municipal market, *BAID* 9 (Oct. 1933), p. 17 (Avery); a small county courthouse, *BAID* 10 (Dec. 1933), p. 16; a new thousand-dollar bill, *BAID* 10 (Jan. 1934), p. 14; an industrial city, *BAID* 10 (Mar. 1934), p. 16; a Baroque fountain, *BAID* 10 (July 1934), p. 13. McLaughlin (interview, Apr. 1982) confirms the limited acceptance of modern design at Yale in these years.

62. *BAID* 9 (Dec. 1932), pp. 9–10; Saarinen's design was not illustrated, and the original drawing is privately owned. "Hood" was presumably Raymond Hood, a visitor to Yale in these years who taught design there early in 1934; "Kahn" was perhaps not Albert, but Ely Jacques Kahn, who was then collaborating with Eliel Saarinen on the Hudnut Building and was also an official in the Beaux-Arts Institute of Design. "Milles" was undoubtedly Carl Milles, and "Eliel Saarinen" would seem likely as the name modestly obscured at the top of the drawing.

63. Walter McQuade, "Eero Saarinen, A Complete Architect," *Architectural Forum* 116 (Apr. 1962), pp. 102–19; also, Karol Yasko, a classmate of Eero's (interview with Elsa Gilbertson, June 9, 1982).

64. Drawings for these and other collaborative projects on which Eero Saarinen worked are in the drawing archives of the Suomen Rakennustaiteen Museo. Eliel Saarinen had originally been given the Swedish Theater commission around 1915; he accepted Eklund as a collaborator in 1929, and resigned in favor of Eklund in 1935, according to correspondence in the archives of the SRM.

65. The importance of the Stockholm Exhibition to the functionalist movement is discussed in Wrede, *op. cit.*, pp. 127–44. It is unclear if Saarinen's drawing relates to a competition for the "Forum" or "Glass Palace" that was built between 1935 and 1936 according to designs by Viljo Revell, Niilo Kokko, and Heimo Riihimäki.

66. As discussed in Pearson, *op. cit.* pp. 77, 151–61.

67. Cranbrook Archives, Cranbrook Academy of Art, Administration Records, Eliel Saarinen to P. D. Merrill, Aug. 14, 1936. The office of Eliel and Eero Saarinen later associated with J. Robert F. Swanson on certain projects, such as the Smithsonian Art Gallery. From 1944 to 1947, the firm was known officially as Saarinen, Swanson, and Saarinen; after 1947, as Saarinen, Saarinen and Associates; and following Eliel's death, as Eero Saarinen and Associates.

68. Among others, Ralph Rapson, who was at Cranbrook from 1938 to 1940 (interviewed in Dec. 1981).

69. The construction dates are documented in Cranbrook Archives, Cranbrook Academy of Art, Administration Records, Sanford Allen to George Booth, Oct. 2, 1936, and Mar. 19, 1937. Saarinen's original perspective of the building, in the Cranbrook Academy of Art/Museum, is dated 1936. In some accounts the building is incorrectly dated 1931; this date refers to an observatory essentially laid out by Booth and approved by the Trustees in 1930 (Trustees Minutes, May 13, 1930). Saarinen's 1932 studies for an addition to this first element were apparently of a preliminary nature (Trustees Minutes, Apr. 31, 1932). The finished building is published in "Institute of Science Building, Cranbrook," *Architectural Forum* 69 (Dec. 1938), pp. 418–424.

70. Though often dated 1938 ff., early designs for Tanglewood are signed and dated 1937, mostly March or June. One original drawing and four photostats of three drawings and one model are in the archives of the Suomen Rakennustaiteen Museo. Original drawings for the project in Flint, also dated 1937, are in the Cranbrook Academy of Art/Museum. Dated photographs of the Fenton building are in the Cranbrook Archives.

71. Kidd and Kidd had been entrusted with the entire design in May of that year, but the directors of the Hall rejected their classically inspired design, and next asked them to prepare construction documents for the Saarinen design begun in October and completed by December; see correspondence, notebooks, and contracts in the archive of the Kleinhans Music Hall, including Edward H. Letchworth, President of the Board of Directors, to Eliel Saarinen, Oct. 19, 1938; F. J. and W. A. Kidd Notes, May 6, 1938; contract between the Director and architects, Dec. 5, 1938. Before selecting Kidd and Kidd in May, the Directors had solicited preliminary drawings from several local firms, including Bley and Lyman, Edward B. Green, and Harbach and Kideney. The groundbreaking was announced in a Buffalo publication, *City Planning* 14 (Nov. 1939) (clipping in Kleinhans archive). The date of the opening is given in *Kleinhans Music Hall* (brochure published by Kleinhans Music Hall Management, Inc., 1942), n.p.

72. The model photograph shows a larger stage enclosure than was actually built.

73. Eliel Saarinen, "The Design," *Kleinhans Music Hall, op. cit.*

74. Several of Bel Geddes' designs were published in Norman Bel Geddes, *Horizons,* Boston, 1932, pp. 140–81. The student project is noted above.

75. The European roots of such details are discussed in Pearson, *op. cit.,* pp. 30–32.

76. Giedion's comments after inspecting design drawings are recorded in the Kleinhans archive, Kidd Notes, Jan. 9, 1939. Hudnut's comments appear in "Kleinhans Music Hall," *Architectural Forum* 75 (July 1941), pp. 35–42. The text is unsigned, but was later published under his name in Joseph Hudnut, "Comment," *Kleinhans Music Hall, op. cit.* Hudnut did find much to praise about the interior.

77. The contract with Perkins, Wheeler and Will was signed in February 1938; other dates and the background of the commission are according to history compiled by the present firm of Perkins and Will. Both correspond with Betty Williams Carbol, *The Making of a Special Place; A History of Crow Island School* [Winnetka, 1980]. Betty W. Carbol was a student at the school when it opened in 1940 and continues to be employed there as a teacher (interview, Dec. 3, 1981).

78. As illustrated in a letter from Eero Saarinen to Florence Schust (Knoll Bassett), c. 1935, in Mrs. Bassett's possession.

79. Hudnut's remarks, together with statements by Carleton Washburne and Frances Presler, then Director of Activities at Crow Island, are published in "Crow Island School," *Architectural Forum* 75 (Aug. 1941), pp. 79–92. A sympathetic addition by Perkins and Will was completed in 1955. Neutra's advanced designs for schools were published in "Public Elementary School, Los Angeles," *Architecture and Building News* 144 (Nov. 22, 1935), pp. 226–27, and "Schools in California," *Architectural Review* 81 (Mar. 1937), pp. 120–121.

80. Contacts with Saarinen are confirmed by the diaries of Mrs. Hugh Th. Miller, a member of the building committee and niece of its chairman, William G. Irwin. I am grateful to Mrs. Miller's daughter, Mrs. Robert S. Tangeman, for confirming them, and to both Mrs. Tangeman and her brother, Irwin Miller, for discussing the history of the commission with me. They explain that it was during the Saarinens' visits to Columbus that Mr. Miller became acquainted with Eero, and not, as sometimes claimed, at Yale, where their periods of attendance overlapped. Among architects considered before February 1939 was Edmund B. Gilchrist, of Philadelphia. A business associate of Mr. Irwin's suggested Eliel Saarinen. Contracts and clippings in the church archives confirm the dates of construction, and contacts with other architects.

81. Irwin Miller first brought this to my attention, an interpretation expanded in a typed manuscript in the church archives, "Our Church is Our People." Among published articles on the

church are "Tabernacle Church of Christ," *Architectural Forum* 77 (Oct. 1942), pp. 35–44; and "Tabernacle Church of Christ," *Architects' Journal* 98 (Sept. 9, 1943), pp. 183–86. For Saarinen's general attitude toward such ornament, Christ-Janer, *op. cit.,* p. 113.

82. Similar church designs of 1927 by Aalto are discussed in Pearson, *op. cit.,* pp. 54–57. Parallels by Bryggmann include the church at Sortavala (1929) and Tehtaapuisto Church, Helsinki (1930). For a series of Finnish designs showing similar motifs, see "Warkauden Kirkkokilpailu," *Arkitekten* 1 (1936) pp. 10–16.

83. Eero Saarinen to Florence Schust (Knoll Bassett), c. 1935, in Mrs. Bassett's possession.

84. The competition for the theater was announced in *Architectural Record* 84 (Nov. 1938), pp. 33–36, and the results in *Architectural Record* 85 (April 1939), pp. 61–64. It was not built. Rapson's comments were made during an interview, Dec. 1981.

85. An announcement of award together with a description of the competition, including names of jurors and finalists, is in "The Smithsonian Gallery of Art Competition," *Architectural Forum* 71 (July 1939), pp. i–xvi. The model was requested after the competition.

86. Lorimer Rich, "A Study in Contrasts," *Pencil Points* 22 (Aug. 1941), pp. 497–516.

87. Controversy surrounding the design is documented by correspondence in the Smithsonian archives, especially dating from 1940 and 1941.

88. Cranbrook Archives, Ellen S. Booth Papers, Ellen S. Booth to Trustees of Cranbrook Foundation, June 22, 1937; Cranbrook Foundation, Trustees Minutes, June 21, 1938, and Oct. 26, 1939.

89. Cranbrook Archives, Cranbrook Foundation, Trustees Minutes, May 2, 1940, and Oct. 22, 1942. Published accounts of the design include Florence Davies, "Cranbrook's New Museum," *Magazine of Art* 36 (Jan. 1943), pp. 6–9; and "Museum and Library, Cranbrook Academy of Art," *New Pencil Points* 24 (Dec. 1943), pp. 36–49. The building was not without influence; see, for instance, "Eisenhower Museum Planned for Four-Acre Site in Abilene [Kansas]," *Architectural Record* 112 (Aug. 1952), p. 22.

90. Given qualified praise in Henry-Russell Hitchcock, "Paris 1937," *Architectural Forum* 67 (Sept. 1937), pp. 158–74.

91. Cranbrook Archives, Cranbrook Foundation, Administration Records, Annual Report, June 13, 1939; and Eero Saarinen to George Booth, Jan. 2, 1942.

92. Cranbrook Archives, Eliel Saarinen Correspondence, George Booth to Eliel Saarinen, Dec. 29, 1941, and Eliel Saarinen to George Booth, Dec. 31, 1941. Booth felt that time given to independent practice conflicted with the Saarinens' academic responsibilities.

93. The design was a collaborative effort between Edward P. Elliott, architect; Theodore Luderowski, landscape architect; B. Schiwetz, sculptor; and Margaret Garceau, painter. The results of this competition were announced and evaluated in "Two Cranbrook Teams Awarded Rome Alumni Prizes," *Pencil Points* 21 (Apr. 1940 supplement), pp. 78–80. The Bel Geddes design is illustrated in Bel Geddes, *op. cit.,* pp. 172–173.

94. The Fabric House project was published in "The New House 194x," *Architectural Forum* 77 (Sept. 1942), pp. 65–152, esp. 87–89.

95. The Art Institute is published in *The Architect and Building News* 197 (Mar. 3, 1950), pp. 228–229; *Progressive Architecture* 30 (Feb. 1949), pp. 62–65; 35 (Apr. 1954), pp. 100–102.

96. The Gidwitz house, which Rapson designed with John Van Der Meulen, is published in "Transformation d'une Maison à Chicago," *Architecture d'Aujourd'hui* 20 (July 1950), pp. 70–72. It incorporated some foundation elements from an earlier house on the site.

97. Rapson collaborated with Robert Tague; the results of the competition are published in "Open Competition for . . . the Legislative Palace of Ecuador," *Arts and Architecture* 61 (Dec. 1944), pp. 23–27. It was not built. A losing entry by Eero Saarinen is published in "Eero Saarinen & Associates," *Michigan Society of Architects Bulletin* 271 (July 1953), pp. 32–57, 35.

98. Although most chronologies list Eames' dates at Cranbrook as earlier, student records and correspondence confirm otherwise; see Cranbrook Academy of Art, Registrar's Office, Records.

99. Eames' attendance at Washington University is confirmed by student records; his associations with Wilbur T. Trueblood (1875?–1937) and Hugo Graf (1888?–1953), Charles M. Gray (1898?–1970), Pauley, and Robert P. Walsh (1899?–1964) by entries in the St. Louis City Directories; additional information from clippings in the archives of the St. Louis Public Library and interview with Charles P. Reay (Walsh's nephew), Dec. 1981.

100. A photograph of the church appears in the *St. Louis Post Dispatch,* Apr. 5, 1936. Working drawings for the Dinsmoor house in Webster Groves, in the possession of the present owner, are dated May 23, 1936.

101. Working drawings for the Meyer house are dated Dec. 14, 1936. The date of the ground breaking—Jan. 3, 1937—is inscribed on the wall of the house. The period of construction, and trips by Eames to Cranbrook to receive criticism of his design from Eliel Saarinen and to coordinate ceramic plaques, rugs, and other items made at Cranbrook are recalled by Mrs. John Meyer (now Mrs. Leigh Gerdine) (interview, Nov. 20, 1981). Dates are also confirmed by correspondence: Cranbrook Academy of Art, Alumni Records, Charles Eames to Eliel Saarinen, 24 [Jan. 1938]. Sheila Burlingame, the sculptor of the plaques named by Mrs. Gerdine, is mentioned in "Alumni Notes," *Academy News* 2 (1940); she is identified as a St. Louis artist and sculptor whose son, John Courtney, was studying at Cranbrook, in "Sheila Burlingame Flays Art Board . . .," *St. Louis Star-Times,* July 9, 1937.

102. Among many articles describing this design are "G.M. Technical Center," *Architectural Forum* 91 (July 1949), pp. 70–78; "General Motors Opens First Completed Buildings," *Architectural Record* 110 (Oct. 1951), p. 12; "General Motors Technical Center," *Architectural Forum* 95 (Nov. 1951), pp. 111–23; and John McAndrew, "First Look at the General Motors Technical Center," *Art in America* 44 (Spring 1956), pp. 26–33. Dated prints at the General Motors Technical Center show an evolutionary stage of the design, and suggest that simplification of the first proposals began late in 1945. Published accounts of Eero Saarinen's independent career include Aline Saarinen, ed., *Eero Saarinen on His Work,* New Haven, 1968; Rupert Spade, *Eero Saarinen,* New York, 1971; and Allan Temko, *Eero Saarinen,* New York, 1962.

103. A history of this series is presented in Esther McCoy, *Case Study Houses, 1945–1962,* second ed., Los Angeles, 1977.

104. The designs were published in "Case Study Houses 8 and 9," *Arts and Architecture* 62 (Dec. 1945), pp. 44–51. Among many articles describing these houses in relation to others in the series is "The Case of a Unique Building Plan—The Case Study Houses," *Interiors* 108 (Sept. 1948), pp. 96–119.

105. The latter design, done in collaboration with Oliver Lundquist, won first prize in a competition also sponsored by *Arts and Architecture;* Charles Eames was a member of the jury. See "Designs for Postwar Living," *California Arts and Architecture* 60 (Aug. 1943), pp. 23–38, 43–44; (Dec. 1943), pp. 22–25.

106. Original drawings of the Rich studio are in the Cranbrook Academy of Art/Museum, and photographs of the project dated February 1941 are in the Cranbrook Archives. Eames and Frances Rich, a Cranbrook student and Irene Rich's daughter, were in California together in 1940; Cranbrook Academy of Art, Alumni Records, Charles Eames to Richard Raseman, July 1940.

107. The city hall project by Eames—part of a series of hypothetical designs requested from different architects—is published in "New Buildings for 194x," *Architectural Forum* 78 (May 1943), pp. 69–152, esp. 88–89. See also "City Hall by Charles Eames," *California Arts and Architecture* 60 (June 1943), pp. 22–23.

108. Photographs of the unfinished house are published in "Case Study House No. 9 Under Construction," *Arts and Architecture* 66 (Jan. 1949), pp. 32–33; it is described as nearly completed, and the Eames house as finished, in "Case Study House for 1949," *Arts and Architecture* 66 (Dec. 1949), pp. 26–39. The earliest date on surviving working drawings in the Eames office is May 1948.

109. Interview with Ray Eames, Aug. 2, 1981. This sequence is also noted in Edgar Kaufmann, jr., "Three New Buildings on the Pacific Coast," in Jane B. Drew and Donna H. Trevor, eds., *Architects' Year Book 4* (London, 1952), pp. 55–63; and Esther McCoy, "On Attaining a Certain Age," *Progressive Architecture* 58 (Oct. 1977), pp. 80–83. The earliest surviving drawings in the Eames office that show the revised design are dated October 1948; construction photographs of the house are published in "Case Study House for 1949: The Steel Frame," *Arts and Architecture* 66 (Mar. 1949), pp. 30–31. Kenneth Acker was consulting architect.

110. For instance, "Steel Shelf with a View," *Architecture Forum* 93 (Sept. 1950), pp. 97–99; and "The Castle-Cabana of John Entenza," *Interiors* 110 (Dec. 1950), pp. 92–99. A more recent analysis of the house and its significance is Geoffrey Holroyd, "Architecture Creating Relaxed Intensity," *Architectural Design* 36 (Sept. 1966), pp. 458–70. This issue is largely devoted to the Eames office.

111. Drawings in the Eames office are dated from January through August 1949. Ray Eames has identified the thumbnail pencil sketch (fig. 58) as hers, and the heavier, blue ink sketch above (fig. 57) as being by Charles. Mr. Wilder's reasons for not building the house were personal (interview with Billy Wilder, Aug. 1981). Kenneth Acker was again consulting architect.

112. I am grateful to the client and to Kevin Roche for explaining these and other aspects of the design in interviews conducted during 1981 and 1982.

113. Dan Kiley was the landscape architect. The house is compared to the Villa Rotunda in "A Contemporary Palladian Villa," *Architectural Forum* 109 (Sept. 1958), pp. 126–31. It is also published in "Etats-Unis: une demeure conçue par un des grands architectes contemporains," *L'Oeil* (Oct. 1962), pp. 66–73; and "Eero Saarinen, Miller House," in Yukio Futagawa, ed., "Houses in U.S.A.," *Global Interior* no. 1 (1971), pp. 114–15.

114. The program for the competition, records of entrants, jury reports, and correspondence are in the archives of the National Park Service, Jefferson National Expansion Memorial National Historic Site, St. Louis, Missouri.

115. The program encouraged a collaborative effort; working with Eero were J. Henderson Barr, associate designer; Dan Kiley, landscape architect; Alexander Girard, painter; and Lilian Swann Saarinen, sculptor. Fred N. Severud served as structural engineer. A resemblance between Eero's arch and a design published in 1939 for an Italian exhibition was noted at the time: "St. Louis Arch Likened to '42 Mussolini Plan," *New York Herald Tribune,* Feb. 26, 1948. Publications of the arch (as well as other entries to the competition) include "Jefferson National Expansion Memorial Competition," *Architectural· Forum* 88 (Mar. 1948), pp. 14–18; "Competition," *Progressive Architecture* 29 (May 1948), pp. 51–73; "Engineering of Saarinen's Arch," *Architectural Record* 133 (May 1963), pp. 188–91; "The St. Louis Memorial Arch," *American City* 81 (Jan. 1966), pp. 141–42; and George McCue, "The

Arch: An Appreciation," *American Institute of Architects Journal* 67 (Nov. 1978), pp. 57–63.

116. Although Eliel Saarinen's entry was not among the finalists, a copy of the fabled congratulatory telegram that was mistakenly addressed to him rather than Eero and sent on September 26, 1947, is in the St. Louis archives. The mistake was quickly corrected. In addition to Eero, architects named as finalists were Gordon A. Phillips, Urbana, Illinois; William N. Breger, Woodstock, New York; Harris Armstrong, Kirkwood, Missouri; and T. Marshall Rainey, Cleveland, Ohio. Three alternates named were Percival Goodman, New York City; Pilafian and Montana, Detroit, Michigan; and Hugh Stubbins, Jr., and G. Holmes Perkins, Lexington, Massachusetts.

117. Documents in the M.I.T. Museum archives that confirm these dates include a memorandum from R. M. Kimball to the Building Committee, Oct. 11, 1950; and the M.I.T. Planning Office Notebook. The dedication of the buildings on May 2, 1955, was reported on that day in the *Boston Daily Globe* and on May 9 in the *Christian Science Monitor*. The Auditorium has twice been re-roofed: in 1963 with lead plates, and after 1979 with copper.

118. Structural engineers were Ammann and Whitney; acoustical engineers, all on the M.I.T. faculty, were Bolt, Beranch, and Neuman. The finished designs of both Auditorium and Chapel were published together with earlier schemes in "Saarinen Challenges the Rectangle," *Architectural Forum* 98 (Jan. 1953), pp. 126–33. Among many articles evaluating the finished buildings is "The Three Critics Discuss M.I.T.'s New Buildings," *Architectural Forum* 104 (Mar. 1956), pp. 156–57, 174, 178, 182.

119. The Stephens project is published in "Chapel for a Women's College," *Progressive Architecture* 32 (June 1951), pp. 15–16. According to Saarinen's associate, Glen Paulsen, Saarinen mentioned an Italian Romanesque prototype as his precedent (interview with John Gerard, May 18, 1982). The scarcity of centralized chapels in Italy during the Romanesque period, and the frequency with which Early Christian chapels are confused with Romanesque examples, suggest that Saarinen may have referred to an Early Christian precedent.

120. Later examples include sculpture by Seymour Lipton at IBM, Yorktown; Constantino Nivola at the Stiles-Morse Colleges; and Oliver Andrews at the Ingalls Rink. These buildings are discussed below.

121. As quoted in "Recent Work of Eero Saarinen," *Zodiac* no. 4 (1959), pp. 31–67.

122. Among Saarinen's statements relating these beliefs to modern architecture as he defined it are Eero Saarinen, "Function, Structure and Beauty," *Architectural Association Journal* 73 (July-Aug. 1957), pp. 40–51; and "Problems Facing Architecture," text of an address delivered by Saarinen at the University of Pennsylvania, Dec. 8, 1960;

deposited in the Saarinen Archive, Yale University Library. For a particularly clear statement on the importance of relating a building to its setting, see Eero Saarinen, "Campus Planning," *Architectural Record* 128 (Nov. 1960), pp. 123–30.

123. A major article on concrete shells—and apparently one of the first to appear in an American periodical—is "Shell Concrete for Spanning Large Areas," *Architectural Forum* 91 (Dec. 1949), pp. 101–06. Saarinen's M.I.T. Auditorium is included in articles on early uses of concrete shells, including Mario G. Salvadori, "Thin Shells," *Architectural Record* 116 (Nov. 1954), pp. 217–23; and Lawrence Lessing, "The Rise of Shells," *Architectural Forum* 109 (July 1958), pp. 106–11.

124. This change in direction is discussed in relation to earlier currents of modern architecture, and illustrated partly by Eero Saarinen's work, in Henry-Russell Hitchcock, "American Architecture in the Early Sixties," *Zodiac* no. 10 (1962), pp. 5–17.

125. The development of the design is described in "Research in the Round," *Architectural Forum* 114 (June 1961), pp. 80–85.

126. These studies are in the Saarinen Archive of the Yale Library. Similar studies of fenestration patterns for the much earlier Swedish Theater project are in the drawing archives of the Suomen Rakennustaiteen Museo. Procedures followed in Saarinen's office are discussed by such associates as Joseph Lacy (interview with John Gerard, Sept. 1981); and model-maker James Smith (interview with John Gerard, Apr. 8, 1982).

127. Among published accounts of these colleges are "New and Old at Yale," *Architectural Record* 132 (Dec. 1962), pp. 93–100; and Walter McQuade, "The New Yale Colleges," *Architectural Forum* 117 (Dec. 1962), pp. 104–11.

128. According to Kevin Roche (interview, Nov. 12, 1981). The structural engineer with whom Saarinen collaborated was Fred N. Severud. A slightly earlier American example utilizing suspended roof construction is Matthew Nowicki's Livestock Judging Pavilion, Raleigh, N.C. (1949–53).

129. The building is appraised in Walter McQuade, "Yale's Viking Vessel," *Architectural Forum* 109 (Dec. 1958), pp. 106–11.

130. As quoted in "Recent Work . . .," *op. cit.,* p. 54.

131. For a general account of Mendelsohn's career, see Arnold Whittick, *Eric Mendelsohn,* second ed., London, 1956. Mendelsohn's tendentious relationship with German Expressionism is inadequately examined in Wolfgang Pehnt, *Expressionist Architecture,* New York, 1973. Dulles is also linked to sketches by Mendelsohn.

132. As reported in "Breakdown at Sydney," *Builder* 192 (Mar. 1, 1957), pp. 397–407.

133. Minoru Yamasaki, the principal designer, was reportedly assisted by Gyo F. Obata, who studied at Cranbrook in 1946 (interview with Charles P. Reay of Hellmuth, Obata and Kassabaum, Nov. 20, 1981).

134. Saarinen's contract with TWA for architectural services is dated December 5, 1956, according to Rose Scotti of TWA (letter of June 30, 1982). The complex process of development of the Terminal is partly recounted in "TWA's Graceful New Terminal," *Architectural Forum* 108 (Jan. 1958), pp. 78–83. Construction photographs appear in "Shaping a Two-Acre Sculpture," *Architectural Forum* 113 (Aug. 1960), pp. 118–23. The finished building is evaluated in Edgar Kaufmann, jr., "Inside Eero Saarinen's TWA Building," *Interiors* 121 (July 1962), pp. 86–93.

135. The contract commissioning Eero Saarinen and Associates to begin preliminary designs for Deere and Company is dated January 31, 1957. Construction began in late 1961 and was finished by Spring 1964. Records of design and construction are maintained in the Deere Co. archives. The early proposals were described during interviews on April 30, 1982, with Deere officials connected with the development of the building; these included Joseph Hanson, Joseph Dain, and Robert Bolt.

136. Publications describing the building include "Bold and Direct, Using Metal in A Strong, Basic Way," *Architectural Record* 136 (July 1964), pp. 135–42; "John Deere's Sticks of Steel," *Architectural Forum* 121 (July 1964), pp. 76–85; and Forrest Wilson, "Pavilion in an Industrial Xanadu," *Interiors* 124 (Jan. 1965), pp. 78–91. A more recent discussion is Donald Canty, "Evaluation: The Wonders and the Workings of Saarinen's Deere and Company Headquarters," *American Institute of Architects Journal* 65 (Aug. 1976), pp. 18–21. The sympathetic addition designed by Kevin Roche, John Dinkeloo and Associates is published in "Deere and Company, West Office Wing," *Architecture and Urbanism* 105 (June 1979), pp. 19–34.

137. Ammann and Whitney were the structural engineers. Among many publications, design drawings appear in "A New Airport for Jets," *Architectural Record* 127 (Mar. 1960), pp. 175–82; the completed building is published together with Saarinen's comments in "Dulles International Airport," *Architectural Record* 134 (July 1963), pp. 101–10. The controversial addition by Hellmuth, Obata and Kassabaum is discussed in "Plans for Dulles Include Elongated Catenary Roof," *American Institute of Architects Journal* 67 (Feb. 1978), p. 14; and "Whither Dulles?" *Progressive Architecture* 59 (Mar. 1978), p. 28.

138. Several related studies in the Saarinen Archive at Yale University show alternate column arrangements; some are dated October 31, 1960. Frank Stanton has recalled Saarinen's early proposals for an exposed concrete structure (interview with R. Craig Miller, Mar. 1982).

139. As Saarinen described the scheme in a letter to Frank Stanton, Mar. 31, 1961, CBS Executive Files.

140. E.g., Paul Bonatz's office building for the Sturm-Konzern, Düsseldorf, 1923–25, published in Gustav Platz, *Die Baukunst der Neuesten Zeit,* Berlin, 1927, p. 358.

141. Publications of the completed building include Bethami Probst, "CBS: Somber Power on Sixth Avenue," *Progressive Architecture* 46 (July 1965), pp. 187–92; and "Saarinen's Skyscraper," *Architectural Record* 138 (July 1965), pp. 111–18. It is related to the history of the skyscraper in Eric Larrabee, "Saarinen's Dark Tower," *Harper's Magazine* 229 (Dec. 1964), pp. 55–61.

142. Among articles elevating Saarinen to this position are "The Maturing Modern," *Time* 68 (July 2, 1956), pp. 50–57; Robin Boyd, "The Counter-Revolution in Architecture," *Harper's Magazine* 219 (Sept. 1959), pp. 40–48; and Lawrence Lessing, "The Diversity of Eero Saarinen," *Architectural Forum* 113 (July, 1960), pp. 94–103.

143. Among articles on Saarinen's office is Nancy Lickerman Halik, "The Eero Saarinen Spawn," *Inland Architect* (May 1981), pp. 14–43. Other recent assessments of Eero Saarinen include Paul Goldberger, "Eliel and Eero Saarinen," in Joseph J. Thorndike, Jr., ed., *Three Centuries of Notable American Architects,* New York, 1981, pp. 300–17; and Andrea O. Dean, "Eero Saarinen in Perspective," *American Institute of Architects Journal* 70 (Nov. 1981), pp. 36–51.

144. Robert Venturi, *Complexity and Contradiction in Architecture,* New York, 1966. The manuscript for this now-famous tract was completed several years before its publication.

145. Among the early critical appraisals is Reyner Banham, "The Fear of Eero's Mana," *Arts* 36 (Feb. 1962), pp. 70–73. A more benign view is taken in Walter McQuade, "Eero Saarinen, A Complete Architect," *Architectural Forum* 116 (April, 1962), pp. 102–19.

146. Construction on the house—near Muskoka, Ontario—began in May 1962, and was completed by July 1963, according to the client (name withheld on request; interviews, Apr. and June 1982). Dated drawings in the Weese office support these dates. The house is included in a publication devoted to Weese's extensive practice: "Harry Weese: Humanism and Tradition," *Process: Architecture* no. 11 (1979), pp. 26–31. Additional information from interviews with Mr. Weese, Nov. 1980, Oct. 1981, and Apr. 1982.

147. The plan for Center City and Bacon's role in formulating that plan during the 1940s and 1950s is summarized in Edmund N. Bacon, "Downtown Philadelphia: A Lesson in Design for Urban Growth," *Architectural Record* 129 (May 1961), pp. 131–46. Additional information from interview with Mr. Bacon, Apr. 9, 1982. His theories are fully presented in *idem, Design of Cities,* rev. ed., New York, 1974. For a moving tribute to Eliel Saarinen, see *idem,* "Eliel Saarinen," in Muriel Emanuel, ed., *Contemporary Architects,* New York, 1980, pp. 697–99.

5. INTERIOR DESIGN AND FURNITURE

R. Craig Miller

1. In a purely art historical sense, the terms Art Deco, *moderne,* International Style, or modernism are descriptive of stylistic movements of the period. I am using the term Art Deco to describe the work which was produced in the early part of the twentieth century in reaction to the Art Nouveau and which reached its apex at the "Exposition Internationale des Arts Décoratifs et Industriels Modernes" held in Paris in 1925. Art Deco was largely a decorative style and relied on the revival of historical forms for furniture and a highly stylized neoclassical vocabulary for interiors. It favored traditional luxury materials. Art Deco is perhaps best epitomized by the work of the French designer Jacques-Emile Ruhlmann (1879–1933). The term *moderne* is used to describe a contemporaneous movement more concerned with industrial design and the machine, though often in a superficial way. It favored industrial materials such as steel, glass, or plastics; its ideal was geometric forms that could be mass produced. Decorative details tended to geometric patterns or streamlined curves. The most influential practitioners were architectural designers such as Robert Mallet-Stevens (1886–1945) or Pierre Chareau (1883–1950). See Yvonne Brunhammer, *Les Années 25,* Paris: Musée des Arts Décoratifs, 1966, and *1925,* Paris, 1976; Martin Greif, *Depression Modern,* New York, 1975; Bevis Hillier, *The World of Art Deco,* New York, 1971; Alain Lesieutre, *The Spirit and Splendour of Art Deco,* New York, 1974; and *Thirties,* London: Arts Council of Great Britain, 1979. The term modern is used to describe the largely architectural movement so concerned with the machine aesthetic. It was christened the International Style following an exhibition at The Museum of Modern Art in 1932 (Feb. 9–Mar. 23), and its most influential school was the Bauhaus. See Henry-Russell Hitchcock and Philip Johnson, *The International Style: Architecture since 1922,* New York, 1932; Hans M. Wingler, *Das Bauhaus,* Cologne, 1962; and Reyner Banham, *Theory and Design in the First Machine Age,* London, 1960.

2. One thinks of such designers as Joseph Urban, Rudolph Schindler, Paul Frankl, Richard Neutra, Raymond Loewy, William Lescaze, and Kem Weber around World War I. During the late thirties Marcel Breuer, T. H. Robsjohn-Gibbings, Ludwig Mies van der Rohe, Hans Knoll, and Walter Gropius emigrated.

3. For a concise history of the careers of Eliel and Eero Saarinen, see the author's entries on them in: Adolf K. Placzek, ed., *Macmillan Encyclopedia of Architects,* 4 vols., New York, 1982.

4. Eliel Saarinen, "Project for Lake Front Development of the City of Chicago," *American Architect* 124 (Dec. 5, 1923), pp. 487–514.

5. *Thumb Tack Club of Detroit,* 1924, 4th Annual Architectural Exhibition Catalogue, Nov. 17–30.

6. Jessica Ayer Hay, "The Story of the Two Artists Who are Designing Cranbrook School," *Afterglow* 3/9 (Sept. 1927), p. 17. Swanson was paid $100 in March 1928; Cranbrook Archives, Cranbrook School Records, p. 20.

7. The panels were carved by the Wolverine Stone Co. *Ibid.,* pp. 26–27, 32–33.

8. It is not altogether clear who executed these windows to Saarinen's design, although G. Owen Bonawit, Inc., of New York did other work at the school for boys. Cranbrook Archives, Cranbrook School Art Work, Bonawit to Henry Booth, May 12, 1927; also Cranbrook School Correspondence, Bonawit, Box 19, Bonawit to George Booth, July 16, 1928, and Booth to Bonawit, July 23, 1928.

9. The fixtures were originally to have been brass but were made up from standard fixtures in the Orrefors catalogue with the assistance of Edward Hald (b. 1883), the noted Swedish glass designer. Eliel Saarinen, "The Story of Cranbrook," unpublished manuscript, 1950, no. 86. See also Cranbrook Archives, Records of the Cranbrook Architectural Office, File P, Booth to Swedish Arts & Crafts Co., June 4, 1928; Correspondence between J. L. Oliver and Tage Palm, Oct. 5, 1928– Apr. 22, 1929, Cranbrook School Records, pp. 20, 28–29, 38–39.

10. Initial correspondence was with W. and J. Sloane, New York, but there is some question as to whether the furniture was subcontracted to Stickley Bros., Grand Rapids. Cranbrook Archives, Purchases-Miscellaneous, Correspondence-Cranbrook School, Box 19, A. C. Estes to G. Booth, June 28, 1927. The bronze panels in the backs of the chairs were made by Barton Brass Works, and the glides supplied by W. S. Brown Co. Cranbrook Archives, Cranbrook School Records, pp. 28–29, 32–33. A drawing of the armchair and side chair is dated 05/18/28. Cranbrook Archives, Cranbrook Architectural Office, Boys School, no. 127.

11. See Gillian Naylor, *The Arts and Crafts Movement,* London, 1971, and Ken and Kate Baynes, *Gordon Russell,* London, 1981.

12. Saarinen House, however, is quite conservative if compared to the contemporaneous Lovell House, Los Angeles (1929) by Richard Neutra (1892–1970) or Villa Savoy, Poissy (1929–30) by Le Corbusier (1887–1966). In form it is very much an urban rowhouse and has a U-shaped plan with a courtyard to the rear. The Cranbrook Museum has a reproduction of an early plan showing an L-shaped concept with the furniture arrangement indicated. Notable differences from the executed house are a square entrance hall with inlaid floor, a "beamed" ceiling in the living room, and a living room fireplace with a herringbone brick hearth.

13. Saarinen House was refurbished in the 1970s; while it retains many of its original fur-

nishings, most of its colors and finishes are new. Colors and finishes cited in this essay are based on contemporary accounts. Henry P. Macomber, "The Michigan Home of Eliel Saarinen," *House Beautiful* 74 (Oct. 1931), pp. 133, 136.

14. *Ibid.*

15. The tea table was used in an alcove to the right of the fireplace with two lounge chairs; a drawing of the table is dated 3-28/30-29. Cranbrook Archives, Cranbrook Architectural Office, Furniture, no. 205.

16. The sets were divided between Cranbrook Academy of Art (1951.108–110, 127–128; 1951.112–116; 1951.117–121; 1951.122–126; 1951. 129–133) and Suomen Rakennustaiteen Museo (hereafter referred to as SRM), Helsinki (#092/1–5, 6–10, 11–15, 17–21, 22–26).

17. The executed design is quite similar to the set of drawings SRM 092/17–21. The tables are in the collection of the Cranbrook Academy of Art/Museum (No. 1972.18, 1972.22, 1977.3, and 1977.4). Berglund was brought by Booth to run the cabinet shop. It was initially hoped that the shop could be put on an independent financial basis as with the Silver and Weaving departments, but the Depression must have severely limited the demand for such expensive work. Berglund worked at Cranbrook from Mar. 25, 1929, through Aug. 1, 1932. He primarily executed custom designs for Saarinen House and Kingswood. Cranbrook Archives, Cranbrook Foundation, Trustees Minutes, Jan. 21, 1931, vol. 1, p. 102; Oct. 7, 1931, vol. 1, p. 100; Apr. 21, 1932, vol. 1, p. 125. Berglund also executed a *moderne* design by Eero Saarinen for a painted wood table (dated Sept. 1930) used in the master bedroom at Saarinen House. The table is also in the Cranbrook collection, though not accessioned.

18. Cranbrook Archives has two drawings of the dining room: an early version, sheet no. 203 dated Apr. 11, 1929, and the final version, sheet no. 203–A dated Feb. 11, 1930. Cranbrook Archives, Cranbrook Architectural Office, Residence No. 1.

19. Macomber, *House Beautiful, op. cit.,* p. 136.

20. The Company of Master Craftsmen was the deluxe furniture division of W. and J. Sloane. The history of the firm is still somewhat uncertain, but it is clear that they were one of the major cabinet shops in New York. The firm did extremely fine Duncan Phyfe-revival furniture and also more contemporary Art Deco and *moderne* pieces; an Art Deco armoire (no. 1980.333) is in the collection of The Metropolitan Museum of Art. A check of the telephone books showed the following information by year: 1925, no listing; 1930, Lawrence St., Flushing; 1938, 3630 Lawrence, Flushing; and 1948, no listing. Correspondence between Saarinen and Sloane seems to have begun in December 1929, and a final agreement was signed on May 14, 1930. Cranbrook Archives, Correspondence between Eliel Saarinen and William Coffin, Dec. 7, 1929 through Aug. 21, 1930.

21. The drawings are in Helsinki: SRM 092/50 and SRM 092/51. Cranbrook records show that the cabinet shop also made a set of extension leaves for the dining room table: Job. No. 314, Sept. 16, 1930 for $241.84. Cranbrook Archives, Cranbrook Academy of Art, Craft Shops 1930–31, Series 1, Box 3.

22. Both the table piers and the chairs with their beautiful fluted backs were to have had ebony inlay on the ridges. This proved to be difficult, and W. and J. Sloane changed the design to black painted decoration, apparently without Saarinen's permission. Cranbrook Academy of Art, Sloane File, W. Coffin to E. Saarinen, Aug. 21, 1930. Four drawings of the chairs survive: one in Helsinki (SRM 092/16) and three at Cranbrook (Cranbrook Academy of Art, nos. 1951.111, 1955.391, 1955.392).

23. It is indeed difficult to name many American designers during the 1920s and thirties who could rival Saarinen as a furniture designer, particularly in regard to craftsmanship. Eugene Schoen (1880–1957), the New York designer, is one of the few notable exceptions.

24. Saarinen's concern for lighting is evidenced in a letter written by George Booth: ". . . Mr. Saarinen regards it as a distinct error that any room in which we work should not have a chance to receive the sunlight at least a portion of the day. He evidently deems sunlight at least of equal importance to the quiet and steady light usually obtained from the northern exposure." Cranbrook Archives, University of Michigan, Correspondence with Burton, Little, Lorch, etc., 1923–27, Box 13, Booth to Lorch, May 5, 1926.

25. "The Kingswood School for Girls," *Architectural Forum* 56 (Jan. 1932), p. 39.

26. *Ibid.* The finishes noted below are based on contemporary accounts.

27. *Ibid.,* p. 56.

28. *Ibid.,* p. 39.

29. This collection of thirty-five sketches by Eero Saarinen affords an interesting comparison with the almost contemporary drawings done by the elder Saarinen for the living room furniture at Saarinen House. The Kingswood sketches were for side chairs, armchairs, and lounge chairs; they range in style from rather traditional *bergères* and Federal lolling chairs to more contemporary Art Deco or *moderne* designs. The drawings are in the collection of the Cranbrook Academy of Art/Museum: nos. 1951.134 A, B; 1951.135 A, B; 1951.136 A, B; 1951.137; 1951.138 A, B; 1951.139; 1951.140; 1951.141 A, B; 1951.142 A, B; 1951.143 A, B; 1951.144 A, B; 1951.145; 1951.146; 1951.147 A, B; 1951.148 A, B; 1951.149; 1951.150; 1951.151; 1951.152 A, B; 1951.153 A, B, C; 1951.154 A, B. It should perhaps be noted here that Eero Saarinen was an extremely facile draftsman and, in fact, could draw with both hands at the same time; carbon paper was required if he wrote with his left hand, since it was in reverse.

30. A bill from Loja Saarinen dated June 2, 1931, notes that the upholstery was designed and

supervised by Maja Wirde. Papers of Loja Saarinen, property of Ronald Swanson.

31. "Kingswood School for Girls," *op. cit.,* p. 56. The manufacturer for the armchair is not certain; an exhibition catalogue listed "Metal Chairs/Designed by Eero Saarinen/Manufactured by Ypsilanti Reed Furniture Company" under Kingswood School (*Cranbrook Exhibition at the Detroit Institute of Art* [sic], Detroit, 1931, n.p.). Other tubular metal designs attributed to Saarinen were for the Headmistress' Office: two tables, an armchair with two loose cushions, and a side chair with caning, which recall Breuer's designs of the late 1920s. For the Bruno chair, see Ludwig Glaeser, *Ludwig Mies van der Rohe,* New York: The Museum of Modern Art, 1977, pp. 62–63.

32. The dormitory furniture was made by Stickley Brothers, Grand Rapids, Michigan. *Cranbrook Exhibition, op. cit..*

33. Saarinen worked on several projects, none of which were executed: Business Complex for Amos Anderson, Helsinki (1928); Central Library, Helsinki, with Jarl Eklund (1930–31); Swedish Theater, Helsinki, with Eklund and Eero Saarinen (1934–36); and the Alko Warehouse Competition (1935–36).

34. Saarinen studied at the Grande Chaumière, Paris (1929–30) and at Yale from Sept. 1931 to June 1934.

35. Some of the more noteworthy exhibits in New York were the "International Exhibition of Art in Industry" at R. H. Macy's (1928), the "Exhibition of Twentieth-century Taste" at B. Altman and Co. (1928), and the American Designers' Gallery Inc. (Nov. 1928–Feb. 1929).

36. For more than three decades, Richard Franz Bach (1887–1968) was a leading advocate of modern design in America. He held the position of Avery Librarian when he was asked to join The Metropolitan Museum of Art in 1918 as Associate in Industrial Arts (Joseph Breck was Curator of Decorative Arts and Assistant Director). *Bulletin of the Metropolitan Museum of Art* 13 (Sept. 1918), pp. 208, 210. He was also an associate editor of *Good Furniture* and the *American Magazine of Art.*

37. The show was scheduled for Feb. 11–Mar. 24 but was extended to Sept. 2, 1929 because of its popularity. *Bulletin of the Metropolitan Museum of Art* 24 (Aug. 1929), p. 168, and (Oct. 1929), p. 298. For a general account of the 1929 exhibition, see Charles R. Richards, "Exhibition of American Contemporary Design," *Bulletin of the Metropolitan Museum of Art* 24 (Mar. 1929), pp. 69, 71–78, and Penelope Hunter, "Art Deco and the Metropolitan Museum of Art," *Connoisseur* 179 (Apr. 1972), pp. 273–281.

38. H. W. Kent, "The Motive of the Exhibition of American Industrial Art," *Bulletin of the Metropolitan Museum of Art* 24 (Apr. 1929), p. 97.

39. Richard F. Bach, "American Industrial Art, An Exhibition of Contemporary Design," *Bulletin of the Metropolitan Museum of Art* 24 (Feb. 1929), p. 40.

40. Newspaper clipping in Cranbrook Academy of Art/Library, "Saarinen Room Praised by Critics," *Detroit News,* Feb. 1929.

41. The rug was made by Barrymore Seamless Wiltons, Inc., Philadelphia, and was later used in the dining room at Saarinen House. *The Architect and the Industrial Arts,* New York: The Metropolitan Museum of Art, 1929, p. 61.

42. *Ibid.* The paper was made by Orinoka Mills, Philadelphia.

43. These chairs were also made by the Company of Master Craftsmen. Other manufacturers included: lighting fixtures (Edward F. Caldwell, Inc., New York); andirons (Sterling Bronze Company, Inc., New York); chinaware (Lenox, Inc., Trenton, New Jersey); glassware (Corning Glass Works, Steuben Division, Corning, New York); silver centerpiece (International Silver Company, Meriden, Connecticut); and silver flatware (International Silver Company; Reed & Barton, Taunton, Massachusetts; Rogers, Lunt and Bowlen Company, Greenfield, Massachusetts; Towle Manufacturing Company, Newburyport, Massachusetts). The tapestry was designed and woven by Loja Saarinen. *The Architect and the Industrial Arts, op. cit.,* p. 61.

44. International expositions such as the 1933 World's Fair in Chicago contributed significantly. "A Century of Progress Exposition, Chicago 1833–1933," *Architectural Forum* 59 (July 1933), pp. 1–70; "Century of Progress," *Architectural Forum* 61 (July 1934), pp. 1–34.

45. The exhibit ran at The Metropolitan Museum of Art from Nov. 5, 1934 to Jan. 6, 1935. Richard F. Bach, "Contemporary American Industrial Art, 1934," *Bulletin of the Metropolitan Museum of Art,* 29 (Oct. 1934), p. 162; 30 (Jan. 1935), p. 18. For a general account of the show, see "Contemporary American Industrial Art: 1934," *Bulletin of the Metropolitan Museum of Art* 29 (Dec. 1934), pp. 201, 203–05.

46. "Clearly Contemporary," *Country Life* 67 (Jan. 1935), p. 65.

47. The silver was made by International Silver Company. Other furnishings were as follows: furniture (Robert W. Irwin Company); wall hanging (Studio Loja Saarinen); and dress (Pipsan Saarinen Swanson). "Contemporary Quinquennial," *Architectural Forum* 61 (Dec. 1934), p. 412.

48. Drawings for the building are in the Kahn Archives at the Avery Library, Columbia University.

49. The finishes noted below are based on a contemporary account. See "The Hudnut Building," *Architectural Forum* 55 (Oct. 1931), p. 417. Unfortunately, none of the original furnishings are known to survive.

50. Saarinen's other projects were for the Post Office Competition, Helsinki (1934), and the so-called "Forum" (c. 1934) in Helsinki (fig. 40).

51. Eero Saarinen's drawings for the Swedish Theater were discovered by the author in 1977 in the Jarl Eklund papers at SRM. They included dozens of sketches for the exterior of the building very much in the manner of Eric Mendelsohn and furniture studies. The neoclassical theater was originally built by G. T. Chiewitz about 1860. For a history of the Swedish Theater, see Erik Lucander, "Svenska Teaterns, nya palats," *Byggaren* 13/11 (1936), pp. 126–34, and Marius af Schultén, *Svenska Teatern, Benois Teaterhus,* Helsinki, 1970.

52. There are a few interior perspectives of the restaurant dated 1936: SRM 045/215-7.

53. The following drawings have been catalogued: Empire Revival, dated July 1936 (SRM 092/117); Louis XVI Revival, dated Mar. 1936 (SRM 092/93, 109, 110); theater seating, dated Mar., May, June, Sept. 1936 (SRM 092/70–80, 92–97, 118–19, 123–24); Windsor chairs (SRM 092/98–100); and restaurant furnishings, dated Mar. 1936 (SRM 092/81–91, 101–08, 111–16, 125–26).

54. "A Combined Living-Dining Room-Study," *Architectural Forum* 67 (Oct. 1937), pp. 303–05.

55. The built-in cabinets may also be seen as a precursor of Saarinen's interest in modular wood units, even though they have a continuous top in this instance. Moreover, the elaborate model with miniature furniture showed that even in the late thirties Saarinen had begun to rely on models to work out his ideas three-dimensionally. Most importantly, Eero Saarinen in the thirties actually owned an example of Aalto's no. 41 armchair (1930–33) designed for the sanatorium at Paimio. In an interview with Jill Mitchell, who was a student at Cranbrook (1939–41), Mitchell recalled that she and her husband, Wallace Mitchell (subsequently Director of Cranbrook), were later given the chair by Saarinen. It is unfortunately now lost. Interview with Jill Mitchell, Aug. 24, 1982.

56. See "Kleinhans Music Hall, Buffalo, New York," *Architectural Forum* 75 (July 1941), pp. 35–42.

57. The Saarinen office used this wedge-shaped auditorium form in many projects through the 1940s; an early example was a project for the Cultural Center for Flint, Michigan (begun c. 1937). Perhaps one of the earliest examples of this constructivist auditorium was Marcel Breuer's Kharkov Theater Project of 1930. By the late forties, the Saarinen office invariably used domed spaces for concert halls·and auditoriums, as will be seen below.

58. Much of the furniture was a curious juxtaposition of innovative and traditional: sofas, lounge chairs, etc., were rather heavy upholstered forms but had slender chromium legs. The conference table for the Board Room had an elaborate inlaid top but tapered legs of nickel bronze.

59. Specifications called for a northern white maple frame and one-inch foam latex padding cemented to a molded plywood seat panel. Bids were sent out on Aug. 25, 1939, and due on Sept. 8, 1939. A contract was signed in October 1939 with Vernon M. Page, Inc., Calvert and Redwood Strs., Baltimore, Maryland. What appears to be a prototype for the chair may be seen in a photograph in the Cranbrook Archives of the Design Studio at Cranbrook; it is dated April 4, 1940, and shows a young Charles Eames.

60. I am referring to the no. 403 armchair made by Artek, Finland. See John McAndrews, Preface, *Aalto, Architecture and Furniture,* New York: Museum of Modern Art, 1938, p. 28. I am indebted to Marja Pystynen for information on dating Aalto's furniture. Correspondence with Pystynen, July 30, 1982.

61. I am referring to a chair (retail no. C2601-C; contract no. C2794-C) made for Heywood-Wakefield, Gardner, Massachusetts. See David A. Hanks, *Innovative Furniture in America From 1800 to the Present,* New York, 1981, pp. 64–66. I am indebted to Frank Parish, formerly of Heywood-Wakefield, for information on Rohde's furniture. Correspondence with Parish, Aug. 27, 1979.

62. Saarinen's lounge chair is a variation of the armless sofa shown in the project for a living-dining room for *Architectural Forum* (1937). Unfortunately most of the furniture designed for the bar has been removed from the building and has not been located. For the Aalto no. 400 lounge chair see *Aalto, op. cit.,* p. 29. For Mies' Tugendhat chair, see Glaeser, *Ludwig Mies van der Rohe, op. cit.,* pp. 54–57.

63. In Finland competitions are often held for the design of public buildings; during the twenties and thirties, in particular, they aroused considerable controversy among younger designers advocating modern architecture for public buildings and traditionalists. Bryggman was one of the leading advocates of the International Style in Finland, and Eero Saarinen was well aware of his projects during the 1930s. See Miller, *Macmillan Encyclopedia, op. cit.* Further evidence of Eero Saarinen's importance in the design of the Columbus church is a set of drawings sent by Saarinen from Europe to Florence Knoll in the 1930s. One design shows a rectangular mass with a campanile quite similar to the massing of the Columbus church. A second drawing shows an "A-frame" design which was later used by Eero Saarinen for the chapel at Concordia College (1953–58). Interview with Florence Knoll Bassett, Feb. 16, 1982. Moreover, Irwin Miller recalls that many of the details for the church were done by Charles Eames and the younger Saarinen. Interview with Irwin Miller, June 10, 1982.

64. The piers are covered in mosaic, and the mechanical registers are detailed around their tops as a discreet horizontal line.

65. Doors in the low screen open to reveal a baptismal pool.

66. While this detailing might have some acoustical properties, it also provides a subtle patterning that seems to show the hand of the elder Saarinen in creating ornamentation integral to the materials.

67. They were, in fact, repeated in Christ Lutheran Church, Minneapolis, Minnesota (c. 1949). While the exterior is somewhat weak, the splendid interior has all the motifs of the Columbus church condensed into a much smaller building. Likewise, the project for Christ Church, Cincinnati, Ohio (1946), was similar in plan and detailing. One important variation here is what appears to be an enclosed courtyard, which is reminiscent of Östberg's Stockholm City Hall.

68. See "Crow Island School, Winnetka, Illinois," *Architectural Forum* 75 (Aug. 1941), pp. 79–92.

69. Aalto had used an undulating ceiling in his library at Viipuri (1927–35) and by the late thirties was increasingly using rich combinations of materials in buildings such as his own home, Munkkiniemi (c. 1937), and the Villa Mairea, Noormarkku (1938).

70. Saarinen developed the motifs of the Cranbrook Museum and Library further in his designs for the Edmundson Memorial Museum, Des Moines, Iowa (1944–48), and a project for the Fort Wayne Art School and Museum, Fort Wayne, Indiana (c. 1945–46).

71. "Museum and Library, Cranbrook Academy of Art," *New Pencil Points* 24 (Dec. 1943), p. 45.

72. *Aalto, op. cit.* p. 26. Saarinen's side chairs—unlike the Aalto design—are not a continuous laminated piece of plywood and have upholstered seat and back pads.

73. Formal classes in interior design were begun in 1934 by Rachel de Wolfe Raseman, wife of Richard Raseman, Secretary of the Academy. The Cranbrook catalogues list Raseman as teaching from Mar. 1934–June 1935; she was listed as an art instructor at Kingswood from 1933–36. As in several other departments at Cranbrook, the design students seem initially to have been local women. Prior to the end of World War II, the number of students or graduates formally enrolled in design was limited: 1934, two; 1935, one; 1937, two; 1938, four; 1939, four; 1940; two; 1941, seven; 1942, two; 1943, four; and 1944, two. After the War, the enrollment grew considerably: 1945, six; 1946, eleven; 1947, nine; 1948, seven; 1949, eight; and 1950, ten. These figures are compiled from the Alumni Directory published by Cranbrook in Fall 1973. The other formal design class taught at Cranbrook in the mid-thirties was a course on the contemporary design of interiors and furnishings given by Pipsan Saarinen Swanson in Winter 1935. With the inauguration of the Intermediate School, William Comstock was added as a design instructor in September 1936. Comstock studied architecture at Cranbrook from 1932–33; he taught in the Intermediate School from 1936–39 and intermittently at the school for boys and Kingswood.

74. Eero Saarinen's resignation in 1942, Eames' departure for California in 1941, and Eliel Saarinen's offer to step down from the Presidency of the Academy in 1943 are indicative of the situation. The Design department went through a series of heads of equally brief tenure—Frank Greer (1942–43), Howard Dearstyne (1944–46), and Norman Nagle (1946–48)—and only achieved some stability with the appointment of Theodore Luderowski (1949–56). At one point (1943–44) during the War, the Design department was actually closed.

75. In an interview with R. Craig Miller, Nov. 19–20, 1981, Alice Meyer Gerdine noted that Eames had visited Eliel Saarinen at Cranbrook on several occasions and had received various suggestions on the design of the house. This seems to be confirmed in an undated letter (probably written in 1937) from Eames to Saarinen stating that ". . . you were kind enough to criticize a design for me . . ." Cranbrook Academy of Art, Alumni Records, Charles O. Eames, Eames to Saarinen, Monday 24.

76. While the architectural spaces in the Meyer house survive largely unaltered, the original finishes and furnishings have been changed. The description noted below of Eames' interior design was supplied by Mrs. Gerdine in the above interview. Unfortunately, no professional photographs of the major rooms exist from the 1930s.

77. Frei was a noted stained glass maker in the St. Louis area with whom Eames collaborated in the thirties. Gerdine interview, *op. cit.*

78. A bust by Carl Milles hung over the marble surround; in addition, Eames designed acanthus leaf andirons for the fireplace. *Ibid.*

79. Mrs. Gerdine has stated that the suite was made by John Rausch, a St. Louis cabinetmaker. *Ibid.*

80. Eames' whereabouts in the year prior to enrolling at Cranbrook are not clear. In later years, he stated that he had attended Cranbrook as early as 1936–37. See "Nelson, Eames, Girard, Propst: The Design Process at Herman Miller," *Design Quarterly* 98/99, p. 58, and "Eames Celebration," *Architectural Design* 36 (Sept. 1966), pp. 433–42. There are unfortunately no St. Louis architectural directories for the year 1937. In an interview with Jill Mitchell, she recalled that Eames later told her that he had been in New York during part of 1937 working on stage designs. Mitchell thought that it was during this time that Eames made his initial contacts in the entertainment business which were to prove helpful to him on his move to Los Angeles in 1941. Mitchell interview, Aug. 24, 1982, *op. cit.*

81. Cranbrook Archives, Cranbrook Academy of Art, Annual Reports 1933–42, Series 1, Box 3, p. 9, R. Rasemen to C. Billington, Jan. 23, 1940.

82. "3 Chairs/3 Records of the Design Process," *Interiors* 117 (Apr. 1958), p. 118. This article is a concise summary by Eames of his furniture designs.

83. Cranbrook Academy of Art/Museum, "Jill Mitchell Speaks with Barbara Price," Apr. 1982, p. 11.

84. Eames had been married to Catherine

Woermann; he married Ray Kaiser on June 20, 1941.

85. The show was on view Dec. 1–29, 1939. "Exhibition of the Work of the Academy Staff," *Academy News* (1940), n.p.

86. The competition was announced on Oct. 1, 1940. Saarinen and Eames placed in category A (living room seating) and B (other furniture for a living room). See Eliot F. Noyes, *Organic Design in Home Furnishings,* New York: The Museum of Modern Art, 1941.

87. One might add, at the age of thirty and thirty-three, respectively.

88. For a concise history of the "modern chair," see R. Craig Miller, "Frank Lloyd Wright and Modern Design: An Appraisal," *Frank Lloyd Wright Newsletter* 3/1 (First Quarter 1980), pp. 1–6.

89. See Christopher Wilk, *Marcel Breuer: Furniture and Interiors,* New York: The Museum of Modern Art, 1981, pp. 35–41.

90. For the twentieth-century architect, the chair has always been the primary furniture form. As the most widely used piece of furniture in homes and offices, it offers a large market for mass production. Most importantly, the chair lends itself readily to the expression of architectural concepts, new materials, and technological innovations. This accounts, in fact, for the large number of chairs in the Cranbrook exhibition; Eames, Saarinen, Rowland, and others have largely devoted their energies to the design of chairs.

91. I am referring to Breuer's B32 sidechair made by Thonet (1928) and Mies van der Rohe's "MR" chairs (1927). See *Marcel Breuer, op. cit.,* pp. 70–78, and Glaeser, *Ludwig Mies van der Rohe, op. cit.,* pp. 20–23.

92. I am referring to designs such as Aalto's no. 41 armchair (1930–33) and Breuer's Isokon series (1935–36). See *Aalto, op. cit.,* p. 30, and *Marcel Breuer, op. cit.,* pp. 126–32. There were, however, earlier three-dimensionally molded shell-forms such as John Henry Belter's laminated wood side chair (patented 1858), Gio Ponti's "Lotus armchair" (c. 1937), and Hans Coray's aluminum "Landi armchair" (c. 1930). See, respectively, Hanks, *Innovative Furniture, op. cit.,* pp. 52–53; Nathan H. Shapira, *Design Quarterly* 69/70 (1967), p. 14; and Clement Meadmore, *The Modern Chair,* New York, 1975, pp. 80–84. The Eameses, in fact, owned an example of the Landi chair (fig. 104, rear) and perhaps were influenced by Corey's design in their metal shell chairs for the "Low-cost Furniture Competition" (1947–50) discussed below.

93. Aline B. Saarinen, *Eero Saarinen on His Work,* New Haven and London, 1962, p. 66.

94. The competition entries had fabric designed by Marli Ehrman; the German-born textile designer also won a first prize in the competition for woven fabrics. Noyes, *Organic Design, op. cit.,* pp. 13, 15, 38. The plywood shells were made by the Haskelite Corporation in Chicago and upholstered by the Heywood-Wakefield Company.

Ibid., p. 13. Unfortunately, none of the Saarinen/Eames entries were commercially manufactured.

95. George Nelson has noted that a similar rubber shock mount was developed almost simultaneously by two Italian designers, Cristiani and Fratino. George Nelson, *Chairs,* N.Y., 1953, pp. 120–21.

96. The side chair was, of course, a much simpler form. Noyes, *Organic Design, op. cit.,* pp. 14–15. An interesting aside on the working relationship between Eames and Saarinen was related by Ralph Rapson, who was at Cranbrook when the designs were done. He recalled that Saarinen had lots of ideas about various chair forms but little idea then of construction methods; Eames, on the other hand, had a great interest in technology and detailing. Interview with Ralph Rapson, May 1, 1982. This seems to be confirmed in the comments of Buford Pickens, who was teaching at Wayne University at the time of the Organic Design competition. He has recalled that Eames went to Grand Rapids to study the manufacture of bent plywood theater seating. Interview with Buford Pickens, Nov. 18, 1981. Other people who worked on the Organic Design entries include Ray Eames, Don Albinson, and Harry Bertoia.

97. Noyes, *Organic Design, op. cit.,* pp. 9, 26–30.

98. As with the armchairs, the sofa units were executed with wood legs and with fabric over the exposed shell. *Ibid.,* pp. 10, 16–17.

99. Baldwin and Weese won first prize in category F (furniture for outdoor living) and honorable mentions in categories B (other furniture for a living room) and D (furniture for a bedroom). Unfortunately, The Museum of Modern Art retained few of their entries for its collection, and the designs are known mostly through drawings and photographs. *Ibid.,* pp. 34–37.

100. The Baldwin/Weese prototypes were made by the Lloyd Mfr. Co. For the Aalto tea cart, see *Alvar Aalto, 1898–1976,* Helsinki, 1978, p. 58.

101. The lamp was in production from Dec. 1950–1953; correspondence with George W. Hansen, Feb. 1, 1983.

102. The original webbing was cotton with a herringbone pattern of four V's.

103. Interview with Rapson, *op. cit.* For Mathsson's "Pernilla" series, see *Design Quarterly* 65 (1966), pp. 13, 15, 18.

104. See Eric Larrabee and Massimo Vignelli, *Knoll Design,* New York, 1981. p. 44.

105. Eero Saarinen resigned from the faculty in Feb. 1942 and completely devoted his time to private practice in Bloomfield Hills. Charles and Ray Eames moved to California in 1941 and were soon joined by Harry Bertoia and Don Albinson. Weese and Baldwin settled in the Chicago area; the latter, however, subsequently practiced in New York, Montgomery, Chicago, and back in New York. Likewise, Rapson practiced in Chicago, New York, Boston, Europe, and finally Minneapolis. Florence Knoll settled in New York in the early

forties.

106. The web is indeed quite intricate. Harry Weese married Ben Baldwin's sister, Kitty. Eero Saarinen's second wife, Aline Bernstein Louchheim, was a cousin of Edgar Kaufmann, jr., then Curator of Design at The Museum of Modern Art. During the 1940s and fifties, the Museum was at the center of developments in avant-garde design and was especially helpful in fostering the careers of Charles and Ray Eames. Likewise, many of the designers worked either for Herman Miller or Knoll and often collaborated on projects for clients such as Irwin Miller (Cummins Engine Co.) and William A. Hewitt (John Deere). Even today, Ben Baldwin's furniture is sold through Jack Larsen's company.

107. What was probably Eero Saarinen's most articulate speech on design was an address given at the Schöner Wohnen Congress, Munich, on Oct. 24, 1960. This quote (p.1) and the design concepts outlined below are taken from this paper. A copy is in the Saarinen Archive at Yale University. See also *Eero Saarinen on His Work, op. cit.*

108. Saarinen practiced as an interior designer per se on only two occasions: the remodeling of his own houses in Bloomfield Hills, Michigan, and New Haven, Connecticut. The former was an Italianate farmhouse for which Saarinen designed rather austere interiors (c. 1955). The sparse furniture was mostly prototypal pieces of his own design; color was provided by paintings and sculpture. See "A Modern Architect's Own House," *Vogue* 135 (Apr. 1, 1960), pp. 172–73, 175–79. Saarinen died before he could move into the Connecticut house (1961); no photographs are known to survive.

109. Schöner Wohnen address, *op. cit.,* p. 4.

110. *Ibid.,* p. 3. In fact, this advocacy of impersonal spaces seems to be more typical of Saarinen's work in the late 1940s and early fifties. The interiors of his late buildings (discussed below) increasingly received highly individual treatments.

111. One thinks, in particular, of Harry Bertoia and Alexander Girard, respectively. Other artists who collaborated on projects with Saarinen include Marianne Strengell, Alexander Calder, Theodore Roszak, Oliver Andrews, Seymour Lipton, Jacques Lipchitz, and Antoine Pevsner.

112. Starting from the early forties, furniture designers who worked with Saarinen include Harry Bertoia, Don Albinson, Niels Diffrient, Don Petitt, and Warren Platner. For architects in the Saarinen office, see Nancy Lickerman Halik, "The Eero Saarinen Spawn," *Inland Architect* (May 1981), pp. 14–45.

113. Examples include the Bristol Pavilion (1936) by Breuer and Yorke and the Haggerty house (1938), Cohasset, Massachusetts, by Breuer and Gropius. The dining room suite from the Wermuth house was sold at Christie's, New York, on May 30, 1981 (no. 280) and offered again on April 3, 1982 (no. 216); it was designed by Eliel Saarinen. The Bell house seems to have been largely the work of Eero Saarinen, although the Wermuth house was produced by the Saarinen office.

114. "Designs for Postwar Living," *California Arts and Architecture* 60 (Aug. 1943), pp. 20–33, 43.

115. Again, the houses were begun as part of a competition for *Arts and Architecture* in 1945. See "Case Study Houses 8 and 9," *Arts and Architecture,* 62 (Dec. 1945), pp. 43–51. The Eames house is discussed below.

116. "Case Study House," *Arts and Architecture* 67 (July 1950), pp. 26–39, 43–46. Also, see "The Castle-cabana of John Entenza," *Interiors* 110 (Dec. 1950), pp. 92–99. The built-in sofa is a precedent for the sunken conversation pit used in the Irwin Miller house (1953–57). Eero Saarinen felt that he had invented the seating pit, but it would perhaps be more accurate to say that he popularized it at mid-century. Schöner Wohnen address, *op. cit.,* p. 8. What appears to be an early American example is shown in the Isabel Perkins Anderson studio, Brookline, Massachusetts. See Clay Lancaster, *The Japanese Influence in America,* New York, 1963, pp. 219, 222.

117. The strong Miesian influence on the GM Technical Center should also be mentioned. For the Farnsworth house, see Arthur Drexler, *Ludwig Mies van der Rohe,* New York, 1960, figs. 78–80.

118. Saarinen and Girard had worked together earlier on a Canadian vacation house (c. 1949) for the Millers. Saarinen very much relied on Girard for his sense of color and accessories. Kevin Roche, Saarinen's principal associate, was responsible for much of the complex detailing of the building. Interview with Miller, *op. cit.*

119. The conversation pit was Saarinen's alternate to numerous sofas; the colors are changed seasonally: beige and light cottons for summer, reds and rich fabrics for winter. The dining room table has a concrete pedestal, a marble top supported on a steel frame, and a center pool; the original dining chairs were Eames plastic shells on "Eiffel Tower" bases. See "A Contemporary Palladian Villa, *Architectural Forum* 109 (Sept. 1958), pp. 126–31. The overall concept of the Miller house is, in fact, quite similar to Saarinen's ideas for his own projected residence as recorded in his Schöner Wohnen address, *op. cit.,* pp. 7–9.

120. This quote is from a speech given at Dickinson College, Dec. 1, 1959, and is reprinted in *Eero Saarinen on His Work, op. cit.,* pp. 6, 8.

121. The earliest example of a circular church by the office was Eliel Saarinen's project for a chapel at Stephens College, Columbia, Missouri (c. 1947–50); that design is reminiscent of Josef Hoffmann's Hanak Museum, Vienna (c. 1945). Eero Saarinen's first usage of a circular chapel seems to have been one for Drake University, Des Moines, Iowa, in the mid-fifties.

122. See *Eero Saarinen on His Work, op. cit.,*

pp. 52–55. One should also recall the sketch for an A-frame church by Eero Saarinen noted earlier (note 63). A worthy contemporary was the chapel at the U.S. Air Force Academy, Colorado Springs, Colorado (1956–62), by Gordon Bunshaft.

123. The chapel for Stephens College (1953–57), finally executed by Eero Saarinen, is of a similar design.

124. Charles Eames, "General Motors Revisited," *Architectural Forum* 134 (June 1971), p. 26.

125. The vibrant glazed bricks in shades of red, yellow, black, etc., were also used on the exteriors of the buildings.

126. The stair designs, as well as receptionists' desks, have traditionally been attributed to Kevin Roche.

127. The wall treatment seems to have been inspired by Aalto's wooden versions. The extruded metal sections have a contrasting painted and metallic finish which gives them a three-dimensionality; a similar extruded metal section is used for the walls of the auditorium. The sculptural wood built-ins may be seen as a precedent for the equally organic seating in the TWA Terminal (1956–62). The wood armchairs used in the offices have traditionally been attributed to Finn Juhl.

128. The no. 71 armchair will be discussed below.

129. The sofas were made in several sizes. The construction of the lounge chairs is surprising in that they have traditional wood frames with webbing; Saarinen had by this time used molded fiberglass for the womb (no. 70) chairs. Furthermore, there are two versions in the series: one with a continuous seat cushion (fig. 98) and the other with a loose cushion (fig. 99). The sofas and lounge chairs in the lobby of the Process Development Administration Building had loose cushions upholstered in white plastic. "A Tour of the GM Technical Center Interiors," *Architectural Record* 119 (May 1956), 151–58. For the Grand Confort, see *The Modern Chair, op. cit.*, pp. 58–61.

130. Of particular interest is Eero Saarinen's predilection in the fifties for Japanese gardens which provided a non-Western formality for the grounds of corporate complexes; the Watson Research Center, Yorktown, New York (1951–61) had Japanesque gardens by Sasaki, Walker, Associates. *Eero Saarinen on His Work, op. cit.*, p. 80. Likewise, Saarinen had a great interest in Japanese houses and their interiors. In talking about the plans for a house he wished to build for himself, he frankly acknowledged the influence of Japanese architecture. Schöner Wohnen address, *op. cit.*, pp. 7–9. There was, in fact, a great vogue for Japanese design in the 1950s, and Isamu Noguchi—to name but one contemporary—often did Japanesque gardens for Skidmore, Owings, and Merrill then.

131. Interview with Joseph Hanson, Robert Bolt, and Joseph Dain, Apr. 30, 1982.

132. *Eero Saarinen on His Work, op. cit.*, p. 76.

133. One of the earliest examples was John Portman's Hyatt Hotel in Atlanta, Georgia (c. 1967). See "Regency Hyatt," *Interior Design* 38 (Sept. 1967), pp. 136–49.

134. Other designs featuring domed structures for auditoriums were the Detroit Civic Center (c. 1947); Brandeis University, Waltham, Massachusetts (c. 1948–50); and the North Campus at the University of Michigan, Ann Arbor, Michigan (1954).

135. *Eero Saarinen on His Work, op. cit.*, p. 60.

136. Allen Temko has cited Matthew Nowicki's Livestock Judging Pavilion, Raleigh, North Carolina (1949–53) as a precedent for the Ingalls Rink. Allen Temko, *Eero Saarinen*, New York, 1962, p. 43. Niels Diffrient, in fact, remembered that Nowicki worked in the Saarinen office in the early 1950s and that he did a series of remarkable sketches of suspended-cable buildings and interiors. Interview with Niels Diffrient, Aug. 5, 1982.

137. *Eero Saarinen on His Work, op. cit.*, p. 68.

138. Edgar Kaufmann, jr., "Inside Eero Saarinen's TWA Building," *Interiors* 121 (July 1962), pp. 86–93.

139. By 1950, the roster of furniture designers included: Franco Albini, Hans Bellman, Pierre Jeanneret, Donald Knorr, Ludwig Mies van der Rohe, George Nakashima, Isamu Noguchi, Elias Svedberg, and Ilmari Tapiovaara, among others.

140. Interview with Florence Knoll Bassett, Feb. 1, 1982.

141. The numbers noted with furniture produced by Knoll are, in fact, the names by which the designs are properly known; popular names are noted on occasion to help the general reader. Likewise, Herman Miller used a series of initials to designate the furniture of Charles and Ray Eames. Also, it should be noted that the company archives at Knoll are not complete so it is difficult to precisely date when designs were begun, manufactured, modified, or dropped.

142. One should say reinforced plastic—or what is commonly called fiberglass—to be precise. In the 1940s and fifties, plastics by themselves were not strong enough to be made into shells of thin section and compound curves and required a bonding agent for strength.

143. "Modern Doesn't Pay, or Does It?" *Interiors* 105 (Mar. 1946), pp. 66–74.

144. Mies produced a series of variations in sketch form of the conchoidal chairs, none of which were executed. Philip Johnson and Arthur Drexler have in the past dated these drawings c. 1946; Ludwig Glaeser now dates them to the early 1940s. Johnson mounted a large Mies retrospective at The Museum of Modern Art in 1947 (Sept. 16–Nov. 23) and the accompanying catalogue illustrated several of the sketches. Whether

Mies' drawings were known beforehand is not certain, but they clearly had an important influence on the development of the plastic shell chair. See Philip C. Johnson, *Mies van der Rohe,* New York: The Museum of Modern Art, 1947, pp. 172–73; Drexler, *Ludwig Mies van der Rohe, op. cit.,* fig. 30; and Glaeser, *Ludwig Mies van der Rohe, op. cit.,* pp. 16, 76–85.

145. Dates are from Christine Rae, ed., *Knoll au Louvre,* New York, 1971, n.p.

146. In an interview with Mrs. Bassett, Feb. 1, 1982, *op. cit.,* she noted that the chair had a hole in the back due to the cone molding process and that the shell had to be completely upholstered due to the rough finish of the fiberglass. The shells were made by the Winner Manufacturing Company, Trenton, New Jersey, of fibers bonded with Paraplex P–43 resin. "Chemistry Builds a Chair," *Rohm & Haas Reporter,* Nov.-Dec. 1951, pp. 2–4.

147. Photographs of the prototypes are in the Saarinen Archive, Yale University. Don Petitt, who worked with Saarinen on his furniture designs, has noted that the metal base was required for the "womb chair" to make the large shell rigid. Interview with Don Petitt, June 2, 1982.

148. Date is from *Knoll au Louvre, op. cit.,* n.p.

149. Mrs. Bassett has recalled that she suggested the sofa to Saarinen; the settee is, in fact, a chair cut in half with a wood filler panel. Interview with Bassett, Feb. 1, 1982, *op. cit.* An article in *Interiors* (109 [June 1950], p. 95) noted that a three-seater sofa was envisioned at one point, though it was never introduced.

150. Niels Diffrient was Saarinen's assistant on the design of the chair. He recalled that the design was underway when he joined the office in Summer 1949 and that a final design was shown to Knoll in Summer 1950. Saarinen's general working method was 1) to begin with pencil sketches; 2) then to make miniature models of paper or sheet metal; 3) to build full-size models in clay, plaster, or sheet metal; and 4) to create full-size prototypes in the production material. Interview with Diffrient, Aug. 5, 1982, *op. cit.*

151. Early versions of the back panel were made of resin reinforced with sisal, a rough fiberglass shell which had to be upholstered; with improvements in technology, later chairs had a smooth plastic back which could be exposed. *Ibid.* Knoll advertisements note that the backs were available in black, blue, yellow, red, and grey. Diffrient also stated that a bent plywood back was envisioned at one point for a dining chair, although this was apparently never put into production. Interview with Niels Diffrient, Aug. 18, 1982.

152. The no. 71 armchair and no. 72 side chair were made in many versions by Knoll; they came with four-legged and pedestal bases of metal or wood.

153. There is some confusion as to when the design was begun. Rae notes that the "pedestal chair had its beginning around 1953." *Knoll au Louvre, op. cit.,* n.p. Don Petitt, Saarinen's assistant,

has offered a different chronology of the chairs: 1) sketches were begun in 1955; 2) full-size models were made by Aug./Sept. 1955; and 3) final models were completed by Summer 1956. The table versions were then made. Interview with Petitt, *op. cit.* While the pedestal chairs were Saarinen's last executed designs, Frank Stanton had hoped that he would design a unique chair for the CBS Building (1960–65), but Saarinen died before the interiors were begun. Interview with Frank Stanton, Mar. 22, 1982.

154. *Eero Saarinen on His Work, op. cit.* p. 66.

155. This was a problem that had fascinated designers since the zigzag chair (c. 1934) by Gerrit Rietveld. See Daniele Baroni, *The Furniture of Gerrit Thomas Rietveld,* Woodbury, 1978, pp. 136–39. One of the first one-piece chairs in molded plastic was the prototype made by the Lewis, Prestini, and Armour team for the "Low-cost Furniture Design Competition" held at The Museum of Modern Art (1948). See Edgar Kaufmann, jr., *Prize Designs for Modern Furniture,* New York: The Museum of Modern Art, 1950, pp. 44–46. Perhaps the first plastic one-piece chair to be mass produced was the 276 S chair designed by Verner Panton in 1960 but not put into production by Herman Miller until c. 1967.

156. The no. 150 armchair and no. 151 side chairs have a foam rubber cushion and were also available upholstered on the inside of the shell. Knoll press releases (undated) note the original shell colors as white, light grey, beige, and charcoal. There was also the no. 152 stool in the series; Petitt attributed the stool form to Florence Knoll. Interview with Petitt, *op. cit.*

157. The tables are also a "purer" design since there is no contradiction—as noted above in the chairs—with the materials used for the top and base.

158. Charles Eames, Foreword to Shapira, *Design Quarterly, op. cit.,* p. 3.

159. Both Harry Bertoia and Don Albinson worked in the Eames studio for extended periods, and their contribution has been the subject of some controversy.

160. Sketches in the Eames Archives show a free-standing fireplace in the living room, which was apparently eliminated as construction began. The idea of an inglenook with a built-in sofa came, of course, from Eliel Saarinen, who had used it initially in his Finnish house, Hvitträsk (1902 ff.) and had repeated it in Saarinen House at Cranbrook. Both Eero Saarinen and Eames continued to use inglenooks in their domestic commissions in the 1940s; the former eventually developed this motif into a sunken conversation pit in the Miller residence as noted earlier.

161. I am paraphrasing Adolf Loos' *Ornament und Verbrechen* of 1908.

162. Drawing #33-P-56-C-3.9 in the Eames Archives shows a table quite similar to Saarinen's pedestal table of 1955–57. The plan of the Wilder residence is, in fact, quite similar to Mies van der Rohe's Tugendhat house, Brno, Czechoslovakia

(1930), which also had a built-in pedestal dining table. See Johnson, *Mies van der Rohe, op. cit.,* pp. 76, 83.

163.   The major exhibitions were the Eames exhibit at The Museum of Modern Art (1946) and the Good Design shows done with Edgar Kaufmann, jr., at the Merchandise Mart, Chicago (1949), and at The Museum of Modern Art (1950). The Eameses, of course, did numerous showrooms for Herman Miller starting with their Beverly Hills building in 1949.

164.   The show was organized by Alexander Girard and ran from Sept. 10-Nov. 20, 1949. Florence Knoll designed a living/dining room and bedroom; other Cranbrook faculty and alumni participating included Pipsan Swanson, Benjamin Baldwin, Harry Bertoia, Lilian Swann Saarinen, Harry Weese, Maija Grotell, and Marianne Strengell. See A. H. Girard and W. D. Laurie, Jr., eds., *An Exhibition for Modern Living,* Detroit: The Detroit Institute of Arts, 1949.

165.   La Chaise was an entry in the Low-cost Furniture Competition noted earlier. See Kaufmann, *Prize Designs, op. cit.,* p. 59.

166.   The Eameses initially formed an experimental group with John Entenza, editor of *Arts and Architecture,* and others. They produced a series of molded plywood body splints for the U.S. Navy during the War and, later, airplane sections.

167.   See Eliot Noyes, "Charles Eames," *Arts and Architecture* 63 (Sept. 1946), pp. 26–45.

168.   The examples shown in The Museum of Modern Art exhibit "New Furniture by Charles Eames" (Mar. 13–Apr. 14, 1946) were refined before mass production. Interviews with Ray Eames, Mar. 11, 1980, and Dec. 11, 1980. For the executed collection see George Nelson, *The Herman Miller Collection,* Zeeland, 1948.

169.   The rectangular CTW (coffee table wood) table is included in this exhibition. See fig. 117, left, for an illustration.

170.   Aalto's wood folding screen (mid-1930s), though different in construction, was certainly not unknown to the Eameses.

171.   The shells were originally made of birch, walnut, or ash; birch stained red or black; and upholstered in leather or cowhide. See Noyes, "Charles Eames," *op. cit.*

172.   Don Albinson, who worked in the Eames studio from Dec. 1945 through 1959, recalled that the DCM and LCM were not completed by the time of the New York exhibit. Interview with Albinson, Aug. 24, 1982.

173.   In particular, Scandinavian designers such as Arne Jacobsen and Poul Kjaerholm seem to have studied the Eameses' work quite carefully. For the Larkin chair, see David A. Hanks, *The Decorative Designs of Frank Lloyd Wright,* New York 1979, pp. 36, 87–88.

174.   The competition was announced on Oct. 23, 1947, and ran from Jan. 5–Oct. 31, 1948. Winners were announced on Nov. 28, 1948, and the results exhibited from May 16–July 16, 1950.

The Eameses' entries were co-winner of a second prize for seating units. The team included Charles and Ray Eames; Don Albinson; Frances Bishop; James Connor; Robert Jakobsen; Charles Kratka; Frederick Usher, Jr.; University of California, Los Angeles Campus, Department of Engineering: L. M. K. Boelter, Dean; Morris Asimow; Don Lebell; Wesley L. Orr. Kaufmann, *Prize Designs, op. cit.,* pp. 6, 8–9, 19–23. Included in the Eames entry was a little-known prototype for a "minimal chair," a reductionist design that on first glance looks as if it were made for a Giacometti sculpture.

175.   The fiberglass shells were initially made by the Zenith Plastics Co., Gardena, California, for Herman Miller. Interview with Albinson, Aug. 24, 1982, *op. cit.* The first fiberglass shells were available in a variety of colors: off-white, medium grey, gun-metal, and a light grey-brown. Kaufmann, *Prize Designs, op. cit.,* p. 20. Herman Miller expanded the color range and variety of bases for mass production. See George Nelson, *The Herman Miller Collection,* Zeeland, 1952, pp. 94–96.

176.   Edgar Kaufmann, jr., *What is Modern Design?,* New York, The Museum of Modern Art, 1950, p. 11.

177.   Wire had, of course, been used for nineteenth-century garden furniture. Those chairs and settees, however, generally featured wire bent in only two dimensions and were generally woven, not welded.

178.   For the Eames wire shell series, see *Herman Miller Collection* (1952), *op. cit.,* pp. 97–99.

179.   There were distinctive differences between the Eames and Bertoia designs. A photograph of an Eames prototype (c. 1950) in the Eames Archives shows a single rod for the edging and a triangular gridwork. The executed version, however, has a double ring of rods around the perimeter of the shell; the rods forming the grid are perpendicular to each other and do not fill the entire shell. The Bertoia chairs have a single rod edging and a diamond grid (except for the side chair) filling the entire shell. Don Petitt and Richard Schultz assisted Bertoia in the development of the wire shell chairs: Petitt recalls that the prototypes were exhibited in New York in 1952 and went into production the following year. Interview with Petitt, *op. cit.* See "Bertoia: His Sculpture, His Kind of Wire Chair," *Interiors* 112 (Oct. 1952), pp. 118–21.

180.   See *Herman Miller Collection* (1952), *op. cit.,* pp. 102–07.

181.   They were, unfortunately, sold assembled, which created shipping problems with the bending of the steel frame.

182.   Drexler has rightly noted that the design evolved from the built-in sofa in the Eames house. Arthur Drexler, *Charles Eames,* New York: The Museum of Modern Art, 1973, p. 38.

183.   This chair was not designed for Billy Wilder as has so often been noted; it was a narrow

chaise lounge (1968) that was designed by the Eameses for their good friend, Wilder.

184. This prototypal lounge chair has traditionally been dated c. 1944. See Drexler, *Charles Eames, op. cit.,* pp. 26–27. Don Albinson recalled that it was one of the first projects he worked on in the Eames studio and dates it to 1946. He also recalled that one of the three-piece chairs was given to Billy Wilder. Interviews with Albinson, Aug. 24, 1982 and Jan 13, 1983.

185. Again, Don Albinson recalled that Charles Eames wanted to design a soft, comfortable lounge chair reminiscent of a traditional club chair. The three-piece shell form was worked out rather quickly; the problem came in the design of the armrest, which is a steel plate that holds the two lower shells together. The aluminum base was developed from a four-legged pedestal base used earlier in the 1950s for plastic shell chairs; one modification was the use of a five-legged base for the Eames lounge chair, which is nondirectional. Interview with Albinson, Jan. 13, 1983, *op. cit.*

186. The dining and coffee tables were originally available with tops of Botticino marble, slate, or white glass, uncharacteristically rich materials for the Eameses. See "3 Chairs," *Interiors, op. cit.,* p. 121.

187. *Ibid.,* p. 119.

188. The prototype required no mold since a flat sheet of plastic was heated and bent. The Knoll version was available in red, black, or yellow enamel; it could also be upholstered. Kaufmann, *Prize Designs, op. cit.,* pp. 13–14.

189. Interview with Rapson, *op. cit.* For Rapson's work with Knoll, see "Forum of Events," *Architectural Forum* 82 (Jan. 1945), p. 62.

190. Unfortunately, few of his designs were manufactured, an exception being an office chair series for Westin-Nielsen, St. Paul, Minnesota (c. 1957).

191. Rowland's working method is to begin with sketches on three-by-five index cards and then proceed to wire and paper models. This is followed by details at ¼″ on graph paper and then full-size models. Interview with David Rowland, Feb. 2, 1982.

192. David Rowland, "The Moral Basis of Design," *Industrial Design* 16 (Apr. 1969), p. 80.

193. Rowland studied as a young man with László Moholy-Nagy at a summer session in 1940 at Mills College, Oakland. Rowland also recalled what a great influence the book *Bauhaus 1919–1920* (New York: The Museum of Modern Art, 1938), had on him as a young man. Interview with Rowland, *op. cit.*

194. See *Marcel Breuer, op. cit.,* pp. 45, 62.

195. Prototypes of the chair had seat and back panels initially of Saran and then fiberglass; the version manufactured by General Fireproofing (1964) had steel panels with a vinyl finish. Subsequent versions have wood panels also. Interview with Rowland, *op. cit.*

196. Saarinen's and Eames' sofa design for the Organic Design competition had flat springs, and

Carl Koch submitted a spring chair design in the Low-cost Furniture competition. See Kaufmann, *Prize Designs, op. cit.,* pp. 49–52.

197. Rowland's initial work was done at Cranbrook with a chair for the No-Sag Spring Company in Detroit (c. 1950–51). Subsequent models were made in the 1950s and sixties. See "The Padded Spring Chair that Isn't," *Interiors* 113 (Nov. 1953), p. 100. The Sof-Tech chair was finally manufactured by Thonet in c. 1979. See Olga Gueft, "Thonet Sof-Tech Stacker," *Interiors* 139 (Aug. 1979), pp. 66–67, 84.

198. Wilk notes that the Breuer remark was originally published in the *Bauhaus Journal* (1926), no. 1, p. 3. *Marcel Breuer, op. cit.,* p. 188.

199. One should note that Baldwin has done a few designs intended for mass production: textiles for Arundell Clarke in the 1940s, the Solo paper cup in the 1950s, and a furniture series for Jack Lenor Larsen in the 1970s.

200. The furniture was made by Thonet. Baldwin also commissioned textiles by Strengell and art work from Joan Miró, Alexander Calder, and Saul Steinberg. See "Cincinnati's Terrace Plaza," *Architectural Forum* 89 (Dec. 1948), pp. 81–96.

201. Interview with Baldwin by C. Ray Smith, n.d. Baldwin kindly supplied a copy of the transcript.

202. *Ibid.* In talking about his first trip to Japan, Baldwin remarked: "I felt as if it had all been designed for me." Interview with Ben Baldwin, May 15, 1982.

203. While at Kingswood, Knoll did her first architectural project (c. 1932), a house for herself designed under the supervision of Rachel Raseman. With her parents' death, she became a part of the Saarinen family and traveled on occasion with them to Europe during the summers. Interview with Bassett, July 27, 1982.

204. Knoll was initially enrolled at Cranbrook from Sept. 1934 to July 1935. Her enrollment at Columbia (Fall 1935) was limited to a few months due to health problems. Cranbrook dates are based on records in the Registrar's office (letter from John Gerard, Jan. 11, 1983) and an interview with Bassett, Jan. 13, 1983, *op. cit.* Attendance dates at Columbia and the Architectural Association were confirmed by letters from the registrars, dated respectively Feb. 15, 1983, and Aug. 6, 1982.

205. Cranbrook Academy of Art Alumni Records, Florence Schust, F. Schust to R. Raseman, Feb. 11, 1940.

206. A letter from the Registrar (dated Aug. 4, 1982) confirms that Knoll was enrolled from Sept. 1940 to June, 1941.

207. Interview with Bassett, Feb. 16, 1982, *op. cit.*

208. There is some confusion as to when the Knolls were married; in the above interview, Knoll stated that they were married in Aug. 1946. Hans Knoll died in 1955, and Knoll subsequently married Harry Hood Bassett in 1958. For general

articles on the company, see "Modern Doesn't Pay, or Does It?" *Interiors, op. cit.,* pp. 66–75; John D. Morse, "The Story of Knoll Associates," *American Artist* 15 (Sept. 1951), pp. 46–50; and "Florence Knoll and the Avant Garde [sic]," *Interiors* 116 (July 1957), pp. 58–66. Also, see *Knoll Design, op. cit.*

209. For the early work of the Knoll Company, see *Knoll Design, op. cit.,* pp. 18–23, 40–49.

210. Interview with Bassett, Feb. 16, 1982.

211. *Knoll Design, op. cit.,* p. 77. For general information on Knoll's career and the Planning Unit, see pp. 76–89, 126–47.

212. Many of the furniture series in the succeeding decades were available with similar wood or metal bases; wood was thought to be more "domestic" and to appeal to more conservative clients.

213. Metal rod was used for the no. 75 stacking stool, and black tubular steel bases were used on the no. 33 sofa series.

214. In the 1940s, large T-angles were used for the no. 155 coffee table and the no. 300 dining table. In the succeeding decade an assortment of low tables were made with T-angles in various finishes.

215. See "Knoll's Spare Parallel Bar System," *Interiors* 115 (Jan. 1956), pp. 106–07.

216. See "CBS Offices by the Same Designer," *Architectural Forum* 102 (Jan. 1955), pp. 134–39.

217. Knoll refined the "Parson's table" form further during the fifties in the no. 303 table with its decidedly Miesian edging. Mies designed a low, "Parson's" style table in 1930, which is illustrated in Johnson, *Mies van der Rohe, op. cit.,* pp. 55.

218. Boat-shaped tables were made in the forties, but the most famous example is the no. 1581 series. Likewise, the most elegant table desks are two pedestal designs: the no. 2480 oval table and the no. 2485 rectangular desk.

219. See *Marcel Breuer, op. cit.,* P. 62.

220. See Johnson, *Mies van der Rohe, op. cit.,* pp. 80–84.

221. Examples are the all-wood no. 125 unit and the no. 523 series, which have steel bases.

222. Knoll was quite fortunate to have a series of extraordinary clients. One of her most important domestic designs was the remodeling of Nelson Rockefeller's apartment in New York during the mid-1940s. Such an influential client was obviously helpful to a designer still in her twenties. Knoll recalled that one of the most striking features was a freestanding semicircular wall in the manner of the dining room from the Tugendhat House (1930) by Mies. Unfortunately no photographs exist of the Rockefeller apartment, and the interiors have been destroyed.

223. See "Knoll Associates Move Into the Big Time," *Interiors* 110 (May 1951), pp. 74–83.

224. See "Knoll, Chicago: New Tune in the Same Key," *Interiors* 113 (Feb. 1954), pp. 46–51.

225. See Louise Sloane, "Two Showrooms," *Progressive Architecture* 139 (July 1958), pp. 137–42.

226. See "The Knoll Interior," *Architectural Forum* 106 (Mar. 1957), pp. 137–40, and "Knoll's Newest Showroom," *Interiors* 120 (Mar. 1961), pp. 138–39.

227. Once again, Mies' influence during the 1940s seems to be evident. He had used curved walls for exhibitions (Silk Exhibit, "Exposition de la Môde," Berlin, 1927, in collaboration with Lilly Reich) and in several house designs (for example, the Tugendhat House [1930] noted earlier and a project for the second Ulrich Lange house, Krefeld, Germany [1935]). A particularly revealing detail is Knoll's use of a curved, cantilevered wall shelf as in the Tugendhat House. See Johnson, *Mies van der Rohe, op. cit.,* pp. 76, 83, 116.

228. The detailing of the wood frames for the glass walls is one of the few instances where Eliel Saarinen's direct influence can be seen in Knoll's work.

229. For an illustration of a model, see *Knoll Design, op. cit.,* p. 135. Interview with Bassett, *op. cit.*

230. The building was designed by Skidmore, Owings and Merrill. See "Insurance Sets a Pattern," *Architectural Forum* 107 (Sept. 1957), pp. 113–27.

231. "It's the Detailing that Counts," *House and Garden* 131 (Feb. 1967), p. 132.

232. See "Model of Office Planning," *Progressive Architecture* 43 (Mar. 1962), pp. 151–57.

233. See Mildred F. Schmertz, "Distinguished Interior Architecture for CBS," *Architectural Record* 139 (June 1966), pp. 129–34; *Office Design* 4/3 (May 1966), pp. 20–43; John Vaughan, "Clear Image," *Queen* (Jan. 18, 1967).

6. METALWORK AND BOOKBINDING

J. David Farmer

1. The metalworking department has carried a number of names in its history and, in fact, its proper name is sometimes inconsistent within Cranbrook records and publications at any one time. In the early years it was known as either the Silversmithing or Silver department. Under Harry Bertoia, it was listed first as the Metalwork and then as the Metalcraft department. After 1948, with Richard Thomas as head, official references title it the Metalsmithing department.

2. George G. Booth, *The Cranbrook Press. Something about the Cranbrook Press and on Books and Bookmaking; also a List of Cranbrook Publications with Fac-simile pages from* *the same,* Detroit, 1902.

3. Interview with Elia Eschmann and Alice Eschmann Schweitzer, Jan. 13, 1982.

4. The only published biography of Eschmann is Genevieve Miller, "Medicus Librorum. Jean Eschmann, Restorer of Rare Books," *Bulletin of the Cleveland Medical Library,* 3, 1 (Jan. 1956), pp. 3–8.

5. E.g., Cranbrook Archives, Cranbrook Foundation, Administration Records, Agreement between Cranbrook Foundation and Jean Eschmann, Oct. 1, 1931.

6. Cranbrook Archives, Cranbrook Foundation, Administration Records, Costs of Bindery Shop Jobs Completed in October 1932.

7. Cranbrook Archives, Cranbrook Academy of Art, Administration Records, 1931–66, George Booth to Richard Raseman, n.d.

8. Mostly brought by Eschmann, as noted in a letter, Cranbrook Archives, Cranbrook Foundation, General Records, Jean Eschmann to H. P. Macomber, April 4, 1929.

9. Interview with Eschmann and Schweitzer, *op. cit.*

10. E.g., Betty Lorch (daughter of Emil Lorch, professor of Architecture at the University of Michigan), who bound books which still remain at Cranbrook.

11. Cranbrook Archives, Cranbrook Foundation, Trustees Records, 1927–54, George G. Booth to Mrs. Jean Eschmann, July 15, 1933.

12. Cranbrook Archives, Papers of George G. Booth, Correspondence between George G. Booth and Samuel Yellin, 1917.

13. Cranbrook Archives, Papers of George G. Booth, Correspondence between George G. Booth and Georg Jensen and Karl Larsen, 1922 and 1927.

14. Cranbrook Archives, Papers of George G. Booth, Statement by George G. Booth, n.d.

15. There is no published biography of Kirk. Most biographical information in this essay is based on an interview with Vera Kirk and Marion Kirk Jones, Oct. 17, 1981, and Kirk's own résumé.

16. Interview with Margaret Biggar by John Gerard, March 21, 1981.

17. Cranbrook Academy of Art/Museum, nos. 1933.33a–c.

18. Walter Rendell Storey, "Antiques that Illustrate Art History," *New York Times Magazine,* Feb. 26, 1933, p. 14.

19. Cranbrook Academy of Art/Museum, no. 1933.37. Cranbrook Archives, Cranbrook Academy of Art, Craftshop inv., 1929–33, job no. 30, 1929.

20. Among many ecclesiastical commissions are appointments for Christ Church, Grosse Pointe; Cathedral of St. Paul's, Detroit; National Cathedral, Washington, D.C.; Chapel of the Little Flower, Syracuse; St. Joseph's, Detroit. His work was shown in a number of special exhibitions of ecclesiastical art: "Exhibition of Ecclesiastical Art," Denver Art Museum, 1931, nos. 20–34;

"Religious Art of Today," Dayton Art Institute, 1944, nos. 86–87; "First Annual Liturgical Art Show," St. Thomas University, Houston, 1950, nos. 50a–d.

21. Detroit Public Library, Burton Historical Collection, Kate Thompson Bromley Papers, 1941.

22. His work has been shown in special exhibitions; note especially "Arthur Nevill Kirk—Retrospective Exhibition," The Detroit Institute of Arts, 1950 (no catalogue), and *Arts and Crafts in Detroit, 1906–1976. The Movement, the Society, the School,* Detroit: The Detroit Institute of Arts, 1976, p. 87, nos. 53–55.

23. *St. Louis Post-Dispatch, Sunday Magazine,* Jan. 26, 1930.

24. Cranbrook Archives, Papers of George G. Booth, Handwritten note on letter from M. W. Childs to George G. Booth, Jan. 27, 1930.

25. *Cranbrook Announcement,* Oct. 1932.

26. Cranbrook Archives, Cranbrook Foundation, Trustees Records, 1927–54, Richard Raseman to Foundation, Jan. 18, 1933.

27. E.g., a catalogue of c. 1912 from the Taidetakomo Koru firm in the collection of the Taideteollisuusmuseo, Helsinki, with accessories designed by a number of Finnish artists.

28. Cranbrook Archives, Administration Records, 1931–66, Eliel Saarinen to Barbara Reed, April 14, 1936. Saarinen described a service manufactured by Taidetakomo. A letter dated May 28, 1981, from Marianne Aav, Curator, Taideteollisuusmuseo, Helsinki, stated that Saarinen probably meant the firm of Taito Oy, sometimes known as Taidetakomo Taito Oy.

29. Many examples in both the Cranbrook Academy of Art/Museum and the Suomen Rakennustaiteen Museo, Helsinki.

30. Cranbrook Academy of Art/Museum, Cranbrook Architectural Office drawings 107, 107A, 107B, 107C.

31. Cranbrook Archives, Papers of George G. Booth, Correspondence between George G. Booth and Oscar Bach, 1928.

32. E.g., in Kenneth Reid, "Eliel Saarinen—Master of Design," *Pencil Points* 17 (Sept. 1936), p. 485.

33. Cranbrook Academy of Art/Museum, no. 1933.50. Cranbrook Archives, Cranbrook Academy of Art, Craftshop inv., 1929–33, job no. 164, 1930.

34. Cranbrook Academy of Art/Museum, no. 1933.51.

35. Interview with Biggar, *op. cit.*

36. Eliel Saarinen, in *The Architect and the Industrial Arts,* New York: The Metropolitan Museum of Art, 1929, pp. 58–61.

37. The centerpiece is similar but not identical to a footed bowl in the Cranbrook Academy of Art/Museum, no. 1933.49.

38. E. P. Hogan, Historian, International Silver Co., to John Gerard, June 29, 1981. A thirteen-inch-diameter bowl is in the Cranbrook Academy of Art/Museum, 1936.4.

39. *The Architect and the Industrial Arts, op. cit.,* p. 61.

40. The Contempora pattern by Reed and Barton.

41. Patent nos. 84654 and 84655.

42. *The Architect and the Industrial Arts, op. cit.,* p. 61.

43. "Fine Examples of Hand-Wrought Iron are Made at Cranbrook," *Detroit News,* July 20, 1930.

44. E.g., Suomen Rakennustaiteen Museo, Helsinki, no. 92/30, and Cranbrook Academy of Art/Museum, no. 1951.106.

45. Executed by Edward F. Caldwell and Co.

46. Also executed by Caldwell. The drawing for the lamp is in the Suomen Rakennustaiteen Museo, Helsinki, no. 92/46.

47. The room is illustrated in *Architectural Forum* 61 (Dec. 1934), pp. 412–13.

48. Described and illustrated in the *Detroit News Rotogravure,* May 12, 1935.

49. An oblong silver-plated centerpiece, silver-plated finger bowl, silver-plated dish, gold-plated nut dish, brass centerpiece, brass shallow bowl, and a brass fluted bowl; listed in Cranbrook Archives, Cranbrook Academy of Art, Administration Records, 1931–66, Inventory, 1935. It does not seem that Nessen offered the pieces commercially.

50. *Academy News,* 1941, photograph of the May 12 annual tea, in which the urn occupies a prominent place on the table with other metalware.

51. Cranbrook Archives, photographs nos. 2703–704.

52. Cranbrook Archives, Alumni Records, Richard Raseman to Harry Bertoia, May 3, 1937.

53. Cranbrook Archives, Alumni Records, Richard Raseman to Harry Bertoia, May 5, 1937.

54. There is no published study of Bertoia as a metal designer and craftsman.

55. Interview with Brigitta Valentiner Bertoia, April 7, 1981.

56. Cranbrook Academy of Art/Museum, no. 1938.8.

57. "Hand-wrought Forms in Pewter and Brass Shown at Artists Market," *Detroit News,* Apr. 9, 1939.

58. E.g., in *Modern Handmade Jewelry,* New York: The Museum of Modern Art, 1946; see *Arts and Architecture* 63 (Dec. 1946), pp. 31–33, for illustrations. Also at the Alexander Girard Gallery in May 1947; see *Detroit News,* May 7, 1947.

59. Several times at the Nierendorf Gallery, New York; see review in *Art News* 46, 3 (May 1947), p. 48.

60. Cranbrook Archives, Cranbrook Academy of Art, Administration Records, 1931–66, Richard Raseman to Cranbrook Academy of Art trustees, Oct. 7, 1942.

61. Cranbrook Archives, Cranbrook Academy of Art, Administration Records, 1931–66, Trustees' executive committee minutes, Feb. 2, 1943.

62. Cranbrook Archives, Cranbrook Academy of Art, Administration Records, 1931–66, Zoltan Sepeshy to Cranbrook Academy of Art Board of Trustees, Jan. 8, 1946.

63. Cranbrook Archives, Cranbrook Academy of Art, Administration Records, 1931–66, Henry Booth to Zoltan Sepeshy, Jan. 9, 1947.

64. Interviews with Mr. and Mrs. William Whitney, June 2, 1981, and Richard Thomas, June 3, 1981.

65. Most information on Thomas in this essay comes from undated interviews between Thomas and Joy Hakanson; Michael Hall and John Gerard, Jan. 4, 11, and 16, 1980; and the author, Feb. 18 and June 3, 1981.

66. Archives of American Art, roll 926, nos. 213–4, Letter from Richard Thomas to D. Kenneth Winebrenner, July 31, 1950.

67. See, e.g., *Alumni Exhibition,* Bloomfield Hills: Cranbrook Academy of Art/Museum, 1951, and issues of the *Cranbrook Newsletter.*

68. Richard Thomas, *Metalsmithing for the Artist-Craftsman,* Radnor, 1960; *idem, Metal Raising: A Course of Study,* New York, 1961; *idem, Raising Techniques,* New York, 1961.

69. E.g., *American Church Silver,* Bloomfield Hills: Cranbrook Academy of Art/Museum, 1952, in which a number of students participated in a laboratory project for Trinity Lutheran Church, Detroit.

70. Archives of American Art, roll 926, nos. 65–68, Correspondence between Bishop Page and Richard Thomas, 1961.

71. Interview with Hakanson, *op. cit.*

7. TEXTILES
Christa C. Mayer Thurman

1. Cranbrook Archives, Papers of George G. Booth, Inventories and Appraisals for Cranbrook House, 1914; 1915–18; 1921; 1921–25; 1933; 1937; 1949.

2. *Arts and Crafts in Detroit 1906–1976. The Movement, the Society, the School,* Detroit: The Detroit Institute of Arts, 1976, p. 22.

3. Cranbrook Archives, Box 11; purchased May 14, 1920.

4. Cranbrook Archives, Papers of George G. Booth, Morris and Company, H. C. Marillier to G. G. Booth, 1911–Dec. 1926.

5. *Ibid.,* Albert Herter to G. G. Booth, 1918–20.

6. Cranbrook Archives, Box 12–14; Inventories.

7. The term "tapestry" is often misused. Its correct usage implies that an item was constructed in the tapestry weave (also referred to as weft-faced plain weave). As the Cranbrook-made textiles discussed here do not include the tapestry

weave, the term "hanging" has been used to refer to them.

8. Cranbrook Archives, Papers of George G. Booth, G. G. Booth to H. C. Marillier, Nov. 1, 1922.

9. *Ibid.*

10. Cranbrook Archives, Papers of George G. Booth, G. G. Booth to H. C. Marillier, Jan. 16, 1925.

11. *Ibid.*

12. *Ibid.,* H. C. Marillier to G. G. Booth, Jan. 30, 1925.

13. Detroit Public Library, Burton Historical Collection, Diary of Kate Thompson Bromley [c. 1930–54], n.p.

14. Cranbrook Archives, Papers of George G. Booth, H. C. Marillier to G. G. Booth, Feb. 3, 1925.

15. *Ibid.,* J. H. Dearle to H. P. Macomber, Oct. 14, 1929.

16. *Ibid.,* Henry S. Booth to H. C. Marillier, Apr. 12, 1932.

17. *Birmingham Eccentric,* Mar. 24, 1932. The tapestries hang to this day at Christ Church Cranbrook.

18. Cranbrook Archives, Papers of George G. Booth, G. G. Booth to A. Herter, 1918–1920.

19. Alice M. Zrebiec, "The American Tapestry Manufactures: Origins and Development 1893–1933," unpublished Ph.D. dissertation, New York University, 1980, p. 2.

20. Cranbrook Archives, Papers of George G. Booth, G. G. Booth to A. Herter, Aug. 30, 1918.

21. *Ibid.,* Mar. 3, 1919.

22. *Ibid.,* Feb. 5 or 8, 1919.

23. Cranbrook Academy of Art/Museum, no. 1944.83; sketch, no. 1920.4; 13 ft. × 10 ft. 4 in.; cotton, wool, and silk with gold and silver threads for highlights; 20.2 warps per in., 80 wefts per in.; weaver's name (J. B. Baule) woven into lower left corner, with the initials H. L. (Herter Looms) and the year 1920. Booth's pencil sketch has no accession number. According to Alice Zrebiec, the inclusion of a weaver's name was most unusual at the Herter Looms (*op. cit.,* p. 146). What is even more unusual is the fact that only one name occurs although it is known that "three men had been constantly employed for the entire time" (Cranbrook Archives, Papers of George G. Booth, Frank W. Richardson to G. G. Booth, June 26, 1920).

24. Cranbrook Archives, Papers of George G. Booth, G. G. Booth, undated lecture notes, p. 1.

25. *Ibid.*

26. *Ibid.*

27. Booth dealt with John Wise, Ltd., Heeramaneck Galleries, Dikran G. Kelekian, Inc., and others; see Cranbrook Archives, Papers of George G. Booth, "The Cranbrook Foundation, List of Old Fabrics" (Textile Inventory), Nov. 28, 1927.

28. Undated account by Florence Davies, Art Critic for the *Detroit News,* p. 3, among personal papers of Loja Saarinen, property of Ronald S. Swanson.

29. *The Saarinen Door. Eliel Saarinen, Architect and Designer at Cranbrook,* Bloomfield Hills: Cranbrook Academy of Art, 1963, p. 61.

30. Interview of Dipl. Ing. von Pfaler by Christa Thurman, Apr. 2, 1982, at his home in Borgå, Finland.

31. *The Saarinen Door, op. cit.,* pp. 62–63.

32. John Gerard, *Studio Loja Saarinen,* Bloomfield Hills: Cranbrook Academy of Art/Museum, 1980.

33. *Handarbetets Vänner 100 år,* Stockholm, 1974, under "H. V. Tekniken." In 1909, fifty-two out of eighty furnishing material orders were done there in this technique. Cärin Wastberg was largely reponsible for the subtle color compositions.

34. From extant pieces attributed to Studio Loja Saarinen and part of the Cranbrook Museum's collection, sixteen are attributable to Loja herself, seven attributable as joint ventures of Eliel and Loja Saarinen, three as having been designed by Eliel Saarinen, eleven by Wirde; six cannot as yet be fully identified and are therefore attributed to the Studio. The Wilton Seamless machine-woven carpet is not included in these counts.

35. Cranbrook Archives, Cranbrook Foundation, Trustees Records, Series I, Box 3, Cranbrook Academy of Art (Correspondence, Reports) 1930–1949 Folder, "Plan for Operation of Textile Department at Cranbrook for one year from October 1, 1930," undated manuscript.

36. Immigration papers for Maja Andersson Wirde.

37. The 1927 exhibition was preceded by the 1925 Paris Fair. As the Paris Fair did not come to the United States, it was decided to bring an exhibition entitled "Swedish Contemporary Decorative Arts" to New York (The Metropolitan Museum of Art) and thereafter to Detroit and to Chicago (The Art Institute of Chicago). George G. Booth was instrumental in getting this exhibition to the United States. Wirde is listed in the catalogue as Maja Andersson (p. 12, entry 57, ill. p. 48).

38. Föreningen Handarbetets Vänner, *Arsberattelser* (Annual Reports), 1904–30, and obituraries in the following Swedish newspapers: *Sydsvenska Dagbladet* Snällposten, Feb. 15, 1952; *Svenska Dagbladet,* Feb. 14, 1952; and *Smålandsposten,* Feb. 14, 1952.

39. Cranbrook Archives, Miscellaneous Cranbrook Academy of Art Correspondence, Box 15, List of staff at Cranbrook compiled by John Gerard, furnishes the following names and rates of pay for the weavers in the Studio in 1930: Lilly Bjerkin (60¢ per hour, part-time); Ruth Ingvarson (60¢ per hour, part-time); Walborg Nordquist (Smalley) (78¢ per hour, $32 per week, or 60¢ per hour); Lillian Holm ($30 per week, 73¢ per hour); Hilda Franzen ($100 per month, 56¢ per hour); Kerstein Berglund ($3.82 per day); Elizabeth Edmark ($3.82 per day); Esther Broberg, Gerda Nyberg (47½¢ per hour); Maja Andersson Wirde ($1.46 per hour, $260 per month);

and other weavers: Marie Bexell, Ragnhild Johnson (1929), Anna Danielson, and Peggy Buckberrough.

40. Cranbrook Archives, Papers of George G. Booth, Box 6, "Writings on the Cranbrook Ideal 1924–1939"; M. W. Childs, "A Detroit Millionaire's Attempt to Restore the Hand Crafts," *St. Louis Post-Dispatch,* Jan. 26, 1930.

41. R. J. Bilaitis, Chairman, Department of Art and Art History, Wayne State University, to Christa Thurman, June 2, 1982.

42. Florence Davies, "An Old Art Flourishes," *Detroit News,* Dec. 26, 1937.

43. Due to its size (18 ft. 11 in. × 72 ft.) the Living Room Carpet, although still extant, could not be included in the exhibition. Curiously, it was excluded from an earlier exhibition in favor of a Kingswood carpet; see Cranbrook Archives, Cranbrook Architectural Office, Saarinen temporary exhibition at The Detroit Institute of Arts, 1931, Drawing No. 332–ABC.

44. Like most other decorative arts departments, the Museum carpet collection did not include the nineteenth and twentieth centuries until fairly recently. By the time this oversight was acknowledged it was too late to find prime examples of the 1920s–40s as they had either worn out or been discarded. Within the textile field the Kingswood carpets are unique and warrant serious attention in regard to their future.

45. The *Festival of the May Queen* hanging could not be included in this exhibition due to its size (18 × 16 ft.). The cartoon and weaving sample were both hanging in Studio Loja Saarinen in 1933, as per Cranbrook Archives photograph no. 2373. A label attached to the reverse of the weaving sample and printed in ink in Loja Saarinen's handwriting states: "This is a sample of the large (16′ × 18′) tapestry at Kingswood School Dining Hall. It was woven at Cranbrook Academy of Art in 1932. It was designed by Eliel and Loja Saarinen."

46. See dated photographs identified in her handwriting, Lund, Kulturen, Archives. There was a round and a rectangular carpet which she designed in 1928 for first-class accommodations on the Swedish ship *Kungsholm,* and there are other textiles at the Nordiska Museet of this period that identify Wirde without question as the creator of all these designs. The Wirde textile holdings from Handarbetets Vänner were recently transferred to the collections of the Nordiska Museet. Examples of woven and embroidered textiles are included, as well as rug samples and a few lace pieces.

47. John Gerard to Christa Thurman, May 5, 1982. Column 1, Row 1 shows Cranbrook School Dormitory Pergola (it relates to Column 2, Row 3); Row 2 illustrates Cranbrook School Dining Hall; Row 3 introduces Cranbrook Academy with the Crafts Court Archway; Row 4 presents Cranbrook School (similar to Column 3, Row 2). Column 2, Row 1 shows Christ Church Cranbrook with its tower; Row 2 interprets Cranbrook Pavilion; Row 3 presents Cranbrook School Dormitory Pergola (similar to Column 1, Row 1); Row 4 portrays the Greek Theater. Column 3, Row 1 illustrates Christ Church Cranbrook; Row 2 shows Cranbrook School (similar to Column 1, Row 4); Row 3 introduces the Mill Race; Row 4 presents Brookside School with Tower and Meeting House. Column 3, Row 3 was identified by Mary Riordan.

48. Archival material by Maja Wirde at the Smålands Museum, Växjö.

49. The sketch was found by the author among archival material at Smålands Museum, Växjö, in April 1982.

50. I am indebted to John Gerard for interpreting the motifs included in this hanging (Feb. 1982).

51. Hvitträsk hanging, Cranbrook Academy of Art/Museum, no. 1979.2.

52. John Gerard has suggested this identification of the black-booted bear (conversation, June 1981).

53. Obituary of Loja Saarinen, Apr. 24, 1968, property of Ronald S. Swanson.

54. Cranbrook Archives, Cranbrook Foundation, Administration Records, Richard P. Raseman to Cranbrook Foundation, June 8, 1936; Cranbrook Academy of Art Annual Reports 1933–1942.

55. Cranbrook Archives, Cranbrook Academy of Art Papers, Class Announcement 1939–1940.

56. Cranbrook Archives, Cranbrook Academy of Art Papers, List of looms, Feb. 18, 1941, and Jean D. White to Sanford H. Allen, Feb. 1941.

57. Cranbrook Archives, Cranbrook Academy of Art Papers, Ledger, Weaving Room, Material Inventory May–Dec. 1929. The listings of "rayon" are most puzzling as Loja Saarinen supposedly did not use any synthetic fibers in her weavings. "Lustrone" [sic] is "Lustron" and was manufactured by the Lustron Company (or Lustron Comp.), Inc., 44 K Street, South Boston, Massachusetts; it appears as "Lustron Rayon Yarns" in the *Official American Textile Directory* (compiled by Textile World, 1927), p. 236, but does not appear listed in 1929. Davison's *Textile Blue Book* (1926), p. 536, lists a "Lustron artificial silk" with the stipulation of "sell direct" (does not appear listed in 1928). This substantiates the information that Lustron was discontinued in the 1920s. It is referred to as "Lustra-cellulose" in J. Merritt Matthews, *The Textile Fibers,* New York, 4th ed., 1923, p. 673. I acknowledge Jane Hutchins' help in regard to this information. In the twenties the synthetics were in their infancy. In 1884 the first artificial fiber, known as artificial silk, had been introduced in France. From there it reached England and ultimately was brought to the United States in 1910 where it was manufactured by the Viscose Company of America, a firm renamed shortly thereafter as American Viscose Corporation. The substance for this man-made fiber was cellulose and the first synthetic available was "rayon." Charles H. Rutledge and Louisa

Bellinger, "Man-Made Filaments and Chemistry," in *Threads of History,* New York, 1967, pp. 44–45.

58. See Chronology, and Cranbrook Archives, Announcement of Classes 1932–33 Folder, which states: "Capable and serious students may obtain instruction in Weaving and Textiles. Also design of textiles with special consideration of color, one three-hour lesson two dollars." During 1931, Wirde had seven students, according to Cranbrook Academy of Art Papers, "Report covering the Activities at the Weaving Department, 1931."

59. Cranbrook Archives, Cranbrook Foundation, Series 1, Box 6, Katherine Rogers Adams to Cecil Billington, Feb. 2, 1932.

60. Keeping the weaving studio open had to do in part with commissions and also undoubtedly with the fact that Loja was the wife of Cranbrook's President.

61. Cranbrook Archives, Cranbrook Foundation, Trustees Records 1927–1954, R. Raseman to Foundation Trustees, Feb. 24, 1933.

62. Correspondence in regard to her salaries earned for that year at Cranbrook was directed to 181 Michigan Avenue, Chicago; the letters were signed by Helen McIlroy, July 31, 1933. Another reference to Wirde's departure can be found in the Kate Thompson Bromley Diary (*op. cit.*), about 1930–54. It states: "She [Maja Wirde] left here for the Chicago Century of Progress where she was all summer in the Swedish Building, returning to Sweden, when the season of 1933 finished there." The Diary further reveals this information: "Under her [Wirde's] tutelage Mrs. Saarinen had perfected her skill in weaving so that she would be able to take her place."

63. Cranbrook Archives, Announcement of Classes, September 1935–June 1936; also Cranbrook Academy of Art Papers, and Cranbrook Academy of Art Intermediate School Announcement 1936–1937.

64. Cranbrook Archives, Kingswood School Cranbrook Catalogue, 1935–1936, p. 28; Cranbrook Academy of Art Intermediate School Announcement 1936–1937.

65. Cranbrook Archives, Cranbrook Academy of Art Papers, Series 1, Box 3 (Annual Reports 1933–1942), Report of Cranbrook Academy of Art, 1933–1934; and Kingswood School Cranbrook Catalogues, 1933–1966.

66. *Flint Journal,* May 17, 1942.

67. Christopher R. Young, Curator of Collections and Registrar, Flint Institute of Arts, to Christa Thurman, July 22, 1981. No further information is available on Lillian Holm. The accession number of the piece is 1965.14; it was a gift of Lillian Holm in memory of Ralph T. Sayles, brother of a local patron, Miss Mary Sayles.

68. See photographs of the Kingswood Auditorium in the Cranbrook Academy of Art/Museum.

69. See photograph of Kingswood Ballroom in Cranbrook Academy of Art/Museum.

70. Cranbrook Archives, Cranbrook Foundation, Administration Records, Minutes of meeting of the Cranbrook Foundation, Apr. 21, 1932.

71. Diary of Kate Thompson Bromley, *op. cit.*

72. Property of Ronald S. Swanson.

73. Accession no. 1979.8a–w; a total of twenty-three watercolor and pencil sketches exist. They were a gift to the Cranbrook Academy of Art/Museum made by Pipsan Saarinen Swanson shortly before her death.

74. Cranbrook Archives, Cranbrook Academy of Art Papers, Announcement of Courses: Weaving, Interior Design, with new course listed with Pipsan S. Swanson as Instructor.

75. Résumés of Pipsan Saarinen Swanson covering the years 1923–70, Cranbrook Academy of Art/Museum, and earlier résumés, Papers of Loja Saarinen, property of Ronald S. Swanson.

76. *Detroit Free Press,* Sept. 28, 1947; *Detroit News,* Feb. 23, 1947; *Herald Tribune Home Institute,* Oct. 28, 1947; *House and Garden,* Oct. 1947.

77. Pipsan Swanson résumés, *op. cit.*

78. Ex.: Birmingham and Bloomfield High Schools, Mental Health Research Building and Psychiatric Unit of Children's Hospital at University of Michigan, Dormitories and Lecture Halls at Eastern Michigan University, the First Baptist Church at Flint, Michigan, etc.

79. Pipsan Swanson résumés, *op. cit.*

80. Victoria and Albert Museum, London, information sheet describing the room at time of installation (1974); and Valerie Mendes, Division of Textiles and Costume, to Christa Thurman, Sept. 29, 1981. The room was dismantled during the late 1950s and thereafter Edgar Kaufmann, jr., the son of the patron, presented it to the Victoria and Albert Museum.

81. Cranbrook Academy of Art/Museum, Transcript of Anssi Blomsted interview with Charles Eames, Dec. 1976. The designs for the house were completed in 1936, construction was started in 1937 (see De Long).

82. M. Dismore, First Christian Church Librarian, to Christa Thurman, May 26, 1982.

83. *Ibid.,* May 21, 1982.

84. Diary of Kate Thompson Bromley, *op. cit.,* Sunday, Feb. 1942: ". . . finished it was twelve feet by thirty-five feet [the actual size given by the Church is thirty-five feet by ten feet] . . . Before it was started, Mrs. Saarinen had been to her [Lillian Holm] four different times to urge her to weave it. But it was not until she was finally assured that she would receive full credit publicly, would she agree. That had not always been the case. This beautiful piece is unfortunately to be hung in a very smoky, dirty manufacturing town; so that curtains are to be drawn over it, except during services and when it is to be shown." It still hangs behind curtains today.

85. Cranbrook Archives, photograph no. 2444 shows a large carpet identified as a Chrysler Showroom commission. The actual pieces for this showroom and for the Richard Hudnut Salon or

the Yardley Shop could not be located.

86. Cranbrook Archives, Papers of George G. Booth, Loja Saarinen to G. G. Booth, Aug. 28, 1942.

87. Cranbrook Archives, Cranbrook Academy of Art Papers, *Cranbrook Bulletin,* 1945.

88. Christa Thurman interview with Marianne Strengell, May 6, 1981.

89. Cranbrook Archives, Cranbrook Academy of Art Papers, R. P. Raseman, Mar. 13, 1937.

90. Cranbrook Archives, Marianne Strengell, First contractual letter, Mar. 25, 1937.

91. Her title became Director of the Weaving Department with Robert D. Sailors as Instructor—a position he filled until 1947.

92. In Cranbrook Archives, Cranbrook Foundation, Administration Records, Minutes of meeting of The Cranbrook Foundation, June 11, 1938, she is mentioned as ". . . having done a very excellent job, and merits an increase."

93. Thurman interview with Strengell, *op. cit.*

94. Cranbrook Archives, Cranbrook Academy of Art Papers, Class Announcements 1942–1943.

95. Cranbrook Archives, Cranbrook Academy of Art Papers, Tentative Plan for Division of Work during Five Years (manuscript), Dec. 5, 1942, mentions that both courses were to take place during the second semester.

96. *Ibid.*

97. Miriam Kellogg Fredenthal to Christa Thurman, Jan. 18, 1982 (includes statement by M. K. Fredenthal).

98. For further technical description see text. All pictorial hangings for Kingswood, etc., were executed in this technique.

99. Thurman interview with Strengell, *op. cit.*

100. Cranbrook Archives, Cranbrook Foundation, Trustees Records 1927–1954, Cranbrook Academy of Art Trustees Record 1, June 1, 1944, pp. 95–6.

101. Cranbrook Archives, Cranbrook Academy of Art Papers, "Cranbrook Academy of Art, Bloomfield Hills, Michigan" (manuscript), 1943, p. 1.

102. John Gerard to Christa Thurman, June 3, 1982, and June 18, 1982. Also see note 42. Nyberg worked from 1930 to 1942 for Loja Saarinen. Prior to 1945 she also worked on and off for Marianne Strengell; from 1945 until sometime in the sixties she worked full-time for Strengell.

103. J. I. Biegeleisen and Max Arthur Cohn, *Silk Screen Techniques,* New York, 1958, pp. 12–13.

104. *Christian Science Monitor,* Oct. 1, 1940.

105. *Annual International Textile Exhibition 1944,* Greensboro: Weatherspoon Art Gallery, [p. 7].

106. Program of "The First Biennial Exhibition of Contemporary Textiles and Ceramics," Feb. 3–28, 1946, Cranbrook Academy of Art/Museum.

107. Tentative Plan for Divison of Work . . . , *op. cit.*

108. Marianne Strengell to Christa Thurman, Feb. 4, 1982, and illustration in *Art News* 46 (May 1947), p. 36.

109. Cranbrook Academy of Art, *Alumni Directory,* Fall 1973. These included Matthew Kahn, Painting, 1946–49; Ron Fiedler, B.F.A. Design, 1949; Joseph Bobrowicz, B.F.A. Painting, 1951.

110. Thurman interview with Strengell, *op. cit.,* newspaper articles, and correspondence dated Feb. 4, 1982.

111. Two résumés covering the years 1929–81 (the earlier one is from the private papers of Loja Saarinen, property of Ronald S. Swanson); also newspaper accounts, correspondence with Christa Thurman during 1981 and 1982, and interview, *op. cit.*

112. Cranbrook Academy of Art/Museum Records, Catalogue listings and correspondence files pertaining to biennial exhibitions, 1946–54. In 1946 Anni Albers, Marli Ehrman, Lillian Garrett, Noemi Raymond, Robert D. Sailors, Marianne Strengell, and Angelo Testa participated.

113. *Ibid.* Ruth Adler (Schnee), Hollis E. Beasley, Geraldine Funk (Alvarez), Joy Lind, Mary Walker Phillips, Antoinette Lackner Prestini (Webster), Noemi Raymond, Ben Rose, Robert D. Sailors, Marianne Strengell, and Angelo Testa participated.

114. *Ibid.* Anni Albers, Benjamin Baldwin and William Machado, Majel Chance (Obata), Georgia B. Chingren, Marli Ehrman, Geraldine Funk (Alvarez), Trude Guermonprez, Matthew Kahn, Gyrogy and Juliet Kepes, Gale Kidd, Maria Kipp, Lea Van P. Miller, Mary Walker Phillips, Ben Rose, Bernard Rudolsky, Ruth Adler Schnee, Abel Sorensen, Marianne Strengell, Angelo Testa, and Henning Waterstron participated.

115. *Ibid.* The textile section included Anni Albers, Josef Albers (for Arundell Clarke), Rosemary Zettel Antonacci, Michael Belangie (for Menlo Textiles), Kenneth Brosen (for Mitchell-David Co., Inc.), Marli Ehrman (for Edwin Raphael Co.), Espada-Ryder (for Konwiser, Inc.), Alexander Girard (for Herman Miller Furniture Co.), Trude Guermonprez, Eszter Haraszty and Evelyn Hill (for Knoll Textiles, Inc.), Paul Hultberg (for Arundell Clarke), Eleanor and Henry Kluck (for Elenhank Designers), Boris Kroll, Estelle Laverne and Ross Littell (for Laverne Originals), George Nelson (for Schiffer Prints Division of Mil-Art Co., Inc.), Original Textile Co. (for Mitchell-David Co., Inc.), Ruth Reeves (for Konwiser, Inc.), Ben Rose, Norman Ruskin, Pipsan Saarinen Swanson, Angelo Testa, Henning Waterstron and Don Wight (for Greeff Fabrics, Inc.). A selection of items was circulated by the Smithsonian Institution's Travelling Exhibition Service after the Cranbrook showing.

116. All matriculated weaving students who had received their degree by 1951 and who were identified as such in the 1973 Cranbrook Academy of Art Alumni Directory were sent a form letter to determine whether or not they were still active in the textile field. The results of this survey were as follows: sixty-two letters were sent in January

1982. Thirty-one responded, out of whom ten are still active in the textile field; six were active at one time, but present activity is unknown; eight are no longer active; four individuals are no longer alive; three letters were returned and marked addressee unknown; thirty-one did not respond. This information was given to the Cranbrook Academy of Art, July 1982.

117. Cranbrook Archives, Cranbrook Academy of Art Papers, Letter of recommendation to the Trustees by Marianne Strengell, June 18, 1943.

118. Cranbrook Archives, Cranbrook Academy of Art Papers, Cranbrook Academy of Art Trustees Record 1, p. 31, Mar. 30, 1944; also Cranbrook Academy of Art Papers, Cranbrook Foundation Minutes, vol. 2, p. 134, Oct. 26, 1944. In October 1944 further discussion about the purchase of a powerloom is recorded: "Appearing that the ownership of a powerloom would place the Academy in a very advanced position and constitute a desirable addition to its teaching facilities, it was moved, supported, and carried unanimously that the sum of $1,200.00 be set aside."

119. Cranbrook Academy of Art, Registrar's Office, Robert D. Sailors to Palmer Black, Aug. 11, 1944.

120. Christa Thurman interview with R. D. Sailors, Feb. 24, 1982.

121. Cranbrook Archives, Cranbrook Academy of Art Papers, Course Announcements, 1942–1943.

122. Cranbrook Academy of Art, Registrar's Office, Carolyn S. Howlett, Head of Art Education at The School of the Art Institute, to R. D. Sailors, Apr. 1945: ". . . eager to learn more about his adventures into powerloom weaving."

123. Cranbrook Academy of Art, Registrar's Office, Anni Albers to R. D. Sailors, Apr. 23, 1946. She asked him for a report as ". . . we have been thinking about a powerloom for sometime, but have not yet been able to set one up, nor do I myself feel able to handle it."

124. Christa Thurman interview with Mary Walker Phillips, Dec. 14, 1981; Thurman interview with Ed Rossbach, Mar. 11, 1982. As Phillips put it, Sailors was someone who "taught a lot of people a lot about weaving."

125. Private papers of R. D. Sailors, Norma Lee Browning, "Weaving His Way to Wealth," Chicago Tribune, Feb. 13, 1949.

126. Thurman interview with Sailors, op. cit.

127. Private papers of R. D. Sailors, check receipt no. 34277 from George G. Booth for $102.00, Sept. 18, 1946.

128. Thurman interview with Sailors, op. cit. The sample still exists, property of R. D. Sailors. The house is described and illustrated in Architectural Forum, The Magazine of Building 94/1 (Jan. 1951), p. 86. I am grateful to Donald Kalec for identifying the house.

129. Cranbrook Archives, Cranbrook Academy of Art Papers, Cranbrook Academy of Art Trustees Record, p. 174, Jan. 7, 1947.

130. R. D. Sailors to Christa Thurman, May 14, 1982.

131. Cranbrook Academy of Art, Registrar's Office, R. D. Sailors to Noma Hardin, Jan. 5, 1947; Private papers of R. D. Sailors, information folder distributed by Weatherspoon Art Gallery, 1944. The annual international exhibitions at the University of North Carolina continued for ten years. They were juried by Anni Albers, Alexander Girard, Noma Hardin, Dorothy W. Liebes, George E. Linton, Meyric Rogers, Robert Sailors, Marianne Strengell, Leslie Tillett, etc. Faculty, students, and alumni would submit and compete with other institutions teaching weaving or individuals adept in it. Cranbrook faculty, alumni, and students were always well represented, usually winning the top prizes. Among the names which appeared repeatedly were Ruth Adler (Schnee), Majel Chance (Obata), Georgia B. Chingren, Yvonne Delattre, Mildred Fischer, Noma Hardin, Estelle Heller, Gale Kidd, Jack Lenor Larsen, Floyd B. LaVigne, Sonya J. Leach, Joy Lind, Dorothy Meredith, Signe Midelfart (Ortiz), Yvonne Palmer (Bobrowicz), Kenneth Peabody, Mary Pendleton, Mary Walker Phillips, Antoinette Lackner Prestini (Webster), Ed Rossbach, Robert D. Sailors, Ellen Siegel, Marianne Strengell, Azalea Thorpe, etc.

132. Antoinette Lackner Prestini (Webster) had been a weaving student from 1945 to 1947 and taught the 1947 summer session in weaving.

133. Ed Rossbach to Christa Thurman, July 7, 1981, and interview, Mar. 11, 1982.

134. Cranbrook Archives, Papers of George G. Booth, G. G. Booth to Loja Saarinen, July 30, 1942.

135. The New Basketry, New York, 1976, 1980; Baskets as Textile Art, New York, 1973; Making Marionettes, New York, 1938; and The Art of Paisley, New York, 1980.

136. Cranbrook Academy of Art, Registrar's Office, Jack Lenor Larsen, "A Brief Personal History," 1950.

137. Cranbrook Academy of Art, Registrar's Office, Jack Lenor Larsen, Academic Record.

138. Christa Thurman interviews with Jack Lenor Larsen, July 14, 1981; with M. W. Phillips, Dec. 14, 1981; and with Sailors, op. cit.

139. Thurman interview with Larsen, op. cit.

140. Jack Lenor Larsen: 30 ans de création textile, Paris: Musée du Louvre, Musée des Arts Décoratifs, Pavilion de Marsan, 1981.

141. His publications include: with Azalea Thorpe, Elements of Weaving, New York, 1967; with Mildred Constantine, Beyond Craft: The Art Fabric, New York, 1972; with Jeanne Weeks, Fabrics for Interiors, New York, 1975; with Dr. Alfred Buehler and Garrett and Bronwen Solyom, The Dyer's Art-Ikat, Batik, Plangi, New York, 1977; and with Mildred Constantine, The Art Fabric: Mainstream, New York, 1981.

142. Jack Lenor Larsen . . . , op. cit., and publicity information in connection with that exhibition. Also, "An interview with Jack Lenor Lar-

sen on the Occasion of his Firm's Silver Jubilee," *Interior Design* 49 (Apr. 1978), pp. 252–65, and Thurman interview with Larsen, *op. cit.*

143. Cranbrook Academy of Art, Registrar's Office, Jack Lenor Larsen, "Why I select Cranbrook for Graduate Work in Weaving," 1950.

144. *Arts and Architecture* 66 (Mar. 1949), pp. 32–38.

8. CERAMICS
Martin Eidelberg

1. In regard to Booth's extensive patronage of Mrs. Robineau see Peg Weiss, ed., *Adelaide Alsop Robineau, Glory in Porcelain,* Syracuse, 1981, pp. 161–70. Some idea of his purchases from Volkmar can be gathered from the Cranbrook Archives, Papers of George G. Booth, Invoices from the Detroit Society of Arts and Crafts, Feb. 1, 1917; Mar. 1, 1917; Apr. 2, 1917; c. Oct. 1931; also *Arts and Crafts in Detroit 1906–1976, The Movement, The Society, The School,* Detroit: The Detroit Institute of Arts, 1976, nos. 19–21. In regard to the Pewabic Pottery, see the invoices from July 1, 1916, and c. Oct. 1931. Booth also purchased some examples of the work of Charles F. Binns of Alfred University; see the invoice of c. Oct. 1931; also Sotheby, Parke-Bernet, New York, May 2, 1972 (auction cat.), no. 64, and *Arts and Crafts, op. cit.,* nos. 11–12, 14.

2. There is a "Bible fireplace" in the living room of Cranbrook House that was ordered in early 1920; see Cranbrook Archives, Papers of George G. Booth, F. K. Swain to George Booth, Apr. 15, 1920. There is also a large panel of tiles set in an exterior wall of the building. In 1918 Booth asked Mrs. Stratton to fabricate a bathroom with Pewabic tiles, a ceramic stove, and a series of tiled floors (Cranbrook Archives, Papers of George G. Booth, Mary Chase Stratton to George Booth, Oct. 16, 1918; Booth to Stratton, Oct. 12, 1918; Stratton to Booth, Oct. 28, 1918). The cost made him abandon part of the project and Mrs. Stratton was so angered by the idea of combining Pewabic and commercial tile that she refused the commission. Amicable relationships were later restored. Booth was instrumental in having the Pewabic Pottery execute the mosaics in Christ Church Cranbrook (although Mrs. Stratton had worked with Cram and Goodhue on a previous occasion); see Cranbrook Archives, Papers of George G. Booth, George Booth to B. G. Goodhue Associates, June 4, 1926. The tiles on the stairwell floor of the present Academy Administration Offices building appear to be from the Pewabic Pottery and, as discussed below, the Saarinens utilized the Pewabic facilities several times. Mrs. Stratton even served once as a hostess on a tour of Cranbrook ("600 Attend Art Parley," *Detroit News,* May 14, 1937) but, interestingly, she apparently had no hand in the creation of the ce-

ramics program at Cranbrook.

3. Cranbrook Archives, Papers of George G. Booth, Helen Plumb to Mr. Jucker (Director of J. Seligman & Co.), June 30, 1926. There also are extensive invoices.

4. Cranbrook Archives, Papers of George G. Booth, extensive invoices from the Detroit Society of Arts and Crafts, and from the American Federation of the Arts; also Sotheby, Parke-Bernet, New York, May 2, 1972 (auction cat.), nos. 49–51, 55, 57, 60–61, 66, 69, 80, 83, 91, 94, 96, 100–1, 111, 129; also *Arts and Crafts, op. cit.,* nos. 149, 150, 158–59, 163, 183.

5. Cranbrook Archives, Papers of George G. Booth, especially invoices from the Detroit Society of Arts and Crafts, c. May 1930, c. Aug. 1931, c. Oct. 1931; also Sotheby, Parke-Bernet, New York, May 2, 1972 (auction cat.), nos. 74, 104; *Arts and Crafts, op. cit.,* nos. 3–10.

6. Ceramic vases by Willy Finch and Louis Sparre survive at Hvitträsk but their date of acquisition is unknown and they do not appear in early photographs of the interior of the house. Several glass vases by the Orrefors factory have been identified as coming from Saarinen House at Cranbrook but these are unornamented and were probably used only as containers for flowers, unlike the engraved vases which Booth bought as museum pieces.

7. E.g., Eero modeled a series of clay plaques depicting various sports for the entrance hall of the Cranbrook School for boys.

8. Lenox model nos. 2092–94. Apparently only this one exemplar was ordered and the service was not put into commercial production. I am grateful to Elaine Batti of Lenox for her help. Ironically, this company had itself issued Viennese-inspired black and white porcelains a decade earlier; see "The Potters of America: Examples of the Best Craftsmen's Work for Interior Decoration," *Craftsman* 28 (1914–15), p. 298.

9. Executed by Wiener Porzellan-Manufaktur Jos. Böck; illustrated in *Deutsche Kunst and Dekoration* 31 (Nov. 1912), p. 101. See Waltraud Neuwirth, *Österreichische Keramik des Jugendstils,* Vienna, 1974, pp. 276–77, nos. 171–73.

10. Even at the Bauhaus the ceramics department was not as thoroughly integrated with the school as were the other programs. It existed only during the Weimar period and was located outside the school, in a pre-existing workshop at Dornburg; the department was abolished when the school moved to Dessau.

11. Cranbrook Archives, Papers of George G. Booth, Helen Plumb to Henry Macomber, July 29, 1929. Apparently Plumb had been nominating potential ceramic instructors already a year earlier. On Oct. 29, 1928, she proposed the Austrian ceramist Annie Eisenmenger (Cranbrook Archives, Papers of George G. Booth, Helen Fitz Simons to George Booth, Aug. 6, 1929).

12. Mrs. Allen's intention of starting a class in pottery is noted in the *Minutes* of the Cranbrook Foundation, Meeting of May 18, 1931, p. 105. A small brochure announcing the start of the pottery class was printed by the Cranbrook Press (Cranbrook Archives, Cranbrook Academy of Art, Announcements, Cranbrook Press Publications). The brochure is undated but is probably from the late summer or early fall, 1931, since the verso announces the start on October 10 and 13 of her husband's classes. The only other record of this pottery class is a short article, "Class in Pottery Attracts Matrons of Hills Society," *Birmingham Eccentric,* Dec. 15, 1931. No official records concerning Mrs. Allen seem to be in the Cranbrook Archives.

13. "Class in Pottery Attracts Matrons of Hills Society," *op. cit.*

14. There are many extant documents which shed light on how Gregory got his position (Cranbrook Archives, Cranbrook Foundation, Trustees Records). According to Gregory's letter of Nov. 20, 1930, to Cyrus W. Knouff, Manager, Educational Department, American Crayon Company, Sandusky, Ohio, the artist took the initiative and wrote even earlier that autumn, hoping to benefit from Knouff's friendship with Frank Allen. Knouff wrote Allen on Dec. 4, 1930. Allen replied on Dec. 9, 1930, and then Knouff must have sent a copy on to Gregory. The latter sent photographs of his work to Allen, who in turn replied on March 23, 1931, that there was "no active program" and "no opening at the present time." Not easily rebuffed, Gregory and his wife visited Cranbrook in the summer of 1931 and met with Eliel Saarinen (Statement of Eliel Saarinen, Mar. 10, 1933). Saarinen put the artist off, saying that Booth was too occupied with the completion of Kingswood School, but in the fall of 1931 Saarinen and his wife visited the Gregorys in Cleveland and discussed the matter further. Finally, after an exchange of letters and telegrams, Booth gave Gregory an interview at Cranbrook on December 30, 1931, and early the next month the artist was offered a position. Gregory's statement that this occurred "with no warning that he was even being considered" (Robert Bordner, "Waylande Gregory Wins Cranbrook Fellowship," *Cleveland Press,* Jan. 23, 1932) typifies the way the artist rearranged history in his favor.

15. Cranbrook Archives, Cranbrook Foundation, Trustees Records, Cyrus Knouff to Frank Allen, Dec. 4, 1930: "Miss Welling [Jane Betsey Welling, an art educator at Teachers College, Detroit] told me about Mr. Booth's showing her two or three pieces of sculpture which was [sic] done by Waylande Gregory that she said he admired above all others." The only Gregory/Cowan ceramic that the author can find documented at this period is a *Diana and Actaeon* (Cranbrook Archives, Papers of George G. Booth, Invoice from the Detroit Society of Arts and Crafts, c. late Apr. 1930).

16. Cranbrook Archives, Cranbrook Foundation, Trustees Records, Statement of Eliel Saarinen, Mar. 10, 1933.

17. Many of Gregory's early commissions were for architectural sculpture: the Memorial Hall, Salina, Kansas; Roosevelt High School, Wichita, Kansas; the Aztec Room in the Hotel President, Kansas City, Missouri; the Adminstration Building of Kansas University, Lawrence, Kansas; the Cloister of the Theological Seminary of The University of Chicago. While these were not executed in ceramic, there are several indications that Gregory hoped to work on a monumental scale in this medium. For example, he complained that he was not introduced to the architect Raymond Hood when the latter visited the Saarinens (Cranbrook Archives, Cranbrook Foundation, Trustees Records, Statement of Richard Raseman, Jan. 18, 1933). After the artist left Cranbrook he chose Metuchen, New Jersey, for his residence so as to be near the Atlantic Terra Cotta Company's plant, and he maintained a studio in Perth Amboy where he worked in conjunction with that firm (The Detroit Institute of Arts, Museum Archives *BUR/EX 16/8, Waylande Gregory to Clyde Burroughs, c. 1933).

18. Cranbrook Archives, Cranbrook Foundation, Trustees Records, Waylande Gregory to James L. Oliver, Jan. 11, 1932.

19. The kiln was built by the Bellevue Industrial Furnace Company of Detroit. A photograph of it after the first firing with a notation "kiln completed spring 1932" is in the artist's estate. Many of the materials, including glazes, were bought from an auction of assets of the Cowan Pottery in Cleveland. Additional supplies, including clay, were bought from the Pewabic Pottery. These details show how old ties were frequently continued.

20. Cranbrook Archives, Cranbrook Foundation, Trustees Records, George Booth to Waylande Gregory, Jan. 7, 1932. Gregory claimed to have completed "more than 120 pieces" while at Cranbrook; see "Akron Exhibit," *Cleveland Press,* Mar. 25, 1933.

21. The completed work is illustrated in "A New Course," *Detroit News,* Aug. 14, 1932. A photograph of the sculpture is in the Cranbrook Archives (neg. 2164).

22. A photograph of the *Girl with Braids* is in the Cranbrook Archives (neg. 2171). The sculpture should be compared with Milles' *Siren with Fishes,* the fountain behind the Academy's Administrative Offices which Gregory could have known while he was still in Cleveland; see *Bulletin of The Cleveland Museum of Art* 18 (Dec. 1931), p. 1.

23. Although these works have often been thought to date later, primarily because they were exhibited later, their Cranbrook origins can be demonstrated. *Ichabod Crane* was in the Gregory exhibition circulated by The Detroit Institute of Arts; there was no public checklist but there is an itemized listing which was sent to participating museums whereon *Ichabod Crane* appears as no. 52 (The Detroit Institute of Arts, Museum Archives, *BUR/EX 16/7–8). *Kansas Madonna* was exhibited at the Detroit museum in the "Joint Annual Exhibition for Michigan Artists and Society of Independent Artists," Jan. 3–31, 1933, no. 781. *Horse and Dragon* appears as no. 45 on the list for the circulating Gregory exhibition, and several photographs of it are in the Cranbrook Archives (negs. 2168–70).

24. A photograph of one of the reliefs is in the artist's estate; the pair are included on the list for the circulating Gregory exhibition already cited (The Detroit Institute of Arts, Museum Archives, *BUR/EX 16/7–8) as nos. 25–26.

25. A photograph in the artist's estate showing ruined ceramics in the Cranbrook kiln includes a view of the *Europa* seen from behind. This first version differed from the one now in the Everson Museum of Art (pl. 53) in relatively minor features: the support under the bull was a large fish, Europa's right leg was held more parallel to the bull's body, and her right arm rested on her upraised knee. "The large Europa and Bull figure" is mentioned by Raseman (Cranbrook Archives, Cranbrook Foundation, Trustees Records, Statement of Richard Raseman, Mar. 11, 1933). Also, in Gregory's lawsuit against Booth, the artist listed among the works allegedly damaged a "Europa and Jupiter" and another called "Europa and Bull" (District Court, Eastern Division of Michigan, Southern Division, Nov. 19, 1934, Complaint no. 13,612). It seems unlikely that there were two such statues but whether this was an honest error or a way of raising Gregory's claim remains moot. His *Europa* naturally invites comparisons with Milles' different but not unrelated treatment of the same theme (fig. 189 and pl. 57). But there were other precedents, especially in European ceramic sculpture, the most apropos being the group created in 1927 by Jean Gauguin (Erik Lassen, *En københavnsk porcelaensfabriks historie,* Copenhagen, 1978, fig. 84). Even closer at hand geographically, though very different in its romantic presentation, was the bronze by Cleveland sculptor Alexander Blazys (*Arts* 16 [1929–30], p. 568).

26. "Cranbrook Art at Kingswood," *Detroit News,* May 22, 1932; "Cranbrook Artisans, Artists Show Work," *Birmingham Eccentric,* July 2, 1932.

27. A copy of the brochure advertising his sculpture is in the artist's estate; copies of the brochure advertising his class are in the artist's estate and in the Cranbrook Archives, Cranbrook Academy of Art, Announcements, Cranbrook Press Publications. Notices about his class also appeared in local newspapers: "A New Course," *Detroit News,* Aug. 14, 1932; also "Gregory To Offer Ceramics Classes," *Birmingham Eccentric,* Aug. 13, 1932.

28. In January 1933 Gregory calculated that he then had five students taking group lessons and three students taking individual instruction. From these eight students, six of whom were women, he received only $181.50 for a half year's instruction. See Cranbrook Archives, Cranbrook Foun-

dation, Trustees Records, memorandum by Waylande Gregory, Jan. 1933.

29. Cranbrook Archives, Cranbrook Foundation, Trustees Records, George Booth to Dr. Katherine Rogers Adams, Sept. 12, 1932; George Booth to Eliel Saarinen, Sept. 12, 1932; Agreement between Dr. Katherine Adams and Waylande Gregory, Sept. 23, 1932. The artist was obliged to teach a class of not more than twelve girls two mornings a week. His salary of $1,000 was handsome when compared with his earnings from his adult students.

30. The voluminous correspondence detailing some of the complaints and a great deal of the ensuing litigation can be found in the Cranbrook Archives, Cranbrook Foundation, Trustees Records.

31. Cranbrook Archives, Cranbrook Foundation, Trustees Records, Statement by George G. Booth, c. Feb. 16, 1933; Statement by Richard Raseman, Mar. 10, 1933; Statement by James L. Oliver, July 5, 1933.

32. Cranbrook Archives, Cranbrook Foundation, Trustees Records, Statement of Richard Raseman, Mar. 11, 1933.

33. Cranbrook Archives, Cranbrook Foundation, Trustees Records, Austin Purves, Jr., to George Booth, Apr. 6, 1933.

34. The Detroit Institute of Arts, Museum Archives, *BUR/EX 16/7–8. The exhibition was shown at the John Herron Art Institute, Indianapolis; DePauw University, Greencastle; The Art Association of Richmond, Indiana; The Grand Rapids Art Gallery; The Syracuse Museum of Fine Arts; The Rochester Memorial Art Gallery.

35. *Montclair Art Museum Bulletin* (Mar. 1934), p. 1. See also The Detroit Institute of Arts, Museum Archives, *BUR/EX 16/7–8, Waylande Gregory to Clyde Burroughs, Nov. 25, 1933.

36. "Cranbrook Sculptor Wins Memorial Prize," *Detroit Free Press,* May 5, 1933; a clipping is on file in the Cranbrook Archives, Cranbrook Foundation, Trustees Records.

37. "Novel Sculpture Placed on View," *Art News* 32 (Mar. 17, 1934), p. 6.

38. "100 Artists Represented in Ceramic Annual," *Art Digest* 8 (May 15, 1934), p. 16. This work was alternately titled *Head of Girl* and *Head of Child* as indicated by photos in the artist's estate.

39. *Design* 37 (Nov. 1935), p. 34.

40. "Contemporary American Ceramics Assembled by Syracuse Museum for Exhibition in Denmark, Sweden, and Finland," *Design* 38 (Nov. 1936), p. 29. Interestingly, Grotell helped arrange for the exhibition to travel to Finland.

41. "Two New Masters Added to Faculty," *Crane,* Oct. 12, 1933, n.p.: "Mr. Fredericks is carrying on the work in drawing, painting, and sculpture. . . . Work in all media, especially clay, is to be done"; Kingswood School Cranbrook, *Catalogue,* Feb. 1934, p. 7.

42. Cranbrook Academy Administrative Offices, Faculty File, Richard Raseman to Marshall

Fredericks, June 21, 1934: "You are to have the use of the Ceramic Studio and its equipment . . ."

43. Cranbrook Academy Administrative Offices, Faculty File, Richard Raseman to Maija Grotell, Feb. 11, 1938.

44. Cranbrook Academy Administrative Offices, Faculty File, Richard Raseman to Maija Grotell, Oct. 24, 1935. Syracuse University, George Arents Research Library, Papers of Maija Grotell, Richard Raseman to Maija Grotell, Feb. 11, 1935.

45. Copies of the undated invitation are in the Cranbrook Academy Administrative Offices, Faculty File, and in Syracuse University, George Arents Research Library, Papers of Maija Grotell. The exhibition must have opened around December 20. See Cranbrook Academy Administrative Offices, Faculty File, Richard Raseman to Maija Grotell, Dec. 20, 1934. An illustrated notice appeared in *Detroit News,* Dec. 23, 1934, and a smaller notice appeared in *Pontiac Daily Press,* Dec. 31, 1934.

46. Syracuse University, George Arents Research Library, Papers of Maija Grotell, Richard Raseman to Maija Grotell, Feb. 11, 1935. In this letter Raseman lists the nine pieces which were sold, including three to Eliel Saarinen, two to the Cranbrook Museum, and one each to Sepeshy and Raseman.

47. See "Modernism in Art Defended by Editor," *Detroit News,* Nov. 8, 1935; The Detroit Institute of Arts, Museum Archives, BUR 5/21, Robert T. Hatt to E. P. Richardson, Oct. 5, 1935. Also that year the Cranbrook Foundation gave throwing wheels to the Academy and the other schools. An interesting note appeared the following year in the *Cranbrook News Bulletin* 1 (Dec. 1936), p. 6: "As far as the Academy was concerned, no one used them at all until this year."

48. Cranbrook Academy Administrative Offices, Faculty File, Richard Raseman to Maija Grotell, May 18, 1937.

49. Cranbrook Academy Administrative Offices, Faculty File, Maija Grotell to Richard Raseman, May 20, 1937; Raseman to Grotell, May 21, 1937.

50. Cranbrook Academy Administrative Offices, Faculty File, Maija Grotell to Richard Raseman, May 29, 1937.

51. Cranbrook Academy Administrative Offices, Faculty File, Richard Raseman to Maija Grotell, Jan. 28, 1938.

52. Cranbrook Academy Administrative Offices, Faculty File, Maija Grotell to Richard Raseman, Feb. 4, 1938; Raseman to Grotell, Feb. 11, 1938; Grotell to Raseman, Feb. 25, 1938; Raseman to Grotell, Mar. 1, 1938; Raseman to Grotell, Mar. 9, 1938. This year-long exchange refutes Grotell's frequently recounted version of how she was repeatedly offered the position but refused it (e.g., her interview with Jeff Schlanger and Toshiko Takaezu, May 24, 1968).

53. Cranbrook Academy Administrative Offices, Faculty File, Richard Raseman to Maija Grotell, May 25, 1938; also "Brings Her Fine Craftsmanship to Cranbrook," *Detroit News,* Sept. 25, 1938.

54. American Craft Museum, New York, inv. no. 67.26. Another good example is the cylindrical vase in the Cranbrook Academy/Museum, inv. no. 1970.2, which is a taller edition of a design made several years earlier (illustrated in *Design* 38 [Nov. 1936], p. 5).

55. A photograph of this vase (apropos of the faculty exhibition held in December 1939) appeared in *Academy News* 2 (1940), n.p.

56. Other Grotell vases come close to Saarinen's designs: a floor vase with the decoration built in high relief now in the Cranbrook Academy/Museum, inv. no. 1978.16; others with painted decoration can be seen in photographs in the Grotell Papers at Syracuse University, *op. cit.*

57. During her first summer in this country she attended Charles F. Binns' course at Alfred University to see how ceramics were taught here in preparation for her own intended career. Although she depended upon the sale of her pottery while she worked at the Henry Street Settlement House, she valued the certitude of a guaranteed salary.

58. For her various teaching posts see her Biography. Even her position at Rutgers University was a relatively menial one, for although her official title was "Instructor and Research Assistant," her job was to teach ceramic engineering students how to throw and glaze; she was obliged to use glazes prepared by the department—something which chafed her greatly (interview with Schlanger and Takaezu, *op. cit.*).

59. A photograph of Grotell helping youngsters model clay animals at the Henry Street Settlement appeared in the *New York Sun,* Dec. 12, 1935. Grotell herself modeled ceramic figurines in her early career. "Bowls, vases and small figures" are listed on the invitation to her December 1934 exhibition at Cranbrook. Such figures are visible in her portion of the December 1939 faculty exhibition; see *Academy News* 2 (1940), n.p., and Cranbrook Academy Archives, neg. 5447–2. Late in her life she said candidly, "At that time it was terrible ceramic sculpture, really. These figurines with brilliant glazes, . . . more humorous than anything else" (interview with Schlanger and Takaezu, *op. cit.*). However, this should not be taken to mean that she disapproved of ceramic sculpture as a whole. She certainly admired major artists like Carl Walters. What she disliked were the trivial aspects of ceramic sculpture and these would be especially evident in student work. She always encouraged and supported serious students like Nancy Leitch, a ceramic animalier who was her assistant for several years. Moreover, the problem gradually abated after William McVey installed a separate kiln for the Sculpture department.

60. Her prior work as a sculptor in bronze partially prepared her for this work in glazed ceramic. Her relief sculpture for the Rome Collaborative Program was ceramic; see *Academy News* 1 (1939), n.p. Photographs of the *Anteater* and of the artist looking at other Crow Island School reliefs on display at the student exhibition appeared in *Academy News* 2 (1940), n.p. For the artist's views see Lilian Saarinen, "Clay Has Flight," *Interiors* 104 (Oct. 1944), pp. 48–49, 98, 100.

61. Recent discussions have tended to over-emphasize the unstructured nature of Grotell's instruction as though it were a truism throughout her career. This is due in part to the fact that information was gathered from interviews with her later students. The many photographs of classes from her first years at Cranbrook suggest a more orthodox approach; this has been affirmed by early students and by Grotell's interview with Schlanger and Takaezu, *op. cit.*

62. Charles F. Binns, *The Potter's Craft,* New York, 1922; *idem, Lectures on Ceramics,* Alfred, 1937; Cullen W. Parmelee, *Clays and Some Other Ceramic Materials,* Ann Arbor, 1937; Bernard Leach, *A Potter's Book,* London, 1940; Alfred B. Searle, *An Encyclopedia of the Ceramic Industries,* London, 1922.

63. A good index is suggested by some of the bachelor's and Master's theses done under her supervision and inspiration: Florence Chang, "Experiments with Michigan Clay as a Slip Glaze" (1943); Edna Vogel, "Glazing in a Reducing Atmosphere" (1943); Halden Thurn, "The Use of Wood Ashes in a Low-Fire Matt Glaze" (1944); Emma Langseth, "Clays and Slips with Emphasis on Minnesota Clay" (1944); Mildred Glaubis, "A Simple Method for Producing Copper Reds" (1944); Lydia Winston, "A Study of Vermont Kaolin" (1944); Carmen Brooks, "Glazing Stone" (1946); Martha Middleton, "An Experiment in the Local Reduction of Copper and Iron Oxides in Ceramic Glazes" (1947).

64. E.g., she was amused by the way Mrs. Stratton of the Pewabic Pottery carefully guarded her secret formulae for iridescent glazes. For Grotell the important issue was not the formula (she believed that any effect could ultimately be obtained with experimentation) but the way one used it.

65. Cranbrook Academy Administrative Offices, Alumni Records, Statement of c. May 13, 1941.

66. The vase must date to late 1939 or early 1940; it was photographed in a completed state about April 2, 1940 (Cranbrook Archives [neg. 5495-1]). Also in Cranbrook Archives are many photographs of Watson's early vases, almost all imitating Grotell's style, and one example of his sculpture.

67. Grotell had to take over Marshall Fredericks' modeling and ceramics classes at Kingswood when he left for the War. Here too she changed the curriculum. Whereas the school's catalogues through the 1942–43 edition (pp. 30–32) emphasized a sculpture curriculum and carried a photograph of young girls executing small sculptural projects, the subsequent edition (1943–44, p. 30)

introduced as the third course in the normal sequence one wholly devoted to ceramic form with "throwing on the wheel, slab and coil building . . . " And starting in the next year's catalogue (1944–45, p. 32) there were new illustrations, one of girls modeling small figures and the other of girls throwing on potter's wheels. In short, this is a microcosmic repetition of the way Grotell transformed the Academy ceramic program.

68. Feb. 7-Mar. 2, 1952; a twelve-page catalogue was published. The ceramist had had another exhibition in the Cranbrook Museum in February 1947 but nothing is known about it save for a listing in a 1946–47 "program."

69. See Marion H. Bemis, "Maija Grotell Decorates A Pot," *Ceramics Monthly* 5 (May 1957), pp. 18–19, 32.

70. According to Grotell (interview with Schlanger and Takaezu, *op. cit.*), Eliel Saarinen approached her one Sunday morning, asking whether she could produce a glaze for bricks like the copper red glaze inside a bowl of hers which he owned. She refused at first, but her reverence of Saarinen caused her to reconsider and accept the project. She received a mere $50 to cover the cost of materials necessary for the experiments to obtain the red and other colors. Grotell was given an additional commission to make four large cachepots for indoor shrubbery. A General Motors advertisement placing a new-model Pontiac alongside her vases because they both won "styling honors" (*Life* 42 [Feb. 28, 1957], p. 128) is, at best, an unfortunate merger of art and industry.

71. Lydia Winston Malbin, daughter of architect Albert Kahn, a pupil of Grotell's from 1941 to 1950, and an integral member of the Cranbrook community, joined forces with the Saarinen-Swanson design group; see "Art, Architecture and Decoration merge ideally in Saarinen-Swanson modern," *House and Garden* 92 (Oct. 1947), pp. 152–57, *passim* incl. p. 15. According to the artist (interview, June 15, 1982), Grotell heartily approved and encouraged her in this venture. Likewise, John Glick (interview, Aug. 26, 1981) tells that Grotell approved of his interest in functional tableware and a pottery shop geared to production. What Grotell disapproved of was facile commercialism. For example, if she saw students making small, easy-to-sell objects just before the Ceramic department's annual Christmas sale, she strongly remonstrated, threatening them with expulsion. Perhaps most insightful is a tale which Grotell herself told (interview with Schlanger and Takaezu, *op. cit.*) of how a potential client asked her to produce a dozen bowls, with the promise of future commissions once the first dozen sold. She refused the offer, and the angered man asked Saarinen to fire her. When she explained that she did not have the time for "mass production," Saarinen supported her stance.

72. Interview with Schlanger and Takaezu, *op. cit.* The anecdote is also told by Rhoda Lopez,

who says that she was the student in question (Elaine Levin, "Maija Grotell," *American Ceramics* 1 [Winter 1982], p. 44) but since Grotell was prone to repeat parables it may have been used apropos of other students as well.

73. A color photograph of the ceramic students at work in the ceramic studio, including Littleton decorating what may be this very vase, appeared in an advertisement for Dow Chemical in *Saturday Evening Post* 223 (Sept. 9, 1950), p. 89. A photograph of the vase appears in the artist's 1951 Master's thesis and also in "Michigan-Craftsmen," *Art Digest* 25 (Apr. 15, 1951), p. 13.

74. Littleton developed a technique of compressing the clay as he threw to align the kaolinite particles in accord with their flatness as revealed by electronic microscope analysis; see Warrington W. Colescott, "Harvey Littleton," *Craft Horizons* 19 (Nov.-Dec. 1959), p. 20.

75. See Harvey K. Littleton, *Glassblowing: A Search for Form,* New York, 1971, pp. 8–12. Littleton's discovery of glass was more of a rediscovery, for his father had been Director of Research at the Corning Glass Works, and Littleton had tried his hand at making cast glass sculpture in 1942 and 1945.

76. Earlier in her career McVey had made humorous, bird-shaped ashtrays and it is easy to imagine the relationship between such forms and her later work.

77. "Most pots have been designed as 'containers' for flower arrangements, a prescribed number of red apples. . . . These extraneous objects are needed to complete the design. . . . I prefer completing the unit myself. This feeling . . . has led to my incorporating stopper-accents in many of my designs" ("Leza McVey," *Everyday Art Quarterly* 27 [1953], p. 20).

78. Prior to her arrival she had taught for four years at the Honolulu YWCA Adult Education program, and had worked commercially for three years each at the Hawaiian Potters' Guild and the Honolulu Planning Mill. She had exhibited once at the Syracuse Ceramic National, twice at Wichita, and had had a one-person exhibition at the Library of Hawaii.

79. Conrad Brown, "Toshiko Takaezu," *Craft Horizons* 19 (Mar.-Apr. 1959) p. 23. A similar statement is quoted by Joseph Hurley, in "Toshiko Takaezu, Ceramics of Serenity," *American Craft* 39 (Oct.-Nov. 1979), p. 3.

80. Described by Takaezu in Hurley, *op. cit.,* pp. 4–5. The close relationship between her teapots and spouted vases can be seen in a contemporary photograph in Joy Hakanson, "Another Look at Craft Exhibition," *Detroit News,* Mar. 13, 1955. See also the photographic sequence presented by Brown, *op. cit.,* p. 22. Takaezu also suggested analogies with birds' necks and with pre-Columbian pottery in the Cranbrook Academy/Museum (one of the few occasions when a student acknowledged the possibility of being influenced by the Museum's collection); see Joy Hakanson, "Ceramist Views Nature of Clay," *Detroit News,* July 31, 1955.

81. E.g., Harold Riegger (see *Ceramics Monthly* 1 [Sept. 1953], pp. 13–15); Louis Gonet (working at Cranbrook!) (see *Ceramics Monthly* 2 [Oct. 1954], p. 23); Aaron Bohrod and F. Carlton Ball, (see *Ceramics Monthly* 3 [June 1955], pp. 16–17); Konrad Sadowski (see *Craft Horizons* 14 [Nov.-Dec. 1954], p. 14); David Weinrib (see *Craft Horizons* 16 [Jan.-Feb. 1956], p. 16.

82. Although initially she formed these on the wheel, she then paddled and even deflated and reinflated the still wet clay until satisfied. Photographs showing the artist at work appear in Brown, *op. cit.,* pp. 24–25. According to Susan E. Meyers, "The Pottery of Toshiko Takaezu," *American Artist* 33 (Feb. 1969), p. 42, "To Toshiko, symmetry is cold and mechanical, and she will deliberately *distort* a perfect form. She prefers to capture the *essence* of roundness; the *idea* of roundness; shapes that will give the illusion of fullness."

83. She was Grotell's assistant during the 1953–54 academic year and taught the 1954, 1955, and 1956 summer sessions.

84. What Grotell wrote in 1941 well summarizes her attitude: ". . . we should recognize the fact that it is not another school of design that is so much needed, as a school where creative expression will have greater freedom based on fundamental knowledge. It was this opportunity that was part of the ideal in the founding of the Academy, as I understand it . . . " (Cranbrook Archives, Cranbrook Foundation, Trustees Records, "File of Letters Regarding Mr. Walter Baermann's Report Dated October 13, 1941," p. 12).

9. SCULPTURE AND PAINTING
Joan Marter

1. In 1930, for example, Stanley Casson wrote: "[Milles] can be considered more than any other as the sculptor *par excellence* of the twentieth century. In the gradual development of his work from mode to style and from the conventions of a period to the personality of an individual, he stands out as the most important figure in modern art." Stanley Casson, *XXth Century Sculptors,* London, 1930, p. 25. Early monographs on Carl Milles include: Conrad Köper, *Carl Milles,* Stockholm, 1913, and M. P. Verneuil, *Carl Milles, Sculpteur Suédois,* 2 vols., Paris and Brussels, 1929.

2. For letters regarding Geza Maroti's employment at Cranbrook see Cranbrook Archives, Cranbrook Academy of Art Correspondence, Box 15, Maroti, George Booth to Geza Maroti, Dec. 3, 1926. Also see Papers of George G. Booth, Society of Arts and Crafts I, Box 14, Correspondence Business, George Booth to Helen Plumb, Feb. 1, 1927.

3. For more information on Geza Maroti's work at Cranbrook see "The Story of the Two Artists Designing Cranbrook School," *Afterglow* (Sept. 1927); "Maroti Exhibit Opens Tuesday," *Detroit News,* June 28, 1931.

4. Templin Licklider and Carleton McLain, "The Gift of Knowledge (to Youth), 1928 by Geza Maroti," Feb. 11, 1961 (unpublished manuscript in Cranbrook Academy of Art/Library, Maroti file).

5. Cranbrook Archives, Cranbrook Academy of Art Correspondence, Box 15, Maroti, George Booth to Hon. Harry Hawley (American Consul), Nov. 9, 1927. Booth requested an extension of Maroti's visa: "Professor Maroti convinced all parties at interest of his personal high qualities and his quite extraordinary artistic abilities, and we deem the possibility of retaining his services as a most valuable contribution to the architectural and art educational work of the United States."

6. See Albert Kahn, "The Fisher Building," *American Architect* 135 (Feb. 20, 1929), pp. 211–219.

7. Cranbrook Archives, Cranbrook Academy of Art Correspondence, Box 15, Maroti, Geza Maroti to George Booth, Jan. 10, 1929.

8. For more information on David Evans at Cranbrook, see "English Sculptor on Cranbrook Staff," *Detroit News,* Nov. 2, 1929; "British Sculptor Exhibits at Cranbrook Academy," *Detroit News,* Jan. 19, 1930. Letters and statements on Evans' employment can be found in the Cranbrook Archives, Cranbrook Academy of Art Correspondence, Box 15.

9. For photos of the relief, see "Sculptor Completes Work on Cranbrook Bronze Relief," *Birmingham Eccentric* (May 15, 1930), and *New York Times,* April 19, 1931. American sculptors such as Paul Manship and Lee Lawrie created similar stylizations for architectural sites (see, for example, *Sculpture: Lee Lawrie,* Cleveland, 1936).

10. Cranbrook Archives, Cranbrook Foundation, Series I, Box 5, Evans, George Booth to David Evans: "On February 4, 1930 an understanding was reached between Mr. Booth and Mr. Evans that Mr. Evans is free to leave Cranbrook at any time on fair notice, and that the Foundation has the same right at any time to terminate Mr. Evans' connection with Cranbrook." The ensuing dispute between Evans and Booth was resolved by Booth paying return passage to England for the sculptor. See the Cranbrook Archives for all relevant letters.

11. Millesgården Archives, George Booth to Carl Milles, May 12, 1930. This letter and correspondence relating to Milles' years at Cranbrook are stored at the artist's home in Lidingö, Sweden.

12. In December 1930 an article on Cranbrook included a photograph of *Orpheus* installed in the court of the workshops. See "Cranbrook Academy of Art," *Architectural Record* 68 (Dec. 1930), p. 448. *Sunglitter* by Carl Milles (wrongly identified as *Triton*) is also illustrated in this article. On August 29, 1930, George Booth wrote to Carl Milles: "In response to a recent letter of mine to Mr. Palm, I received a cable advising me that it was agreeable to you to let us have the bronze "Orpheus" at a price of $4000.00. I am enclosing herewith a draft for that amount payable to your order" (see Millesgården Archives).

13. In 1926 Milles was given a solo exhibition at the Tate Gallery in London, his first exhibition outside Sweden. In the fall of 1929, Milles made his first trip to the United States. A letter from Hakon Ahlberg, Stockholm, to John Holabird, dated March 28, 1929, states: "I wish to tell you that Professor Carl Milles intends to go to America this autumn, probably in September. He is much interested in modern American architecture and hopes to communicate with some of the important architects" (see Millesgården Archives). For additional information on Carl Milles' work during the Cranbrook years, see Meyric R. Rogers, *Carl Milles, an Interpretation of His Work,* New Haven, 1940.

14. Charles Marriott, "The Art of Carl Milles," in Verneuil, *op. cit.,* p. 152: ". . . if we speak of Milles as a Northern Bernini, it is to suggest his power of handling a large and extended composition."

15. Milles' frequent circulation among those working in private studios was noted by his former students (interview with Svea Klein, July 7, 1981). In an interview with Roy Slade on February 24, 1981, Frances Rich recalled: "And Carl would come to see us and he would stop in each little cubicle and of course we were all ears to hear what he had to say from every cubicle to the other. And we all used to laugh because he would come through and they'd all be doing these nude figures."

16. Marshall Fredericks was Instructor in Modeling from 1934 to 1942. Janet de Coux held the position of Instructor in Sculpture from 1943 to 1944; Jon Jonson from 1945 to 1947; and William McVey from 1947 to 1953.

17. See Arvid Andrén, *Greek and Roman Marbles in the Carl Milles Collection,* Rome, 1972: 77: "[Milles] acquired a number of statues and heads which he justly admired as fine specimens of ancient sculpture. . . . But he also bought some pieces which pleased his eye by forms which to the expert are but faint and marred shadows of a great formal tradition better preserved in other works. There are also some items which, on closer examination, must be set down as forgeries or as pieces of doubtful antiquity."

18. "Cranbrook Sculptor's Collection to Go to Museum, Sells Sweden Art Treasures for $165,000," *Detroit News,* Sept. 26, 1948: "Sweden disclosed that all of the 73-year-old sculptor's statues, paintings, ceramics, precious glassware, and priceless assortment of art objects will be transferred to the Milles Museum in Stockholm [sic] there to be kept for the enjoyment of the

Swedish people."

19. Letters in the archives of Millesgården document his whereabouts in these years. In January 1933, Milles dismissed all of his assistants at Cranbrook. Within months, all of the craft workshops had also closed.

20. Millesgården Archives, Carl Milles to George Booth, Apr. 1934. Other correspondence related to this purchase can also be found in these archives.

21. See Millesgården Archives, Agreement between Carl Milles and the Cranbrook Foundation, July 24, 1934. $120,000 was the purchase price for over sixty bronzes included on a list attached to the contract.

22. Other early works at Cranbrook are the *Triton with Shell Fountain* and *Sunglitter,* both installed there by 1931.

23. See Ulf Abel, *Carl Milles-Form, Idé, Medalkonst,* Stockholm, 1980, pp. 132–35. In an English summary, Abel wrote of Milles' "using a naturalistic language of forms . . . to materialize the immaterial, to embody a vision." Milles was influenced by the astronomer and religious philosopher Camille Flammarion whose "belief in the existence of the soul 'as a real being, independent of the body' brought him to spiritism." Milles was sent a copy of the Swedish spiritualist society journal *Spiritualisten* by Rolf Carleson, the editor and a leading figure of this group. In his reply Milles wrote: "I have been interested in spiritual matters ever since I started when young to study astronomy." My thanks to Ulf Abel for a personal discussion of this topic in Stockholm, July 14, 1981.

24. See, for example, a metope from the Parthenon, *Lapith and Centaur Attacking,* in R. Lullies and M. Hirmer, *Greek Sculpture,* New York, 1957: figs. 144–45.

25. Records, related drawings, and photographs of all of Milles' American commissions can be found at Millesgården.

26. For the *Peace Memorial* see Millesgården Archives for a statement prepared by the St. Paul Area Chamber of Commerce: "The figure . . . represents the thought that out of conference and understanding comes the hope of peace."

27. For a review of Milles' exhibition in St. Louis, see *American Magazine of Art,* 23 (Aug. 1931), pp. 163–64. For additional details on this commission see letters from Mrs. Louis P. Aloe to Carl Milles, 1931–39, other related correspondence, and the contract with the city of St. Louis dated April 8, 1936, in the Millesgården Archives. Also see B. Boxerman, "Louis Patrick Aloe," *Bulletin of the Missouri Historical Society,* 31 (Oct. 1974-July, 1975) pp. 41–54. My thanks to Georgia Buckowitz, Acting President, Board of Public Service, who supplied the original blueprints and construction records for this fountain.

28. See minutes of the joint meeting of the Municipal Art Commission and Aloe Plaza Committee, Nov. 25, 1938, in the St. Louis Art Museum

Library: "Mr. Carl Milles . . . sent a scale model of his revised scheme for the inspection of the Committee and had authorized Mr. Charles Eames to act as his representative." Meyric Rogers, then Director of the City Art Museum of St. Louis, advised Milles on the project, made suggestions about the theme for the fountain, and served on the committees overseeing the execution of the design. On November 17, 1938, he wrote to Milles at Cranbrook: "The city is now pressing for the work to go ahead as they say that unless it begins almost immediately they will lose the W. P. A. grant of funds which is necessary to carry on the work, so quick action seems to be necessary. I believe [St. Louis architect] Charles Nagel telephoned Charlie Eames about this yesterday so this gives you a week to talk the matter over with Saarinen and get his advice about this new problem."

29. For critical reaction to the Aloe Plaza Fountain, see vertical files, St. Louis Public Library and Cranbrook Academy of Art/Library. Initially there were problems with jets of water which soaked pedestrians and cars along Chestnut Street.

30. For later examples of sculpture functioning as part of an architectural plan for the revitalization of a city, see Donald Thalacker, *The Place of Art in the World of Architecture,* New York, 1980.

31. For more information on the cemetery, designed by Walter Marlowe, and Milles' *Fountain of Faith,* see "Hovering Sculpture," *Architectural Forum,* 97 (Dec. 1952), pp. 112–13.

32. See, for example, Runge's *Morning,* 1809, and his engraving for *Four Times of Day,* 1803, in *German Masters of the Nineteenth Century,* New York: The Metropolitan Museum of Art, 1981, pp. 191 and 257.

33. For further information on this competition, see "Smithsonian Competition, Winners of First Stage," *Architectural Forum* 70 (June 1939), p. 28. The model with Milles' maquette as a silver casting is illustrated in *Academy News* 2 (1940), n.p.

34. Milles is quoted in "Improbable Horse," *Time* 54 (July 18, 1954), p. 54.

35. I regret that it is not possible to illustrate and discuss works by more of Milles' students. For sculptures produced by Frances Rich and Lilian Swann Saarinen for the 1939 New York World's Fair, see *American Art Today,* New York, 1939, figs. 736, 769. Also see Merle Armitage, *The Sculpture of Frances Rich,* Manzanita, 1974.

36. For additional information on Fredericks, see "Levi Barbour Memorial Fountain, Marshall Fredericks Sculptor," *Pencil Points* (Feb. 18, 1937), pp. 92–95, and Ernest W. Watson, "Marshall Fredericks, Sculptor to the People," *American Artist* 18 (Sept. 1954), pp. 36–41.

37. For correspondence and newspaper clippings related to construction delays, see Fredericks' personal files, Royal Oak, Michigan. My thanks to the artist for supplying this material.

38. See Marshall Fredericks to John Robbins of the *Cleveland Press,* Apr. 16, 1951, in the artist's personal files for a lengthy explanation of this work.

39. Interviews with Tony Rosenthal, June 23, 1981, and Apr. 12, 1982. For additional information on the artist, see Sam Hunter, *Rosenthal: Sculptures,* New York, 1968; and *Tony Rosenthal at Cranbrook,* Bloomfield Hills: Cranbrook Academy of Art/Museum, 1980.

40. From an unpublished statement in the artist's personal files.

41. See Rosenthal's personal files for letters and clippings related to the installation and purchase of this sculpture. My thanks to Tony Rosenthal for supplying me with these materials.

42. Interview with Mrs. Brigitta Bertoia, May 8, 1981.

43. *Ibid.* For additional discussion of Bertoia, see June Kompass Nelson, *Harry Bertoia, Sculptor,* Detroit, 1970; "Harry Bertoia Drawings," *Arts and Architecture* 62 (May 1945), pp. 22–23; and *Harry Bertoia, an Exhibition of His Sculpture and Graphics,* Allentown: Allentown Art Museum, 1976.

44. See Nelson, *Bertoia, op. cit.,* fig. 74.

45. Interview with Paul Cummings for the Archives of American Art, June 20, 1972.

46. For wire sculpture from the late 1940s which is related to Calder's constructions, see Nelson, *Bertoia, op. cit.,* fig. 19.

47. "Sonambient: The Sound Sculpture of Harry Bertoia" (film directed by Jeffery Eger, Kenesaw Films, 1971).

48. Bertoia, "Sonambient" (Recording LPS 10570).

49. Frank L. Allen, who was Director of Art Education at Cranbrook from November, 1930 to June 1932, also taught some painting classes at the Academy. John Cunningham became an instructor in painting and drawing in 1932. He stayed for one year and also directed the summer session. Later he was Visiting Instructor in Industrial Design at Mills College. Sepeshy was appointed in 1931, and continued in the Painting department until his retirement in 1966.

50. Interview with William Woolfenden for the Archives of American Art, Jan. 13, 1963. For additional information on Sepeshy, see L. Schmeckebier, *Zoltan Sepeshy, Forty Years of His Work,* Syracuse, 1966.

51. Interview with Dennis Barrie for the Archives of American Art, Apr. 26, 1973.

52. *Ibid.*

53. These lectures were recalled by Daniel Dickerson, a student of Sepeshy, now on the faculty of the National Academy of Design; interview, Aug. 22, 1981. See Zoltan Sepeshy, *Tempera Painting,* New York, 1946.

54. Sepeshy's former students remember him as being supportive of their personal artistic development (interviews with Robert Beauchamp and Bill White, Jan. 9, 1981).

55. See Dorothy Seckler, "Wallace Mitchell," *Art News,* 48 (Jan. 1950), p. 47. See also *Wallace MacMahon Mitchell, A Memorial Exhibition of Paintings and Painting-Constructions 1936–1976,* Bloomfield Hills: Cranbrook Academy of Art/Museum, 1977.

56. This exhibition for the Salon des Réalités Nouvelles was shown in Paris at the Palais des Beaux-Arts in 1947, and in the following year it was circulated throughout Germany by the Solomon R. Guggenheim Foundation.

57. Eliel Saarinen, "My Point of View of our Contemporary Architecture," in *The Saarinen Door,* Bloomfield Hills, 1963, p. 59.

AFTERWORD
Roy Slade

1. Dennis Barrie, *Cranbrook U.S.A.,* Bloomfield Hills: Cranbrook Academy of Art/Museum, 1982.

2. Charlene Wetzel Kull, "Cranbrook Tales," *Michigan History* 66/2 (Mar.-Apr. 1982), p. 29.

3. Martin Filler, "Where the Teacher is Beauty," *House and Garden* 154/4 (Apr. 1982), p. 116.

4. "Cranbrook," in Eric Larrabee and Massimo Vignelli, *Knoll Design,* New York, 1981, p. 16.

5. Wolf Von Eckardt, "The Cranbrook Academy of Art," *New Republic* (June 24, 1978), p. 29.

6. Daniel Libeskind, Head, Department of Architecture, in conversation with Roy Slade, Summer 1981.

7. Barrie, *op. cit.*

8. Arthur Pound, *The Only Thing Worth Finding* (interview with George G. Booth by Cyril Arthur Player), Detroit, 1964, p. 381.

9. Commencement remarks by Lynn Barnhouse, graduating design student, Cranbrook Academy of Art, 1981.

BIBLIOGRAPHICAL NOTE

For reasons of length, a full bibliography has not been included in this volume. All references—whether to archival sources or to previous publications on the Cranbrook Academy of Art, its faculty and students, and their participation in (and influence on) the development of modern American art, architecture, and design—are contained in the notes which accompany each chapter.

INDEX

A page number in *italic type* refers to an illustration, with colorplate page numbers preceded by an asterisk (*).

F

G

H

Hagen, G. B., 91

hallway carpet, for Kingswood School
    Cranbrook, layout for (Saarinen, Eliel),
    181; *183*

Hammarstrom, Olav, 200

Handarbetets Vänner, Stockholm, Sweden
    (Friends of Handicrafts Association),
    177, 180, 181, 183, 187, 211

hand mirror (Kirk, A. N.), 153; **151*

hanging (Fredenthal and Kellogg), 196;
    195; sketch for (Fredenthal), 196; *193*

hanging lamp, study for (Saarinen, Eliel),
    156; *154*

hanging showing Cranbrook map
    (Saarinen, Eliel and L.), 183, 187;
    *frontispiece

Hans, Norman, 204

Hansen, George W., New York City, 112

Hanson, Duane, 258

Hardin, Noma, 204

Harkness Quadrangle, Yale University,
    New Haven, Connecticut (Rogers), 92

Harrison and Abramovitz, New York City,
    133

Haskelite Manufacturing Corporation,
    Chicago, Illinois, *110*

Hebbeln, Henry, 200

Heinz, H. J., Co., Pittsburgh,
    Pennsylvania, interiors for (Knoll, F.),
    142

Helsinki, Finland, 16, 17

Herter, Albert, 173

Herter Looms, New York City, 173

Heywood-Wakefield Company, Gardner,
    Massachusetts, *110*

Hoffman, Mrs. Max, 163

Hoffmann, Josef, 21, 27, 48, 215; Austrian
    Pavilion, preliminary sketch for, 27, 70;
    26

Hofmann, Hans, 109, 121

Holabird and Root, 246

Holm, Lillian, 180, 187–88, 190, 192;
    193; First Sight of New York, 188, 221;
    *191

Hood, Raymond, 47

Horan, Claude, 234

Horse and Dragon (Gregory), 217

House Beautiful magazine, 16

Howe and Lescaze, Philadelphia, 31

Howells, John Mead, 47

Hudnut, Joseph, 66, 67, 69

Hudnut Building (Richard Hudnut Salon),
    New York City (Saarinen, Eliel, and
    Kahn, E. J.), 61; interiors for, 99,
    101–102, 192

Hulse, Dorthea, 205

Hvitträsk, near Helsinki (Saarinen, Eliel),
    16, 18, 56, 88, 176, 238

H. V. weaving technique, 177

I

IBM Building, *see* Watson, Thomas J.,
    Research Center for IBM, Yorktown,
    New York (Saarinen, Eero, and
    Associates)

Ichabod Crane (Gregory), 217

Illinois Institute of Technology, Chicago
    (Mies van der Rohe), 72, 133

Imperial Hotel, Tokyo (Wright, F. L.), 60

Industrial Revolution, 28, 113

Ingalls Hockey Rink, Yale University, New
    Haven, Connecticut (Saarinen, Eero,
    and Associates), 82, 117–18; exterior,
    82; plan of, *82*

Ingvarson, Ruth, 147, 180–81, 187, 190;
    193

Inland Architect magazine, 16

interior design, 91–93, 95–98, 102–10,
    114–18, 121–22, 130, 134, 137–38, 140,
    142–43

Interiors magazine, 120

International Silver Co., 162, 163

International Style, 47, 63, 66, 69, 98, 110,
    138

"International Textile Exhibition,"
    University of North Carolina,
    Greensboro, 197, 204

Interplay (Larsen), 210; *210*

Island House, Muskoka, Ontario (Weese
    and Associates), 88; elevations of, *89*;
    exterior, *88*; design diagrams for, *89*

ivory comb, sketch for (Peche), 27; *27*

R

T–angle frame tables (Knoll, F.), 134; *135*

Teague, Walter Dorwin, 142–43

tea wagon (Baldwin and Weese), 33, 111; *32*

Teet, Del, Seattle, Washington, 208

Tengbom, Ivan, 241

Terrace Plaza Hotel, Cincinnati (Baldwin), 130

textiles, 40, 95, 103, 109, 110, 160, 173–211

Testa, Angelo, 197

Thaibok Fabrics, Ltd., 208

These United States (Gruening), 18

Thomas, Richard, 167, 169–71; chalice, 169; *169*; pastoral staff, 169–70; *170*; punch bowl, 170–71; *171*

Thomsen, Edward, 91

Tiffany, Louis Comfort, 143, 149

Tomalka, Edward, 203

Tonal (Bertoia), 256, 258; *256*

Towle Manufacturing Company, 162

Trans World Airlines Terminal, John F. Kennedy Airport, New York (Saarinen, Eero, and Associates), 33, 82–83, 84, 118; exterior, *83*; interior, 118; *117*

triptych, silver (Kirk, A. N.), 150, 152; *149*

Triton Pool (Milles, C.), 27, 54, 70, 245, 246; *264*

Trueblood and Graf, St. Louis, 71

Tugendhat chair (Mies van der Rohe), 105

Tugendhat house, Brno (Mies van der Rohe), 134

TWA Airlines Terminal, *see* Trans World Airlines Terminal

U

United States Embassy, London (Saarinen, Eero), 81; *see also* American Embassy, London (Saarinen, Eero)

Unity Temple (Wright, F. L.), 91

University of Chicago, Law School (Saarinen, Eero), 81

University of Michigan, architectural program at, 36–37, 38, 42, 43, 50

University of Pennsylvania, Women's Dormitories at (Saarinen, Eero), 116–17

Untitled (Mitchell), 261; *259*

Untitled, monoprints (Bertoia), 166, 254–55; *257, *260, *261*

upholstery material (Rossbach), 205; *208; *203, *207*

upholstery material (Sailors), 203; *204*

upholstery material (Strengell, M.), 197; *196, 197*

Urban, Joseph, 31

urbanization, 16–17

urn (Saarinen, Eliel), 99, 101, 163; *164*

U.S. Glass Company, 189

Utzon, Joern, 82

V

valance, for Saarinen House (Saarinen, L.), 177; *175*

Valentiner, Brigitta, 254

Valentiner, William, 254

vase (Bertoia), 166; *168*

vase (Littleton), 232; *233*

vase (Watson), 225; *227*

vases (Grotell), 220–21, 222–23, 229; *218, 230; *212, *224, *228*

vases (Takaezu), 235; *235; *229*

Velde, Henry van de, 28

Velonis, Anthony, 197

Venturi, Robert, 87

Victoria and Albert Museum, London, 189; *see also* South Kensington Museum, London

Vienna, Austria, 22, 28

Villa Keirkner, Helsinki (Saarinen, Eliel), 48, 93; *49*

Vogel, Edna, 226

Volkmar, Leon, 44, 213, 221

Voulkos, Peter, 232

V'Soske, 109, 142, 199

W

Wagner, Otto, 23

Wallace, R., and Sons, 163

wall-covering material (Strengell, M.),
197; *197*

Walsh, Robert P., 71

War Memorial Fountain, Cleveland
(Fredericks), 252–53; *251*; model for,
252

Warren, Edward Perry, 150

Washburne, Carleton, 67

Watson, Thomas J., Research Center for
IBM, Yorktown, New York (Saarinen,
Eero, and Associates), 81, 116; exterior,
80

Watson, William, 225, 226; vase, 225;
227

weaving, *see* textiles

Webster Groves, Missouri, house in
(Eames, C., and Walsh), 71

Weese, Harry, 33, 70, 78–79, 87, 88, 111,
237; chairs, drawings for, 111; *110*;
Island House, 88; *88, 89;* tea wagon,
33, 111; *32*

Weese, Harry, and Associates, *88, 89*

Wermuth house, Fort Wayne, Indiana
(Saarinen, Eero), 73, 113

West, Andrew Fleming, 27

Wheaton College Art Center competition,
design for (Saarinen, Eero), 68, 72

Whitaker, Charles Harris, 41

White, William Alan, 18

Wiener Werkstätte, 25, 27, 28, 160, 176

Wieselthier, Vally, 214, 215

Wilder, Billy, house, project, Beverly Hills
(Eames, C. and R.), 75, 77, 121–22;
aerial perspective, *75;* interior
perspectives, *76;* perspective of
entrance, *75;* plan perspective, *75*

Wingspread house (Wright, F. L.), 88

Winston, Lydia, 189

Wirde, Maja Andersson, 180, 183, 187,
189, 219; *Animal Carpet,* 187; *187;*
*186; carpet, curtain, and upholstery
materials, for Library, Kingswood
School Cranbrook, 59, 98, 187; *188;*
study hall carpet, Kingswood School
Cranbrook, 183; *185;* *14*

Wissenschaft, Industrie und Kunst
(Semper), 28

womb furniture (Saarinen, Eero): chairs,
113, 120; settee/sofa, 113, 120; *118*

Woo, Marie, 235

Woodland Crematorium, Stockholm
(Asplund), 70

Workers' Club, Jyväskylä (Aalto), 66

Works Progress Administration (WPA),
197, 219, 248

Wright, Frank Lloyd, 44, 67, 68, 189; as
architect, 16, 21, 60, 88, 91, 114, 122,
124, 192, 203; furniture by, 99, 124;
influence on: Saarinen, Eero, 113;
Saarinen, Eliel, 27, 60, 68; photograph
of, *45*

Wright, Russel, 99, 198

Y

Yale University, architectural program, 63

Yamasaki, Leinweber, and Associates, 82

Yardley Shop, New York City, textiles and
carpets for (Studio Loja Saarinen), 192

Yellin, Samuel, 148